HUMAN RIGHTS: BACKGROUND AND ISSUES

ACCESSING JUSTICE THROUGH MENTAL HEALTH LAW REFORM IN THE PACIFIC

HUMAN RIGHTS: BACKGROUND AND ISSUES

Additional books in this series can be found on Nova's website
under the Series tab.

Additional e-books in this series can be found on Nova's website
under the eBooks tab.

HUMAN RIGHTS: BACKGROUND AND ISSUES

ACCESSING JUSTICE THROUGH MENTAL HEALTH LAW REFORM IN THE PACIFIC

HELEN J. MÉNARD

nova publishers
New York

Library of Congress Cataloging-in-Publication Data

Names: Menard, Helen J. author.
Title: Accessing justice through mental health law reform in the pacific /
Helen J. Menard (Legal Consultant, Picnic Bay, Queensland, Australia).
Description: Hauppauge, New York : Nova Science Publisher's, Inc., 2016. |
Includes bibliographical references and index.
Identifiers: LCCN 2016008528| ISBN 9781634849333 (hardcover) | ISBN
9781634849562 (ebook)
Subjects: LCSH: Mental health laws--Oceania
Classification: LCC KVC689 .M46 2016 | DDC 344.9504/4--dc23 LC record available at http://lccn.loc.gov/2016008528

Published by Nova Science Publishers, Inc. † New York

Blessed are the cracked, for they shall let in the light.

Groucho Marx (1890-1977)

Driftwood

My life so resembles this broken tree
Knocked over by life's flood brought to its knee
Lying face down in the slush and mud
Eye to eye with paragrass, weed and scrub

Perhaps this is one nightmarish dream
To be torn from your roots carried downstream
Flung though the rapids onto some monstrous boulder
Then far out to sea with bruised body and shoulder

To float for days in the burning sun
No place to turn to, nowhere to run
Then one day you know you're out of the deep
Washed ashore in a bay where the currents will keep

You are safe and with love renamed
Driftwood

Leibling Marlow 1983
Taken from *Fright or Light: Surviving Mental Illness*
Leadership Fiji, 2006 and Psychiatric Survivors Association of Fiji

CONTENTS

FIGURES AND TABLES

PREFACE

Much of the mental health legislation in the Pacific region is archaic, pays no attention to the rights of mental health consumers and is long overdue for reform. A small number of countries in the Pacific has recently undertaken such reform. This work analyses the provisions of past and present mental health statutes in selected Pacific countries to establish, firstly, whether the new legislation has prima facie created or improved pathways for access to justice for mental health consumers and, secondly, whether these pathways offer any practical benefit for those subject to involuntary detention. The research is based on field work involving interviews and correspondence with mental health professionals, court officials, law reformers, lawyers and other professionals in the Pacific region.

For mental health consumers, involuntary detention involves significant deprivation of liberty and more often than not invasive treatment without consent. In these circumstances accessing justice via the law and the legal system is critical both at the time of admission and subsequently throughout continuing confinement. It is argued that access to justice for mental health consumers under detention pivots around the provision of *information*, *representation* and effective *participation* in the legal processes. Each of these elements is examined with particular reference to the admission criteria for involuntary detention and the legal mechanisms available for review of and appeal against detention. The study of reform is limited to the Pacific island countries of Tonga, Samoa and Fiji—being the only jurisdictions in the region to have undergone recent mental health law reform—while Vanuatu is chosen as the counterfactual case, illustrative of mental health law yet to undergo reform.

Reform of mental health laws in Pacific island countries has largely been inspired by international human rights movements, global world health initiatives and, on occasions, a few key individuals in a position to influence political decision making. Legislative reform has created a variety of rights based frameworks throughout the region, which have delivered limited practical improvements for mental health consumers. In terms of consumers' ability to access justice through the utilisation of those rights, the reforms have been primarily aspirational rather than substantive. Lack of political commitment together with limited financial and professional resources constitute major impediments to the capacity of the legislation to change substantially the lives of mental health consumers in these countries. Likewise, culture and customary practices still have significant influence in the management of mental health in Pacific communities and, when mental health initiatives are presented in a human rights context, often create substantial barriers.

Effective realisation of human rights based initiatives in the facilitation of access to justice for mental health consumers is best achieved through the application of culturally appropriate ideals—the acceptance and implementation of which will necessitate significant efforts to increase social awareness and recognition of human rights based principles and the nature and treatment of mental illness. Otherwise, rights based legislation will only serve as 'window dressing' and can do little to promote meaningful access to justice for those subject to involuntary detention.

ACKNOWLEDGMENTS

The rights of mental health consumers have played a large part in my professional life as a health professional, a lawyer and an academic. The challenges faced by mental health consumers at every level of society are enormous. Overcoming these challenges can only ever be achieved by increasing social awareness and acceptance of mental illness as an everyday part of the human condition for which all deserve to share equal rights within the community. I hope that in some small way this work contributes to that objective for the benefit of all mental health consumers in the Pacific.

I am immensely grateful to all those professionals in the region—in particular those in Tonga, Samoa, Fiji and Vanuatu—who gave willingly and generously of their time and shared their experiences and knowledge and, in the process, helped to capture a moment in mental health history. This also includes all those who assisted in locating and retrieving information not readily available from accessible sources and those who contributed anonymously but no less generously. They are too many to name and to forget any one would unfairly diminish his or her contribution.

I am also indebted to Professor Brian Opeskin and Emeritus Professor Terry Carney for their wisdom, direction and enthusiasm for the project especially at times when it all seemed 'too hard'.Without their encouragement and gentle coercion I may still be wandering in the wilderness.

Most importantly I extend my sincere and heartfelt thanks to my life partner Ian for living through the highs and lows, for providing invaluable technical assistance and tireless proof reading, and for never once failing to be supportive or doubting my ability to reach the end. Thank you.

ABBREVIATIONS

AusAID	Australian Agency for International Development
BMHV	Board of Mental Health Visitors
CAT	Convention against Torture and Other Cruel, Inhuman or Degrading Treatment or Punishment
CMHO	Chief Mental Health Officer
CRC	Convention on the Rights of the Child
CRPD	Convention on the Rights of Persons with Disabilities
CTO	Community Treatment Order
DPO	Disabled Persons Organisation
ECT	Electro convulsive therapy
FLRC	Fiji Law Reform Commission
FNU	Fiji National University
FSM	Fiji School of Medicine
FSPI	Foundation of the Peoples of the South Pacific International
GDP	Gross Domestic Product
ICCPR	International Covenant on Civil and Political Rights
ICESCR	International Covenant on Economic, Social and Cultural Rights
ITO	Inpatient Treatment Order
MHRB	Mental Health Review Board
MHRT	Mental Health Review Tribunal
MI Principles	UNHCR Principles for the Protection of Persons with Mental Illness and the Improvement of Mental Health
MoH	Ministry of Health
NGO	Non-government organisation
NMHC	National Mental Health Council/Committee
NSW	New South Wales
NZ	New Zealand
NZAID	New Zealand Agency for International Development
PacLII	Pacific Islands Legal Information Institute
PCDF	Partners in Community Development Fiji
PIFS	Pacific Islands Forum Secretariat
PIMHnet	Pacific Islands Mental Health Network
PITS	Pacific Islands Treaty Series

PNG	Papua New Guinea
PVCH	Port Vila Central Hospital
RRRT	Regional Rights Resource Team
SA	South Australia
SOAD	Second opinion of an appointed doctor
SPC	Secretariat of the Pacific Community
UDHR	Universal Declaration of Human Rights
UK	United Kingdom
UN	United Nations
UNDP	United Nations Development Programme
UNICEF	United Nations International Children's Emergency Fund (now United Nations Children's Fund)
Vic	Victoria
WHO	World Health Organisation
WHO Ten Principles	WHO Mental Health Care Law: Ten Basic Principles

PART I: BACKGROUND AND CONTEXT

Chapter 1

INTRODUCTION

1. OVERVIEW

Mental health care has great potential for abuse of human rights. History is littered with vivid examples of institutional and systemic abuse associated with unlawful detention and treatment.

The very nature of psychiatric treatment

> alter(s) the functioning of the human mind and... can be seen as an interference in human autonomy ... the powers accorded to psychiatric medicine give rise to unnecessary and unwanted intervention in the lives of persons whose situation, although unusual, may be tolerable from their point of view.[1]

Although the legal framework in which modern psychiatry sits has arguably restricted the circumstances under which abuse can occur, some contend that the law merely masks the interventionist approach and still leaves the mentally ill vulnerable.[2] If a person is deemed to be suffering from a mental illness, the legal ramifications can be quite extreme. It can involve detention against a person's will; treatment without consent; seclusion and physical restraint; the administration of powerful mind altering drugs; highly invasive medical procedures including electro convulsive therapy and behaviour modification therapy.

All of these actions, without appropriate legislative endorsement and protection constitute, at a minimum, grave violations of civil human rights at the hands of the State. Involuntary detention and treatment of a person without his or her consent is only justified where the person satisfies a statutory definition of mental illness or mental disorder that necessitates compulsory admission to a psychiatric facility or detention within the community. However, people may demonstrate symptoms that are mistakenly classified as a mental illness or disorder and, as a result, are inappropriately detained and treated without their consent. It is for these reasons that the legal processes by which a person is detained against his or her will deserve the closest examination. In the same the way, the legal mechanisms available to detainees to appeal against their detention or have it reviewed,

---

1 J Mason and G Laurie, *Mason and McCall Smith's Law and Medical Ethics* (Oxford University Press, 7th ed, 2006) 710.

2 Ibid.

should ensure optimum access to justice. This means that review mechanisms should be readily available to all detainees—both on request and by way of periodic review—and effective access to these processes should be facilitated by the provision of *information, representation* and *participation*. The hard reality for many Pacific jurisdictions is that limited professional and financial resources frequently impact on their ability to maximise these processes.

In the face of the overall shortage of mental health care and treatment options in the Pacific—either in an institutional or community setting—mental illness remains significant. Although some writers suggest the incidence of mental illness in the Pacific does not differ greatly from the incidence in more affluent Western societies, it is often difficult to quantify. In most countries reliable statistical information is not available, especially where there are no formal mental health services or no inpatient facilities. In other instances, the incidence may depend on what is considered to be a mental illness; how many of those people actually seek treatment; and the nature of treatment sought. The 'treatment gap,' being the percentage of individuals who require care but do not receive treatment,[3] is estimated to range from 90 percent in Fiji[4] to 99 percent in Vanuatu.[5] The lack of formal and optimal treatment alternatives constitutes a denial of social justice for mental health consumers in terms of accessing appropriate care and protection for themselves and the community. However, there is also evidence of denial of justice with respect to the functioning of legal mechanisms when consumers are detained in mental health facilities—where they exist—or within the community.

2. Research Context

When the World Health Organization (WHO) published its Regional Strategy for Mental Health in 2002 it found 'a dearth of any reliable or substantive empirical data on the incidence and profile of mental illness in the Pacific Region.'[6] However, since that time there has been an increasing amount of material emerging, particularly in relation to the socio- cultural issues that underpin mental health in the region.[7]

Awareness of mental health as a priority health issue in the Pacific really only came of age following the WHO's Situational Analysis of Mental Health Needs and Resources in Pacific Island Countries in 2005.[8] This project had its origins in the World Health Report

3 R Kohn et al. 'The Treatment Gap in Mental Health Care' (2004) 82 *Bulletin of the World Health Organisation* 858, 859.

4 TemoL, *St Giles Hospital to Be Turned into a Regional Mental Health Institute* (Fri, 23/10/2009,0936) <www.connectme.com.fj/news/national/St-Giles-Hospital-to-be-turned-into-a-regional-mental-health-institute (accessed 29 March 2011)>.

5 J Benson et al. 'A New Era in Mental Health Care in Vanuatu' (2011) 2011 *International Journal of Family Medicine* 15.

6 World Health Organisation, 'Regional Strategy for Mental Health' (WHO, Western Pacific Region, 2002) 20.

7 See a series of papers in *Pacific Health Dialog* Vol.15. No 1. 2009; P Culbertson, M N Agee and C Makasiale (eds), *Penina Uliuli: Contemporary Challenges in Mental Health for Pacific Peoples* (University of Hawaii Press, 2007); D Taylor, 'Tonga National Disability Identification Survey' (Tonga Disability Action Committee, 2006); World Health Organisation, 'Situational Analysis of Mental Health Needs and Resources in Pacific Island Countries' (WHO, Centre for Mental Health Research, Policy & Service Development, 2005).

8 World Health Organisation, above n 6.

2001[9] that followed the influential work by Desjarlais whose concern was that 'changes in the human and social environment are affecting mental health adversely. They are increasing the risk of mental disorders and making their prognoses worse. Social support that has maintained people in the community is crumbling.'[10]

In focusing its 2001 report on worldwide mental health issues, the WHO found that there was a significant gap between the current global burden of mental disorders and the policy, services and resources available to address this burden. The project was aimed at addressing this gap by providing technical assistance to countries for the development of mental health policy and services.[11] In turn, this led to the Western Pacific Regional Strategy for Mental Health in 2002[12] and the abovementioned Pacific analysis in 2005. The formation of the Pacific Islands Mental Health Network (PIMHnet) followed in March 2007—despite calls for the establishment of such a regional association some thirty years earlier[13]—with a charter to assess and address some of the critical mental health issues in the Pacific Region.[14] Since then a number of WHO funded projects have been undertaken in various countries under this mandate. Some have been instrumental in effecting legislative change and others have focused on training and awareness programs for mental health personnel and improvements to service delivery.

The WHO also identified policy and legislation as one of the key approaches for achieving its regional strategy to provide principles and guidance for countries when responding to challenges posed by mental health issues in the region.[15]

> Legislation regulating compulsory or voluntary treatment of people with mental disorders is lacking in several countries and is in need of review in many others. The appropriate legal protection for individuals with mental disorders needs to be ensured. Laws that respect the rights of individuals with mental disorders to dignified and effective care … are needed.[16]

Increasing global consciousness of human right issues has also created a platform for change in the region. Significant international instruments surfaced in 1966 with the *International Covenant on Economic, Social and Cultural Rights*[17] and the *International Covenant on Civil and Political Rights*[18] and continued with the *Convention on the Rights of*

---

9 World Health Organisation, 'World Health Report' (WHO, 2001).

10 R Desjarlais et al. *World Mental Health: Problems and Priorties in Low Income Countries* (Oxford University Press Inc, 1995), quoted in World Health Organisation, above n 6, 7.

11 World Health Organisation, 'Report on the Mental Health Policy Project: First International Training Forum on Mental Health Policy and Services' (WHO, 2002).

12 World Health Organisation, above n 6.

13 HBM Murphy, *Mental Health Trends in the Pacific Islands: A Report on a Tour of Pacific Territories* (South Pacific Commission, 1978) 56.

14 WHO Regional Office for the Western Pacific Press Releases, *New Network Seeks to Improve Mental Health Care in Pacific Islands Countries* <www.wpro.who.int/NR/exeres/6C2C3583-BBA7-4E61-B64B-7BBF8372AB67.htm>.

15 World Health Organisation, above n 6, 19.

16 Ibid.

17 *International Covenant on Economic, Social and Cultural Rights*, opened for signature 16 December 1966, 993 UNTS 3 (entered into force 3 January 1976).

18 *International Covenant on Civil and Political Rights*, opened for signature 16 December 1966, 999 UNTS 171 (entered into force 23 March 1976).

the Child[19] in 1989, UNHCR *Principles for the Protection of Persons with Mental Illness and the Improvement of Mental Health Care*[20] in 1991 and, more recently, the *Convention on the Rights of Persons with Disabilities*[21] in 2006.

Although the only direct reference to any of these documents in regional mental health laws is in Fiji, it is clear that some of the instruments have influenced the drafting of new mental health legislation in both Tonga and Samoa.

3. Research Objectives

Much of the mental health legislation in the Pacific region is archaic, pays little heed to the rights of mental health consumers and is long overdue for reform. A handful of countries in the Pacific have recently undertaken such reform. This work comparatively analyses the relevant provisions of past and present mental health statutes in each of the selected countries in order to explore the answers to several questions. The study is limited to four Pacific island countries. Three of these—Tonga, Samoa and Fiji—are the only jurisdictions in the region to have undergone recent mental health law reform, while the fourth, Vanuatu, is chosen as the counterfactual case—illustrative of mental health law within Pacific countries yet to undergo reform.

The questions under examination are twofold:

> To what extent has new mental health legislation in the Pacific created or improved access to justice for mental health consumers subject to involuntary detention?
>
> If statutory pathways have been created or improved, have they conferred any real benefit on those mental health consumers subject to involuntary detention under the legislation?

Access to justice will be measured principally by reference to the provision of *information*, *representation* and effective *participation* in the legal mechanisms which govern admission criteria for involuntary detention and the review of and appeal against detention. Each of these elements is examined with particular reference to the relevant admission criteria and the review and appeal procedures.

Reform of mental health laws in the Pacific has been driven by highly aspirational international human rights norms; by more realistically expressed global world health initiatives; and, in one or two instances, by a few key individuals in a position to influence local political decision making.

In addition, legislative reform in three of the target countries—Tonga, Samoa and Fiji—has created a variety of rights based frameworks founded primarily on 'western' style statutory models. However, these frameworks are fundamentally shown to be unrealised, while there has been no statutory reform of mental health legislation in Vanuatu.

---

19 *Convention on the Rights of the Child*, opened for signature 20 November 1989, 1577 UNTS 3 (entered into force 2 September 1990).

20 Office of the High Commissioner for Human Rights, *Principles for the Protection of Persons with Mental Illness and the Improvement of Mental Health Care*, GA Res 46/119, (17 December 1991).

21 *Convention on the Rights of Persons with Disabilites*, opened for signature 13 December 2006, 2515 UNTS 3 (entered into force 3 May 2008).

Some of the major impediments to the capacity of legislation to change substantially the lives of mental health consumers in these countries include culture and customary practice—which still have significant influence in the management of mental health in Pacific communities—especially when mental health initiatives are presented in a 'Western' health paradigm or a 'Western' style human rights context. These factors also influence policy development and the prioritisation of mental health on domestic government agendas. Furthermore, limited professional and financial resources in the region seriously impact on the capacity to deliver mental health initiatives and services and as a result access to justice, even when they do form part of government policy.

Effective realisation of human rights based initiatives and the facilitation of access to justice for mental health consumers can be best achieved through the incorporation of culturally appropriate values as part of mental health care policy and mental health legal services. It is imperative that there be significant efforts to increase social awareness and acceptance of the nature and treatment of mental illness and human rights based principles. Systemic community education—driven at a government policy level and adequately funded—is essential if, in time, the prioritisation of mental health services on domestic political agendas is to be achieved. If this does not occur, rights based legislation in the region will only ever serve as 'window dressing' and can do little to promote meaningful access to justice for those mental health consumers subject to involuntary detention.

4. Structure and Contents

Part I contains a number of chapters that set the background and context of the work and mental health in the Pacific.

Chapter 1 presents the work in the Pacific context and outlines the structure of the work as well as the research methodology employed and explores some of the limitations on research in the region.

Chapter 2 discusses the prevalence of mental illness in the region and some of the factors that impact on the existence and reporting of mental illness.

Chapter 3 describes international influences on mental health law in the Pacific, namely the application of various human rights treaties and principles.

Part II comprises a series of chapters that explore the legal landscape in mental health in the Pacific, both generally and within each of the target countries.

Chapter 4 examines the history of mental health legislation in the region and explores some of the philosophical debates about who is and who is not considered to be 'mentally ill'—from both the legal and medical perspectives.

Chapters 5-8 evaluate the legislative structures in existence in each of the selected countries prior to reform; the principles and philosophies that motivated the process of reform; and, by way of comparative analysis, the current legislative provisions in each jurisdiction. This evaluation also involves a review of the operation of legislative mechanisms by discussing relevant case law, where it exists. Finally, critical issues seen as impacting on the ability of mental health consumers to access justice are identified as future challenges in each jurisdiction.

Part III examines the essential elements of access to justice and the challenges the region faces in realising access to justice for mental health consumers.

Chapter 9 introduces the core concept of access to justice and its scope for the purpose of this work.

Chapter 10 discusses access to justice in the context of this study in detail and assesses the ability of the new legislation to meet its stated objectives; the implementation of prescribed review mechanisms and their effectiveness in enhancing access to justice; differences between the review models adopted; the challenges of delivering mental health services and accessing justice in the Pacific; international trends in mental health and the Pacific's position on the global mental health spectrum.

Chapter 11 explores the significance of culture and the conceptual conflict involving the application of 'Western' style human rights principles as impediments to the realisation of access to justice for mental health consumers in the Pacific. This includes the interplay between culture and mental illness as a means of devising culturally appropriate legislation and legal mechanisms for mental health consumers, while recognising that culture plays a fundamental role in managing mental health in most Pacific communities.

Chapter 12 analyses existing legal and human rights frameworks in the target countries, where they relate to accessing justice for mental health consumers, and the extent to which these frameworks comply with international human rights instruments.

Chapter 13 looks at the role that resources and regional policy play in obstructing access to justice for mental health consumers. It sketches the availability of mental health services and professional resources, the distribution of finances and government mental health policy as a context in which to place mental health legislation and appropriate reform.

Part IV contains concluding remarks in relation to themes surrounding the research and discusses future pathways towards accessing justice in the region.

5. Terminology

This study is limited to an examination of legislation in the Pacific island countries of Tonga, Samoa and Fiji—being the only jurisdictions in the region to have undergone recent mental health law reform—and, by contrast, Vanuatu where there has been no such reform. Accordingly, references to 'the Pacific' or 'the region'—unless otherwise indicated—will only refer to these countries. While many of the problems explored are common throughout the entire Pacific, no claims regarding access to justice are made in relation to countries other than those under discussion.

In general, the term 'mental health consumer' is used to describe those persons defined under the various statutes as 'mentally ill' or 'mentally disordered' or 'of unsound mind' and who are detained involuntarily—either within the community or in a mental health facility. While it is conceded that 'mental health consumer' is not a widely used term in the region and is not universally accepted by all mental health groups in other jurisdictions, in the author's opinion it is the term that carries the least stigma and endeavours to place these people within the broader health community in a non-discriminatory setting.

Finally, in order to avoid confusion with the use of the term 'traditional' in relation to mental health services, the term 'informal' will be used to describe mental health care and support services provided by NGOs, faith based organisations and traditional or 'custom' healers. 'Formal' mental health care will include those services based on modern (or traditional) psychiatric medicine and provided by government health departments and registered private mental health care practitioners.

6. METHODOLOGY

The primary focus of this project concerns the rights of mental health consumers within the relevant statutory frameworks and their impact on a person's ability to access justice. As such, this study does not endeavour to scrutinise every aspect of mental health legislation in the designated jurisdictions. The provisions that impact directly on creating pathways to justice—in terms of the law and the legal system—are the central theme. These include those legislative mechanisms that facilitate access to justice or a legal solution for mental health consumers, with particular reference to criteria for involuntary detention and treatment; mechanisms for appeal against and periodic review of involuntary detention; and some specific rights based provisions.

Wherever possible, as much up to date material as is available has been used to outline the history of mental health in the region as well as selected demographics of the target countries. The sources of this material include published texts, academic articles, government and non-government reports, Internet sources and online government and non-government databases. The history of regional mental health law, including statutes, case law and law reform reports, has been sourced from online databases such as PacLII (Pacific Islands Legal Information Institute) and general library resources.

Consumer information relating to accessing mental health services has also been obtained from the relevant mental health service providers and samples of this documentation appear in Annexures 1-11.

6.1. Interviews

Aside from reviewing published literature and online sources, key personnel in each of the target countries—who are or have been involved in assisting mental health consumers to access justice—have been identified and interviewed. Given the small number of mental health professionals in these jurisdictions it was not appropriate to undertake probability sampling with a view to making the survey conclusions generalisable. In ideal circumstances it would have been desirable to interview the entire population of mental health professionals in the target countries; however, this was not possible because of limitations imposed by their location, availability and willingness to be interviewed. As a result, a non-probability survey methodology is adopted in which respondents have been selected based on convenience and the author's judgement.[22] Respondents were selected to ensure that, where possible, both legal and medical professionals were included from each jurisdiction.

[22] *StatPac Survey Sampling* < http://www.statpac.com/surveys/sampling.htm (accessed 19 December 2013)>.

In some cases, representation of all categories of respondents was not possible due to the nature of the system in operation. For example, in Fiji, where there was no mental health legal system in place, it was not possible to interview legal practitioners. A similar situation arose in Samoa, where only one case has come before the court under the legislation. In Samoa and Vanuatu, where the number of mental health professionals is very small, those interviewed represented the total population available.

Where feasible, professionals were also selected on the basis of having had experience under both the new and old legislative schemes in order to provide comparative information. This was most relevant in Tonga where the new legislation has been in operation for the longest period.

In summary, those sampled include a cross section of mental health professionals (three psychiatrists, two senior nurses and two psychologists), court officials (a senior magistrate and two court registrars), law reformers (parliamentary counsel and a mental health policy officer) as well as academics and lawyers in the nominated countries. The reality is that mental health is poorly resourced in the region and so, by definition, the pool of key people with first hand and accurate information regarding the questions at hand is small. This is particularly so in lesser-populated countries. This may be considered a positive feature in that the survey captures a large portion of the available population but, conversely, it limits the amount of comparative data.

In a few instances, individuals who may have access to strategic information were unavailable or unwilling to participate in the research. Regrettably, this has limited access to raw data on a small number of issues but, where possible, attempts have been made to obtain the information from indirect sources. Respondents from Fiji—experienced and senior stakeholders in the mental health arena—opted to participate on an anonymous basis due to the restrictions on freedom of speech which prevailed in that country at the time.[23]

Finally, due to the logistical, ethical, cultural and legal complexities involved there has been no attempt to knowingly gather primary data from any person who is or who has ever been a consumer of psychiatric services in the region.

7. Target Countries

This work is limited to a study of particular jurisdictions in the Pacific region. Tonga, Samoa and Fiji have been chosen because they are the only jurisdictions in the region to have undergone law reform and implemented new legislation in the area of mental health. They are discussed in the chronological order in which reforms were introduced—Tonga in 2003, Samoa in 2007 and Fiji in 2010. These countries are contrasted with Vanuatu as a country in which there has been no mental health law reform in over fifty years. There are other countries in the region in a similar position to Vanuatu—Cook Islands, Kiribati, Nauru, Papua New Guinea, Solomon Islands and Tuvalu—but the scope of this project has been restricted by the time and cost involved in extending the research beyond the designated countries. The population size and socio-cultural issues in Vanuatu are similar to the other countries under

[23] The Fijian Constitution was abrogated in 2009 taking with it any rights in relation to freedom of expression or speech. See *Fiji Constitution Amendment Act 1997 Revocation Decree 2009* (Fiji Islands) and also *Media Industry Development Decree 2010* (Fiji Islands); J Fraenkel, 'Melanesia in Review: Issues and Events, 2010, Fiji' (2011) 23(2) *The Contemporary Pacific* 456, 457–8.

discussion. Furthermore, as Vanuatu has ratified more human rights treaties—including the *Convention on the Rights of Persons with Disabilities*—than any other country in the region, it has a platform from which to launch legislative and human rights reform making it a pertinent case study. The various legislative models implemented by the target countries are evaluated with a view to providing a possible benchmark for reform for those yet to undertake the process.

7.1. Geography

The geographical spread of islands throughout the target countries and the sparse allocation of resources to remote areas constitute two of the major obstacles to the optimum delivery of mental health care services in the region and these are discussed further in Chapter 12. A brief geographical sketch of the target countries follows.

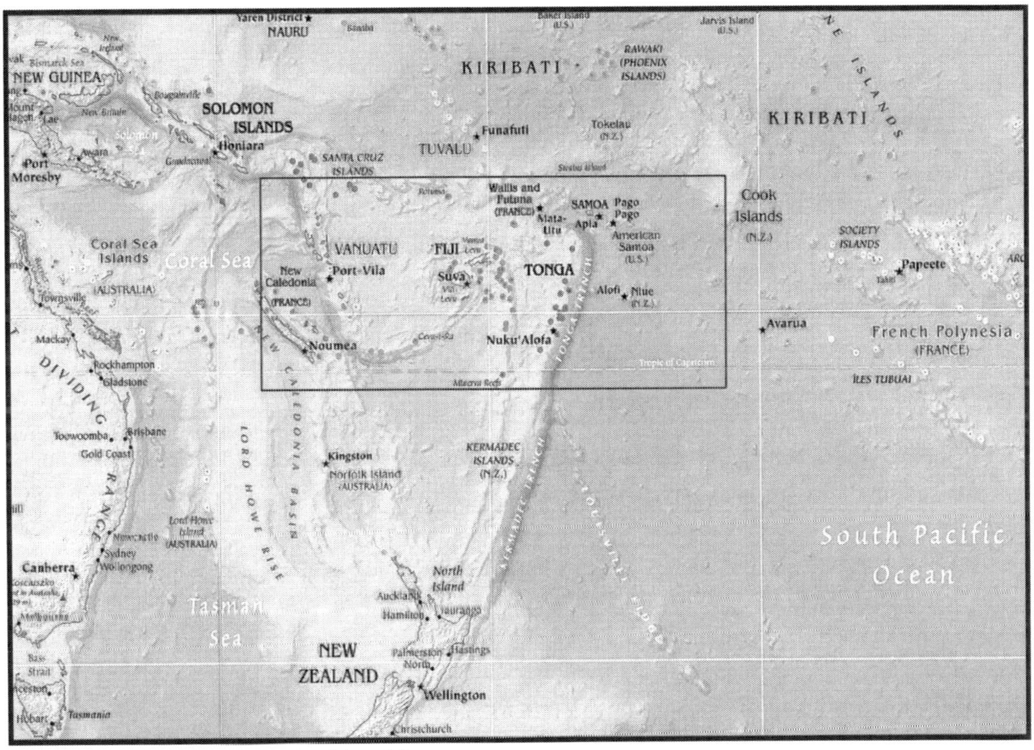

Oceania Map <www.geopgraphicguide.com>.

Figure 1. Map of the South Pacific Region.

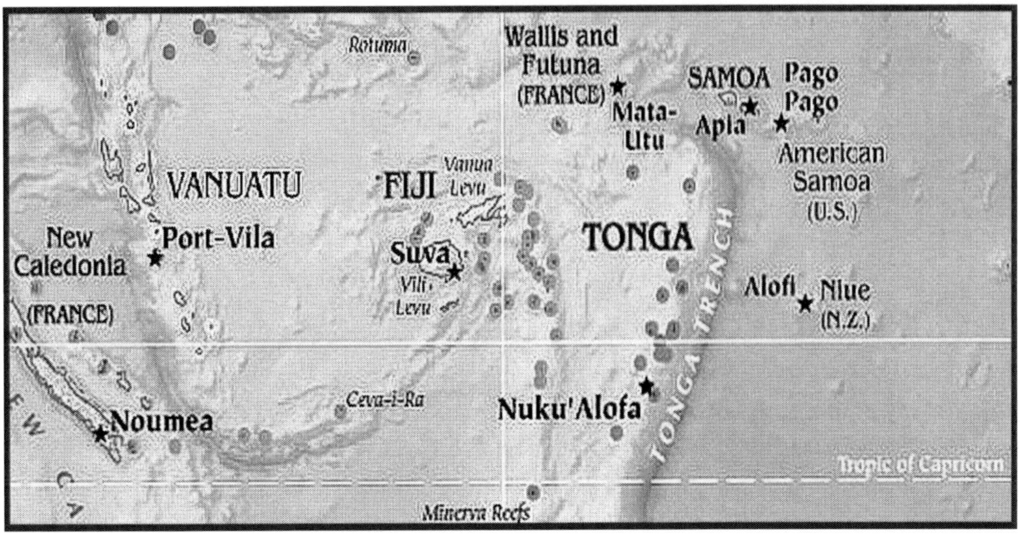

Oceania Map <www.geopgraphicguide.com>.

Figure 2. Map of target Pacific countries.

Tonga is an archipelago of 176 islands—of which only 36 are inhabited—spread over 800 kilometres. The islands are divided into three groups—the northernmost group Vava'u, the middle group Ha'apai and the southernmost group Tongatapu. Approximately 70 percent of Tongans live on the main island of Tongatapu on which the capital, Nuku'alofa, is situated.[24]

While Samoa consists of ten islands, the population is predominantly spread across the two main larger islands of Upolu and Savaii which are separated by Apolime Strait—a distance of approximately 20 kilometres. The capital, Apia, is situated on the smaller of the main islands, Upolu.

Fiji comprises around 332 islands of which only 110 are inhabited. The population is concentrated on the two largest islands of Viti Levu and Vanua Levu.[25] The country is spread across 18,000 square kilometres of which only 11 percent is arable. The capital Suva—located on Viti Levu—is the largest city in the country and contains 10 percent of the total population.[26]

Vanuatu is also an archipelago of 82 islands spread over a north-south distance of 2,500 kilometres. Only 65 of the islands are inhabited and more than 25 percent of the population lives on the central island of Efate, on which the capital, Port Vila, is situated. In fact, nearly 75 percent of the population in Vanuatu lives in rural areas outside the two main urban centres on the islands of Efate and Santo.[27]

---

[24] O Guttenbeil-Likiliki and Foundation of the Peoples of the South Pacific International, 'Youth and Mental Health in Tonga: A Situational Analysis' (2009) 13.

[25] WHO Western Pacific Region, *Fiji* <www.wpro.who.int/countries/fij/2010/FIJ.htm (accessed 14 March 2011)>.

[26] Ibid.

[27] Vanuatu National Statistics Office Ministry of Finance and Economic Management, *National Census of Population and Housing Summary Release* <www.vnso.gov.vu/images/stories/2009_Census_Summary_release_final.pdf (accessed 1 April 2013)>.

7.2. Government

Currently, a variety of governments exist across the region ranging from a military-led regime in Fiji to a longstanding stable democracy in Samoa. While there have been regular interruptions to the democratic process in Vanuatu, Tonga is in the process of transitioning from an enduring constitutional monarchy to democracy. At times when the governing processes are in turmoil, attention is drawn away from what are seen to be non-essential initiatives—the end result being, at best, that implementation is delayed or, at worst, that projects wither on the vine. Legislative mental health reform in Vanuatu and Fiji has suffered this fate.

Tonga has been a constitutional monarchy since 1875 with almost absolute power given to the King of Tonga as head of state.[28] The pro-democracy movement has been active since the early 1990s and, after violent pro-democracy demonstrations in November 2006, King George Tupou V ultimately pushed through a package of substantial constitutional reforms. For the first time, in 2010, a majority of seats in the legislative assembly was elected by universal suffrage.[29] King George Tupou V died on 19 March 2012 and has been succeeded by his younger brother King Tupou VI who, in the past, has not been known to share his older brother's democratic ideals.

Prior to 1889, Samoa (formerly Western Samoa) was ruled by the paramount chiefs and later the King. In 1889 Samoa became a condominium under the control of Britain, Germany and the United States and soon after a German protectorate from 1900.[30] In 1921, following the Treaty of Versailles, the League of Nations transferred control of Samoa from Germany to New Zealand, initially as a mandate and later a trust territory.[31] Following independence from New Zealand in 1962, all previous constituent laws were repealed and replaced by the Constitution of Western Samoa.[32] The political situation in Samoa is recognised as stable, with the country having been under the control of the Human Rights Protection Party for over 25 years.[33]

Fiji was a British colony from 1852 until 1970 when it attained independence and became a democratically elected sovereign state. However, since 1987—when Fiji became a republic—there have been a series of military coups and several constitutions. Following the most recent coup d'état of 5 December 2006, a military-led regime governed Fiji. In April 2009, the Constitution was finally abrogated and until 2014 the country was administered by special presidential decrees.[34] Promised democratic elections in 2009 were aborted. A new constitution was enacted in 2013 and Fiji finally went to the polls in 2014 electing the Fiji

---

28 J Corrin Care, T Newton and D Paterson, *Introduction to South Pacific Law* (Cavendish Publishing Ltd, 1999) 12.

29 G Powles, 'Political and Constitutional Reform Opens the Door: The Kingdom of Tonga's Path to Democracy' (2012) 18 *Comparative Law Journal of the Pacific* 193; J Maloney and J R Struble, 'A New Day in Tonga: The Judiciary, The Reformers & the Future' (2007) 11(2) *Journal of South Pacifc Law* 151; Ménard H, *LW112 Legislation Course Book* (Course Materials School of Law, University of the South Pacific, Suva, Fiji, Rev. July 2011) 4.5.

30 Corrin Care, Newton and Paterson, above n 28, 12.

31 Ibid 22.

32 Ibid 15–16; all references to Western Samoa were amended to Samoa in accordance with the provisions of *Constitution Amendment Act (No. 2) 1997* (Samoa).

33 F Hope Eseta and Foundation of the Peoples of the South Pacific International, 'Youth and Mental Health in Samoa: A Situational Analysis' (2009)14, citing the Asian Development Bank 2007.

34 *Fiji Constitution Amendment Act 1997 Revocation Decree 2009* (Fiji Islands); *Executive Authority of Fiji Decree 2009* (Fiji Islands).

First Party led by Josaia Voreke Bainimarama, previously the military commander following the coup in 2006 and later self-appointed interim Prime Minister.

Prior to independence in 1980, Vanuatu (formerly the New Hebrides) was governed as a joint condominium between Britain and France. Upon independence, Vanuatu became a democratically elected republic operating under a Westminster model of parliament and adopting the common law legal system. The constitution incorporated British and French laws in force immediately before independence and wherever possible taking due account of custom.[35] Even though French laws remain 'on the books' in Vanuatu, they are rarely used.

8. Research Limitations

8.1. Content

This research specifically excludes an examination of Pacific legislation as it relates to mentally ill offenders within the criminal justice system. This is largely due to the constraints of time and space but it is also as a reflection of the fact that most writers in this area of law tend to deal with mentally ill offenders as a discrete class of persons with a distinct range of issues. The key issue with respect to mentally ill offenders is the extent to which the particular mental disorder affects a person's responsibility for criminal conduct and in particular, the connection between the commission of the crime and the mental disorder. Mentally ill offenders in the Pacific region are largely managed within the prison system due to the complete absence of dedicated forensic facilities.

Nor is it within the scope of this study to examine mental health consumers' rights of access to appropriate psychiatric care and treatment options, nor their right to consent to or refuse such treatment. Questions of consent and capacity to consent are principally contentious in the milieu of involuntary detention and treatment. This study is focused on the methods employed to review those orders for detention and treatment.

Some mental health consumers who are involuntarily detained under community treatment orders and are living within the community may have other legal problems—such as housing, debt, family law, employment or criminal law—requiring legal solutions. However, general access to the legal system is, again, beyond the scope of this project. Nonetheless, studies in other jurisdictions strongly suggest that the concerns facing mental health consumers—when attempting to interact with the legal system—are comparable regardless of the point of access to the legal system.[36]

Detailed field research has not been conducted on socio-cultural issues relating to mental health as the scope of such research is well beyond the parameters of this work. This means that interviews have not been conducted with government or non-government officials regarding mental health care or mental health care policy and reliance has been primarily on published reports.

---

35 *Constitution of the Republic of Vanuatu* ss 95(1)-(3).

36 See M Karras, 'Access to Justice and Legal Needs Vol. 4: On the Edge of Justice: The Legal Needs of People with a Mental Illness' (Law and Justice Foundation of New South Wales, 2006); Australian Government Attorney General's Department, 'A Strategic Framework for Access to Justice in the Federal Civil Justice System, Report by the Access to Justice Taskforce' (Commonwealth of Australia, 2009).

In depth discussion of the conflicting ideologies underpinning some of the human rights treaties examined in the following chapters is also beyond the realm of this research. Debates around concepts such as cultural relativism are limited to those notions that construct barriers to accessing legislative justice for mental health consumers in the region as illustrated by the tension between rights individualism and collectivism.

It is not the intention to explore or propose culturally appropriate ways of achieving access to justice for mental health consumers in any given Pacific community—to the extent that such methods might be seen as proper. This might include the ways in which and the places at which review hearings are conducted; the constitution of the review panel; and who may be present at the hearing. Where culture or custom *is* seen to be an integral part of the legal process, then it should be for that particular community to develop and oversee ways of ensuring its integration.

8.2. Background Materials

Due to the lack of primary materials and the presence of other mental health bodies in the region, WHO publications or reports commissioned by the WHO are a significant source of literature on mental health in the Pacific. Fiji's draft mental health bill in 2006 is said to have relied heavily on the WHO Resource Book on Mental Health, Human Rights and Legislation[37] and individual governments frequently rely on WHO data in their strategic plans and annual reports. The difficulty is that information presented in WHO reports is not always accurate and—while some data can be verified from alternate sources—much of the statistical data cannot. As such, the material is best used as a guide only and not in any definitive sense. By way of illustration, the WHO's Situational Analysis of Mental Health Needs and Resources in Pacific Island Countries was published in 2005 after an audit of 19 Pacific countries.[38] Information provided under the section 'mental health laws' for Tonga states:

> Mental health [sic] Act 1992. This is the only law enacted regarding 'disability' as all other types are expected to be cared for at home by family/community.
>
> 2004 bill passed to amend act problems with English translation.[39]

Even taking into account the acknowledged limitations with the collection of data in the region,[40] in the context of the report this is a significant error. The *Mental Health Act 2001* (Tonga)—a very different piece of legislation from the 1992 Act—came into force on 1 September 2003,[41] well before the publication of the WHO report. There were no amendments to the *Mental Health Act 1992* (Tonga) as implied and the *Mental Health (Amendment) Act 2004* (Tonga) served merely to correct a number of syntactical errors in the English version of the 2001 Act.

---

37 M Freeman, *WHO Resource Book on Mental Health, Human Rights and Legislation* (World Health Organisation, 2005).

38 WHO, 'Situational Analysis of Mental Health Needs and Resources in Pacific Island Countries' (2005) 10.

39 Ibid 23, 111.

40 Ibid 2.

41 Government of Tonga, Gazette No. 22 of 2003.

The same WHO report also ascribes to Tonga '7 x psychiatric nurses'.[42] In fact, there are no mental health trained nurses in Tonga even today—a fact easily established by speaking with the staff—and those working in the mental health unit at Vaiola Hospital are general trained nurses only with 'on the job' mental health experience ranging from five to twenty years.[43]

Further review and analysis of some of these reports is contained in the discussion in Chapter 13.

NZAID has funded a number of projects on youth and mental health in the region. These studies have been produced in partnership with agencies such as the Foundation of the Peoples of the South Pacific International (FSPI), the Tongan Community Development Trust and the Samoan Nurses Association[44] and the Tonga Red Cross Society and the Tonga Disability Action Committee.[45] The Masculinity Mental Health and Violence Project, also funded by NZAID in partnership with FSPI and Partners in Community Development–Fiji (PCD-F), produced Masculinity, Mental Health and Violence in Vanuatu: Situation Analysis, 2004 and Youth, Mental Stress & Violence in Fiji: Situation Analysis, 2005.

In general, these studies used standard research methodologies involving the collection of both quantitative and qualitative data which is analysed in depth, and they present comprehensive findings and recommendations for future policy direction. These studies are discussed and reviewed in detail in the relevant chapters where the appropriate information appears.

Another key source of information in the region comes from government publications and annual reports. While this material is not strictly scholarly 'literature', it is often the only data available on a given subject and, as such, warrants some examination. Nonetheless, it is often poorly presented; some data is unsupported by evidence and frequently unsourced; and at times information is simply inaccurate. For example, the Vanuatu Mental Health Policy and Plan (2009-2014)[46] cites suicide trends based on a survey carried out in rural and urban areas. However, there is no independent reference to, or verification of, the study referred to and the accuracy of the figures quoted has been questioned by local health professionals.[47] The survey appears to be based on Dupré-Wheeler's findings in 2001, which suggested that 130 successful suicides occur every year—that is, one every three days. Despite the limitations on this study discussed earlier in this chapter, it remains the only research of its kind from which to gauge community trends. Even so, allowing for public policy restrictions on the publication of suicide statistics, this pattern would seem to be of such significance that at least some incidents might be reported in the local media—they are not.

Again, more comprehensive review and analysis of various government reports, plans and policies is contained in Chapter 13.

---

42 WHO, above n 38, 112.

43 V Sione et al. 'Walking Apart Towards the Same Goal? The View and Practices of Tongan Traditional Healers and Western Trained Tongan Mental Health Staff' (2009) 15(1) *Pacific Health Dialog* 89, 91.

44 O Guttenbeil-Likiliki and Foundation of the Peoples of the South Pacific International, 'Youth and Mental Health in Tonga: A Situational Analysis' (2009); Hope Eseta and Foundation of the Peoples of the South Pacific International, above n 33.

45 D Taylor, 'Tonga National Disability Identification Survey' (Tonga Disability Action Committee, 2006).

46 Republic of Vanuatu Ministry of Health, 'Vanuatu Mental Health Policy and Plan (2009-2014)' (2009) 9.

47 Interview with Carlie Dodds, Clinical Psychologist, Vanuatu (Port Vila, 28 June 2012)

8.3. Practical Issues

There have been many practical challenges in undertaking this type of research in this region. Written materials and resources in relation to mental health often do not exist or are difficult to access, particularly those that predate the availability of information on the Internet. Record keeping is frequently non-computerised, erratic and seldom prioritised. Even where information is available, for example, on individual government websites, the sites are often incomplete or out of date, thus hampering access to some data. Regional published research into mental health is barely fifteen years old, and research on mental health law in the Pacific is extremely limited. International travel throughout the Pacific is restricted and costly. Electronic communication is regularly problematic due to inadequate bandwidth, slow connection speeds and unreliable local service providers. Key personnel with mental health experience are few in number—even fewer have specialist professional training—and are not always easily accessible. For personal or socio-political reasons, some relevant personnel have elected not to participate in this research or have provided information on an anonymous basis. While every attempt has been made to obtain as much original information as possible, there may well be gaps or unintended inaccuracies in some aspects of the material presented.

Chapter 2

MENTAL HEALTH IN THE PACIFIC

1. OVERVIEW

Mental health struggles for recognition at all levels of society in the Pacific.[1] The Pacific Islands Mental Health Network (PIMHnet)—an initiative of the World Health Organisation (WHO)—was established in March 2007 to assess and address some of the critical mental health issues in the Pacific Region.[2] As part of an analysis of mental health needs in the Pacific in 2005, the key mental health concerns included:

- difficulty discussing topics around mental health;
- poor understanding of appropriate care;
- stigmatisation and neglect;
- lack of professional skills and interest in working in the area of mental health and
- low priority for government funding compared to pressing physical health issues.[3]

Regardless of the causes, where mental health resources and services are inadequate and there is a reluctance to prioritise mental health on the domestic political agenda, the ability of mental health consumers to exercise their legal rights—and, therefore, access justice—is compromised.

This chapter explores the prevalence of mental illness in the Pacific in terms of both statistical and diagnostic profiles in each country, together with the significant factors affecting the occurrence of mental illness in the region. In this context, prevalence will be used as referring to the overall existence of disease, or mental illness, within a given population (as opposed to 'incidence' which is used to describe the occurrence of *new* disease within the community).[4]

---

1 WHO Regional Office for the Western Pacific Press Releases, *New Network Seeks to Improve Mental Health Care in Pacific Islands Countries* <www.wpro.who.int/NR/exeres/6C2C3583-BBA7-4E61-B64B-7BBF8372AB67.htm>.

2 Ibid.

3 World Health Organisation, 'Situational Analysis of Mental Health Needs and Resources in Pacific Island Countries' (WHO, Centre for Mental Health Research, Policy & Service Development, 2005) 18.

4 M Ibrahim et al. 'Incidence v Prevalence' (June 1999) (2) *ERIC Notebook* 1.

The prevalence of ill health should be an obvious driver for the provision of health services—in this instance, mental health services. It is the existence, or not, and the quality of these services that also determine the extent to which the rights of mental health consumers are realised under mental health legislation. Throughout the region, the promotion, funding and administration of mental health legislation fall under the health ministries which, by definition, are also responsible for ensuring that mental health consumers are able to exert their rights under the legislation.

2. The Prevalence of Mental Illness

Until recently there has been very little published material on the prevalence of mental illness in the Pacific and reliable statistics for the region in terms of identified, diagnosed and treated cases of mental illness are few and far between.

The WHO Regional Strategy for Mental Health in 2002[5] noted that in the Western Pacific, while physical health had improved significantly in 50 years, mental health had worsened.[6] The same report maintained that worldwide, mental and behavioural disorders represented 11 percent of the total disease burden in 1990, and this was predicted to increase to 15 percent by 2020.[7] In the Western Pacific Region, the burden is even higher than in some other parts of the world. In the more affluent countries of the Region, mental and neurological disorders account for 27 percent of the total disease burden and in the other countries the figure is 15 percent. As a proportion of the total, the burden caused by mental disorders is less in developing countries, mainly because of the large burden of communicable, maternal, perinatal and nutritional conditions. Even so, the burden of mental disorders is heavy and increasing.[8]

Fifteen years on and little has changed. The WHO maintains that 'health systems have not yet adequately responded to the burden of mental disorders; as a consequence, the gap between the need for treatment and its provision is large all over the world.'[9] In May 2012, the Sixty-fifth World Health Assembly adopted resolution WHA65.4 on the global burden of mental disorders and the need for a comprehensive, coordinated response from health and social sectors at the country level[10] resulting in the WHO's Mental Health Action Plan 2103 – 2020.[11] There is some evidence to suggest that the presentation of persons suffering from mental illness to mainstream health care services in the Pacific is not common and diagnosis and treatment even less so. However, that is not to say there is no mental illness in these communities. Traditional healers are frequently consulted by people with mental disorders and their families.[12]

---

5 World Health Organisation, 'Regional Strategy for Mental Health' (WHO, Western Pacific Region, 2002)

6 F Hope Eseta and Foundation of the Peoples of the South Pacific International, 'Youth and Mental Health in Samoa: A Situational Analysis' (2009) 15, citing World Health Organisation, above n 5.

7 World Health Organisation, above n 5.

8 Ibid.

9 World Health Organisation, 'Mental Health Action Plan 2013 - 2020' (2013) 8.

10 *World Health Organisation Sixty-Fifth World Health Assembly*, Comm A, 1st report, 9th plen mtg, Res WHA65.4, WHA65/2012/REC/1 (adopted 25 May 2012)

11 World Health Organisation, above n 9.

12 World Health Organisation, above n 5, 17

Murphy, in his seminal study of mental health trends across 13 Pacific countries in the late 1970s, found that hospitalisation rates for major mental illness were only about one-fifth of the rates observed in developed countries.[13] Even so, he concluded that inaccessibility to services was not a relevant factor[14] and admission to an inpatient unit was only ever sought when the community was no longer able to accept or manage the person's behaviour.[15] This appears to be consistent with the more traditional Pacific practices of extended family and community based care and the lack of understanding of the origins of some forms of mental illness.

As will be seen from the discussion on the interaction between culture and mental health in Chapter 11, the gradual erosion of traditional community practices and the move away from communal living—with all its consequences—have increased the demand for mental health services in some countries.

It is prudent to make a distinction between the *recorded* prevalence of mental illness and the *actual* prevalence of mental illness in any society. The information presented in the following paragraphs relates almost exclusively to the *recorded* prevalence of mental illness. Some of the literature suggests that the recorded levels of mental illness in the Pacific have been significantly lower than in Western communities. However, there is an implication that the actual prevalence of such illness in Pacific communities may be masked by the customary community care model and the disinclination of people to present to formal mental health services unless, and until, there is a pressing need to do so. Where these community support structures are gradually dissolving, the recorded prevalence levels may eventually begin to approach actual prevalence levels.

2.1. Statistical and Diagnostic Profiles

The World Mental Health Survey in 2004 estimated that 13 percent of the world's adult population is likely to have a mental disorder, three percent of them severe.[16] Yet, for example, in 2007 only 48 people in Vanuatu out of a population in excess of 200,000 were recorded as having received treatment for a mental disorder,[17] indicating a treatment gap of over 99 percent.[18] The Ministry of Health in 2009 conceded that 'while no study has systematically documented mental health problems in Vanuatu, there is general concern [about] mental health problems including alcohol and substance abuse disorders.'[19] Disappointingly, this concern has not yet generated any tangible result in terms of either documenting or providing services for mental health in that country.

13 HBM Murphy, *Mental Health Trends in the Pacific Islands: A Report on a Tour of Pacific Territories* (South Pacific Commission, 1978) 4–5.

14 Ibid 6.

15 Ibid 3.

16 WHO, Geneva, 'A Mentally Healthy Nation with Accessible Care for All, The Country Summary Series. Vanuatu, Mental Health Improvements for National Development' (2009).

17 Ibid.

18 J Benson et al. 'A New Era in Mental Health Care in Vanuatu' (2011) 2011 *International Journal of Family Medicine* 1, 5.

19 Government of the Republic of Vanuatu Ministry of Health, 'Vanuatu Mental Health Policy and Plan (2009-2014)' (2009) 19.

As can be seen from the material discussed below, recorded information on the prevalence of mental illness in the Pacific is, at best, inaccurate, inconsistent and unreliable—at worst, non-existent.

2.1.1. Tonga

Murphy's 1970s study in Tonga found very low reported levels of major mental illness, specifically the psychoses.[20]

It has been suggested that Dr Mapa Ha'ano Puloka, currently the only practising psychiatrist in Tonga, was instrumental in significantly increasing the recorded prevalence of mental illness in Tonga in the mid-1990s.[21] Puloka, an indigenous Tongan, promoted folk healing practices and collaboration with traditional healers as part of the milieu for mental health care and treatment. He also set out to 'Tonganise' psychiatric concepts and disorders and, in the space of two years from 1996 to 1998, the annual diagnosis rate for schizophrenia rose from 5.8 to 34, taking Tonga from one end of the global scale (median 15.2 per 100,000) to the other.[22]

A national disability survey in Tonga in 2006 found that, of an estimated 4800 different disabilities within a group of 2782 people with disabilities—representing 2.8 percent of the population—only five percent of the disabilities involved a mental illness.[23] It is easy to understand why physical and vision impaired disabilities are prioritised over mental illness, when there is a limited resource pool and those disabilities represent 36 and 24 percent respectively[24] of the total number of disabilities in the community. A later study of youth and mental health in 2009,[25] did not contain any data in relation to the prevalence, reported or otherwise, of mental illness within the community. However, it did refer to a study carried out by UNICEF in 2001[26] that surveyed 2880 students in Tonga and found that almost 30 percent confirmed experiencing a period of sadness or depression beyond their control in the previous six months.[27] When the same youth focus groups were asked similar questions five years later, their responses had not altered.[28]

Puloka stated in this same report that Tongan youth presented with the typical range of mental illnesses including anxiety disorders, conduct disorders, depression, psychosis, obsessive-compulsive disorders and alcohol and substance abuse.[29]

---

[20] H Murphy and B Taumoepeau, 'Traditionalism and Mental Health in the South Pacific: A Re-examination of an Old Hypothesis' (1980) 10 *Psychological Medicine* 471, 480.

[21] Email from Dr Mike Poltorak, Kent University, to Helen Ménard 12 June 2013; Excerpts from an unpublished paper.

[22] Ibid.

[23] D Taylor, 'Tonga National Disability Identification Survey' (Tonga Disability Action Committee, 2006) 22.

[24] Ibid.

[25] O Guttenbeil-Likiliki and Foundation of the Peoples of the South Pacific International, 'Youth and Mental Health in Tonga: A Situational Analysis' (2009).

[26] UNICEF, 'State of Healthy Behaviour and Lifestyle of Pacific Youth: Kingdom of Tonga Report' (2001).

[27] Guttenbeil-Likiliki and Foundation of the Peoples of the South Pacific International, above n 25, 88.

[28] Ibid 8.

[29] Ibid 20.

The Ministry of Health's annual report for 2010 suggests that *manually* recorded annual inpatient admissions increased from 114 in 2006, to 181 in 2008 and 194 in 2010. However, these figures do not correlate with those cited in the Ministry's 2009 report being 155 in 2006 and 225 in 2008,[30] thereby highlighting the inaccuracy of the recorded data.

Of the total number of admissions to the mental health unit in 2010, 54 percent involved persons suffering from schizophrenia and 24 percent involved persons suffering from bipolar disorder. The admissions also included five persons diagnosed with intellectual disability, two with acquired brain injury and one with a borderline personality disorder.[31] This report also attributes 261 admissions for the period for 'mental and behavioural disorders' being the ninth highest cause for any hospital admission[32] and states:

> Admission [sic] related to Mental and Behavioural Disorders were not usually found at [sic] the 10 leading causes of admission in past years. However, part of this increase is caused by an improvement in the coding of disease practices delivered by the Medical Records Section.[33]

These figures are significantly inconsistent with those manually recorded by the mental health unit—being 194 for the same period.[34] What is unknown, for example, is whether the hospital and the mental health unit use similar diagnostic criteria; whether the hospital figures include mental health admissions in general medical wards as well as the mental health unit; or the extent to which multiple admissions for the same person are recorded.

There is no indication in the 2010 Health Ministry report whether those admitted were classified as voluntary, involuntary or forensic patients or if there were multiple admissions for the same person or for the same reason. Nor is there any analysis of data on the basis of age, gender or location. Finally, there is no material relating to persons detained under community treatment orders (CTOs) or any reference at all to community based care or treatment.

More reliable statistics are not readily available but one respondent estimated that approximately 1,000 people currently access mental health services across Tonga, with as few as 20 people being treated under CTOs.[35]

The Ministry's most recent report for 2011-12 did not distinguish admissions to the mental health unit in any way except to state the total number of admissions for the year at 215 with an average length of stay of 54 days and an average bed occupancy of 79 percent.[36] Nor did it state whether these admissions related to new admissions or repeat admissions for the same person. Again, highlighting the inaccuracy of reporting, the same report had a total of 259 admissions for the period pursuant to section 23 of the *Mental Health Act*[37] with no

---

30 Government of Tonga, 'Report of the Minister of Health for the Year 2009' (2009) <www.health.gov.to/sites/default/files/AR2009.pdf> 116.

31 Government of Tonga, 'Report of the Minister of Health for the Year 2010' (2010) <www.health.gov.to/sites/default/files/AR2010.pdf> 103.

32 Ibid 22.

33 Ibid 22.

34 Ibid 103.

35 Loupua Sefokuli, Interview with Ilaivatu Mafi, Sister in Charge MHU (Tonga,13 June 2012)

36 Government of Tonga, 'Report of the Minister for Health for the Financial Year 2011/2012' (2011) 34.

37 23. Where a police officer or town officer –(a) has reasonable grounds to believe that a person has within the last 48 hours attempted to inflict serious injury or bodily harm –(i) on himself, or (ii) on another person, or (b) has reasonable grounds to believe that a person has inflicted or is likely to inflict serious injury or bodily harm,

indication as to how many of these resulted involuntary or voluntary status.[38] The same report states that 126 CTOs were issued for the period which is a significant increase on the previous estimates but with no suggestions as to how many were new orders or renewals of existing orders.[39] In addition, only 45 home visits in the community were made[40] which, at an average of less than one a week, seems somewhat incongruous with the number of consumers in the community on CTOs who might require treatment support. While the recording of the new data is a positive step further clarification and consistency would enable it to be used as a more effective tool.

2.1.2. Samoa

One study by a physician-specialist in Samoa over a twelve month period from 1973-1974, estimated that four percent of outpatient consultations were psychiatric problems and one percent of inpatient admissions involved a psychiatric diagnosis.[41] There is no current official data to support any change in this information.

Speaking at a meeting of the Samoa Medical Association and the Samoa Association of General Practitioners in June 2014, Dr Tuitama maintained that

> [the] Mental Health unit in Samoa has a total of about 286 patients who most are currently undergoing treatment and management ... These patients also include referrals from other wards and coral reef patients ... of these 286 patients majority of them are schizophrenic patients who makes up a total of 188, 29 suffer depressions, 9 are bipolar, 9 are ADHD, 8 epilepsy, 5 bipolar with schizoaffective disorder, 4 dementia, 3 PTSDD and the rest are phobias with other personality disorders [sic].[42]

A study of youth and mental health in 2009[43] revealed that, of 149 registered cases of people with mental illness in Samoa, 70 percent were between the ages of 14 and 40.[44] As the total figure represents less than one thousandth of the overall population, it would tend to suggest that the majority of cases are not surfacing within the mental health system or are not being accurately recorded. However, these are the same figures are quoted in the Samoan Mental Health Policy 2006, which was supposedly based on records obtained from the mental health unit in 2005.[45] Notwithstanding the government's concession that there is very limited data on mental health in Samoa, much of which is 'anecdotal,'[46] there does not appear to have been any attempt by the authors of the 2009 report to obtain more current and relevant data.

---

then the officer and any person called in assistance of him may without warrant remove that person from any public or private place to a mental health facility using reasonable force as necessary.

Note: the figures quoted in this section of the report refer to 83 admissions by police and 176 by others although 'others' is not specified. It is presumed to be family members or relatives despite the fact that section 23 does not allow for this.

38 Government of Tonga, above n 36, 35.

39 Ibid.

40 Ibid.

41 R Grigor, 'The Physician-Specialist in Western Samoa' (1975) 82 *New Zealand Medical Journal* 161.

42 Deidre Taotua Fanene, 'There Is No Health, Without Mental Health,' *Samoa Observer* (Apia, Samoa), 1 June 2014, <http://www.samoaobserver.ws/other/community/10367-there-is-no-health-without-mental-health (accessed 6 September 2015)>

43 Hope Eseta and Foundation of the Peoples of the South Pacific International, above n 6.

44 Ibid 11.

45 Government of Samoa Ministry of Health, 'Samoa Mental Health Policy' (2006) 5.

46 Ibid 20.

Samoa's part time psychiatrist, Dr Ian Parkin, suggests that the incidence of people registered and treated for mental illness appears to be well below international standards for those with some form of mental disorder. However, as most people treated for a mental illness in Samoa are treated for schizophrenia, the incidence at approximately 0.07 percent—while lower than international levels of around 0.4 percent—in his view is not extraordinarily low.[47] He maintains that:

> Schizophrenia is the predominant disorder we treat. We do not see much mania and we see extraordinarily low levels of depression. People with anxiety disorders rarely present for treatment. Most people with mental disorders do not present and I suspect are not even aware that there is a service which could help them. In general people are taken to traditional healers first and only when they do not help the person do we get to see them.[48]

Despite the currently low numbers of presenting cases, it would seem that mental health is recognised as a growing concern for this community. The government's mental health policy concedes that mental illness is becoming more visible in Samoan society as the community ties weaken: 'There are people who wander aimlessly in town and public places that [sic] often spend days away from their homes. Some families insist on seeking and taking their relatives back home but some do not bother anymore.'[49]

The Ombudsman, who has jurisdiction over human rights issues in Samoa, in his inaugural human rights report of 2015 stated that 'mental health is not widely discussed in Samoa, but trends discovered in the Survey [The Human Rights Survey 2014-2015] suggest that it should be.'[50] The report made recommendations in different areas of human rights including disability but, in relation to mental health, suggested that, as an 'emerging issue', more data and public dialogue was necessary before any recommendations could be made. The matters deserving consideration were 'providing a basic understanding of what mental health is and the services available, addressing the link between mental health and abuse and expanding suicide prevention strategies.'[51]

2.1.3. Fiji

There is a shortage of comprehensive data in Fiji regarding the national prevalence and epidemiology of mental disorders.[52]

47 Email questionnaire from Dr Ian Parkin, Psychiatrist Samoa, to Helen Ménard, 15 April 2011

48 Ibid; see also Government of Samoa Ministry of Health, above n 40.

49 Government of Samoa Ministry of Health, above n 45, 7.

50 Government of Samoa Office of the Ombudsman, 'State of Human Rights Report 2015 ' (2015) <http://www.paclii.org/ws/cases/WSNHRIRp/2015/1.html#fn185 (Accessed 5 September 2015)>

51 Ibid.

52 S Singh et al. 'WHO Profile on Mental Health in Development (WHO proMIND): Fiji.' (World Health Organisation, 2013) <http://www.who.int/mental_health/policy/country/countrysummary/en/index.html (accessed 2 January 2016)> 22.

A study of admission statistics by race over a 20 year period up to 1963, found that the admission rate for Indo-Fijians was twice that of indigenous Fijians—and even higher again for others (Europeans, Chinese and Rotumans)—and argued that 'the greater Europeanisation of Indians made them more likely to be admitted for psychiatric treatment than the Fijians [who] were still being taken care of at the "tribal" level.'[53]

A follow up study in 1976 found similar trends, in that hospital admission rates for Indo-Fijians were double that of indigenous Fijians, even though Indo-Fijians only made up 51 percent of the total population compared to 43 percent for indigenous Fijians.[54]

A study in 2002 reported a reversal in trends, recording that 51 percent of psychiatric admissions were indigenous Fijians and 45 percent Indo-Fijians, which may merely reflect the ethnic distribution of the population at that time.[55] The most recent census in Fiji in 2007 found that 57 percent of the population was made up of iTaukei (indigenous Fijians) and 37 percent Indo-Fijian.[56] The reasons for this change in population dynamics are discussed in Chapter 13.

None of these figures take into account people treated for psychiatric disorders in the general hospital system. Aghanwa's study in 2000 at the Colonial War Memorial Hospital, Suva found that 0.4 percent of all hospital admissions were referred for psychiatric services within that hospital and the referrals mainly involved non psychotic type disorders.[57]

The Ministry of Health's annual report in 2010 indicated there were a total of 490 psychiatric admissions with an average length of stay of 110 days—compared to 102 days in 2009—and a bed occupancy rate of 108 percent—compared to 101 percent in 2009.[58] These increases in bed occupancy and stay length rates from 2009 to 2010 were accompanied by a decrease in the number of trained mental health workers for the same periods.[59] There were 12,967 registered psychiatric outpatient attendances in 2010.[60]

While there were slightly fewer psychiatric admissions for 2013 (438), the Ministry's report noted that the bed occupancy rate for psychiatric beds reduced from 104.12 percent in 2012 to 42.48 percent for the same period in 2013. This decrease of 59 percent was attributed to 'a combination of reporting, decentralisation of psychiatry services and establishment of stress wards.'[61] However, there appears to be no independent evidence available to support this assertion.

---

53 G Wilson, "Europeanisation' and Admission to a Mental Hospital in the Fiji Islands' (1965) 64 *New Zealand Medical Journal* 364, 365.

54 E Seru-Puamau, 'Utilisation Review of First Admissions in 2002: St Giles Psychiatric Hospital, Suva, Fiji' (2006) 13(2) *Pacific Public Health* 79, 80 citing J Price and I Karim, 'Matiruku, a Fijian Madness: An Initial Assessment' (1978) 133 *British Journal of Psychiatry* 228.

55 Seru-Puamau, above n 54, 83.

56 Fiji Bureau of Statistics, <www.statsfiji.gov.fj/ (accessed 31 August 2012)>.

57 H Aghanwa, 'Consultation-Liaison Psychiatry in Fiji' (2002) 9(1) *Pacific Health Dialog* 22.

58 Ministry of Health Fiji Islands, 'Ministry of Health, Annual Report 2010' (2010) 17.

59 Ibid 17.

60 Ibid 20.

61 Ministry of Health Fiji, 'Ministry of Health Annual Report 2013' (2014) <http://www.health.gov.fj/PDFs/Annual%20Report/Annual%20Report%202013.pdf (accessed 7 September 2015)> 17.

Table 2.1. Admission statistics for St Giles 2009 – 2013[62]

Year	Outpatient visits	No. Beds	Admissions	Discharges	Occupancy rate	Daily bed state	Alos	Total patient days
2009	7,659	136	493	n/a	101	138	102	50,329
2010	12,967	136	490	n/a	108	147	110	53,734
2011	7,654	136	452	n/a	110	149	70	31,064
2012	5,931	136	509	n/a	104	141	59	30,019
2013	5,609	136	438	380	42.5	58	55.5	21,089

Although the issue is not outlined in the Ministry's report, a senior staff member at St Giles reported that first time admissions increased significantly in 2011 and 39 percent of inpatient admissions in 2011 were iTaukei males. In addition, there was a total of 7964 recorded cases of mental illness for the year 2011 compared to approximately 5000 for 2010.[63] These are unofficial figures and there is no indication whether the 'recorded cases' relate to individuals or the number of attendances—either as an inpatient or an outpatient. However, the Ministry concedes that '[t]here has been a large increase in the utilisation of mental health services in St. Giles. This has been attributed in part to increased awareness of mental disorders in the community and improved diagnosis by health workers in the periphery' and that '[t]he high demand for mental health services has been such that it has led to overutilisation of services and long waiting lists at the divisional hospitals.'[64]

The Ministry's 2013 report published statistics, for the first time, on the number of cases of depression seen in public facilities from 2000 to 2013.[65] These ranged from 34 in 2000 to 12 in 2005, 28 in 2008, 16 in 2010 and 25 in 2013. Given the low numbers, presumably these only relate to general public hospitals and health centres although there is no indication where the public facilities were, whether the numbers represented outpatients or inpatients or how the statistics were collected or recorded.

2.1.4. Vanuatu

Few studies on mental health have been carried out in Vanuatu over the past ten years and even fewer reliable statistics have emerged. Murphy's study in 1970 found that, while reports of major mental illness were rare, admission rates were much the same as for the rest of the region. He also found that proximity to an inpatient facility did not have a significant effect on admission rates.[66]

A study on masculinity and mental health in Vanuatu in 2004 reported that young people with mental illness generally

62 Ministry of Health Fiji, 'Ministry of Health, Annual Report 2009' (2010) <ww.health.gov.fj/PDFs/Annual%20 Report/Annual%20Report%202009.pdf (accessed 10 September 2015)> 28; Ministry of Health Fiji Islands, 'Ministry of Health, Annual Report 2010' (2011) 20; Ministry of Health Fiji, 'Ministry of Health, Annual Report 2011' (2012) <http://www.health.gov.fj/PDFs/ Annual%20Report/Annual%20Report%202011.pdf (accessed 10 September 2015)> 71; Ministry of Health Fiji, 'Ministry of Health, Annual Report 2012' (2013) <http://www.health.gov.fj/PDFs/ Annual%20Report/Annual%20Report%202012.pdf (accessed 9 September 2015)> 51; Ministry of Health Fiji, above n 58, 54.

63 Fiji Times, 'Mind Matters,' *Vanuatu Daily Post* (Port Vila, Vanuatu), Thursday July 19 2012, 6.

64 Ministry of Health Fiji Islands, 'Shaping Fiji's Health: Strategic Plan 2011-2015' (2011); see also Singh et al. above n 52, 22.

65 Ministry of Health Fiji, above n 61, 62.

66 J Allen and J Laycock, 'Major Mental Illness in the Pacific: A Review' (1997) 4(2) *Pacific Health Dialog* 105, 114 citing Murphy, above n 13.

> escape notice from the community if they are not violent nor act out. [In] most cases they remain unseen and receive no help until it is too late. Those who do act out and cause concern are usually brought to the hospital by their family or the police.[67]

Given the estimate that approximately 37 percent of the population in Vanuatu is under 14 years,[68] one of the primary catchment areas for youth mental illness should be in schools. Primary and secondary education is neither compulsory nor free in Vanuatu and, as such, is inaccessible to many children.[69] School dropout rates in 2004 were estimated at 53 percent due to lack of available places. Even for those who do attend school, no counsellors exist in schools and the education department has no policy to deal with children at risk of mental illness.[70] The end result is that there are no early intervention strategies in schools and those outside the education system are unlikely to receive any treatment unless their behaviour is unacceptably socially disruptive or criminal.

Vanuatu's most recent national housing and population census in 2009 reported that, while almost 90 percent of children aged between 8 and 11 years attended school, this dropped to 60 percent by age 15 and 30 percent by age 18.[71] In addition, 20 percent of males between the ages of 15 and 19 were reported as regularly consuming kava—a social drug with sedative and hypnotic effects, the overuse of which is linked to some forms of mental illness in young males. This rate increased to 55 precent of males between the ages of 20 and 24.[72]

2.1.5. Pacific Islanders overseas

Much of the recent literature on mental health in the Pacific, particularly in relation to Samoa, focuses on the experiences of Samoan populations in New Zealand, rather than in their home country. There do not appear to be any studies undertaken directly comparing the prevalence and causation of mental illness within Pacific and migrant Pacific communities. An in depth comparative analysis of the impact of culture on mental illness in these populations is well beyond the ambit of this work, but some general observations are appropriate.

Kokaua et al. in a study of the prevalence of mental disorders among New Zealand born and migrant Pacific people noted that 'there is a lack of information and research on Pacific peoples' migration experiences and mental health' and 'most research has been undertaken on the immigration experiences of refugees, which does not include Pacific people.'[73] The study found that, while the burden of mental disorder was highest among Pacific people in New Zealand (compared with Maori and European populations), their use of mental health services

[67] D Hughes and Foundation of the Peoples of the South Pacific International, 'Masculinity, Mental Health and Violence in Vanuatu: Situation Analysis' (2004) 27.

[68] Secretariat of the Pacific Community, *Statistics for Development Program, Pacific Islands Populations Estimates, May 2011* <www.spc.int/sdp (accessed 28 December 2011)>.

[69] Hughes and Foundation of the Peoples of the South Pacific International, above n 67, 23.

[70] Ibid 15.

[71] Vanuatu National Statistics Office Ministry of Finance and Economic Management, *National Census of Population and Housing Summary Release* <www.vnso.gov.vu/images/stories/2009_Census_Summary_release_final.pdf (accessed 1 April 2013)>.

[72] Ibid.

[73] J Kokaua et al. 'Twelve-Month Prevalence, Severity and Treatment Contact of Mental Disorders in New Zealand Born and Migrant Pacific Participants in Te Rau Hinengaro: The New Zealand Mental Health Survey' (2009) 12(1) *Pacific Health Dialog* 9, 10.

was lower.[74] Pacific people born in New Zealand, or those who migrated to New Zealand as children, displayed higher levels of mental disorder but were also more likely to utilise services than older migrants.[75] Kokaua's study contends that issues of identity for younger Pacific peoples are far more significant than for older migrants as youth attempt to balance pressures to retain a cultural heritage while living in a multicultural and contemporary society.[76]

The 2006 New Zealand Mental Health Survey found that Pacific Island peoples living in New Zealand experienced mental disorders at higher proportions than the general population and close to half of that group had experienced a mental disorder at some stage during their lifetime.[77] The same study showed that only 25 percent of Pacific peoples with a serious mental disorder accessed mental health services compared with 58 percent of the total New Zealand population.[78] Furthermore, Pacific Island people were found to be more likely to use acute inpatient units and to stay longer compared to the general population, and while they comprised only six percent of the total New Zealand population, they constituted 12 percent of all involuntary inpatient mental health consumers.[79]

The results of Kokaua's study, while acknowledging that further research was necessary, suggests that 'early exposure to the New Zealand environment is strongly associated with high levels of mental disorder among Pacific people' and these levels are likely to be affected by the social, cultural and economic pressures of adjustment and acculturation.[80]

Foliaki examined the effects of migration on the mental health of Tongans, suggesting that social support and cultural integration, rather than acculturation, were protective factors for Tongans migrating to other communities.[81]

2.2. Factors Affecting the Prevalence of Mental Illness

The surveyed literature clearly indicates that cultural change and socio-economic transition are among the primary mental health stressors in Pacific communities today. The importance of these issues within any given community may vary depending on the prevailing political and economic circumstances. Nonetheless, they are recurring themes across the region.

2.2.1. Changes in the Cultural Landscape

Murphy concedes that a shift from more communalistic to individualistic living should, on average, lead to more mental illness. He explains the theory as follows:

---

[74] Ibid, 15.
[75] Ibid.
[76] Ibid 10.
[77] MA Oakley-Browne, JE Wells and KE Scott (eds), *Te Rau Hinengaro: The New Zealand Mental Health Survey* (Ministry of Health, 2006).
[78] Ibid 185.
[79] Ibid.
[80] Kokaua et al. above n 73, 15.
[81] S Foliaki, 'Migration and Mental Health: The Tongan Experience' (1997) 26(3) *International Journal of Mental Health* 36.

> The more individualist a person (and his society) is, the more he has to take decisions for himself and seek emotional gratification by his own efforts. The more he and his society live communally the more it is the group which provides the decision and the emotional input. If a person has a defect in his information-processing and decision-taking processes, such as we know to characterise the schizophrenia prone, he is likely to get into less trouble and to produce fewer symptoms if it is the group that takes the decision, than if it is himself. Similarly, if his ability to obtain such gratification is defective, as seems to be the case in those prone to affective disorders, then this is more likely to cause a manifest disorder if he has to obtain such gratification for himself than if he is bathed in the emotional interchanges of a communalistic society.[82]

When compared with a more individualistic and competitive society such as Australia, Murphy contends that Tongan rural communalism—especially as it existed in the 1970s—served to protect schizophrenia-prone individuals from the stresses imposed by an individualistic and industrialised life-style.[83]

> When decisions are shared, where prestige accrues with age, and where life today is still very much the same as it was in one's youth, brain defects are much less important both to daily functioning and to self-image than where one has been taught to depend almost entirely on one's own mental abilities, where past memories may have little relevance to present conditions, and where one is valued on the basis of present actions rather than for whatever one has been and done in the past.[84]

In a study on Samoan youth and mental health, many of the factors noted as contributing to an increased prevalence of mental illness, are common features throughout the Pacific.[85] While culture and family were significant factors among young Samoans, parental violence was seen as a cause of extreme stress and impairment to mental health.[86]

It has been suggested that the reason indigenous Fijian hospital admissions in the 1970s were more than twice the length in duration as Indo-Fijians may be attributed to the fact that 'Indians tend to live in nuclear as opposed to extended families, thus the loss of an adult member of the household was particularly difficult to sustain.'[87]

2.2.2. Urbanisation and Socio Economic Influences

Allen predicted that urbanisation, migration and population growth would increase the profile of chronic mental illness in Pacific communities.[88] On the other hand, Murphy argued that, although rapid social change may make people more vulnerable to mental disorders, in some instances it may result in lower levels by 'removing traditional stresses and making it easier for people to achieve the limited goals they had previously perceived for themselves.'[89]

---

82 Murphy, above n 13, 38.
83 Murphy and Taumoepeau, above n 20, 481.
84 Ibid.
85 Hope Eseta and Foundation of the Peoples of the South Pacific International, above n 6, 16.
86 Ibid 12.
87 Allen and Laycock, above n 66, 106 citing J Price and I Karim, 'An Evaluation of Psychiatric After-care in a Developing Country (Fiji)' (1976) 129 *British Journal of Psychiatry* 155.
88 Allen and Laycock, above n 66, 105.
89 HBM Murphy, 'Rapid Social Change and the Vulnerable of Elites' (1978) 21(3) *Papua New Guinea Medical Journal* 276, 277.

Nonetheless, there is little evidence to suggest that Allen's predictions were inaccurate or that socio-cultural change has had a beneficial impact on the prevalence of mental illness in the region.

Roberts, in reviewing studies on youth, mental health and violence in the Pacific, found that contributing factors in Fiji included the stresses of cultural and socio-economic transition; urbanisation; unemployment and lack of employment opportunities; and the pressures related to living in crowded accommodation and squatter settlements.[90]

The features of overcrowded and un-serviced squatter settlements in Fiji were more significant in Indo-Fijian communities which are being pushed more and more into these settlements as their land leases expire and the land is resumed by iTaukei. This section of the population was estimated to be in the vicinity of 100,000 in 2005—almost 12.5 percent of the population—and increasing. In addition, with the increased 'urban pull,' iTaukei are slowly taking over these settlements, leaving the Indo-Fijians even more marginalised and with no sense of belonging.[91] Mental health stressors under these conditions—well beyond the reach of mental health services—are starkly described as follows:

> Often a family of 8 will live in one room. In some areas, people sleep in shifts while their other family members vacate the dwelling to roam the streets. Houses are close together, with 50 to 80 makeshift homes in a small land area. Many boundary disputes arise over small garden plantations, so that some people live in a continual state of tension with their neighbours.
>
> Hygiene and sanitation is poor and government/local government services are not provided to these areas. Living conditions are so poor that outbreaks of diarrhoeal and dermatological disease are common. Many children do not attend child health clinics or school, and go on to experience the health conditions and social exclusion determined by their position on the social gradient.
>
> Children witness all of their parent's behaviours, including sexual activity, abuse and arguments. They observe their fathers returning home drunk and demanding food that they have not been able to provide. Marriages are under stress from the lack of family resources and the absence of services.
>
> The settlements have become a breeding ground for crime. Boys resort to stealing and girls to prostitution. Glue sniffing is on the rise amongst youth with nothing to do. Mental health services do not reach into the squatter settlements. Despite the stress of living in these conditions some families are unwilling or unable to move on to rental accommodation. On the other hand, they are also reluctant to make improvements in their 'temporary' living conditions. [92]

While the 2009 national census in Vanuatu reported that there had been significant urban drift over the previous decanal census period and 25 percent of the total population lived in urban areas, there was no indication of how many people or households were living in informal settlements without basic services.[93] The urban drift in Vanuatu and ultimately the

90 G Roberts, 'Masculinity, Mental Health and Violence in Papua New Guinea, Vanuatu, Fiji and Kiribati' (2007) 14(2) *Health Promotion in the Pacific* 35, 37.

91 Partners in Community Development-Fiji, 'Youth Mental Stress & Violence in Fiji: Situation Analysis' (2005) 38.

92 Ibid.

93 Vanuatu National Statistics Office Ministry of Finance and Economic Management, above n 71.

socio-cultural issues associated with mental illness are exacerbated as those lacking education find it difficult to get employment.[94] The breakdown in society, as seen in the urban areas of Vanuatu, is associated with low education levels, high unemployment, youth urban migration and dilution of cultural bonds.[95] Accordingly, violence and mental health issues must only increase in the face of inadequate allocation of resources. One survey carried out in the rural and urban areas of Vanuatu concluded that 'jealousy, poverty and cramped houses were cited as the main reasons for attempting suicide.'[96]

2.2.3. Cultural Perceptions of Mental Illness

One factor that could affect the *recorded* prevalence of mental illnesses is the way in which a given society views mental illness. Bridgman rightly contends that, in the same way Pacific cultures may recognise forms of mental illness not recognised within a European framework, some of the illnesses identified by Western psychiatry seem to have no counterpart in Pacific cultures. This includes eating disorders and phobias, panic and anxiety attacks and obsessive compulsive disorders—common among European women but rarely diagnosed in Pacific people.[97]

The 2006 Tongan National Disability Identification Survey[98] reported a low prevalence of mental illness suggesting that this could be due to mental illness not being recognised and the stigma associated with such conditions. While the report contended that there is a strong degree of fear and shame associated with mental illness—possibly exacerbated by international media depictions of violence associated with mental illness[99]—this alleged causal connection was not substantiated with examples or explored in any detail.

Cultural perceptions of mental health and illness and the ways which they impede access to justice for mental health consumers will be canvassed in more detail in Chapter 11.

3. SUMMARY

Despite the fact that documented information is frequently inaccurate, outdated and unreliable, the *recorded* prevalence of mental illness throughout the region still appears to be increasing—in part, due to the dilution of traditional cultural practices and the disintegration of communalism in some Pacific societies. This exists regardless of the fact that cultural views of mental illness prevent sections of the community presenting to formal mental health services. In some countries, the effects of urbanisation and increasing levels of poverty, unemployment and social upheaval are having a greater impact than others. Even so, traditional healers and families still play a significant role in the informal treatment and care of those suffering from mental disorders.

For all these reasons, it is more important than ever that mental health consumers are able to exercise their rights and access justice where legislative reform has created mechanisms for them to do so.

---

94 Hughes and Foundation of the Peoples of the South Pacific International, above n 67, 10.

95 Ibid 33.

96 Government of the Republic of Vanuatu Ministry of Health, above n 19, 20.

97 G Bridgman, 'Mental Illness and Pacific People in New Zealand' (1997) 4(2) *Pacific Health Dialog* 95, 104.

98 Taylor, above n 23.

99 Ibid 45.

Chapter 3

International Influences on Mental Health Law

This Chapter shifts focus to the normative impact of relevant international instruments in contributing to shaping mental health legislation and services in the region. There are a number of human rights instruments that impact on the rights of mental health consumers in terms of their ability to access justice under mental health legislation in the Pacific. Few countries in the region have ratified major human rights treaties—a fact that may be partly attributed to the ideological tension between Pacific cultural traditions and 'Western style' human rights doctrines. However, in some instances, even where countries have not formally committed to specific treaties, the principles have still influenced mental health policy and legislation. Yet, the practical implementation of these legislative initiatives paints a different picture. As will be discussed in later chapters, Samoa and Fiji have incorporated progressive realisation type clauses into their legislation; yet neither of these countries is a State party to the CRPD. Whether the provisions of the CRPD will be construed as being suitable for such limitations is a question that has yet to be answered. Resources at all levels and socio-political commitment will ultimately determine the ability of Pacific countries to comply with international standards and deliver access to justice for those subject to mental health legislation.

1. International Standards in Mental Health

There are a number of international covenants, conventions and principles that have the potential to impact on the rights and treatment of mental health consumers and those who are held under involuntary detention. At the broadest level, these include:

1) Universal Declaration of Human Rights (1948) (UDHR)
2) International Covenant on Economic, Social and Cultural Rights (1966) (ICESCR)
3) International Covenant on Civil and Political Rights (1966) (ICCPR)
4) Convention against Torture and other Cruel, Inhuman or Degrading Treatment or Punishment (1984) (CAT)
5) Convention on the Rights of the Child (1989) (CRC)

6) Convention on the Rights of Persons with Disabilities (2006) (CRPD)
7) Optional Protocol to the Convention on the Rights of Persons with Disabilities (2006)
8) Body of Principles for the Protection of All Persons under Any Form of Detention or Imprisonment (1988)
9) UNHCHR Principles for the protection of persons with mental illness and the improvement of mental health care (1991) (MI Principles)
10) UN Standard Rules on the Equalisation of Opportunities for Persons with Disabilities (1993) (Standard Rules)
11) WHO, Mental Health Care Law: Ten Basic Principles (1996) (WHO Ten Principles)

This discussion will only focus on those instruments that affect the rights of mental health consumers in the Pacific, with particular reference to either creating or improving their ability to access justice under domestic mental health legislation. It is necessary to examine the existence of rights based treaties in the region, as it is the perceived conceptual conflict between Pacific cultural practices and 'Western style' human rights principles that constitutes an important barrier to accessing justice under mental health legislation. Even when this perceived conflict is not openly stated in government policy, nevertheless, it is one of the factors that lies beneath regional resistance to the adoption of international rights based treaties.

In some cases, even where countries have *not* committed to specific treaties, it is obvious the principles have still influenced mental health policy and legislation.

1.1. UDHR

The Universal Declaration of Human Rights (UDHR)[1] was born out of the horrors and human atrocities of World War II and, under the guidance of the member states of the newly formed United Nations, aimed to promote and protect human rights.[2] Even though the UDHR was considered to be the founding document of the modern human rights movement, there has been ongoing debate about whether the standards contained therein 'are inherently "Western" or whether they have a more universal foundation.'[3] Some writers assert that the UDHR was drafted by westerners and western trained representatives from Africa and Asia, and the membership of the UN in 1948 (some 58 member States) reflected the fact that most African, Asian and Pacific people were still under Western colonial rule.[4]

Even though the UDHR was adopted without a dissenting vote and was the first international instrument in which rights accorded to all individuals were articulated, debates about its enforceability and standing in international law continue.[5] The history of the creation of the UDHR strongly suggests the need to strike a balance between 'individual freedoms and

---

1 *Universal Declaration of Human Rights*, GA Res 217A (III), UN GAOR, 3rd sess, 183rd plen mtg, UN Doc A/810 (10 December 1948).

2 Law Commission New Zealand, 'Converging Currents: Custom and Human Rights in the Pacific, Study Paper 17' (2006) 61.

3 Ibid 61.

4 Ibid 62.

5 RKM Smith, *Textbook on International Human Rights* (Oxford University Press, 2nd ed, 2005) 39.

the rights of others and between individual freedom and the legitimate demands of the community and the state.'[6] This is reflected in article 29 of the UDHR, which emphasises the duties individuals have to the community and the legal restrictions on stated rights and freedoms.[7]

It is beyond the realm of this work to canvass the many arguments surrounding the universalism versus cultural relativism debate; in short, universalists maintain that human rights represent moral values that are applicable to all societies and cultural relativists hold that any set of moral judgements cannot be designed to fit across all cultures.[8] While this debate focuses on the application of human rights principles in non-Western countries, most modern constitutions in the Pacific contain a Bill of Rights closely based on the provisions of the UDHR. The conceptual conflict between the individualistic nature of the civil and political rights expressed in the UDHR and aspects of Pacific culture predicated on collectivism—as one of the principal barriers to accessing justice for mental health consumers in the Pacific—is discussed in Chapter 12.

1.2. ICCPR and ICESCR

It was almost 20 years before the ICCPR[9] and the ICESCR[10]—as legally binding instruments to give effect to the UDHR—were adopted by the United Nations General Assembly in 1966. They did not enter into force until ten years later in 1976.[11] Smith argues that, as they were intended to supersede the UDHR—by transferring the provisions of the UDHR into legally binding instruments—the non-universal acceptance of the ICCPR and the ICESCR means that the continuing value of the UDHR cannot be underestimated.[12]

These two treaties contain a broad platform of individual rights pertaining to civil, political, cultural, economic and social issues, which build on the general bank of rights outlined in the UDHR and are predicated on self-determination, equality and non-discrimination, and protection of rights.[13] The distinction between the two instruments has been partly attributed to the prevailing political climate at the time. In the post war era states of the Western bloc were more interested in civil and political rights—those which required the state to refrain from certain actions against individuals—while the Eastern bloc members favoured economic, social and cultural rights—those requiring the state to provide the goods and services necessary for the enjoyment of those rights.[14] The rights under the ICCPR are usually seen as being more fundamental and inalienable than those of the ICESCR, which are viewed as more idealistic and subject to progressive realisation and available resources.[15]

---

6 Law Commission New Zealand, above n 2, 63.

7 Ibid 63.

8 Ibid 70.

9 *International Covenant on Civil and Political Rights*, opened for signature 16 December 1966, 999 UNTS 171 (entered into force 23 March 1976).

10 *International Covenant on Economic, Social and Cultural Rights*, opened for signature 16 December 1966, 993 UNTS 3 (entered into force 3 January 1976).

11 Law Commission New Zealand, above n 2.

12 Smith, above n 5, 45.

13 Law Commission New Zealand, above n 2.

14 Ibid 64.

15 Smith, above n 5, 46–7.

Apart from broad principles encompassing the rights to respect and dignity; cultural participation; independent and impartial decision making; freedom from inhumane treatment and unlawful detention—all in a non-discriminatory framework—there are no principles within either of these treaties dealing specifically with the rights of mental health consumers under involuntary detention. There is, however, a general right to the 'enjoyment of the highest attainable standard of physical and mental health' under the ICESCR.[16] Even so, the international acceptance and application of this right varies enormously and Tobin, in acknowledging the challenges faced by many countries and advocating a middle ground, maintains that 'the right to health as a concept has matured over the past decade or two and holds immense promise as both a normative and operational framework.'[17] The CESCR Committee in General Comment 14 stresses the importance of offering all health services on a non-discriminatory and equal basis[18] but the only explicit reference to mental health is that States must respect best practice international standards including the *MI Principles*.[19]

Of the four countries under examination, Vanuatu and Samoa are the only State Parties to the ICCPR and none of the countries under discussion is even a signatory to the ICESCR. The reasons for and effects of this low commitment rate are discussed in Chapter 12. It is not the aim of this work to explore the underlying theories and application of cultural rights in the region. Nonetheless, Hunt asserts that, while there is much dispute about the definition of cultural rights, with the primary focus on individualism, there are co-existing dimensions of individualism and collectivism present in many instances[20] and the ICCPR could be used to develop both and individualist and collective orientation to cultural rights in the Pacific region.[21]

1.3. MI Principles

As the inaugural international statement addressing rights of people with mental illness, the UNHCHR Principles for the Protection of Persons with Mental Illness and the Improvement of Mental Health Care (*MI Principles*) were highly persuasive when released in 1991[22] but, over time, have been subject to criticism given their reinforcement of the medical model of mental health care. Weller contends that 'on their face the MI Principles construct a coherent human rights framework for mental health care'[23] and '[enshrine] a broad discretion to impose medical treatment on persons who are subject to involuntary detention procedures which is limited only by the standards of medical practice and the principle of best interest.'[24]

---

16 *International Covenant on Economic, Social and Cultural Rights*, opened for signature 16 December 1966, 993 UNTS 3 (entered into force 3 January 1976) art 12.

17 J Tobin, 'Melbourne Legal Studies Research Paper No.562, Introduction: The Right to Health in International Law' (2011) *Melbourne Law School* <http://ssrn.com/abstract=1948850 (accessed 24 June 2013)>.

18 CESCR Committee, *General Comment No.14: The Right to the Highest Attainable Standard of Health (Art. 12 of the ICESCR),* 22nd sess, UN Doc E/C.12/2000/4 (8 November 2000) [18], [26].

19 Ibid [34].

20 P Hunt, 'Reflections on International Human Rights Law and Cultural Rights' in M Wilson and P Hunt (eds), *Culture, Rights, and Cultural Rights: Perspectives from the South Pacific* (Huia Publishers, 2000) 25, 29.

21 Ibid 42.

22 P Weller, 'Lost in Translation: Human Rights and Mental Health Law' in B McSherry and P Weller (eds), *Rethinking Rights Based Mental Health Laws* (Hart Publishing, 2010) 51, 64.

23 Ibid 62.

24 Ibid 64.

The author further maintains that the *MI Principles* were not lauded by consumers because of their 'uncritical acceptance of the medical model of disease and treatment and their related endorsement of involuntary detention and treatment.'[25]

However, despite these conceptual shortcomings, and in the current context, the *MI Principles*[26] do recognise the right to a diagnosis of mental illness in accordance with internationally accepted medical standards (Principle 4.1); the right to treatment in a cultural setting (Principle 7.3); the right to be informed of his or her rights at law (Principle 12.1); the right that involuntary detention be limited by law (Principle 16); and the right to periodic review of involuntary detention by an independent and impartial review body, with its decisions subject to a right of judicial appeal (Principle 17). The *MI Principles* also provide for a person's right to *participate* in hearings; free legal *representation* and interpreter services; alternate medical opinions; access to medical records and written reasons for decisions (Principle 18). General access to *information* is provided for under Principle 19.

1.4. WHO Ten Principles

The *WHO Ten Principles*—adopted in 1996 to assist in the interpretation of the *MI Principles*—include the promotion of mental health and prevention of mental disorders; access to basic mental health care; mental health assessments in accordance with internationally accepted principles; provision of the least restrictive type of mental health care; self-determination; the right to be assisted in the exercise of self-determination; availability of review procedures; automatic periodical review mechanisms; qualified decision-makers and respect of the rule of law.[27]

In 2001 the WHO followed with the World Health Report[28] focusing on international mental health issues and a discussion paper in 2004 canvassing the role of international human rights in mental health law.

This led to the publication of the WHO Resource Book[29] in 2005 outlining the fundamental aims of mental health legislation and upon which it seems at least Fiji based its law reform in this area.[30] These fundamental aims include promotion and protection of the rights of persons with mental disorders and the reduction of stigma and discrimination by protecting human rights; protecting the right to treatment; developing procedural protections; and integrating people with mental disorders in to the community.[31] These principles should be further achieved by supporting the rights of equality and non-discrimination, the right to individual autonomy and the rights to information and participation.[32]

Despite all this, Weller asserts that the WHO model 'replicates the contradictions and limitations of rights based legalism' and that its continued preoccupation with the imposition

25 Ibid.

26 Office of the High Commissioner for Human Rights, *Principles for the Protection of Persons with Mental Illness and the Improvement of Mental Health Care*, GA Res 46/119, (17 December 1991).

27 World Health Organisation, 'Mental Health Care Law: Ten Basic Principles' (1996).

28 World Health Organisation, 'World Health Report' (WHO, 2001).

29 M Freeman, *WHO Resource Book on Mental Health, Human Rights and Legislation* (World Health Organisation, 2005).

30 Fiji Law Reform Commission, 'Issue Paper No. 1 – Purpose, Principles and Definitions – Review of the Fiji Mental Treatment Act' (2006) 1.

31 Freeman, above n 29, 63.

32 Ibid 39.

of medical treatment as the primary response to mental illness is now 'fundamentally challenged' by the CRPD.[33]

Indeed, later resources developed by the WHO are directly aligned with the themes of the CRPD in promoting the human rights of people with mental disabilities in mental health care[34] as is the WHO Mental Health Action Plan 2013 -2020.[35]

1.5. CRPD

The *Convention on the Rights of Persons with Disabilities* (CRPD) was adopted by the UN General Assembly in 2006 and entered into force in 2008.[36] In May 2013 there were 130 State parties, including Vanuatu. Fiji, Samoa and Tonga have signed but not ratified the Convention. The stated purpose of the CRPD is to 'promote, protect and ensure the full and equal enjoyment of all human rights and fundamental freedoms by all persons with disabilities, and to promote respect for their inherent dignity.'[37] Persons with disabilities are defined to include 'those who have long-term physical, mental, intellectual or sensory impairments which in interaction with various barriers may hinder their full and effective participation in society on an equal basis with others.'[38]

The CRPD is founded on a platform of full realisation of human rights through non-discrimination, equality and social inclusion for those affected by disability.[39] The provisions of the CRPD are wide ranging and provide an ambitious spectrum of objectives with the potential to impact on every aspect of a person's life. They are closely aligned to the *MI Principles* in terms of the provision of health care services and the protection of rights, including non-discrimination on the grounds of mental illness. However, as noted previously, the CRPD moves well beyond the medical framework in which the *MI Principles* are set into a broader social setting that supports a more extensive mandate for equality and social inclusion.

With particular reference to the central questions under discussion, the CRPD provides for 'effective access to justice for persons with disabilities on an equal basis with others ... including in all legal proceedings'[40] and that persons not be 'deprived of their liberty unlawfully or arbitrarily.'[41] The CRPD recommends appropriate safeguards to prevent abuse in relation to the exercise of legal capacity and that any restriction to a person's rights in this regard be subject to 'regular review by a competent, independent and impartial authority or judicial body.'[42] Article 21 provides for disabled persons to access to information on an equal basis and article 30(4) confirms an entitlement to recognition and support of a person's 'cultural and linguistic identity'.

---

33 Weller, above n 22, 68.

34 M Funk and N Drew, *WHO QualityRights Tool Kit: Assessing and Improving Quality and Human Rights in Mental Health and Social Care Facilities* (World Health Organisation, 2012)

35 World Health Organisation, 'Mental Health Action Plan 2013 - 2020' (2013)

36 *Convention on the Rights of Persons with Disabilites*, opened for signature 13 December 2006, 2515 UNTS 3 (entered into force 3 May 2008).

37 Ibid art 1.

38 Ibid.

39 Ibid art 4.

40 Ibid art 13.

41 Ibid art 14.

42 Ibid art 12.

1.5.1. Optional Protocol to the CRPD

The Optional Protocol to the CRPD also entered into force in 2008.[43] Its primary objective is to empower the Committee on the Rights of Persons with Disabilities to receive and consider communications from or on behalf of individuals or groups of individuals subject to its jurisdiction who claim to be victims of a violation by a State Party of the provisions of the Convention.[44] The relevance of the Protocol so far is limited in the Pacific, as it has not yet been ratified by any of the four countries under discussion.[45] As a result, disabled persons in Vanuatu—the only country in the region that is a State party to the CRPD—have no right of access to an individual complaints procedure before an international body, should the country be in breach of the Convention.

2. Rights Based Legalism v. the CRPD

Rights based legalism or 'new legalism' or 'positive legalism'[46] are terms that have emerged relatively recently in the mental health context in Western countries as a progression from legalism—which itself replaced the medical paternalism model that pervaded mental health legislation until the 1960s.

There appears to be a degree of overlap in the use and application of the term 'rights based legalism' throughout the literature. There is little dispute that, in the context of mental health, *negative* rights refer to protection of a person from unwanted or inappropriate treatment or detention at the hands of the State—including the right to refuse treatment—whereas *positive* rights focus on the right to receive appropriate treatment in a socially inclusive setting.[47]

Earlier forms of legalism, or what some refer to as 'negative legalism,' focus on the protection of the mentally ill against wrongful treatment and confinement.[48] Yet others also refer to this as 'rights based legalism' in the sense that it creates a legal framework recognising certain rights as applicable to the mentally ill. On the other hand, some equate rights based legalism to 'positive legalism,' which revolves around the positive rights of 'human dignity, non-discrimination, social inclusion, independent living, education and employment.'[49] These positive rights form the central platform of the CRPD wherein article 14 specifically prohibits as discriminatory the deprivation of liberty based on the existence of any disability, including mental or intellectual disability.[50]

---

43 *Optional Protocol to the Convention on the Rights of Persons with Disabilities*, opened for signature 13 December 2006, Doc.A/61/611 (entered into force 3 May 2008).

44 Ibid art 1.

45 *United Nations Treaty Collection* <http://treaties.un.org/Pages/ViewDetails.aspx?src=TREATY&mtdsg_no=IV-4&chapter=4&lang=en (accessed 9 November 2012)>.

46 P Fennell, 'Institutionalising the Community: The Codification of Clinical Authority and the Limits of Rights Based Approaches' in B McSherry and P Weller (eds), *Rethinking Rights Based Mental Health Laws* (Hart Publishing, 2010) 13, 17, 21.

47 M Donnelly, 'Review of Treatment Decisions: Legalism, Process and the Protection of Rights' in B McSherry and P Weller (eds), *Rethinking Rights Based Mental Health Laws* (Hart Publishing, 2010) 275, 277–8.

48 Fennell, above n 46, 20.

49 Ibid 21.

50 *Convention on the Rights of Persons with Disabilites*, opened for signature 13 December 2006, 2515 UNTS 3 (entered into force 3 May 2008).

Fennel maintains this is completely at odds with most current mental health legislation, which allows for the involuntary detention and treatment of mentally ill persons and is in compliance with other human rights laws.[51] Bartlett agrees and goes so far as to suggest that 'UK mental health legislation is [not] remotely compliant' with the CRPD which on its face requires the abolition of all laws allowing detention based, in whole or in part, on mental disability.[52]

While the term 'rights based legalism' appears to be used by some writers to describe either form of legalism, the model that necessitates compliance with the CRPD is, by definition, a much broader form of legalism based on the *positive* right of social inclusion and the right to refuse psychiatric treatment, in a context where the only justifiable discrimination is based on lack of capacity. It might more aptly be described as 'disability free legalism' or 'inclusive legalism'. However, even the concept of capacity appears to be contentious in the context of the CRPD.

Nonetheless, the distinction is rather semantic as access to justice—in the context of review or appeal against detention—is a right enshrined in both general human rights instruments, including the *MI Principles*[53]and the CRPD.[54]

2.1. The CRPD and Legal Capacity

A person's capacity to consent to medical treatment assumes a critical degree of significance when he or she is subject to involuntary detention and is exposed to the likelihood of treatment without consent. In fact, some of the legislative criteria for detention require an assessment of whether or not the person has the capacity to give such consent. While this study is concerned with a person's ability to access justice under mental health legislation using the statutory mechanisms provided, his or her legal capacity to consent to treatment will often be one of the criteria under review. How this determination is made may be central to any decision to continue to detain a person.

Weller poses that 'challenging the strict distinction between capacity and incapacity, and the consequences of that determination, is the principal contribution of contemporary human rights thinking to the mental health field.'[55]

Much has been said in recent literature about rights based legalism and statutory compliance with international human rights treaties, including their impact on the rights of mental health consumers and whether rights based legalism is the definitive solution. Indeed, some authors have suggested that to comply with the CRPD—by treating those with mental illnesses in the same way as those with physical illnesses—mental health laws, as we know

[51] Fennell, above n 46, 48.

[52] P Bartlett, 'The United Nations Convention on the Rights of Persons with Disabilities and Mental Health Law' (2012) 75(5) *Modern Law Review* 752, 754.

[53] Office of the High Commissioner for Human Rights, *Principles for the Protection of Persons with Mental Illness and the Improvement of Mental Health Care*, GA Res 46/119, (17 December 1991) [17].

[54] *Convention on the Rights of Persons with Disabilites*, opened for signature 13 December 2006, 2515 UNTS 3 (entered into force 3 May 2008) [13], [14].

[55] Weller, above n 22, 62.

them, should be abandoned altogether.[56] They also contend that, in cases where legal capacity is the sole remaining issue, substituted decision making powers could be utilised through guardianship laws.[57] Rees maintains that this has the advantage of shifting the decision making from a public official to a family member, friend or statutory guardian and

> [t]his change may promote the dignity and autonomy of a person who loses capacity because of mental illness as in many cases the substitute decision maker would be a close and trusted person rather than an unfamiliar doctor at a psychiatric hospital.[58]

Dawson and Szmukler contend that substituted decision making should apply to both detention and treatment and that there should not be separate criteria for detention for mental illness compared to any other illness as it is simply discriminatory to have separate laws governing psychiatric treatment.[59] But their views do not have universal support.

Where legal capacity to participate effectively in decision making processes is the only issue separating those with a mental disorder from the general population, advancing the argument one step further, Carney suggests that

> the principles of consent to health care (and competence as a basis for substitute decision-making) are already capable of balancing competing interests in mental health care as in somatic health care generally.[60]

Minkowitz extends the effect of the CRPD's non-discrimination rationale even further and argues that

> the CRPD takes a holistic approach to human rights and provides for supportive measures to facilitate individual development and autonomy with equal rights and responsibilities as fundamental to human dignity.[61]

She asserts that the CRPD supersedes the *MI Principles*—which allow 'the imposition of coercive measures in the supposed "best interests" of an adult person with a disability'—and the *MI Principles* should be abandoned.[62] On this point Carney disagrees and maintains that 'rhetorical' language in article 12 of the CRPD 'can [not] dispel *prior explicit* language in previous international instruments expressly addressing mental health care, given accepted principles of treaty interpretation.'[63]

Minkowitz further asserts that article 12 of the CRPD does not in fact champion substituted decision making—where the right to make the decision is given to another

---

56 T Minkowitz, 'Abolishing Mental Health Laws to Comply with the Convention on the Rights of Persons with Disabilites' in B McSherry and P Weller (eds), *Rethinking Rights Based Mental Health Laws* (Hart Publishing, 2010) 151, 151.

57 N Rees, 'The Fusion Proposal: A Next Step?' in B McSherry and P Weller (eds), *Rethinking Rights Based Mental Health Laws* (Hart Publishing, 2010) 73, 74.

58 Ibid 87.

59 J Dawson and G Szmukler, 'Why Distinguish "Mental" and "Physical" Illness in Involuntary Treatment?' in M Freeman and O Goodenough (eds), *Law, Mind and Brain* (Ashgate, 2009) 173, 174–5.

60 T Carney, 'Involuntary Mental Health Treatment Laws: The 'Rights' and Wrongs of Competing Models?' in B McSherry and P Weller (eds), *Rethinking Rights Based Mental Health Laws* (Hart Publishing, 2010) 257, 257.

61 Minkowitz, above n 56, 151.

62 Ibid 153.

63 Carney, above n 60, 258.

person—but that 'a person who experiences difficulties with decision making must be supported to make his or her own decisions.'[64] This advances the process even further along the spectrum of realising human rights for persons who lack legal capacity from *substituted* decision making to *supported* decision making. The latter concept does not mean that the person's decision must be carried out but that the presentation of information to the person must be accessible by that person and his or her self-expression must be respected.[65]

Nonetheless, the concept of supported (or assisted) decision making does assume the existence of either a supportive personal network that is both willing and able to facilitate the process without abuse or compromise, or a sophisticated network of social services and community resources to achieve the same end. Yet, it is the very lack of personal networks that so often contributes to a person's need for involuntary detention and removal from the community. Victoria was the first state in Australia to undergo a wide-ranging review of its guardianship laws and the Victorian Law Reform Commission, in an extremely well researched and comprehensive report, recommends a number of different methods to facilitate decision making for people with disabilities to cover a range of different and changing circumstances—involving individual and state representatives.[66] In the Pacific this might prove to be a challenge. Still, supported decision making is clearly the preferred model espoused by the WHO in its benchmarking criteria for improving human rights in mental health care.[67]

Donnelly argues that an autonomy based rights approach to treatment for mental disorders fails to protect patients who lack the capacity to consent to treatment because of its focus on capable patients[68] and 'does little in terms of delivering appropriate care to patients.'[69] She asserts that 'reformers should not regard the delivery of autonomy as the primary goal of rights protection and that a rights framework must be broader, encompassing the needs of people lacking capacity.'[70]

Donnelly further argues that differential treatment of persons with mental disorders has traditionally been justified on the grounds that the right to refuse treatment must take into account the prevention of harm to others; and the autonomy of a person with a mental disorder is already limited by his or her mental disorder and the role of medical intervention is to restore autonomy.[71] The restoration of autonomy ultimately justifies this limitation on the patient's right to refuse treatment—in other words the end justifies the means.

The more compelling argument is posed by Donnelly and moves towards a more inclusive approach to decision making involving the wishes of the patient lacking capacity and based on dignity and privacy:

---

64 Minkowitz, above n 56, 157.

65 Ibid 164.

66 Victorian Law Reform Commission, 'Guardianship: Final Report 24' (2012). See also Shih-Ning Then, 'Evolution and Innovation in Guardianship Laws: Assisted Decision Making' (2013) 35 *Sydney Law Review* 133.

67 M Funk and N Drew, *WHO QualityRights Tool Kit: Assessing and Improving Quality and Human Rights in Mental Health and Social Care Facilities* (World Health Organisation, 2012) 81.

68 M Donnelly, 'From Autonomy to Dignity: Treatment for Mental Disorders and the Focus for Patient Rights' (2008) 26(2) *Law in Context Special Issue: International Trends in Mental Health Laws* 37.

69 Ibid 49.

70 Ibid 38.

71 Ibid 41–3.

> [t]he argument that treatment will lead to the restoration of autonomy is inevitably speculative... [and] some patients may prefer the limitations of their illness, even if it means detention, to the forced imposition of treatment. While this may seem an unreasonable response to most people, the premise of autonomy is that capable people should be permitted to make unreasonable decisions. If the law is happy to accept unreasonable choices in other respects, it is difficult to find a justification for rejecting such choices in the mental health arena alone.[72]
>
> Further, a focus on autonomy does not recognise the fact that a patient found to lack capacity does not make the imposition of treatment any less traumatic for the patient if he or she does not want the treatment... [especially] highly invasive treatment such as ECT...[73]

In essence, capacity is a threshold issue in many legal situations, not only in relation to consent to medical treatment. For example, a person requires legal capacity to enter into a contract or make a will; the inappropriateness of the terms of the contract or will is largely irrelevant. The fact that a person has a physical illness, a mental illness or no illness at all, should be of no consequence. A person with a medical condition, such as hypertension, has the right to elect whether or not to take prescribed medication and suffer the consequences, even if this results in episodes of uncontrolled agitation that could impact on the safety of others. Equally, people in the community engage in legal risk taking behaviour on a daily basis from driving a motor vehicle, to consuming excessive amounts of alcohol, to participating in adventure sports—and all with the risk of injuring themselves and others.

Why then should the decision of a person with a mental disorder—who refuses treatment for reasons associated with his or her own comfort but which may involve some risk to others—be any different? The answer must lie in identifying the potential risks and developing strategies to minimise them, rather than depriving the person of the right to make the decision.

3. The CRPD and the Future

Minkowitz claims quite properly that, in compliance with the social model of disability posed by the CRPD—as opposed to the medical model—traditional healing centres as 'social institutions integrated into the community' could be integral in building an alternative service system.[74] This concept is already well developed in some regions of the Pacific as a phenomenon that has occurred naturally within the social fabric rather than the end result of a complex and tortuous journey of socio-legal discovery. The quality of care within that framework is a different matter. So what is the answer for the future?

It is clear that the preference for community treatment alternatives and non-coercion are now part of international law for countries that have ratified the CRPD.[75] Any decentralised community based model that gives maximum effect to the CRPD and shifts the balance from

72 Ibid 44.

73 Ibid 49.

74 Minkowitz, above n 56, 164.

75 P Bartlett and V Hamzic, 'Reforming Mental Disability Law in Africa: Practical Tips and Suggestions' (Human Rights Law Centre, The University of Nottingham, 2010) 6.

coercive isolation to social inclusion will need to involve serious commitment by relevant governments to appropriate levels of funding in order to sustain the social infrastructure necessary for success. Even in more affluent countries with relatively well-funded health systems and social welfare safety nets, rights based models demand additional resources from an increasingly over-stretched mental health care budget.[76] When health professionals argue that resources should be prioritised into clinical care, governments are often reluctant to divert funds, for example, to the evaluation and implementation of a more 'rights friendly' and potentially more costly review process[77] aimed at promoting the expression of rights and access to justice for mental health consumers.

If, as many writers suggest, the intention of the CRPD is that existing mental health legislation that provides for involuntary detention and treatment based on disability offends the spirit of the CRPD and ought to be abolished, something short of a revolution will be required in the Western mental health arena. While it is relatively early days for the CRPD, nonetheless, as Bartlett points out, many of the longer term solutions remain problematic. He contends that while disability-neutral legislation might be one way of dealing with issues of capacity and dangerousness in a way that is not linked to disability, this may compromise the civil rights of the broader community and open the gates for human rights abuse in more autocratic regimes.[78] As discussed previously, dangerousness is extraordinarily difficult to predict and preventive detention is a highly sensitive issue even in relation to those who are not mentally disordered. Bartlett quite accurately maintains that even with disability-neutral preventive detention legislation, those people with mental disorders will end up with a criminal record and be exposed to the harshness of the prison system, with even less prospect of being reintegrated into the community on release.[79] This would all seem to be counter-productive.

However, as Bartlett also asserts, it is possibly too early to predict how the provisions of the CRPD will be interpreted. While the CRPD reinforces the international trend away from reliance on institutional care towards community based alternatives and the normalisation of the lives of people with disabilities, the extent to which countries will be held to account under the CRPD remains to be seen.[80] Certainly, large scale deinstitutionalisation, as it occurred in some Western countries, without adequate pre-planning and development of community infrastructure, is not likely to enhance or promote the rights of mental health consumers.

For this reason, as Bartlett rightly poses, it may be that the move away from involuntary detention could be interpreted as an obligation subject to progressive realisation rather than one necessitating immediate compliance under the CRPD[81] and akin to many of the rights under the ICESCR.

The CRPD proposes the ideal. The ideal is rarely achievable and the best practical solution will lie somewhere on the continuum. If we accept that there will always be some mentally disabled people who *do not* have capacity and for whom even the most intensive supported decision-making processes will be complicated, it will be the level of acceptable

---

76 Carney, above n 60, 260.

77 N Rees, 'International Human Rights Obligations and Mental Health Review Tribunals' (2003) 10(1) *Psychiatry, Psychology and Law* 33, 39.

78 Bartlett, above n 52, 772–3.

79 Ibid 774.

80 Bartlett and Hamzic, above n 75, 11.

81 Ibid 16.

restrictions placed on them that will be contentious. For those mental health consumers who *do* have capacity to give informed consent, the challenge will be the extent to which they will be allowed to make poor decisions that may affect others—alongside the rest of the community.

3.1. Disability Free Legalism in the Pacific

The position in the Pacific is even more precarious. Health budgets are much smaller—even as a proportion of GDP—and are under constant pressure to fund more visible and pressing health issues such as high infant and maternal mortality rates as well as communicable and non-communicable disease control and prevention. There are few professional resources in mental health—either medical or legal—to advocate for mental health care promotion and reform. Where rights based legislation has been instigated in some cases, rarely have its provisions been given full effect. Community awareness of mental health issues and related human rights, and the capacity to engage in supported decision making, is poor. None of the countries in the region has separate disability legislation nor discrete legal capacity laws.

While Tonga, Samoa and Fiji have signed the CRPD, Vanuatu is the only country in the region with State Party status but it has yet to meet its reporting obligations under the Convention.[82] There is no indication in any of these countries that a legislative reform package to comply with the CRPD is being contemplated or that there is even an understanding of the extent of reform necessary.

In fact, the paradigm shift necessary to comply with the ideology of the CRPD represents a monumental challenge globally. Many Western countries with far greater resources and social infrastructure have barely begun to absorb the reality of how it can be achieved. A handful of Pacific island countries are only just coming to terms with recognising the basic human rights of mental health consumers; accepting that these rights should be exercised in a non-discriminatory social setting is a dawn that has not yet broken.

3.2. Progressive Realisation

A number of international treaties concede that not all State Parties are in an equal position in terms of available resources, cultural beliefs and practices and political and legislative systems. It has long been recognised, for example, that many African governments—despite developing an awareness of the need for rights based change—are constantly thwarted by poor financial and professional resources and minimal levels of legal and medical education necessary to understand, draft and implement rights based legislative reform.[83] Nonetheless, some rights are considered to be inalienable and *immediately effective* and to be prioritised by member States—namely, those under the ICCPR touching on basic civil rights and freedoms, including the right to life, liberty, equality, a fair trial and freedom

[82] Vanuatu ratified the CRPD in 2008 and under Art 35 of the CRPD is required to submit its initial report within two years. See Table 12.1 in Chapter 12.

[83] Bartlett and Hamzic, above n 75.

from torture and cruel and inhuman treatment. In the current context this would include detention according to law; procedural rights to challenge involuntary detention and treatment; access to justice though equal recognition before the law; and procedural fairness. Bartlett argues that, under the CRPD, any laws that discriminate against people with disabilities should be subject to enforcement with immediate effect.[84] The feasibility of this contention in the Pacific is questionable.

Conversely, rights to education, appropriate housing and standards of living and good physical and mental health, as expressed under the ICESCR, are recognised as being dependent on the goodwill and resources of the State and, as such, subject to an evolving program of implementation,[85] referred to as *progressive realisation.*[86] This also encourages more affluent States to provide technical and financial assistance to underprivileged States to facilitate their progress towards meeting their international treaty obligations. The new Constitution of the Republic of Fiji contains a specific provision that

> [t]he State must take reasonable measures within its available resources to achieve the progressive realisation of the right of every person to health, and to the conditions and facilities necessary to good health, and to health care services, including reproductive health care.[87]

Again, in the current context, this notion might relate to the right to access mental health care services in the community in a cultural setting and the right to human rights education.

The concept of progressive realisation anticipates that the development of certain rights will take place over time and, what constitutes, for example, the 'best attainable levels of health care' may also change with time. But States are required to make genuine and serious efforts to develop these rights and not to use the concept as an excuse to delay projects indeterminately. This means providing the best services possible with the resources available. The *Limburg Principles*[88] were developed to assist States in the interpretation of the phrase 'to achieve progressively the full realisation of the rights' under the ICESCR. The obligation has been interpreted to mean State Parties must move as expeditiously as possible towards realisation of the rights with effective use of available resources, and does *not* imply a right to defer indefinitely.[89] However, it should be noted that, even under the ICESCR, there are some rights that must be delivered immediately.[90]

Jalal asserts that the concept of progressive realisation is poorly understood by most Pacific governments and they resist rights implementation on account of financial constraints

---

84 Ibid 13.

85 Smith, above n 5, 46.

86 *International Covenant on Economic, Social and Cultural Rights*, opened for signature 16 December 1966, 993 UNTS 3 (entered into force 3 January 1976) art 2.1.

87 *Constitution of the Republic of Fiji*

88 CESCR, *Limburg Principles on the Implementation of the International Covenant on Economic, Social and Cultural Rights*, E/C.12/2000/13, 24th sess, Provisional Agenda Item 3, (10 February 2000).

89 P Imrana Jalal, 'Pacific Culture and Human Rights: Why Pacific Island Countries Should Ratify International Human Rights Treaties' (2006) <www.rrrt.org/images/pacificcultureandhumanrights.pdf (accessed 5 April 2013)> 19.

90 ESCR Committee, *General Comment No. 3: The Nature of States Parties Obligations (Art. 2, para. 1 of the Covenant),* 5th Sess, UN Doc E/1991/23 (4 December 1990) [5]; 'In addition, there are a number of other provisions in the International Covenant on Economic, Social and Cultural Rights, including articles 3, 7 (a) (i), 8, 10 (3), 13 (2) (a), (3) and (4) and 15 (3) which would seem to be capable of immediate application by judicial and other organs in many national legal systems.'

and because rights are frequently perceived as an obstacle to economic development.[91] The question then becomes how to monitor reform in member States to ensure that it remains on individual political agendas. Bartlett suggests that, in relation to the CRPD, bodies sufficiently independent of governments—but with appropriate expertise to command the respect of governments—need to be established to monitor the development of rights for persons with disabilities.[92] There are currently no such organisations in operation in any of the countries under discussion.

3.3. The Contextualisation of Human Rights

Human rights are often expressed in broad and universal terms but are applied by courts according to local context, thereby developing a community's appreciation of the meaning of human rights. This does not mean that human rights are compromised to accommodate cultural differences.[93] In fact, in many instances, specific cultural practices must change to accommodate human rights. In several Pacific constitutions specific rights have been expressly limited to maintain customary or cultural practices.[94]

While rights impacting on the provision of services are frequently subject to progressive realisation, fundamental personal rights are expected to be implemented immediately. However, there is still a discretion that allows States to adapt those rights to suit the needs or culture of a particular country, which has come to be known as the *margin of appreciation*. The overall responsibility for the protection of individual rights lies with the States, which are acknowledged in international law as being in a better position to balance individual and State interests. This doctrine, in recognising that few rights are absolute, provides a degree of flexibility for States to determine which measures are appropriate.[95] While the margin of appreciation varies with the right in question, the doctrine has been used most commonly in Europe under the European Convention of Human Rights. The doctrine was considered but rejected in Fiji in *Nadan & McCoskar*. In this case, the provisions of the Penal Code prohibiting consenting homosexual acts were challenged as unconstitutional, on the grounds that the then Fijian constitution guaranteed rights of privacy and equality, specifically in relation to sexual orientation. In striking down the relevant provisions of the Penal Code, Winter J stated:

> In my view despite the margin of appreciation given to the State to restrict sexual acts on the grounds of morality, the suggested limitations by criminal sanction are wholly disproportionate to the right of privacy. The criminalisation of carnal acts against the order of nature between consenting adult males or females in private is a severe restriction on a citizen's right to build relationships with dignity and free of State intervention and cannot be justified as necessary.[96]

---

91 Imrana Jalal, above n 89.

92 Bartlett and Hamzic, above n 75, 14.

93 Law Commission New Zealand, above n 2, 168–171.

94 Ibid.

95 Smith, above n 5, 173.

96 *Nadan & McCoskar v State* [2005] FJHC 252. This decision was premised on the fact that Fiji had ratified the ICCPR (which includes the right to privacy). Winter J stated 'Fiji has ratified the International Convention on Civil and Political Rights. The appellants are entitled to expect that I will interpret these rights in accordance

Another means of taking a more contextual or nuanced approach to fundamental human rights and resolving conflicts between rights emerged in 1984 in what became known as the *Siracusa Principles.*[97] These principles outline a uniform set of interpretations of the Limitation Clauses contained in the ICCPR and, while they do not have the force of law, they offer authoritative guidance on when there might be lawful limits on fundamental freedoms. The New Zealand Law Commission, in its analysis of custom and human rights in the Pacific, suggests that these principles would be preferred to the 'margin of appreciation' as a means of moderating concerns about the potentially undermining effects of human rights principles on custom and culture, because the principles require a stronger justification as to the limitation of human rights.[98]

4. SUMMARY

There are a number of human rights instruments that impact on the rights of mental health consumers in terms of their ability to access justice under mental health legislation in the Pacific. Few countries in the region have ratified major human rights treaties—a fact that may be partly attributed to the ideological tension between Pacific cultural traditions and 'Western style' human rights doctrines. However, in some instances, even where countries have not formally committed to specific treaties, the principles have still influenced mental health policy and legislation.. Yet, the practical implementation of these legislative initiatives paints a different picture. As will be discussed in later chapters, Samoa and Fiji have incorporated progressive realisation type clauses into their legislation; yet neither of these countries is a State party to the CRPD. Whether the provisions of the CRPD will be construed as being suitable for such limitations is a question that has yet to be answered. Resources at all levels and socio-political commitment will ultimately determine the ability of Pacific countries to comply with international standards and deliver access to justice for those subject to mental health legislation.

with its provisions.' However, no United Nations or PITS records support this assertion and the judge's comments must be treated with some circumspection. The case did not go on further appeal. The relevant provisions of the Penal Code have since been repealed by the *Crimes Decree 2009* (Fiji Islands).

97 UN Commission on Human Rights, *The Siracusa Principles on the Limitation and Derogation Provisions in the International Covenant on Civil and Political Rights*, E/CN.4/1985/4, (28 September 1984).

98 Law Commission New Zealand, above n 2, 176.

PART II: MENTAL HEALTH LAW AND POLICY IN THE PACIFIC

Chapter 4

THE LEGAL LANDSCAPE IN MENTAL HEALTH

1. LITERATURE

There appears to be no published literature in the Pacific region that deals analytically or comparatively with the operation of mental health legislation; the review of recent legislation; the legal rights of the mentally ill; or access to justice for mental health consumers in the context of involuntary detention. In fact, prior to the WHO health initiatives in the Pacific in 2002, there was relatively very little written about regional mental health at all—particularly so with reference to the countries under discussion.

A recent publication by MacFarlane and Ménard provides a descriptive overview of the legislation and case law governing medical law in the South Pacific.[1] While the monograph discusses the various mental health statutes in the region, it neither evaluates individual provisions with respect to human rights frameworks or access to justice nor provides any comparative analysis of previous legislation. There is therefore room for an examination of new mental health legislation and its ability to improve access to justice for those subject to its provisions.

In 2013, Pathare and Sagade assessed the mental health legislation in Commonwealth member states for rights based compliance with the CPRD but there was no individual examination of country by country legislation and the results were only framed in a statistical format.[2]

This study seeks to determine whether new mental health legislation in the region has improved access to justice for mental health consumers by either creating new pathways to justice or improving existing pathways; and whether or not these legislative frameworks have resulted in any practical changes for mental health consumers subject to involuntary detention. The answers to these questions necessitate a comparative analysis of the old and new statutes in each of the target countries. However, before embarking on an individual country analysis, it is important to look at the history of mental health legislation the region in order to understand its origins and some of the conceptual issues that have beleaguered mental health law reform.

---

1 P MacFarlane and H Ménard, *Medical Law in the South Pacific* (Kluwer Law International, 2014).

2 Pathare S and J Sagade, 'Mental Health: A Legislative Framework to Empower, Protect and Care. A Review of Mental Health Legislation in Commonwealth Member States.' (2013).

2. The History of Mental Health Legislation in the Pacific

Only 75 percent of countries globally have mental health legislation. Of these, 51 percent have only passed laws since 1990 and 15 percent still have laws dating back before the 1960s.[3] Most of the Pacific falls into the latter category. The global target under the WHO Mental Health Action Plan 2013–2020 is that '50% of countries will have developed or updated their laws for mental health in line with international and regional human rights instruments (by the year 2020).'[4]

For the most part, mental health legislation in the Pacific region is long out of date and largely based on obsolete English statutes,[5] which provide minimal protection for the rights of the mentally ill. Instead of the socio-political debate that took place in England and other jurisdictions[6] regarding the passage of mental health legislation, by virtue of the colonisation process in the Pacific, the adoption and application of English laws took a completely passive route consistent with the general approach of colonial legal systems to adopting metropolitan law. This is confirmed by the fact that, once introduced, the legislation lay dormant for many years and—in some countries in the region—remains so.[7]

In general, the *Mental Health Act 1959* (UK) would have applied in several countries in the region as part of the general application or adoption of English laws, prior to and after achieving independence.[8] English legislation that was applied or adopted in this way was often described by the phrase 'the statutes of general application in force in England' at a particular date. This date—known as the 'cut-off date'—varied from country to country in the region. Even countries such as Samoa—which was not under direct British rule at the time of independence and which attained independence from New Zealand—were still affected by the application of English legislation. Thus, the statutes in force in England as at 14 January 1840—the date of colonisation of New Zealand—were applied to Western Samoa as long as they were in force in New Zealand on 7 December 1921.[9]

The authorising legislation stated that 'statutes of general application shall be in force so far only as the circumstances of any particular territory and its inhabitants ... permit and subject to such qualifications as local circumstances render necessary.'[10]

The precise application of legislation in the dependent countries under this provision is ambiguous and, given that all of the target countries have since implemented their own mental health legislation, the only real issue in relation to the countries under discussion concerns Vanuatu. As the 'cut-off date' for Vanuatu was 1976, four years before

[3] M Freeman, *WHO Resource Book on Mental Health, Human Rights and Legislation* (World Health Organisation, 2005) 1.

[4] World Health Organisation, 'Mental Health Action Plan 2013 - 2020' (2013), 12.

[5] *Cook Islands Act 1915* (New Zealand); *Mental Treatment Ordinance* [Cap 56] (Kiribati); *Mentally Disordered Persons Ordinance 1963* (Nauru); *Nuie Act 1966* (NZ); *Mental Treatment Act* [Cap 103] (Solomon Islands); *Mental Treatment Ordinance* [Cap 37] (Tuvalu); *Mental Hospital Act* [Cap 38] (Vanuatu); *Mental Health Act 1959* (UK).

[6] See the history of early mental health legislation in NSW in P Shea, *Defining Madness* (Hawkins Press, 1999) Ch 3–4.

[7] For example, *Mental Treatment Ordinance* [Cap 56] (Kiribati); *Mentally Disordered Persons Ordinance 1963* (Nauru); *Nuie Act 1966* (NZ); *Mental Treatment Ac*t [Cap 103] (Solomon Islands); *Mental Treatment Ordinance* [Cap 37] (Tuvalu); *Mental Hospital Act* [Cap 38] (Vanuatu).

[8] For example, Kiribati, Solomon Islands and Vanuatu.

[9] See *Samoa Act 1921* (NZ) s 349 and *Constitution of the Independent State of Western Samoa 1960*art 114.

[10] *Western Pacific (Courts) Order 1961* (UK) s 15.

independence, it is possible that provisions of the *Mental Health Act 1959* (UK) still apply in Vanuatu, to the extent that they relate to matters not covered under its own legislation. On the other hand, as there are effectively no mental health services available in this country, it remains a moot point.[11] The only relevant legislation in Vanuatu is the *Mental Hospital Act* [Cap 38] enacted by way of joint Anglo-French regulation in 1965.[12]

Most countries in the Pacific region operating under the English common law system included transitional provisions in their constitutions that provided for laws—previously in force in the country—to continue after independence. For example, sections 95(1)-(3) of the *Constitution of the Republic of Vanuatu* state:

> (1) Until otherwise provided by Parliament, all Joint Regulations and subsidiary legislation made thereunder in force immediately before the Day of Independence shall continue in operation on and after that day as if they had been made in pursuance of the Constitution and shall be construed with such adaptations as may be necessary to bring them into conformity with the Constitution.
>
> (2) Until otherwise provided by Parliament, the British and French laws in force or applied in Vanuatu immediately before the Day of Independence shall on and after that day continue to apply to the extent that they are not expressly revoked or incompatible with the independent status of Vanuatu and wherever possible taking due account of custom.
>
> (3) Customary law shall continue to have effect as part of the law of the Republic of Vanuatu.

3. Who Are the Mentally Ill?

The appropriate diagnosis of any mental illness remains a contentious area of debate. Diagnosis of a mental illness or mental disorder is a critical threshold issue as, once a diagnosis is made bringing a person within the scope of the relevant legislation, his or her legal rights are immediately constrained. Access to legal avenues to evaluate these constraints then becomes an equally critical issue. The essence of the question often lies in the underlying tension between the medical and legal views as to what constitutes a mental illness. To frame a definition too widely can result in inappropriate detention of people who are unlikely to benefit from treatment and, conversely, a narrow definition may exclude those who need treatment.[13]

---

[11] MacFarlane and Ménard, above n 1.

[12] Prior to independence in 1980, Vanuatu (formerly the New Hebrides) was governed as a joint condominium between Britain and France pursuant to article 8 of the *1914 Protocol relating to the New Hebrides between Britain and France*. The *New Hebrides Orders in Council* (1922-1970) gave effect to Protocol and gave powers to High Commissioner to make Joint Regulations or Queens Regulations. Laws were a combination of Joint Regulations made by the High Commissioner (UK) and High Commissioner (France) and Queens Regulations made by the High Commissioner (UK) or the High Commissioner (France). All such regulations were given the force of law at independence by virtue of s 95 of the Constitution of the Republic of Vanuatu.

[13] W Brookbanks and S Simpson, *Psychiatry and the Law* (LexisNexisNZ Ltd, 2007) 41.

3.1. Sad, Mad or Bad?

Does every form of depression or sadness, some of which may have its roots in ordinary life experience such as relationship breakdowns, death of family members or career crises, necessarily satisfy the definition of a mental illness? To what extent should persons suffering from drug dependency related psychoses, acquired brain injury or intellectual impairment be caught in the net of compulsory detention under the guise of self-protection?

An even more divisive topic in psychiatric medicine is whether personality disorders—of which there are many types—constitute mental illnesses. This question highlights the polarisation between the legal and medical professions when it comes to defining mental illness and there is no shortage of literature on the topic. If psychiatry were left to its own devices in terms of deciding who was 'mad', many, though not all, in the profession would be comfortable with including psychopathy or anti-social personality disorders under its umbrella.

Prior to the 1980s and the rise of the consumer rights movement, mental health legislation was more focussed on protection of others than on the rights of people with mental illness.[14] With the introduction of rights based mental health legislation, came the attempt to define the undefinable—to frame in comprehensive legal terms the concept of mental illness. In psychiatric terms, this is where the two professions began to diverge. Lawyers are more comfortable with coherence and legal prescription whereas psychiatrists tend to be more philosophical and morally pragmatic—therein lies the divide.

The ethical 'tug of war' in this area is between justice and the rights of the person versus the need for treatment and protection—both in a setting of compulsory detention and treatment without consent. This is not a new game. The natural opponents are the legal and the medical fraternities in what one partial observer describes as a 'cold war'.[15] In trying to determine where it all went wrong, the same observer maintains that the introduction of new legislation in the United Kingdom in 1959 brought with it political and financial support that allowed professionally trained personnel to work in optimum conditions. This did not apply in Australia during the same period, where staff were both poorly trained and insufficiently resourced, leading to patterns of institutional abuse and preventing the legislation from working as it was intended.[16]

Grigor properly maintains that the law can neither cure nor fully protect the mentally ill and, in fact, can be counterproductive when it creates fear and an over cautious approach to diagnosis and treatment. Conversely, he claims that psychiatrists failed to adequately address community concerns about proper care of the mentally ill, which fuelled rights based reformist legislation.[17]

People who do not satisfy the statutory definition of mental illness but whose behaviour would benefit from treatment 'for their own good' pose a difficult ethical dilemma. In many instances, it may involve the elderly and disorientated or those with behavioural problems who disrupt society or the treatment and care of others. They may be unable or unwilling to

[14] Ibid.

[15] J Grigor, 'A Psychiatrist's View of Recent Mental Health Legislation' (Paper presented at the Professional Responsibility in Psychiatry, Psychology and Law: Proceedings of the 7th Annual Congress of the Australian and New Zealand Association of Psychiatry, Psychology and Law, Melbourne, Australia, 1986) 143.

[16] Ibid.

[17] Ibid 145.

consent to treatment, without which their condition may frequently deteriorate. While treatment may often alleviate their symptoms, health professionals are unable to administer treatment without consent. The principle of autonomy is said to prevail in these circumstances but, often, the person's condition will deteriorate until eventually he or she may be admitted for care only after there has been an incident of self-harm or injury to others.

While, in most societies, the 'legalisation' of psychiatry and deinstitutionalisation have reduced the incidence of institutional abuse, access to adequate treatment and community care has largely been denied. Furthermore, the emphasis on individual rights has neither addressed the longstanding issue of stigmatisation of mental illness nor provided community acceptance of those who have been entrusted to its care.

3.2. The Medical View

Mental illness is an exceedingly imprecise term. From a medical standpoint it usually involves symptoms that exhibit a significant degree of impairment of mental function including memory, cognition, emotion and perception. In practice, a psychiatric diagnosis is more often based on the nature of the patient's symptoms in the context of his or her life experiences and the extent to which those symptoms impact on the person's ability to function 'normally' in society or a particular cultural setting. Treatment ranges from cognitive behaviour modification therapy, to antipsychotic or anti-depressant medication, to physical restraint and seclusion, to electro convulsive therapy (ECT) and, as a last resort, to psychosurgery.

There have been a number of models of psychiatric illness used over the years, each with its shortcomings. They include the medical model where the classification of psychiatric illness is in accordance with a series of syndromes most of which have a biological basis; the bio psychosocial model where psychiatric illness is viewed as the result of an interaction between biological and psychosocial factors; and finally the psychosocial model where mental illness is seen as being intrinsically linked to a person's social experiences especially trauma.[18]

Even psychiatrists concede that accurate diagnosis can be arbitrary. Ellard demonstrates this cogently with a series of graduated illustrations in relation to some of the common symptoms of mental illness—delusions, hallucinations, thought disorder and mood.[19] For example:

> Here is someone who hears a loud voice commenting on his actions for most of every day. He has looked everywhere for the loud speakers and cannot find them: he is still looking. There is not much doubt about him.
>
> Here is a man whose wife died two months ago. Yesterday he thought he saw her walk into David Jones' door half a block away…
>
> It is not rare for people with hysteria to hallucinate.[20]

---

18 I Kerridge, M Lowe and C Stewart, *Ethics and Law for the Health Professionals* (3rd ed, 2009) 503.

19 J Ellard, 'The Madness of Mental Health Acts' (1990) 24 *Australian and New Zealand Journal of Psychiatry* 167.

20 Ibid 170.

The late Kathleen Jones, acclaimed English social scientist, once wrote of psychiatrists and their attempts to determine mental illness:

> From the most hard headed proponents of the biochemical view of mental illness to those who dwell on the wilder shores of psychoanalytical thought, they may be cheerfully lumped together as determinists who can be counted on to explain away the most extreme examples of moral turpitude.[21]

3.3. The Legal View

In an ideal world there would be little need for social regulation. We do not live in an ideal world. History has shown that psychiatric medicine alone has not been a responsible guardian of the rights of the mentally ill. However, both the legal and medical professions have struggled to construct legislation in a way that safeguards individual rights while at the same time promoting a therapeutic environment and protecting the community. The repeated and somewhat circular changes to mental health legislation in the United Kingdom from 1959 to 2007, as outlined below, are a case in point.

As Ellard, a prominent Australian psychiatrist, writes, 'those who draft mental health legislation, wise though they may be, cannot be expected to provide definitions which probably do not exist and which no one else has been able to discover.'[22]

The legal definition of what constitutes mental illness has always been, and remains, a highly debatable issue from a legal, social and medical perspective. There is no universally accepted statutory definition of mental illness despite many attempts by many legislators and medical practitioners in many countries, over many years, to find one. The area is simply too complex medically, and the ramifications too extreme legally and socially, to construct an easily workable solution. The resistance to defining mental illness has traditionally come from the health profession, which maintains that the 'diagnosis of mental illness is a matter for psychiatrists not lawyers.'[23] Nonetheless, most common law jurisdictions—in an attempt to satisfy the civil rights movement—have tried to adopt some form of definition, while a few have sought to differentiate between mental illness and mental disorders.[24]

Dawson describes three main methods of legally defining psychiatric disorders that have evolved over time.[25] The first is not to define the terms at all—the most common being unsound mind, mental illness and mental disorder. While he argues this approach has legislative advantages, the inevitable flexibility of an open ended definition leads to unreliable and arbitrary application.[26] The second approach is to 'construct a statutory system of classification of mental disorders' thereby producing a list of disabling conditions.[27] The main weakness with this methodology is that there are frequently inconsistencies between the legal terms used and their meaning in a psychiatric context. The third technique Dawson discusses is the psychopathological approach that involves the 'descriptive language of

21 Grigor, above n 15, 143 quoting Kathleen Jones.
22 Ellard, above n 19, 170.
23 Law Reform Commission of Victoria, 'Report No. 31: The Concept of Mental Illness in the Mental Health Act 1986' (1990) 13.
24 MacFarlane and Ménard, above n 1.
25 J Dawson, 'Psychopathology and Civil Commitment Criteria' (1996) 4 *Medical Law Review* 62.
26 Ibid 66.
27 Ibid 69.

symptomatology or psychopathology—reliance on the major groupings of the clinical signs and symptoms of mental disorders.'[28] Dawson contends this approach has the benefit of assessing mental dysfunction in accordance with recognised clinical signs and symptoms as part of a syndrome[29] rather than attempting to apply artificial definitions of illness.

None of these systems has proven to be the perfect solution and, as can be seen from the discussion in the following chapters on the individual Pacific countries, all of these methods have been adopted at one time or another in those jurisdictions.

3.3.1. Comparative Definitions

As Pacific legislation under discussion in some cases, for example Samoa, has been modelled largely on Australian, and to a lesser extent New Zealand, statutes, it is apt at this point to examine some of those provisions.

The *Mental Health Act 2007* (NSW) s 4(1)[30] defines mental illness in a purely medical framework as follows:

> *mental illness* means a condition which seriously impairs, either temporarily or permanently, the mental functioning of a person and is characterised by the presence in the person of any one or more of the following symptoms:
>
> (a) delusions
> (b) hallucinations
> (c) serious disorder of thought form
> (d) a severe disturbance of mood
> (e) sustained or repeated irrational behaviour indicating the presence of symptoms referred to in paras (a)-(d).[31]

Section 14 of the same Act, in defining a mentally ill person and validating the grounds for detention as being more than simply having a mental illness, states:

> (1) A person is a *mentally ill person* if the person is suffering from mental illness and, owing to that illness, there are reasonable grounds for believing that care, treatment or control of the person is necessary:
> (a) for the person's own protection from serious harm, or
> (b) for the protection of others from serious harm.[32]

---

28 Ibid 71.

29 Ibid 78.

30 Even though new legislation was enacted in 2007, the provisions in relation to the definition of mental illness and criteria for involuntary detention remain as they were in the *Mental Health Act 1990* (NSW).

31 This definition is unchanged from s 3 Schedule 1 of the same Act.

32 Under previous legislation, s 9(1) of the *Mental Health Act 1990 (NSW)* read as follows: A person is a mentally ill person if the person is suffering from mental illness and, owing to that illness, there are reasonable grounds for believing that care, treatment or control of the person is necessary:
(a) for the person's own protection from serious physical harm; or
(b) for the protection of others from serious physical harm,
and a person is also a mentally ill person if the person is suffering from mental illness which is characterised by the presence in the person of the symptom of a severe disturbance of mood or the symptom of sustained or repeated irrational behaviour indicating the presence of that symptom and, owing to that illness, there are reasonable grounds for believing that care, treatment or control of the person is necessary for the person's own protection from serious financial harm or serious damage to the person's reputation.

(2) In considering whether a person is a *mentally ill person*, the continuing condition of the person, including any likely deterioration in the person's condition and the likely effects of any such deterioration, are to be taken into account.

Furthermore, s 15, in defining a mentally disordered person—which may include a mentally ill person—but without defining the term 'mental disorder,' states:

> A person (whether or not the person is suffering from mental illness) is a *mentally disordered person* if the person's behaviour for the time being is so irrational as to justify a conclusion on reasonable grounds that temporary care, treatment or control of the person is necessary:
> (a) for the person's own protection from serious physical harm, or
> (b) for the protection of others from serious physical harm. [33]

And finally, s 16(2), in reference to conduct or beliefs that, of themselves do *not* constitute mental illness or mental disorder, but may be indicative of mental illness, states:

> Nothing in this Part prevents, in relation to a person who takes or has taken alcohol or any other drug, the serious or permanent physiological, biochemical or psychological effects of drug taking from being regarded as an indication that a person is suffering from *mental illness* or other condition of disability of mind.[34]

Section 4 of the *Mental Health Act 2014* (Vic) defines mental illness in broader medical terms as 'a medical condition that is characterised by a significant disturbance of thought, mood, perception or memory' and has similar qualified exclusions in relation to alcohol and drug dependency.[35]

While most other Australian states define mental illness in some form of medical context, s 3 of the *Mental Health Act 2009* (SA)—unchanged from the repealed *Mental Health Act 1993* (SA)—simply states '*mental illness* is any illness or disorder of the mind.' The only limits to this definition, which did not exist under the 1993 Act, reflect the drug and alcohol dependency provisions of New South Wales and Victoria.[36]

By contrast, the *Mental Health (Compulsory Assessment and Treatment) Act 1992* (NZ) takes a very different view and does not use the term 'mental illness' at all, opting simply for mental disorder. In defining this expression in medical terms, s 2 states:

---

33 Section 3 of the same Act defined mental disorder or mental dysfunction as 'a disturbance or defect, to a substantially disabling degree, of perceptual interpretation, comprehension, reasoning, learning, judgment, memory, motivation or emotion.' There is no correlating definition in the 2007 Act.
In relation to mentally disordered person s 10 stated: A person (whether or not the person is suffering from mental illness) is a mentally disordered person if the person's behaviour for the time being is so irrational as to justify a conclusion on reasonable grounds that temporary care, treatment or control of the person is necessary:
(a) for the person's own protection from serious physical harm; or
(b) for the protection of others from serious physical harm.

34 This definition remains unchanged from the *Mental Health Act 1990* (NSW).

35 There was no definition of 'mental illness' in the 1986 Victorian Act until it was amended in 1995. This definition has not changed under the 2014 statute. 'Mental disorder' was also included in the 1995 amendment but was not defined save for the fact that it included a mental illness. The term 'mental disorder' no longer appears in the 2014 legislation.

36 Schedule 1 of the 2009 Act now contains the standard list of conduct or beliefs that, of themselves, do not constitute mental illness.

> *Mental disorder* in relation to any person means an abnormal state of mind (whether of continuous or intermittent nature), characterised by delusions, or by disorders of mood or perception or volition or cognition of such a degree that it –
> (a) Poses a serious danger to the health or safety of that person or of others; or
> (b) Seriously diminishes the capacity of that person to take care of himself or herself;

Finally, under earlier provisions of United Kingdom law, the *Mental Health Act 1983* (UK) s 1(2) defined a variety of terms including *mental disorder* (as including mental illness), *mental impairment, severe mental impairment* and *psychopathic disorder.*[37] The definition of *mental disorder* in the 1983 Act was the same as s 4 of the *Mental Health Act 1959* (UK) but neither the 1959 Act nor the 1983 Act defined the term *mental illness*. The terms *mental impairment, severe mental impairment* and *psychopathic disorder* were introduced into the 1983 statute to replace the terms *subnormality, severe subnormality* and *psychopathic disorder* as defined in the 1959 Act. [38]

Significant amendments were made to the 1983 Act by way of the *Mental Health Act 2007* (UK) and the terms *mental impairment, severe mental impairment* and *psychopathic disorder* were removed. [39] The only replacement was the term *learning disability* which appears to equate to the previous term *mental impairment.*[40]

Under the 2007 Act, the term *mental disorder* is simply defined as 'any disorder or disability of the mind.'[41] There is no definition of mental illness. One may ask, how far is this from the definition of 'lunatic' in the *Lunacy Act 1890* as 'an idiot or person of unsound mind' or 'person of unsound mind' in the *Mental Health Act 1930*? It seems that the legislature has returned to where it started, having gone through a tortuous process of attempting to define the indefinable.

It has often been easier to describe what is *not* considered to be mental illness. New Zealand and all states in Australia,[42] in line with the provisions of the *MI Principles*, have

---

37 *mental disorder* means mental illness, arrested or incomplete development of the mind, psychopathic disorder and any other order or disability of the mind;
mental impairment is a state of arrested or incomplete development of the mind (not amounting to severe mental impairment) which includes significant impairment of intelligence and social functioning and is associated with abnormally aggressive or seriously irresponsible conduct;
severe mental impairment is state of arrested or incomplete development of the mind which includes severe impairment of intelligence and social functioning and is associated with abnormally aggressive or seriously irresponsible conduct;
psychopathic disorder is a persistent disorder or disability of the mind (whether or not including significant impairment of intelligence) which results in abnormally aggressive or seriously irresponsible conduct;

38 These terms were defined under s 4 as: '*subnormality* means a state of arrested or incomplete development of the mind (not amounting to severe subnormality) which includes subnormality of intelligence and is of a nature or degree which requires or is susceptible to medical treatment or other special care or training of the patient;' '*severe subnormality* is state of arrested or incomplete development of the mind which includes subnormality of intelligence and is of a nature or degree that the patient is incapable of living an independent life or of guarding himself against serious exploitation or will be so incapable when of an age to do so;' '*psychopathic disorder* is a persistent disorder or disability of the mind (whether or not including subnormality of intelligence) which results in abnormally aggressive or seriously irresponsible conduct on the part of the patient and requires or is susceptible to medical treatment;' promiscuity and immoral conduct were excluded from the definition of mental disorder (see s 4(5)).

39 *Mental Health Act 2007* (UK) s 3.

40 Ibid s 2(3); a state of arrested or incomplete development of the mind which includes significant impairment of intelligence and social functioning.

41 Ibid s 2.

42 South Australia did not include any of these factors until the new Act in 2009.

incorporated a varying combination of beliefs and practices into their mental health legislation as not, of themselves, amounting to mental illness or mental disorder as follows:

- the expression or refusal to express a political opinion;
- the expression or refusal to express a religious belief;
- the expression or refusal to express a particular philosophy;
- the expression or refusal to express a sexual orientation;
- the engagement in or refusal to engage in a particular political activity;
- the engagement in or refusal to engage in a religious activity;
- the engagement in sexual promiscuity;
- the engagement in immoral conduct;
- the engagement in illegal conduct;
- developmental disability of the mind/intellectual disability;
- addiction to drugs or alcohol;
- anti-social behaviour;
- anti-social personality;
- the person has a particular economic or social status or is a member of a particular cultural or racial group.

While promiscuity, immoral conduct, sexual deviancy and drug and alcohol dependence were excluded from the concept of 'mental disorder' under the *Mental Health Act 1983* (UK),[43] this was reduced to only drug and alcohol dependence under the 2007 Act.[44] In addition, under the 2007 Act, a learning disability is not considered to be a mental disorder unless it is 'associated with abnormally aggressive or seriously irresponsible conduct.' [45]

3.3.2. Personality Disorders and Mental Illness

As previously discussed, it is the issue of personality disorders—in particular anti-social personality disorders—and their place in the mental health landscape about which the medical and legal professions differ from one another, and among themselves. One of the most notorious cases in Australia to highlight this dilemma was the *Garry David* case.[46] While David was a convicted criminal with a long and complex history of violence, the issue revolved around whether he should be detained within the prison system or a psychiatric facility—and this depended on whether he was considered to be suffering from a mental illness as defined under the *Mental Health Act 1986* (Vic). While the Act precluded a person diagnosed only with an 'anti-social personality'[47] from being mentally ill, the argument in this case centred around 'anti-social personality *disorder'* thus creating confusion about the legislature's true intention.[48]

David had been convicted of a number of offences, including two counts of attempted murder—one a police officer—and was sentenced to 14 years imprisonment in February

---

43 *Mental Health Act 1983* (UK) s 1(3).

44 *Mental Health Act 2007* (UK) s 3.

45 Ibid s 2(2).

46 *Attorney General v Garry David (aka Garry Webb)* [1992] 2 VR 46.

47 *Mental Health Act 1986* (Vic) s 8(2).

48 DN Greig, *Neither Bad nor Mad: The Competing Discourses of Psychiatry, Law and Politics* (Jessica Kingsley Publishers Ltd, 2002) 30, 71.

1982. After mandatory remissions, he was due for release from prison in February 1990. While in custody he had carried out innumerable serious acts of self-mutilation and had threatened prison officers and hospital staff with violence. He was alleged to have a deep hatred of authority, in particular the police. He also made general threats against the public at large which were to take place when he was released from prison. He was certified under the *Mental Health Act 1986* (Vic) as a security patient so that he could be detained in a psychiatric facility and not released into the community. He appealed against his detention to the Mental Health Review Board which, after a sixteen day hearing and evidence from eleven psychiatrists, ruled that as he was suffering from a personality disorder—*not* being a mental illness under the Act, as such, he could not be detained in the psychiatric facility and was ordered to be returned to prison.[49]

In the interim, the Victorian government, concerned about releasing David into the community in light of his threatened behaviour, hastily enacted the *Community Protection Act 1990* (Vic) with the sole aim of providing 'safety for the members of the public and the care or treatment and management of Garry David.' Additionally, on the flimsy basis that it was providing a civil form of involuntary commitment rather than providing for a criminal proceeding, the Act abandoned the rules of evidence, thereby allowing the admission of hearsay evidence; dispensed with medical privilege; and lowered the standard of proof to the balance of probabilities. The Supreme Court of Victoria was authorised to make an order for preventive detention for a period not exceeding six months—later extended to twelve months.[50] The Act was initially drafted to operate only for one year, but was subsequently extended until 1994.[51] However, in June 1993 David died as a result of complications arising from repeated, self-inflicted abdominal stab wounds. At the time, he was in custody in prison pursuant to the *Community Protection Act 1990.*

The Victorian government's reaction in this instance was extreme. The extent to which David would have carried out his threats was a source of strong disagreement within the medical profession. While the legal problems arose from the definition of mental illness under the Act, events were set against a backdrop of the Hoddle Street and Queen Street massacres in the inner city areas of Melbourne, Victoria in 1987. Seven and nine people, respectively, were killed by lone gunmen and a further 24 were seriously injured. One of David's threats from prison was to carry out 'another Hoddle Street massacre.' Added to this, was the bombing in 1986 of the Russell Street police headquarters in inner city Melbourne, killing a young policewoman and injuring 22 others, and the underworld 'payback' shooting of two police constables in Walsh Street, South Yarra.[52] There was intense media interest and the government of the day was under enormous pressure to act quickly to provide measures to

---

49 *Statement of Reasons in the Appeal of Gary Ian Patrick Webb (also known as Garry Ian Patrick David) a Security Patient at Aradale Hospital*, Mental Health Review Board No. 230190:X01:300512, 9 May 1990.

50 *Community Protection (Amendment) Act 1991* (Vic) s 8; the validity of the Victorian legislation was never tested. However, a conservative government in New South Wales in 1994 introduced very similar legislation (*Community Protection Act 1994* (NSW) again, to detain one person—Gregory Wayne Kable—whose sentence for manslaughter had expired. The High Court of Australia, by a majority 4:2, in overturning the decision of the NSW Court of Appeal, held that the statute was invalid. The High Court found the Act was inconsistent with the federal Constitution because it imposed functions on the Supreme Court incompatible with the exercise of federal judicial power. See *Kable v Director of Public Prosecutions (NSW)* (1996) 189 CLR 51; [1996] HCA 24.

51 Ibid s 12.

52 Greig, above n 48, 46.

ensure public safety. The Act was seen as a short-term political solution to a problem for which no one had an immediate answer.[53]

Despite a Victorian Law Reform Commission recommendation in May 1990 that the Act be amended to allow an 'anti-social personality disorder' to be considered a mental illness,[54] the legislation in this regard remains largely unchanged.[55]The Commission argued that its aim was

> [not] to detain people who are bad rather than mad ... the Act should apply to *all* people who are mentally ill ... [it] should not arbitrarily exclude a particular group of mentally ill people because psychiatrists classify their underlying condition as a disorder rather than an illness; or because psychiatrists cannot successfully treat them; or because they create major problems for the mental health system.[56]

Nonetheless, the proposal was stridently opposed by the Law Institute of Victoria and the Royal Australian and New Zealand College of Psychiatrists.[57] The depth of the medical profession's sentiment was epitomised by one psychiatrist's response to the report:

> The Law Reform Commission proposal is a thinly disguised introduction of preventive detention achieved by transferring the odium for that process to the mental health care system. The issue of preventive detention is indeed a controversial one and it does raise substantial civil liberties issues. These issues will not go away because of a legislative sleight of hand.[58]

Moreover, in an unprecedented stance,[59] the recommendations of the government's own Social Development Committee did not support the Law Reform Commission's findings[60] and in its final report recommended that 'no changes be made to the involuntary detention provisions of the *Mental Health Act 1986*.'[61]In the lead up to further law reform in the UK, Bartlett warned that '[t]he debate over mental health law reform may continue for years before legislative action is taken. The risk is that discussion will be dominated by a reflex

---

53 R Merkel, 'Dangerous Persons: To Be Gaoled For What They Are, Or What They May Do, Not For What They Have Done' in SA Gerull and W Lucas (eds), *Serious Violent Offenders: Sentencing, Psychiatry and Law Reform* (Australian Institute of Criminology, 1993) 39, 44.

54 Law Reform Commission of Victoria, above n 23, 17.

55 The Act was amended in 1995 to include a definition of mental illness but this did not include a personality disorder. The term mental disorder was also introduced and defined simply to include a mental illness. The new legislation introduced in 2014 removed 'antisocial personality' from the list of exclusions under 'mental illness' and replaced it with 'antisocial behavior.' Arguably, this leaves it open for an 'antisocial personality' or an 'antisocial personality disorder' to come within the definition of mental illness.

56 Law Reform Commission of Victoria, above n 23, 16–17.

57 Greig, above n 48, 103.

58 Ibid 145.

59 Ibid 167.

60 Social Development Committee Parliament of Victoria, 'Interim Report: Inquiry into Mental Disturbance and Community Safety – Strategies to Deal with Persons with Severe Personality Disorder who Pose a Threat to Public Safety' (1990) (v).

61 Social Development Committee Parliament of Victoria, 'Fourth and Final Report: Inquiry into Mental Disturbance and Community Safety' (1992) (vi) recommendation 14.

reaction to perceived problems, rather than a reflective analysis of the broader social and political context.'[62]

3.4. The Pacific Response

Tonga, Samoa and Fiji are the only countries in the Pacific with legislative definitions of mental illness or mental disorder. While the definitions vary, one way and another, they appear to have been influenced by a mixture of Australian and New Zealand statutes. In essence, Samoa and Fiji now *include* mental illness in the broader legislative definition of mental disorder, while Tonga does not. The Tongan legislation defines the terms mental disorder and mental illness separately, but a mental disorder specifically *excludes* a mental illness. Fiji and Tonga define mental illness—largely in a medical framework—Samoa does not. Fiji and Samoa, in seeming compliance with the *MI Principles*, stipulate a range of beliefs and behaviours that do *not* constitute either a mental disorder or mental illness—Tonga does not.

Furthermore, Tonga does not appear to address the issue of personality disorders at all but includes the much wider term 'abnormal behaviour' in the definition of mental disorder. This is particularly significant in Tonga which, as mentioned above, does not have any of the usual belief and practice exclusions. From a definitional perspective this leaves the gate wide open so as to capture an extensive assortment of what may or may not constitute 'abnormal' behaviour at any given time. Samoa excludes 'antisocial personalities' from mental disorder but makes no specific reference to personality disorders. Fiji, on the other hand, includes personality disorders in the definition of mental disorder and only excludes 'antisocial behaviour.' This tends to point to a clear distinction between the concepts of behaviour and disorder, the application of which is unclear but possibly implied in the Samoan provisions.

However, despite the seemingly all-encompassing definitions in Tonga and Fiji, which have the potential to generate a larger group of detainees, the accompanying additional criteria for detention provide a more robust set of safeguards than under previous legislation. The details of these provisions and their implications are discussed in depth on the individual country chapters that follow.

In the earlier style legislation in the Pacific, the most commonly used term was a person of 'unsound mind,' which derives from early English statutes.[63] This expression was defined under previous legislation in Fiji to 'include an idiot.'[64] The only other statutory definition of the phrase was to be found in the now repealed[65] *Prisons Act* (Fiji Islands) where 'unsound mind' was defined as including 'mental disorders and sickness of the mind of any kind whether of a temporary or a permanent nature'.[66]

---

62 P Bartlett, 'The Mental Health Act: Taking Stock of the Current Position and Thinking about the Future' in M Freeman and A Lewis (eds), *Law and Medicine: Current Legal Issues* (Oxford University Press, 2000) 537, 557.

63 *Cook Islands Act 1915* (New Zealand); *Mental Treatment Ordinance* [Cap 56] (Kiribati); *Nuie Act 1966* (NZ); *Mental Treatment Act* [Cap 103] (Solomon Islands); *Mental Treatment Ordinance* [Cap 37] (Tuvalu); *Mental Hospital Act* [Cap 38] (Vanuatu).

64 *Mental Treatment Act* [Cap 113] (Fiji Islands) s 2.

65 *Prisons and Corrections Act 2006* (Fiji Islands) s 55.

66 *Prisons Act* [Cap 86] (Fiji Islands) s 2.

Apart from *Tangata's* case, which is discussed later in Chapter 7 on Fiji,[67] there appears to be no case law in the region that has dealt with the term 'unsound mind' in any detail, and none in the context of a person detained under mental health legislation. The only cases concern the fitness of a person to plead in criminal trials and the application of the test of insanity as espoused by the *M'Naghten* rule. This rule is enshrined in most criminal legislation in the region[68] and is drawn with reference to the law, not to the way in which psychiatrists might necessarily describe mental illness.

It appears, at least within the Western style health services sectors in the Pacific—excluding traditional healers and other informal mental health care service providers—that the classification, description, diagnosis and treatment of mental illness is consistent with the medical models outlined in various international diagnostic manuals, including that referred to by the WHO in the *MI Principles*.[69] It would seem by inference, for example, that this is what is meant in the Tongan legislation when it says that 'a determination that a person has a mental illness shall be made in accordance with internationally accepted medical standards.'[70]

4. Summary

This chapter has examined the origins of mental health legislation the region and some of the theoretical issues that have undermined mental health law reform. All jurisdictions have struggled with the marriage between legal and medical definitions of mental illness—the Pacific is no exception. These definitional tensions have also impacted on law reform in jurisdictions outside the Pacific—sometimes not for all the right reasons. A more detailed analysis of the statutory definitions of mental disorder and mental illness in each of the Pacific jurisdictions and their impact on potential candidates for involuntary detention follows in the next four chapters.

---

67 *Tangata v Speaker of the Legislative Assembly* [1997] CKHC 1.

68 *Rex v Taufa* [2004] TOSC 66; *Police v Fanueli* [1993] WSSC 3.

69 See American Psychiatric Association's *Diagnostic and Statistical Manual of Mental Disorders* (DSM) and *WHO's ICD-10 Classification of Mental and Behavioural Disorders – Clinical Descriptions and Diagnostic Guidelines*.

70 *Mental Health Act 2001* (Tonga) s 17.

Chapter 5

TONGA

The next four chapters undertake a comparative study of the old and new statutes in each of the target countries—specifically in relation to provisions of the legislation that impact on involuntary detention; an examination of the factors motivating change; and an assessment of future challenges.

A comprehensive analysis of the more important elements of justice and the tools necessary to create pathways to justice, together with an overall evaluation of each country's position on the 'access to justice' continuum, appears in Chapter 10.

A comparative analysis of the target countries demonstrates that reform of mental health laws has been primarily driven by international human rights movements, global world health initiatives and a few politically influential individuals. While reform has created an assortment of rights based frameworks in the region, these frameworks are largely aspirational and, thus far, have had little practical effect on the lives of those mental health consumers subject to involuntary detention orders. The obstacles to realisation are identified in general terms in each of the country-specific chapters but are explored in more depth in Chapters 11, 12 and 13.

This chapter explores these issues in relation to the Kingdom of Tonga.

1. THE LAW AS IT WAS

Although a constitutional monarchy from 1875, from 1900 onwards and after the death of King George Tubou I, Tonga entered into Treaties of Friendship with Great Britain, allowing Britain to control the defence and foreign affairs of the country as well as the trials of British subjects and foreigners. In 1970 the treaties were rescinded, Tonga ceased to be a protected state of Britain and returned to a full constitutional monarchy under the original constitution.[1]

Codified laws existed in Tonga from around 1830 until 1870 and were made by the King of Tonga. In 1875, King George Tubou I established the Constitution of Tonga, providing for a legislative assembly and a new legal framework.[2] Apart from s 35 of the Constitution, which prevented any person who was insane or an imbecile succeeding to the Crown,

---

[1] J Corrin Care, T Newton and D Paterson, *Introduction to South Pacific Law* (Cavendish Publishing Ltd, 1999) 12.

[2] WK Horne, *Laws of Tonga,* Preface to the 1929 Edition (1929).

legislative provisions regarding the mentally disordered do not appear until the *Criminal Offences Act* of 1924. Sections 17-20 of the Act—in relation to the test of insanity, unfitness to plead, the insanity defence and custody of the insane under order of the Privy Council—have survived until today, essentially as they first appeared.[3]

Some English Acts were specifically applied in Tonga by the *Tonga Orders in Council 1952-1955* but no mental health legislation came into this category.[4] The *Civil Law Act* [Cap 25] under s 3 adopted 'the common law of England and the rules of equity, together with statutes of general application in force in England.' Although this had the effect of applying legislation in force in England prior to and after 1966, the statute only operated if 'no other provision has been, or may hereafter be, made by or under any Act or Ordinance of the Kingdom.'[5] To this end, as the *Lunatics Detention Act* was already in existence in Tonga, no equivalent English statutes would have been applicable.

Consequently, the earliest mental health legislation in Tonga appears to be the *Lunatics Detention Act* [Cap 80], which was enacted in 1948 and provided for the custody and detention of lunatics.[6] This Act was subsequently repealed by the *Mental Health Act 1992* (Tonga),[7] which appeared to be at least partly modelled on the English legislation of the time,[8] and the 1992 Act was itself repealed by the *Mental Health Act 2001* (Tonga).[9]

1.1. Admission Criteria

The *Lunatics Detention Act* [Cap 80][10] was a very brief piece of legislation and only made provision for procedures involved in the detention of 'lunatics.' This required the production of two certificates signed by qualified medical practitioners or by a medical officer—any officer appointed under the *Medical Services Act* [Cap 76]—and a Tongan medical practitioner, together with an order signed by the Chief Justice or the Chief Police Magistrate.[11] Each of the persons signing the certificate was required to examine the person and declare him or her to be a 'lunatic.' A 'lunatic' was simply defined as 'an idiot or any other person of unsound mind'[12] and the legislation made no specific provision for the criminally insane.[13] There is no definition of the terms 'idiot' or 'unsound mind' in the statute. However, the stipulated Form A under s 3—apart from requiring 'facts indicating

3 *Criminal Offences Act* [Cap 18] (Tonga).

4 Government of Tonga, *Laws of Tonga Revised 1967* (1967) vol. III Appendix.

5 *Civil Law Act* [Cap 25] (Tonga) s 4(a).

6 As this Act did not purport to repeal any previous legislation, it is to be presumed that this was the first legislation of its kind in Tonga. As there was no statutory regime for lawful custody of the mentally ill prior to 1948 in Tonga, it is arguable that a person could have had recourse to a writ of *habeas corpus* under s 9 of the *Constitution of Tonga*.

7 See section 15.

8 *Mental Health Act 1983* (UK).

9 See s 143. This statute came into force on 1 September 2003 [Gazette No.22 /2003 (Tonga) (1 September 2003)].

10 The 1988 Revised Edition of the Tongan legislation refers to the 1948 Act being amended by Act 17 of 1986 but there is no discernible difference between the original 1948 statute and that which appears in the 1988 Revised Edition and, presumably, including the 1986 amendment.

11 *Lunatics Detention Act* [Cap 80] (Tonga) s 3(1).

12 See s 2.

13 The *Criminal Offences Act 1926* (Tonga) contained provisions relating to unfitness to plead and the insanity defence.

lunacy'—refers in the Statement of Particulars to 'first attack of lunacy' and 'whether suicidal' or 'dangerous to others.' These latter two terms suggest that self-harm or harm to others were clinical considerations.[14]

Section 4 provided for the emergency detention of a person—alleged to be a lunatic—for observation and treatment for up to seven days and where it was deemed necessary for the welfare of the alleged lunatic or for public safety.[15]

The later *Mental Health Act 1992* (Tonga) addressed the threshold issues for admission and detention in a more complex manner. Section 9 provided for compulsory admission to hospital for psychiatric *examination* for a non-renewable period of seven days if a person was deemed to be suffering from a severe mental disorder; where the person refused to attend voluntarily; and detention was necessary for his or her safety or the safety of some other person.[16]

Under s 10, a magistrate could order a person to be detained for a period not exceeding 28 days for *observation,* if the magistrate was satisfied that the person was suffering from a mental disorder of a nature and degree warranting detention and observation and the order was necessary in the interests of the person or some other person.[17]

Under s 11, the Supreme Court could order a person to be detained for *treatment* for a period not exceeding two years, but only if the Court was satisfied that the person was suffering from a *mental disorder* of a nature and degree warranting detention and treatment and the order was necessary in the interests of the patient or some other person.[18]

Section 1 defined 'mental disorder' in the broadest possible terms as meaning mental illness, arrested or incomplete development of the mind, psychopathic disorder and any other disorder or disability of the mind.[19] 'Mental illness' was defined as meaning a psychiatric disorder, which substantially disturbs a person's thinking, feeling or behaviour and impairs the person's ability to function.[20]

The Act further defined the terms 'alcoholic,' 'drug addict,' 'mental handicap' and 'psychopathic disorder,' with the net effect of ensuring that every possible disability of the mind came within the ambit of the legislation.[21] In particular, a 'psychopathic disorder' was defined to mean 'a persistent serious disorder of personality resulting in aggressive or antisocial behavior.' This had the effect of removing any practical distinction between different types of mental disorder, thus leaving the gate wide open for anyone with any range of symptoms to be at risk of detention.

In essence, provided they met the criteria under ss 9, 10 and 11, persons could be detained if they:

---

14 *Lunatics Detention Act* [Cap 80] (Tonga) s 3(2), s 2.

15 Ibid s 4.

16 *Mental Health Act 1992* (Tonga) s 9(1)–(4).

17 Ibid s 10 (1)–(4).

18 Ibid s 11 (1)–(4).

19 Ibid s 1.

20 Ibid.

21 'Alcoholic' or 'drug addict' means a person suffering from a disorder or disability of the mind caused by his being so given over to or dependent on the use of alcohol or drugs that he is unable to control himself or is incapable of managing his affairs or endangers himself or others; 'mental handicap' means a state of arrested or incomplete development of the mind which can render a person incapable of independent living.

- demonstrated clinical signs of mental illness;
- were alcohol or drug dependent and exhibited lack of control *or* an inability to manage their affairs *or* endangered themselves or others;
- were mentally handicapped or intellectually disabled *and* incapable of independent living; or
- were afflicted with a persistent serious personality disorder *and* displayed aggressive or antisocial behaviour.

Presumably, admissions under the last category were restricted to 28-day orders under s 10, as admission under s 11 required the 'need for treatment'—a highly debateable issue when it comes to the management of persons with personality disorders.

1.2. The Rights to Appeal and Review

There were no mechanisms for review or appeal against detention or treatment under the 1948 Act. A person could simply be discharged pursuant to a certification procedure that reversed the admission process.[22] It is likely, however, that a detained person would have had access to the Supreme Court via a writ of *habeas corpus*.

Under the 1992 Act, an *observation* order under s 10 could be appealed by the person or a relative to the Supreme Court and a *treatment* order under s 11 to the Court of Appeal.[23] In addition, either of these orders could be renewed by a magistrate or the Supreme Court if the detained person continued to meet the legislative criteria. There was no right of appeal against an *examination* order under s 9. A person detained under ss 9, 10 or 11 could also be released by a medical officer or a psychiatrist, if his or her detention it was no longer considered necessary.[24]

There were no provisions in either of the earlier statutes for a Board of Visitors or equivalent body with general oversight and inspection functions within the mental health facilities.

1.3. The Review Mechanism

There were no specific provisions in either of the earlier statutes enabling periodic reviews or for an inpatient to apply for review of his or her detention or treatment, and certainly no independent legal or quasi-legal review body for people admitted and treated involuntarily.

22 *Lunatics Detention Act* [Cap 80] (Tonga) s 5.
23 *Mental Health Act 1992* (Tonga) ss 10 (5), 11(5).
24 Ibid s 12.

2. Motivation for Change

There is very little official documentation supporting a clear policy direction in relation to the development of the 2001 mental health legislation in Tonga, leading to its implementation in 2003.[25] Similarly, the catalyst for change is somewhat anecdotal and speculative. The best information suggests that credit for driving the movement for change can be attributed to Dr Mapa Ha'ano Puloka—the only qualified psychiatrist in Tonga—and the late Chief Police Magistrate Tapueluele.[26]

Puloka, an indigenous Tongan, was educated in Tonga and studied medicine in Fiji and later New Zealand. He has been practising psychiatry in Tonga for twenty five years; in many ways, Puloka *is* psychiatry in Tonga today. He was instrumental in moving patients from the prison asylum and the building of a security unit in 1993 attached to the mental health unit.[27] Under the earlier legislation, Puloka promoted freedom of movement by establishing an 'open door policy' at the mental health unit. He encouraged patients to 'drop in' or seek respite care without the requirements for formal admission. Puloka also encouraged patients to challenge their detention, thus requiring him to give evidence in open court.[28] He saw this as a way of increasing public awareness of the psychiatric process and to facilitating 'a sense of their own entitlement and rights in relation to government' and to create a sense of public transparency.[29] This approach, particularly in relation to his collaboration with traditional healers, did not always result in government financial support; this then forced Puloka to utilise the media to promote his initiatives.[30]

According to one interview respondent, Puloka was of the view that the earlier legislation had many limitations specifically in relation to human rights. For compelling social reasons—not the least being the increasing prevalence of mental illness and the need for improved psychiatric facilities—Tonga needed to respond to international trends in human rights, which were gathering political momentum in the country at the time.[31] This is an interesting observation considering that the only major human rights treaty that Tonga has ratified to date is the *Convention on the Rights of the Child*.[32]

In particular, Puloka's concerns are said to have centred around respect for human dignity; the right to be free from inhumane and degrading treatment; and the right to liberty.[33] By way of illustration, he maintained that the old legislation contained no provisions for regulating specific forms of treatment nor any penalties for misuse; no provisions covering capacity to consent to treatment or the right to autonomy; no effective mechanisms for review of and appeals against detention; inadequate provisions for community based care and

25 Email questionnaire from Salesi Mafi, Senior Magistrate Tonga, to Helen Ménard,16 September 2011.

26 Interview with Loupua Sefokuli, Law Graduate, (Port Vila, November 2010); Email questionnaire from Salesi Mafi, Senior Magistrate Tonga, to Helen Ménard,16 September 2011.

27 Email from Dr Mike Poltorak, Kent University, to Helen Ménard 12 June 2103. Excerpt from an unpublished paper by the author.

28 Ibid, excerpt from an unpublished paper by the author.

29 Ibid, excerpt from an unpublished paper by the author.

30 Ibid, excerpt from an unpublished paper by the author.

31 Interview with Loupua Sefokuli, Law Graduate, (Port Vila, November 2010).

32 *Convention on the Rights of the Child*, opened for signature 20 November 1989, 1577 UNTS 3 (entered into force 2 September 1990).

33 Interview with Loupua Sefokuli, Law Graduate, (Port Vila, November 2010).

treatment, and lack of treatment options for forensic detainees.[34] Many of these issues have now been addressed in the new legislation.

Puloka has been credited with attempting 'to revolutionise public knowledge of mental illness ... through radio and television broadcasts, newspaper articles and lecture courses at Atenisi University.'[35] He has also been instrumental in organising several WHO sponsored workshops with traditional healers in order to facilitate collaboration with mental health staff in the treatment of mental illness.[36]

Although there is no reference in the 2001 Act to specific human rights principles,[37] it has been suggested that the legislation was revised 'in line with the 10 United Nations Human Rights Principles for the Protection of Persons with Mental Illness and the improvement of mental health care.'[38] A number of studies by the WHO and the United Nations Development Programme (UNDP) were carried out in Tonga from 1999 onwards and it is reasonable to assume that, as with most other countries in the region, these global initiatives influenced the development and progression of mental health policies in Tonga. Certainly, the requirement in s 17 of the Act that the diagnosis of a person's mental illness be made in 'accordance with internationally accepted medical standards,'[39] is a direct borrowing from the *WHO Ten Principles*[40] and many of the features of the Tongan legislation clearly mirror those of the *MI Principles.*

There is no documented evidence to indicate why Tonga opted for the tribunal style model of review, especially given the shortage of medical and legal practitioners in the country, thus reducing the Tribunal's ability to act impartially.[41] It would seem that the legislative intentions were aspirational, if not immediately able to be fulfilled.

3. The Law Now

The *Mental Health Act 2001*[42] completely rewrote the law on mental health in Tonga but does not contain any preamble, explanatory memorandum or detailed statement about the purpose of the legislation. The law has moved from a situation where there was no statutory regime for lawful custody of the mentally ill, to one with broad ranging powers to detain those of 'unsound mind,' to discrete definitions of 'mental illness' and 'mental disorder' and equally discrete admission and detention criteria.

---

34 Ibid.

35 M Poltorak, 'Nemesis, Speaking and Tauhi Vaha'a: Interdisciplinarity and the Truth of "Mental Illness" in Vava'u, Tonga' (2007) 19(1) *The Contemporary Pacific* 1, 3.

36 M Poltorak, 'Traditional Healers, Speaking and Motivation in Vava'u, Tonga: Explaining Syncretism and Addressing Health Policy' (2010) 80(1) *Oceania* 1.

37 The only reference to international standards is to be found in s 17 of *Mental Health Act 2001* which states that 'A determination that a person has a mental illness shall be made in accordance with internationally accepted medical standards.'

38 O Guttenbeil-Likiliki and Foundation of the Peoples of the South Pacific International, 'Youth and Mental Health in Tonga: A Situational Analysis' (2009) 22. As an indication, this report appears to draw heavily on a number of WHO and UNDP projects relating to Tonga from 1999-2008 and little, if anything, by way of government or domestic policy: see 46.

39 *Mental Health Act 2001* (Tonga) s 17.

40 World Health Organisation, 'Mental Health Care Law: Ten Basic Principles' (1996) [3].

41 Email questionnaire from Salesi Mafi, Senior Magistrate Tonga, to Helen Ménard,16 September 2011.

42 The Act did not commence operation until September 2003.

The definition of 'mental illness' adopts a clinical approach whereas 'mental disorder' is restricted to elements of abnormal behaviour and dangerousness. A person satisfying either definition can be detained where there are elements of potential self-harm or danger to others; but those with a mental illness must meet additional criteria. The Act establishes a tribunal based model for the review of and appeal against involuntary detention, as opposed to direct and limited right of application to the Supreme Court.

3.1. Admission Criteria

Under current Tongan law, the grounds for involuntary detention on the basis of mental illness are:

- the person must be suffering from a mental illness;
- the mental illness must require treatment;
- the treatment is available at the mental health facility;
- the person is likely to cause imminent harm to himself or others *or* is likely to suffer serious mental or physical deterioration without detention and treatment;
- the person must lack capacity to give informed consent to treatment *or* has unreasonably refused treatment; and
- there is no less restrictive means of treatment available.[43]

However, a person with a mental disorder—not being a mental illness—may also be detained if his or her behaviour is so irrational that, without detention, treatment *or* care, it could be reasonably concluded that he or she is likely to suffer serious physical harm or cause serious harm to others.[44]

As such, it would seem to be easier to detain a person who, by definition, is not mentally ill. The reason for this is unknown but it may simply be a pragmatic recognition of the difficulty of getting clinical assessments that would provide convincing evidence before a court. To this extent, all that is required is a level of 'abnormal' behaviour together with a 'reasonable' assessment of 'serious' harm. Nonetheless, this is a significantly more restrictive definition than that which existed under the 1992 Act, particularly in relation to persons with an intellectual disability.

The term 'mental illness' is expressed in clinical terms but does not contain any of the socio-political exclusions—such as those outlined in the Samoan and Fijian statutes—and side-steps the contentious medico-legal issue of the placement of personality disorders within the sphere of mental illness.

The definition of mental illness in s 3 appears to be an amalgam of the provisions in the NSW and New Zealand statutes and reads as follows:

> *mental illness* means a condition which seriously impairs, either temporarily or permanently, the mental functioning of a person in one or more of the areas of thought,

[43] *Mental Health Act 2001* (Tonga) s 18.
[44] Ibid s 19.

mood, volition, perception, orientation or memory and is characterised by the presence of at least one of the following symptoms –

(a) delusions;
(b) hallucinations;
(c) serious disorder of the content of thought;
(d) serious disorder of thought form;
(e) serious disturbance of mood; or
(f) sustained or repeated irrational behaviour which indicates the presence of at least one of those symptoms.

The Act also requires that the determination of mental illness be made in accordance with 'internationally accepted medical standards,'[45] in compliance with international principles, reinforcing the medical model in the legislation.

The Tongan legislation defines the term 'mental disorder' to specifically exclude mental illness but to include 'abnormal behaviour' accompanied by an element of dangerousness to self or others.[46] Abnormal behaviour is not defined within the Act and, unlike the 1992 Act, there is no specific reference to personality disorders.

Prima facie it would seem that, even if a person with a less severe personality disorder who does *not* manifest the serious impairment levels of volition and perception—required to come within the definition of mental illness—but who exhibits *some* form of abnormal behaviour, could be caught under the 'abnormal behaviour' provision of the definition of mental disorder. The significance of the distinction lies in the separate criteria for detention for each condition, but is somewhat semantic given that there are no separate treatment facilities to cater for either type of individual in Tonga.

One of the difficulties rests with what is considered to be 'abnormal' and who is responsible for making this determination. According to Bell and Brookbanks, 'the crux of the issue is whether the term should be defined subjectively, that is by reference to the normal position of the individual concerned, or objectively, by comparing his or her thoughts and behaviour with that of the wider community.'[47]

The authors' comments are in relation to the term 'abnormal state of mind' employed in the New Zealand legislation,[48] which differs slightly from that of 'abnormal behaviour' in the Tongan legislation. Nonetheless, it is the meaning of the term 'abnormal' that is critical.[49] The same authors maintain, accurately it is argued, that the more popular objective approach has 'the potential to widen the definition so that almost anyone whose thinking could be construed as abnormal—because it is different, deviant, maladapted, or non-conformist—could be considered mentally disordered.'[50]

---

45 Ibid s 17.

46 Ibid s 3; *"mental disorder"* is a clinical condition in which a person manifests abnormal behaviour that does not meet the criteria for mental illness in this Act but the person is dangerous to himself or to other [sic].

47 S Bell and W Brookbanks, *Mental Health Law in New Zealand* (Thomson Brookers, 2nd ed, 2005) 17.

48 The definition of mental disorder under s 2 of the *Mental Health (Compulsory Assessment and Treatment) Act 1992* (NZ) is stated as 'an abnormal state of mind (whether continuous or an intermittent nature) characterized by delusions or by disorders of mood or perception or volition or cognition of such a degree that it (a) poses a serious threat to the health or safety of that person or of others; or (b) seriously diminishes the capacity of that person to take care of himself or herself.'

49 Bell and Brookbanks, above n 47, 17.

50 Ibid.

The New Zealand Court of Appeal in the *Waitemata Health* case—in which the psychiatric opinion regarding the appellant H was divided—stated that 'a disordered personality per se does not constitute an abnormal state of mind. The abnormal state of mind referred to in the mental disorder definition must be one characterised by delusions or disorders of mood, perception, volition or cognition.'[51]

Those detained under the mental illness provisions in Tonga must only be likely to cause 'imminent' or immediate harm to themselves or others without any prescribed level of harm or danger.[52] Yet, those detained as being mentally disordered are required to exhibit a likelihood of suffering or causing 'serious' physical harm.[53] The term 'serious harm' or danger is yet another term that presents definitional and quantitative challenges; and predicting dangerousness—even in severe cases of violent behaviour—has proven to be notoriously difficult for clinicians and judges alike.

Under the Tongan provisions, while a person who is mentally ill must require treatment *and* that treatment must be available at the treatment facility,[54] a person who is mentally disordered must only require detention, treatment *or* care.[55] This could potentially include those who are not mentally ill and who have some form of personality or behavioural disorder that does not require treatment, or which cannot be treated. It may be that the level of irrationality associated with abnormal behaviour—which, in turn, poses a threat of 'serious' harm—is only designed to encompass the more severe personality disorders. Even so, this provision has all the hallmarks of the 'slippery slope' towards preventive detention.

As cases involving the mental health legislation in Tonga are rare, it serves to examine one recent case despite the fact that it dealt with a mentally ill offender, generally beyond the scope of this work. Sepasitiano Manu was charged with the murder of his father in 2002 while attending a celebration in the family home. Following a series of unexplained and seemingly inexplicable procedural delays—and having been found fit to plead and pleading not guilty to murder—Manu was convicted of manslaughter in November 2011.[56]

Manu had been a regular inpatient in the psychiatric ward at Vaiola Hospital since 1992. Diagnosed with schizophrenia at age 16, he did not always respond well to available psychotropic medication and had 16 inpatient admissions over a ten year period. During his admission in January 2002, Manu's family had requested he be granted 'day leave' to attend a birthday celebration in his honour. Initially, concerned about previous episodes of hostility towards the family, the treating psychiatrist (Dr Puloka) refused; after persistent requests from the family, he relented and granted Manu leave.[57]

In an assessment of his mental condition, three days after the tragic event, Puloka reported that Manu was suffering from paranoid type schizophrenia based on a series of symptoms including thought disorder of delusional content; auditory hallucinations to harm people; mood incongruous with thought content and perception; unpredictable impulse control; normal memory and intellectual functioning; poor judgement but fair insight into his illness. As such, Puloka found him to be 'mentally disordered' within the legal definition under the relevant legislation at the time—the *Mental Health Act 1992*—being a 'mental

---

51 *Waitemata Health v Her Majesty's Attorney General & Ors* [2001] NZCA 312 [45].
52 *Mental Health Act 2001* (Tonga) s 18.
53 Ibid s 19.
54 Ibid s 18.
55 Ibid s 19.
56 *Crown v Manu* [2011] TOSC 34.
57 Ibid.

illness, arrested or incomplete development of the mind, psychopathic disorder and any other disorder or disability of the mind.'[58]

By the time the case went to trial in 2011, the *Mental Health Act 2001* had come into force.[59] Yet, the relevant legislation at the time the offence was committed in 2002, the 1992 *Mental Health Act,* was not considered by the court in its judgment on conviction.

Puloka also contended that Manu was *not* legally insane under the criminal legislation as he considered Manu to have 'planned what he did ... because the defendant waited for all the people to go outside, waiting until his father was alone. He [Manu] took the chopper as his father was reminding him of his medication.'[60] Furthermore, despite experiencing some command hallucinations, 'after one chop, the defendant would know what he was doing and he should have stopped ... generally he knew the difference between right and wrong.'[61] Based on Puloka's evidence, which was not contested by the defence, the Supreme Court found that the defence had not made out its case for legal insanity and that Manu was guilty of manslaughter.

When formulating its decision on sentencing, the Court applied the provisions of the *Mental Health Act 2001* relating to 'mental illness,' which require serious impairment of mental functioning in one or more areas of thought, mood, volition, perception, orientation or memory.[62] The Court found Manu was suffering from a mental illness and that he posed a grave and significant risk to himself and the safety of others, especially his mother and Dr Puloka, both of whom were now on a 'kill' list.[63] Undoubtedly, this was a weighty consideration in the Court's final orders on sentencing. Manu was sentenced to 23 years imprisonment—the maximum being 25 years—together with a treatment order under the *Mental Health Act 2001* 'for the rest of the defendant's natural life'.[64]

One question remains: if Manu satisfied the definition of 'mental illness' under the 1992 Act with the requisite degree of disturbed thinking and impaired ability to function, would he have fully understood his actions so as to satisfy the *M'Naghten* test, especially when he was experiencing command hallucinations at the time of the offence?[65] However, this is a matter of medical evidence, which was uncontested and accepted by the Court.

Nevertheless, there is some evidence that, during the intervening *nine* years it took to bring the matter to trial, the family had petitioned the court on more than one occasion for Manu to be detained in custody.[66] The circumstances of the offence and the indisputable effect on the family and community, together with the ongoing threats against Dr Puloka and the family, undoubtedly influenced the final outcome. Possibly, a criminal conviction—through a failure to satisfy the insanity defence—was added insurance to ensure Manu was

58 *Mental Health Act 1992* (Tonga) s 1.

59 September 2003.

60 *Crown v Manu* [2011] TOSC 34.

61 Ibid.

62 *Mental Health Act 2001* (Tonga) s 2.

63 *Crown v Manu* [2011] TOSC 34.

64 Ibid; see s 67(1) A court may make a treatment order in relation to a person charged with an offence where the penalty includes a term of imprisonment.

65 *R v M'Naghten* (1843) 10 Cl & Fin 200 HL: 'labouring under such a defect of reason, from disease of the mind, as not to know (1) the nature and quality of the act he was doing or if he did know it (2) that he did not know he was doing what was wrong.'

66 It is unclear from the case where Manu was held pending trial but given the repeated references to 'custody' it is assumed to have been Hu'atolitoli prison under monitoring by Dr Puloka. It is also unclear whether at any time Puloka considered transferring Manu back to the secure unit at Vaiola Hospital which is what may have aroused the family's concern.

never released from custody, should he, at any time, fail to meet the criteria for involuntary detention under the Act—as he had many times before. This also raises the question as to why defence counsel did not attempt to present independent evidence in support of the insanity defence. At the time, there was another contracted psychiatrist working in Tonga who, of course, may not have been able to support the defence's position even if asked. Furthermore, to bring an independent psychiatrist from overseas would have been very expensive—a cost the family may have been unable or unwilling to meet in the circumstances, particularly as not one single member of Manu's family attended his trial.

In the final analysis, the end result might not have been any different. Had Manu been found to be legally insane as well as being 'mentally disordered' at the time of the offence, he would have been detained indefinitely at the Prime Minister's pleasure—presumably in the mental health unit or the forensic unit—with little prospect of release. As it stands, with a criminal conviction plus a substantial custodial sentence and a permanent and apparently incurable mental illness, he is now also subject to a security order requiring him to be detained under the *Mental Health Act*—presumably in the mental health unit or the forensic unit for treatment of his mental illness—for the term of this natural life.

The remaining criteria in the Tongan legislation in relation to involuntary detention of those with a mental illness include the capacity for informed consent, unreasonable refusal of treatment and appropriate treatment in the least restrictive environment.[67]

A person is generally agreed to be capable of giving informed consent to treatment if he or she is capable of understanding the *elements* of informed consent; is capable of understanding the *effects* of giving consent; and can *communicate* the decision to consent or refuse treatment to those responsible for the treatment.[68] The *elements* of informed consent include free and voluntary consent without the offer of any inducements.[69] Consent will only constitute 'informed' consent if there has been:

- a clear explanation of the nature of the treatment;
- an adequate description, without concealment, of the benefits, risks and discomforts of treatment and the availability of alternate treatment;
- clear answers to relevant questions asked;
- advice that treatment may be refused or consent may be withdrawn during treatment; and
- advice that independent legal or medical advice regarding the treatment may be obtained.[70]

As part of the criteria for involuntary detention on the grounds of mental illness, s 18(d) requires that 'the person lacks the capacity to give informed consent to treatment for his mental illness *or* the person has unreasonably refused treatment for his mental illness.'

The alternate wording used in s 18 suggests that a person who has capacity to give informed consent—and it would seem refuses treatment—may still be deemed to have unreasonably refused treatment and be detained nonetheless. There is no indication in the

67 *Mental Health Act 2001* (Tonga) s 18(d)(e).
68 Ibid s 34.
69 Ibid s 35(1).
70 Ibid s 36.

legislation as to what might equate to an 'unreasonable' refusal of treatment or who might make such a determination. Nor is there any necessity that the elements of informed consent invoke any standard of reasonableness.

A conundrum arises: if a person (a) is *capable* of informed consent under the legislation, by virtue of the fact that he or she understands the nature and effects of treatment including the risks and benefits; (b) has the ability to communicate his or her decision without coercion; and (c) knowing all this has the right to refuse—how can any refusal then be 'unreasonable'? Surely, the 'capacity' to give informed consent bears with it the right to refuse or consent to treatment regardless of any determination of reasonableness. If the decision to refuse is *so* unreasonable—seemingly displaying a level of understanding that does not properly balance cause and effect—then maybe the person's 'capacity' should be questioned. As one author aptly puts it 'capacity depends on understanding rather than wisdom; the essential feature is understanding, not how wisely it has been applied.'[71]

For example, a person is deemed to have capacity to give informed consent and, in balancing the effects of certain psychotropic medication, exercises his or her right to refuse optimum doses of the medication. The person understands his or her symptoms may not be completely managed and there is a likelihood that this could impact on the safety of others. Irrespective, he or she chooses to balance this against other unpleasant effects of the medication, which significantly reduce his or her quality of life. Does the decision to take a risk with the safety of others, regardless of how small, demonstrate lack of capacity on the basis that accepting such a risk does not display a sufficient level of 'understanding'? Is this an unreasonable decision? Is any decision that has even the smallest risk of impacting on the safety of others unreasonable? Such a decision is really no different to a person who is not suffering from a mental illness but who chooses to legally consume excessive amounts of alcohol, thereby potentially risking the safety of others in a domestic or a social setting.

The origin of this informed consent clause is unclear, as it is not replicated in the context of criteria for admission. Despite the fact that, for example, the 1990 NSW statute included the concept of informed consent in relation to various forms of treatment, and upon which the Tongan statute may have been based, the decision to consent to or refuse treatment was not tied to any form of reasonableness.[72] Nor is there any similar provision in the New Zealand legislation. Nor does Principle 11 of the *MI Principles* outlining consent to treatment impose this restriction.[73] As this legislation predates the CRPD, the possibility of drafting to comply with its terms is irrelevant.

3.2. The Rights to Appeal and Review

The Mental Health Review Tribunal (MHRT) in Tonga must review an inpatient's involuntary status under an Inpatient Treatment Order (ITO) within seven days of admission and the authorised psychiatrist must examine the patient 'regularly.'[74] The MHRT must then

[71] D Court, 'Mental Disorder and Human Rights: The Importance of a Presumption of Competence' (1996) 8(1) *Auckland University Law Review* 1, 5.

[72] *Mental Health Act 1990* (NSW) Ch.7.

[73] Office of the High Commissioner for Human Rights, *Principles for the Protection of Persons with Mental Illness and the Improvement of Mental Health Care*, GA Res 46/119, (17 December 1991).

[74] *Mental Health Act 2001* (Tonga) ss 29–30.

review each involuntary inpatient's status within six months.[75] There is no specific provision for further review after the initial six month review. However, a person subject to involuntary treatment in the community under a Community Treatment Order (CTO) must be reviewed by the MHRT every six months.[76] Under s 15 of the *Mental Health Act 2001,* the MHRT must also review a voluntary patient who is still an inpatient after six months and thereafter once a month.

Section 31 prohibits the administration of psychiatric treatment to an involuntary patient without the authority of the MHRT unless 'the treatment is needed urgently to prevent immediate or imminent harm or behaviour likely to cause immediate or imminent harm to the patient or other persons.'[77] Section 132 gives the MHRT the discretion to *authorise* a treatment plan when reviewing an involuntary patient and the authorised psychiatrist may apply to the MHRT at any time for authorisation or variation of a treatment plan.[78]

Section 31 also prohibits the administration of treatment not authorised by the MHRT unless treatment is urgently needed to prevent harm. Presumably, the MHRT's authorisation would only be necessary when the person did *not* meet the 'harm' provision under s 18(c) and was deemed likely to suffer serious deterioration unless admitted.[79] The current President of the MHRT states the MHRT has occasionally refused to authorise treatment plans but the reasons are unclear—it is to be presumed that such refusals are made within the ambit of the Act.[80]

If, at any time, an inpatient is examined and is found to no longer to meet the criteria for involuntary detention, he or she must be discharged by an order of the Supreme Court.[81] Upon discharge from a mental health facility in Tonga, the authorised psychiatrist must make appropriate arrangements for accommodation and continuing psychiatric treatment.[82] As there are no community mental health facilities or 'half way houses' in Tonga this typically means care within the family or the broader community.

Apart from the previously described periodic review provisions, an inpatient or interested person who wishes to appeal against involuntary detention in Tonga may do so by application for review to the MHRT and the application must be heard within seven days.[83] The Act provides that the person may be legally represented during the review; given access to all medical records;[84] and provided with an interpreter.[85] Any decision of the MHRT, or any failure to make an order within a reasonable time, may be appealed to the Supreme Court of Tonga.[86]

Sourcing definitive figures on the annual number of hearings before the MHRT is problematic as until 2011 neither the MHRT nor the Ministry of Health kept any statistical data. Respondents estimate that appeals against detention are rare, possibly one per month. By far the majority of hearings are by way of periodic review—either after the initial seven days

---

[75] Ibid s 132(b).
[76] Ibid s 132(f).
[77] Ibid s 31.
[78] Ibid ss 32–33.
[79] Ibid s 18(c).
[80] Email questionnaire from Salesi Mafi, Senior Magistrate Tonga, to Helen Ménard,16 September 2011.
[81] *Mental Health Act 2001* (Tonga) ss 30, 142.
[82] Ibid s 91.
[83] Ibid ss 140(1), 133(1)(c).
[84] Ibid ss 134(1), 135.
[85] Ibid s 137.
[86] Ibid s 141(1).

following admission or renewal after six months. The President of the MHRT contends that hearings have only ever been extended beyond the statutory timeframe on one or two occasions when the MHRT could not be convened.[87] The number of hearings appears to range from three to four per week, to none for several months, depending on the number of current admissions.[88] The Ministry's Annual Report in 2011 stated that the MHRT had held 35 court sessions for the year but with no indication as to how many cases were heard in a session or in total for the period; whether they were appeals, periodic reviews, ITOs, CTOs or other matters; or the outcomes of those hearings.[89] However, it was reported that the MHRT approved 131 ITOs during the year with no further information on how many were not approved or were heard in total. The report did not mention reviews of CTOs which is unusual given the relatively large number purportedly in existence (126) and the fact that they are required to be reviewed every six months.[90]

It would also seem that almost cases of initial review within seven days result in orders for continued detention, and the primary reason for admission is that the person presents a danger to him or herself or others.[91] This is unsurprising given that, if a person's symptoms are such as to genuinely meet the criteria for detention, it is unlikely they would have sufficiently abated within such a short period.

Respondents report that many patients are discharged well prior to the six-month periodic review period.[92] This would be consistent with the Ministry's 2011 report quoting the average length of stay in the mental health unit as 54 days.[93] Successful appeals are scarce and usually occur only where there is a treating doctor's recommendation or the person can be adequately supported in the community.[94] This further reinforces the heavy reliance of the MHRT on the medical evidence and, given the lack of opportunity for a second opinion, means continued detention is a forgone conclusion unless the treating doctor thinks otherwise. In such a case, the medical practitioner would have been obliged to discharge the person under the Act anyway, so the review hearing would be unnecessary.

Respondents estimate that less than 80 percent of patients attend their review hearings because 'they are often too ill to follow the discussion,'[95] which is consistent with the fact that this review takes place within seven days of admission. However, when there is an appeal—which is very infrequent—the patient is generally well enough to be present and is asked to attend.[96]

There appears to have been only one case involving an appeal against a decision of the MHRT to the Supreme Court of Tonga.[97] The case did not involve an appeal on the merits under s 41 of the *Mental Health Act* but an application for review of the legality of his detention by way of a writ of *habeas corpus*.[98] The applicant (Dominic Kama) had been

---

87 Email questionnaire from Salesi Mafi, Senior Magistrate Tonga, to Helen Ménard, June 2012.

88 Email questionnaire from Salesi Mafi, Senior Magistrate Tonga, to Helen Ménard,16 September 2011; Email questionnaire from Ma'afu Sefokuli, Court Clerk Tonga, to Helen Ménard, 20 June 2011.

89 Government of Tonga, 'Report of the Minister for Health for the Financial Year 2011/2012' (2011) 35.

90 Ibid.

91 Email questionnaire from Salesi Mafi, Senior Magistrate Tonga, to Helen Ménard,16 September 2011.

92 Ibid.

93 Government of Tonga, above n 89, 35.

94 Email questionnaire from Salesi Mafi, Senior Magistrate Tonga, to Helen Ménard,16 September 2011.

95 Ibid.

96 Ibid.

97 Ibid.

98 *Re Application by Kama* [2007] Tonga LR 76.

detained at Hu'atolitoli prison pursuant to a review order by the MHRT which—in finding that he was mentally ill—was concerned for the safety of the certifying magistrate and various mental health personnel. While the Supreme Court accepted that the applicant was suffering from a mental illness, there was also some discussion about the legality of his detention in the prison, as a nominated mental health facility under the new Act, rather than the mental health unit.[99] The applicant argued that he was classified as suffering from a mental disorder as opposed to a mental illness. However, the Court held this classification was an administrative error and that the applicant met the criteria for detention under s 18; was suffering from a mental illness; and his detention at Hu'atolitoli prison was lawful.[100]

3.3. The Review Mechanism

The 2001 Act in Tonga established a new framework for the hearing of periodic reviews and appeals against detention and treatment by way of the MHRT.[101] The MHRT must consist of the President—a magistrate with a law degree—and two members—a psychiatrist or a medical practitioner with psychiatric experience and another person with relevant experience but not being a lawyer or a medical practitioner—all of whom are appointed by Cabinet.[102] Similar models are used in other jurisdictions including New Zealand, United Kingdom, Canada and Australia.[103]

The quorum of the Tribunal is two but, in exceptional circumstances and at the direction of the President, may consist of only one member.[104] There is no reference to who needs to make up the quorum and, if one member sits alone, who that member should be. The current President states that, in practice, when one member sits it is always the President and, on the rare occasions when there are only two members present, it is usually one of the medical practitioners who is absent.[105] This raises the question as to whether a proper decision can be made about the validity of a person's detention when the criteria for being 'mentally ill' are essentially medical and there is no medical practitioner present to provide evidence or clarification of any written report. This is particularly so in light of the President's comments below regarding the reliance placed on the view of the authorised psychiatrist who is invariably the medical member of the MHRT. The issue of single member tribunals is canvassed in greater depth in Chapter 10.

The functions of the MHRT include:

- review of admission and ongoing detention;
- appeals against detention;
- review, variation and revocation of CTOs;

---

99 Ibid.

100 The court made it clear it did not consider the application to be an appeal and left it open for the applicant to lodge an appeal against the MHRT decision pursuant to s 141 which would raise issues other than the legality of his detention.

101 This body was not established until 2004, after the Act came into operation in 2003.

102 *Mental Health Act 2001* (Tonga) ss 127–128.

103 See, e.g., *Mental Health (Compulsory Assessment and Treatment) Act 1992* (NZ); *Mental Health Act 2007* (UK); *Mental Health Act 2000* (Qld); *Mental Health Act 1990* (NSW); *Mental Health Act 1986* (Vic).

104 *Mental Health Act 2001* (Tonga) s 131.

105 Email questionnaire from Salesi Mafi, Senior Magistrate Tonga, to Helen Ménard, June 2012.

- authorisation of treatment plans; and
- provision of written decisions and reasons.[106]

As with most similar bodies, the MHRT is not bound by the rules of evidence and is required to conduct its hearings as informally as possible.[107] However, there is no specific provision in the Act requiring that the MHRT to be bound by the rules of natural justice. A person may call evidence on his or her behalf but the Tribunal may refuse evidence if it is satisfied that doing so may cause serious harm to the person or put the safety of some other person at risk.[108] Under s 133(2), the person presiding at a review shall decide on the admissibility of evidence and any other questions of law or procedure. The President asserts that

> our policy on evidence is that it must be relevant towards considering whether the person being reviewed is mentally ill and that the recommended medication and place of detention is appropriate for the safety of the patient and support people for these purposes. We rely on the recommendation of the authorised psychiatrist.[109]

The power to 'authorise' treatment plans under the Act[110] must inherently require some degree of review of the plan and, presumably, carries with it the right to refuse to authorise a plan. In practice, it would seem that the MHRT does both authorise and review treatment plans and has, on occasions, refused to authorise them, although reasons for such decisions and precise statistics were not available.[111]

Under the Act hearings are to be held in camera[112] and the MHRT must make and retain audiotapes of the proceedings and provide copies of the tapes to the person if requested, unless there is some risk of harm to any person.[113] The MHRT is also required to provide written reason of its decision within 21 days or within three days of any request by the person or his or her representative.[114]

On the face of it, the overall statutory mechanism would appear to be transparent and accountable with appropriate safeguards in terms of protection of the rights, health and safety of involved individuals. However, it also presupposes an element of independence in order to give effect to the fundamental purpose of any review or appeal process. The obvious predicament for a country such as Tonga is that there is only one specialist psychiatrist and one or two medical practitioners with any psychiatric experience.[115] As these health professionals are invariably involved in the primary care and treatment of patients, as reviewers they must review their own decisions. As such, it is hard to see impartiality, and the appearance of impartiality, in the process.

---

106 *Mental Health Act 2001* (Tonga) s 132.
107 Ibid s 133.
108 Ibid s 136.
109 Email questionnaire from Salesi Mafi, Senior Magistrate Tonga, to Helen Ménard,16 September 2011.
110 *Mental Health Act 2001* (Tonga) s 132(h).
111 Email questionnaire from Salesi Mafi, Senior Magistrate Tonga, to Helen Ménard,16 September 2011.
112 *Mental Health Act 2001* (Tonga) s 138.
113 Ibid s 139.
114 Ibid s 132(k)(l).
115 Email questionnaire from Salesi Mafi, Senior Magistrate Tonga, to Helen Ménard,16 September 2011.

Respondents acknowledge that this is major weakness in the operation of the system but, without sufficient professional resources, they are not in a position to rectify the problem.[116]

Another difficulty is that when the tribunal was established in 2004, there was only one magistrate in the country who met the requirements for the role of President; he is currently serving his second term five year term as he remains the only person qualified to fill the role.[117] This means that longer term patients will appear before the same President—and probably the same medical member—on each occasion, which opens the argument for pre-determined outcomes and, at the very least, a perception of bias. In line with consumer feedback in other jurisdictions,[118] this might be one of the reasons why the number of appeals in Tonga is so low.

3.4. Specific Rights

Part X of the *Mental Health Act 2001* contains a number of provisions relating to patients' rights. These include:

- An explanation of rights under the Act for all persons subject to ITOs or CTOs (s 89)
- Details of prescribed medication including dosages and side effects (s 90)
- Accommodation and treatment planning on discharge (s 91)
- Privacy of phone calls and mail (s 92)
- Confidentiality of medical records with some exceptions (ss 92-93)
- Procedures for handling complaints(ss 94-97)
- Appointment of community visitors to inspect and inquire into and report on complaints or specific matters or the detention, treatment or care of any person within a mental health facility (ss 105-110)
- Provision of information about a person's right to see a community visitor (ss 114-115)
- Appointment of a Mental Health Advisory Committee to advise on matters relating to provisions of the Act and the care and well-being of persons with mental illness or mental disorders (ss 121-126)
- Right to written decisions and reasons by MHRT within specified time frames (s 132 (k)-(l))
- Access to interpreters and representation at MHRT hearings.(ss 134, 137)

Although no reference is made to either document, these provisions appear to be based on various principles contained in the *MI Principles* and the *WHO Ten Principles.*

In reality, it would seem that many of the rights based provisions in the Act do not have any real force. The current—and so far only—President of the MHRT asserts that less than thirty percent of all hearings include representation for the patient and rarely, if ever, does this involve legal representation. He suggests that many of the mentally ill have poor family

116 Ibid.

117 Ibid.

118 See, e.g., V Topp, M Thomas and M Ingvarson, 'Lacking Insight: Involuntary Patient Experience of the Victorian Mental Health Review Board' (2008).

support systems, which accounts for the low levels of representation. However, family members who do appear before the MHRT to assist patients are often able to provide useful information, which condenses the process and is beneficial in terms of making orders.[119]

There are no lawyers in Tonga who specialise in mental health law and no specialist advice services for the mentally ill.[120] In practice, all MHRT hearings are held in private in a room at the mental health unit and the only records of the hearing are the notes taken by the court clerk, which are later placed on the Magistrates' Court file. Interpreters are rarely used, as hearings are held in Tongan (the main spoken language) and the hearings are not tape-recorded.[121] While this occurs more for administrative convenience than consumer preference, it may not necessarily be a negative factor. At least one state in Australia has abandoned the practice of tape recording hearings as consumer studies found the process to be 'too formal and intimidating'.[122]

Only two patients have ever asked for access to their medical records to assist at a hearing and none has sought access to the court files or asked for a tribunal decision in writing.[123] The MHRT's practice is not to give written reasons for its decisions but only to make orders in relation to continuing detention and treatment. In general these orders are not available to the public at large.[124]

It also seems that the community visitor program is not active in Tonga and has never played any role in the representation of mental health consumers before the MHRT.[125]

In short, despite the written law, it seems mental health consumers under detention in Tonga are not able to access their rights to justice in any meaningful way.

4. Challenges for the Future

Tonga was the first country in the region to embark on mental health law reform, despite the fact that it did not graduate from a constitutional monarchy to democracy until 2010. It seems more probable than not that international human rights principles have driven mental health law reform in Tonga and, for the most part, have been championed by Dr Puloka who, as a well-educated and well respected indigenous Tongan, has been in a position to influence domestic mental health policy. Nonetheless, there does not appear to be any dispute among the various respondents that, while the new Act has vastly improved the *notion* of promoting human rights, the day to day reality is quite different.

The facilities at the current mental health unit are stretched to capacity and further expansion is necessary to provide optimum care. There is an acute shortage of trained mental health professionals and independent psychiatrists to assist patients in the appeal and review process, thus enabling access to justice.[126] There is also a greater need for legal training to educate workers, families and the general public about the rights of the mentally ill and a

---

[119] Email questionnaire from Salesi Mafi, Senior Magistrate Tonga, to Helen Ménard,16 September 2011.

[120] Ibid; Email questionnaire from Ma'afu Sefokuli, Court Clerk Tonga, to Helen Ménard, 20 June 2011

[121] Email questionnaire from Ma'afu Sefokuli, Court Clerk Tonga, to Helen Ménard, 20 June 2011

[122] F Clair and S Fisher, 'Powering - and Empowering - Through Change: The Queensland Tribunal's Experience of Transition from Old Systems to New' (2003) 10(1) *Psychiatry, Psychology and Law* 184, 188.

[123] Email questionnaire from Ma'afu Sefokuli, Court Clerk Tonga, to Helen Ménard, 20 June 2011.

[124] Email questionnaire from Salesi Mafi, Senior Magistrate Tonga, to Helen Ménard,16 September 2011.

[125] Ibid.

[126] Ibid; Email questionnaire from Ma'afu Sefokuli, Court Clerk Tonga, to Helen Ménard, 20 June 2011.

critical need for better methods of record keeping within the health and legal systems to support patients' rights to access their records.[127]

What is of most significance in Tonga is that, despite having the legislative framework to do so, the country has essentially been unable to move away from the inpatient care model. In essence, there are no community based mental health services and, if Tonga is to 'progressively realise' the rights of individuals to 'the enjoyment of the highest attainable standard' of mental health, this needs to be a priority. Mental health care has been provided by one psychiatrist in Tonga for almost 25 years and he has been a passionate advocate for mental health consumers and instrumental in influencing national policies on mental health care. His major challenge and, indeed, contribution to mental health has been the development of transcultural psychiatry. Puloka has worked hard at educating the community and traditional healers to recognise that there is a role for modern psychiatric medicine—albeit not an exclusive one. This has resulted in increasing numbers of Tongans seeking formal mental health care and treatment at a level beyond the capacity of available services.

The challenge for the next generation of mental health professionals in Tonga, should they materialise, is to build on the notion of transcultural psychiatry and eventually to complete the circle—to move care and treatment back into a community, hopefully with an enhanced understanding of mental health care and human rights issues. Of course, this is dependent on there being sufficiently trained mental health professionals and financial resources needed to support a community care model. At present, this would simply mean diverting human resources from the inpatient facility, which is already under-resourced and facing an ever increasing demand for its services. It is possible that the development of community based care and treatment is one of the matters alluded to in the Ministry of Health's 2009 report, which lists the objective 'to implement provisions of the Mental Health Act 2001 and formulate a mental health policy.'[128] The Ministry's 2011 report, as part of its mission statement in relation to mental health, states that it is responsible for 'contin[uing] the process of deinstitutionalisation for all psychiatric cases.'[129] Unfortunately, there seems to have been little movement in this regard.

---

127 Email questionnaire from Ma'afu Sefokuli, Court Clerk Tonga, to Helen Ménard, 20 June 2011.

128 Government of Tonga, 'Report of the Minister of Health for the Year 2009' (2009) <www.health.gov.to/sites/default/files/AR2009.pdf> 70.

129 Government of Tonga, above n 89, 32.

Chapter 6

SAMOA

This is the second of four chapters which examines the history of mental health legislation in the region—this time Samoa—as well as the factors that have influenced law reform and the challenges for the future. This examination reveals that despite stated objectives to provide optimum health care services, the legislative model is one that adopts a more pragmatic approach to rights based law, anticipates nominal interaction with formal legal systems and refrains from dealing with issues that are not part of the current treatment profile. Unlike Tonga, Samoa has not opted for the tribunal style model of review and has limited inpatient treatment facilities.

1. THE LAW AS IT WAS

Prior to independence in 1962, Part XII of the *Samoa Act 1921* regulated the custody and treatment of the mentally ill.[1] These provisions governing the custody and treatment of those considered to be of 'unsound mind' and 'criminal lunatics,' were imported from the *Mental Defectives Act 1911* (NZ), later renamed the *Mental Health Act 1911*.[2]

After independence, the *Mental Health Ordinance 1961* was enacted thereby repealing Part XII of the *Samoa Act 1921*[3]. Unfortunately, this Ordinance did not change the law and essentially mirrored the provisions of the antiquated imported New Zealand statutes. In effect, the law in relation to mental health in Samoa remained unchanged for ninety years until it was repealed by the *Mental Health Act 2007*.[4]

Statutes in force in England as at 14 January 1840 were applied to Western Samoa as long as they were in force in New Zealand on 7 December 1921 and were continued under the new Samoan Constitution. However, by 1977, all except one English and a few New Zealand statutes in force in Samoa had been abolished.[5]

---

1 German legislation made in Samoa between 1900–1919 was completely abolished by 1972; see *Samoa Act 1921* (NZ) s 349; see also *Reprint of Statutes Act 1972* (Samoa) s 8; *Constitution of the Independent State of Western Samoa 1960* art 114.

2 *Mental Health Amendment Act 1954* (NZ) s 2(3).

3 *Mental Health Ordinance 1961* (Samoa) s 45.

4 *Mental Health Act 2007* (Samoa) s 38.

5 J Corrin Care, T Newton and D Paterson, *Introduction to South Pacific Law* (Cavendish Publishing Ltd, 1999) 53.

1.1. Admission Criteria

Under the *Mental Health Ordinance 1961,* persons who were considered to be 'mentally defective' could only be detained in 'medical custody' under an order of a judge of the Supreme Court. A mentally defective person was a person 'who owing to his mental condition requires oversight, care and control of himself or his property for his own good or in the public interest.'[6] Mental condition was undefined in the Ordinance.

In making the order, the Court had to be satisfied that the detention was necessary in the person's own interests or for the safety of other persons.[7] A person believed on reasonable grounds to be of unsound mind and to be dangerous to himself or others, could be arrested without a warrant and taken before a judge or magistrate pending an application for a medical custody order.[8] There was no definition of unsound mind in this or any other legislation in Samoa.

It is to be presumed that those of unsound mind were considered to be in a different category to those who were mentally defective. However, as each had to be brought before the Court for a medical detention order, one assumes the Court then had to consider only the person's own interests or the safety of other persons.

1.2. The Rights to Appeal and Review

On application to the Supreme Court, any court order to involuntarily detain a person could be varied, cancelled or reviewed for a further period not exceeding six months.[9] There was no specific right to appeal an order—although to review an existing order could imply an appeal—and the review of medical custody orders did not include any power to review treatment. Presumably, any person would also have had access to the Supreme Court by a writ of *habeus corpus.*

The Ordinance contained general provisions for Visiting Boards—comprised of at least three people, one of whom was required to be a medical practitioner employed by the Department of Health—who were tasked with supervising the personal welfare of detainees and had general powers of inspection of facilities.[10] The Ordinance also required that no fewer than two members of the Board, at least every three months, 'see and examine' every person subject to a medical custody order[11] and report to the Minister, inter alia, on the 'health, welfare and mental condition of the person examined and the attention being given to him.'[12] Following such a report from the Board, the Minister had the power to direct that a medical practitioner examine the person and that an application for variation of a medical custody order be made to the court.[13]

---

6 *Mental Health Ordinance 1961* (Samoa) s 2.
7 *Crimes Ordinance 1961* (Samoa) s 6.
8 *Mental Health Ordinance 1961* (Samoa) s 10.
9 Ibid s 8.
10 Ibid ss 16–20.
11 Ibid ss 18–19.
12 Ibid s 20(2)(c).
13 Ibid s 21.

1.3. The Review Mechanism

There were no specific provisions in the earlier legislation to enable an inpatient to apply for review of his or her detention or treatment and no independent legal or quasi-legal review body for people admitted and treated involuntarily.

2. MOTIVATION FOR CHANGE

A review of literature and government reports in Samoa suggests that the move towards reform was guided by global WHO initiatives in the area of mental health. In committing to mental health as a global priority, the WHO's Regional Strategy for Mental Health in the Western Pacific acknowledged in 2002 that, while there had been improvements in physical health standards over the years, the situation had worsened in respect of mental health over the same period.[14] Compounding the problem in the Pacific region is the scarcity and poor distribution of resources.[15] The development of mental health policy and review of legislation was seen as one of the six key strategies to promote and improve mental health in the region. In particular, legislative reform should be aimed at appropriate legal protection for people with mental disorders and respecting the rights of individuals to dignified and effective care.[16]

Shortly thereafter, in 2003, the WHO Country Cooperation Strategy for Samoa set out strategic directions for 2003-2007 based on a systematic assessment of Samoa's government policies, developmental challenges and health needs—including mental health reform.[17] Increased prevalence of substance abuse and youth suicide within a predominantly young population, together with a general lack of understanding of mental health disorders within the community, were identified as key issues to be addressed.[18]

This was followed by a Ministry of Health symposium on mental health issues in Samoa in April 2003[19] which canvassed a range of issues including culture and mental health, community attitudes to mental health, existing psychiatric services and reform of mental health legislation.

With specific reference to reform of the mental health legislation, the then parliamentary counsel for the Attorney General's Office,[20] Tony Lawson (a former foundation president of Victoria's Guardianship Board), indicated that the program for reform of the 1961 Ordinance would be implemented in 2004 and

> in preparing the new legislation we will draw on the lessons learnt in mental health law reform from within the Pacific region and beyond. Furthermore, we will take into account both the strengths and limitations which Samoa possesses in this area. One of

---

14 *World Health Organisation, 'Regional Strategy for Mental Health' (WHO, Western Pacific Region, 2002).*

15 Ibid 7.

16 Ibid 19.

17 World Health Organisation, 'WHO Country Cooperation Strategy for Samoa' (2003) 2.

18 Ibid 6.

19 Government of Samoa Ministry of Health, 'Summary of Recommendations' (Paper presented at the National Symposium on Mental Health Issues in Samoa, Kitano-Tusitala Hotel, Apia, 2003).

20 A position he held from 2000 to 2007 and which was funded by the Australian Government through AusAID and responsible for the Samoan Government's legislative program reporting to the Attorney General and the Prime Minister.

> those strengths is the aiga (extended family). One of the limitations is the resource constraints, both human and financial, which is part of our reality in Samoa.[21]

It is clear from this statement that community and resources were to be the driving and opposing forces in mental health law reform.

The WHO's situational analysis of mental health needs in the Pacific in 2005[22] identified Samoa as not having a mental health policy despite a highly developed primary health care system, and still being without new mental health legislation.[23] The Samoan Mental Health Policy emerged in August 2006 followed by the *Mental Health Act* in February 2007.

According to Lawson:

> The genesis of the Samoa Mental Health Act and policy behind it came from my time as Parliamentary Counsel in Samoa. I identified the need to update the legislation with a new Act and obtained the approval of the Attorney General and CEO of the Ministry of Health to begin work on drafting a new Act.
>
> It is of note that there was no policy development capacity within the Ministry of Health to provide the drafting instructions for the new Bill. And there was only one psychiatrist in the country, Dr Ian Parkin.[24]

Lawson further stated that he worked with Dr Parkin to develop the legislation and

> used the Victorian and South Australian Mental Health Acts as the models for the Samoan Act and adapted the legislation to address the Samoan realities (namely very limited resources and a range of structural and cultural factors affecting mental health issues and treatment in Samoa).
>
> We developed a draft Act which we sent out for discussion and consultation with interested persons and organisations, principally through the Health Dept. and the CEO Health. Following the consultations I amended the draft Act and submitted it to the CEO Health, Attorney General, Minister for Health for their consideration and approval. Following some further input from Ian Parkin and the Samoan Health professionals, the draft Act was finalised and submitted to the then Minister for Health and CEO Health and the Attorney General for their final approval. This was obtained and the Mental Health Bill went forward to the Parliament in 2007… and became law in the same year.[25]

Samoa's Law & Justice Sector Plan 2008-2012,[26] lists one of its key objectives as improving access to justice, law and legal services, including the establishment of a Law Reform Commission, Community Law Centres, a Human Rights Commission and a Disabled Peoples Rights Unit.[27] However, it makes no specific reference to those suffering from mental disorders. The Plan does state that 'most community life is governed by customary law and

21 Email from Tony Lawson to Helen Ménard, 20 May 2011.

22 World Health Organisation, 'Situational Analysis of Mental Health Needs and Resources in Pacific Island Countries' (WHO, Centre for Mental Health Research, Policy & Service Development, 2005).

23 Ibid 103–7.

24 Email from Tony Lawson to Helen Ménard, 20 May 2011.

25 Ibid.

26 Government of Samoa Office of the Attorney General, 'Samoa Law & Justice Sector Plan 2008-2012: Justice for a Safe and Stable Samoa' (2008).

27 Ibid 3, 11.

the nature of this relationship lies at the heart of law and justice in Samoa'[28] and that the marriage between the formal and the informal structures presents one of the major challenges to the operation of law and justice in the country.[29] This recognition of the existence of two equally viable but potentially divergent structures would also seem to have been a significant factor in drafting appropriate legislation and developing policy in relation to mental health care and services.

While there is no direct reference in either the lead up policy documentation or the legislation itself to compliance with specific international human rights instruments, the mental health policy and the legislation are clearly cognisant of general rights based principles in existence at the time.[30]

3. The Law Now

The *Mental Health Act 2007*[31] was a long awaited reform in Samoa and significantly changed the mental health landscape—at least in theory. The previous statute was scant, at best, and provided no protective mechanisms for the rights of mentally ill persons or supportive platforms for care and treatment. The new framework adopts a definition of mental disorder that includes mental illness but excludes a series of beliefs and activities that, historically, have been the basis of discrimination and persecution of mental health consumers.

The primary focus of the new legislation is the provision of care and treatment in a community setting, but it does not establish any formal independent mechanism for the periodic review of orders for community or inpatient detention or treatment. Appeals against detention orders may be made to the District Court.

Section 3 of the *Mental Health Act 2007* (Samoa) outlines an ambitious set of objectives which are, nonetheless, 'subject to available resources':

> (a) to ensure that persons with a mental disorder receive the best possible care, support and, where required, treatment and protection;
>
> (b) to support families and communities where they are providing care and support for a person with a mental disorder; and
>
> (c) to minimise the restrictions upon the liberty of persons with a mental disorder and interference in their rights, dignity and self-respect, so far as is consistent with their proper care, support, treatment and protection and the protection of other persons;
>
> (d) to work towards ameliorating the adverse effects of mental disorder upon persons with a mental disorder, their families and communities;
>
> (e) to rationalise and co-ordinate services for persons with a mental disorder, their families and communities;
>
> (f) to assist and encourage non-government agencies and organizations to provide care, support and other services for persons with a mental disorder, their families and communities;

---

28 Ibid 23.
29 Ibid 23.
30 See, e.g., *Mental Health Act 2007* (Samoa) s 3.
31 The Act came into force on 2 February 2007.

(g) to assist and encourage the development of services designed to reduce the incidence and adverse impact of mental disorder in the community;

(h) to promote informed public opinion, discussion and understanding of mental disorder;

(i) to eliminate discrimination against, and abuse, mistreatment and neglect of persons with a mental disorder;

(j) to promote a high standard of training of those responsible for the care, support, treatment and protection of persons with a mental disorder; and

(k) to promote research into the problems of mental disorder.

Unsurprisingly, the ability to realise these objectives has very much been limited by available resources and, as discussed in Chapter 13, many of the policy objectives in the Samoan Mental Health Policy remain unfulfilled.

3.1. Admission Criteria

The *Mental Health Act 2007* (Samoa) employs the term 'mental disorder' which is defined in s 2 as follows:

> ['Mental disorder'] includes a mental illness and means a medical condition that is characterized by a significant disturbance of thought, mood, perception or memory, save that a person is not to be considered *mentally ill* by reason of one or more of the following:
>
> (a) that the person expresses or refuses or fails to express a particular political opinion or belief;
>
> (b) that the person expresses or refuses or fails to express a particular religious opinion or belief;
>
> (c) that the person expresses or refuses or fails to express a particular philosophy;
>
> (d) that the person expresses or refuses or fails to express a particular sexual preference or sexual orientation;
>
> (e) that the person engages in or refuses or fails to engage in a particular political activity;
>
> (f) that the person engages in or refuses or fails to engage in a particular religious activity;
>
> (g) that the person engages in sexual promiscuity;
>
> (h) that the person engages in immoral conduct;
>
> (i) that the person engages in illegal conduct;
>
> (j) that the person is intellectually disabled;
>
> (k) that the person takes drugs or alcohol;
>
> (l) that the person has an antisocial personality;
>
> (m) that the person has a particular economic or social status or is a member of a particular cultural or racial group.

Paragraph (k) does not prevent the serious temporary or permanent physiological, biochemical or psychological effects of drugs or alcohol taking from being regarded as an indication that a person has a mental disorder.

While 'mental illness' is included as a mental disorder, mental illness itself is not defined except by exclusion.

According to Lawson, the Victorian and South Australian statutes were used as a model for the Samoan legislation.[32] However, the Samoan definition of *mental disorder*—a broader term and which 'includes a mental illness and means a medical condition that is characterized by a significant disturbance of thought, mood, perception or memory'—appears to be a direct replica of the Victorian definition of *mental illness*, which states 'mental illness is a condition characterised by a significant disturbance of thought, mood, perception or memory.'[33]

There are distinct differences between anti-social behaviour, which any person may engage in from time to time, an anti-social personality and an anti-social personality disorder. Anti-social behaviour is a much wider term and not all anti-social behaviour may be indicative of an anti-social personality or even less so an anti-social personality disorder. The conduct and behaviour exclusions, which now appear in both the Victorian and South Australian statutes, also form part of the Samoan definition, thereby excluding 'antisocial personality' from the definition of mental illness but not the broader definition of mental disorder. Whether this exclusion in Samoa is also intended to extend to antisocial personality disorders or to exclude other types of personalities or disorders is unclear. Nonetheless, it is reasonable to assume that the drafting was intentional and the question of whether an anti-social personality *disorder* is a mental illness is left open—but it could well come within the definition of mental disorder.

Section 8(2) of the 1986 Victorian *Mental Health Act* excluded an 'antisocial personality' from its definition of mental illness and was the only statute in Australia or New Zealand to do so. However, s 4 of the new *Mental Health Act* introduced into Victoria in 2014, removed 'antisocial personality' from its list of exclusions and substituted 'antisocial behaviour'. New Zealand makes no reference at all to the concept and all other Australian states—including South Australia which did not include the term until the passage of amending legislation in 2009—only refer to 'anti-social behaviour' by way of exclusion.[34]

This pattern of legislative drafting tends to demonstrate a marked reluctance to remove anti-social personalities and disorders from the ambit of mental illness and the more encompassing mental disorders. Nonetheless, Samoa has opted for the less popular earlier Victorian approach, which leaves the dichotomy involving anti-social personality disorders and mental illness unresolved.[35] However, it does not mean that such a person can avoid involuntary detention. A person with an anti-social personality disorder may come under the definition of mental disorder and, if the person resisted voluntary care and was assessed as needing available care to protect him or herself or others, could be detained under the Act.

Section 13 requires that detention and treatment in a health care facility under an Inpatient Treatment Order (ITO) in Samoa meet the following criteria:

---

32 Email from Tony Lawson to Helen Ménard, 20 May 2011.

33 *Mental Health Act 1986* (Vic) s 4.

34 *Mental Health Act 2009* (SA) schedule 1.

35 This is not surprising given that Lawson was the President of the Guardianship and Administration Board in Victoria during the height of the furore surrounding the Garry David case.

a) that the person has a mental disorder; *and*
b) that the person is unwilling or unable to receive care, support, treatment or protection for the mental disorder on a voluntary basis; *and*
c) as a result of the mental disorder the person requires care, support, treatment or protection
   i) in the interests of the person; *or*
   ii) to protect another person or persons; *and*
d) the care, support, treatment or protection required under (c)
   i) is available; *and*
   ii) cannot be provided in a less restrictive manner (including but not limited to a Community Treatment Order) than under an Inpatient Treatment Order.[36]

While the Act also defines the term 'mental incapacity,' it is only used in the context of orders of administration under the Act.[37]

3.2. The Rights to Appeal and Review

Under the new Samoan legislation, an Involuntary Treatment Order (ITO) is only valid for six weeks, after which time the patient must be re-examined by a mental health care professional and a new ITO issued.[38] If, at any time, an inpatient is examined and found to no longer meet the criteria for involuntary detention, he or she must be discharged by a mental health care professional—being a medical practitioner, nurse, psychologist or social worker.[39]

According to Parkin, the mental health team has only used involuntary orders on 10-15 occasions since the introduction of the Act and these have been evenly distributed between ITOs and Community Treatment Orders (CTOs). ITOs have rarely, if ever, been renewed beyond the initial six-week period but some CTOs have extended from months to years.[40]

There is no process by which anyone other than a mental health care professional conducts reviews of ITOs or CTOs. Nor is there any requirement that the mental health care professional who reviews an order be different to the person who initiated the order. Samoa is the only Pacific jurisdiction in which an order can be made or reviewed by a person other than a medical practitioner. While it may be a reflection of the lack of available professional resources, Tonga with similar resource issues has not proceeded down this path. Nonetheless, it is a practice adopted in other countries such as South Africa.[41]

On the other hand, the Chief Mental Health Officer (CMHO) has the power to vary or revoke any ITO or CTO where he or she 'considers it appropriate to do so in the circumstances' although there is no indication how the matter might come to the attention of the CMHO.[42] Additionally, there is no requirement under the Act that the CMHO be a

36 *Mental Health Act 2007* (Samoa) s13.
37 "Mental incapacity" in relation to a person, means intellectual impairment, mental disorder, medical disorder, brain injury, physical disability or dementia such that, by reason of the impairment, illness, disorder, injury, disability or dementia, the person is unable to make or communicate reasonable judgments in respect of all or any of the matters relating to the person or the person's circumstances or estate.
38 *Mental Health Act 2007* (Samoa) s 14(2).
39 Ibid s 14(5).
40 Email questionnaire from Dr Ian Parkin, Psychiatrist Samoa, to Helen Ménard, 15 April 2011.
41 P Bartlett and V Hamzic, 'Reforming Mental Disability Law in Africa: Practical Tips and Suggestions' (Human Rights Law Centre, The University of Nottingham, 2010) 17.
42 *Mental Health Act 2007* (Samoa) ss 11(8), 14(9).

medical practitioner. Section 2 merely defines the CMHO as 'a health care professional appointed by the Minister ... with a specialist mental health qualification *or* experience to supervise and manage mental health services.'

A person who wishes to apply for review of a detention order—being either an ITO or a CTO—must obtain leave of the District Court to file an application for review.[43] Leave will be granted subject to the number of applications previously made or hearings already held in relation to that order and provided 14 days have passed since the issuing of an ITO. There is no such time limitation on a CTO.

Review hearings, except in exceptional circumstances, are limited to one per order—being six weeks for an ITO and twelve months for a CTO.[44] While one hearing might be a reasonable restriction for an ITO, it does seem to be less equitable for those detained under a CTO. Leaving aside the obligation on the mental health care professional to discharge the order if the person no longer meets the criteria for detention—and assuming the person is not so discharged—one hearing in twelve months seems unduly restrictive on the person's right to access justice. This is particularly so given the fact that the original order and the review can be made by the same person, thereby depriving the mental health consumer of the benefit of an alternate opinion. Furthermore, there is no indication in the legislation as to what might constitute 'exceptional circumstances' for the purpose of justifying more frequent review.

A person may apply for review of a CTO in the same way and under the same conditions as an ITO.[45] On reviewing an order, the Court 'shall have regard to all the circumstances of the applicant's case'[46] but there is no provision for the Court to review treatment plans or indeed any requirement to have a treatment plan—merely the *need* for treatment under the criteria for detention.

The provisions relating to Visiting Boards in the 1961 Ordinance have not been replicated in the new legislation. As their primary function was to oversee the personal welfare of detainees as well as to exercise general powers of inspection of inpatient facilities, this was presumably considered to be unnecessary given the new policy of community care and the small number of inpatient beds.

3.3. The Review Mechanism

Apart from the right to apply for review of an ITO or a CTO to the District Court, the legislation does not establish a separate formal body within the health or the legal system to facilitate access to appeals against involuntary detention.[47] This is largely a reflection of the lack of professional resources and the preference for community based care and treatment. Parkin maintains the decision was also influenced by the requirement that the reform process be cost neutral and any appeal or review process be seen as 'quick and efficient as well as

[43] The District Court in Samoa is the lowest court with general jurisdiction and is equivalent to the Magistrates' Court in other jurisdictions.

[44] *Mental Health Act 2007* (Samoa) s 21(1),(3),(4),(6).

[45] Ibid s 20.

[46] Ibid ss 20(3), 21(3).

[47] Ibid ss 20–21.

external and independent' and avoid the lengthy delays associated with the previous Supreme Court procedure.[48]

Section 2 of the Act requires that 'the Court' be constituted by a Judge of the District Court and a mental health care professional—any registered medical practitioner, registered nurse, psychologist or social worker appointed by the Minister—sitting as 'advisor' to the Court. An advisor is appointed by the Head of State for renewable terms of three years.

Section 22, in describing the powers and procedures of the Court in this context, grants the Court all the powers in relation to civil proceedings; requires it to act according to equity and good conscience; binds it to the rules of natural justice but not to the rules of evidence; and requires it to conduct proceedings in the least formal manner possible. While this describes a Western style natural justice model, given the realities of the jurisdiction, it is important to ask whether it works in practice.

Since the introduction of the Act, there has been only one instance where a patient's appeal against an initial ITO—on the basis of not meeting the requirements of a mental disorder—was brought before the court. The matter was heard before a judge within a few days. The hearing was held in a courtroom but in a round table format. The judge was assisted by a mental health nurse (as required under s 2) who was not directly associated with the mental health unit or employed by the health sector. The treating psychiatrist, the patient, a nurse from the mental health unit and a family member of the patient were also present. The patient was not represented in any way and made no request for representation. The judge acted to assist the patient but it is unclear whether the patient had access to the medical file. Even though the court upheld the initial detention order, later communication between the patient and the treating team suggested that the patient was satisfied with the process.[49] Since then a small number of other consumers have requested appeals but before the matters came before the court the consumers' symptoms had improved and the orders had been removed.[50]

Although there is no stated right of appeal from a decision of the District Court in the *Mental Health Act,* it is to be presumed that this right exists by virtue of s 70 of the *District Court Act 1969* which states that 'any party to any civil proceedings in a District Court may appeal as hereinafter provided to the Supreme Court against any non-suit or final determination or direction of the District Court.'[51]

3.4. Specific Rights

Part 6 of the *Mental Health Act 2007* deals with a person's rights and reviews. Apart from the review process outlined above, s 19 provides that, where a person is subject to an ITO or a CTO, the health care professional must give the person a copy of the order; a copy of the person's rights in Samoan or English; an application for review;[52] and *subject to*

---

[48] Email questionnaire from Dr Ian Parkin, Psychiatrist Samoa, to Helen Ménard, 15 April 2011.

[49] Ibid; at the request of the respondent, all potentially identifying information in relation to this patient has been withheld.

[50] Email questionnaire from Dr Ian Parkin, Psychiatrist Samoa, to Helen Ménard, 10 January 2016.

[51] 70. Right to appeal - Any party to any civil proceedings in a District Court may appeal as hereinafter provided to the Supreme Court against any non-suit or final determination or direction of the District Court.
75. Procedure on hearing of appeal - (1) All appeals shall be by way of rehearing.

[52] *Mental Health (Treatment Order Forms) Notice 2007* (Samoa), S.R.2007/26 & 27 (7 June 2007).

available resources a verbal explanation of the effect of the order and the person's rights under the Act.

The statement of rights, entitled 'Statement of Rights to Apply to Review Order', makes no reference to anything other than the right to review. The form includes information in relation to who can initiate a review; the right to seek assistance from a health care professional or a lawyer; the process for filing a review; and the powers of the District Court.[53] Although this form states that the person applying for review may 'seek help from' a health care professional or a lawyer, there is no provision in the Act that allows for legal or general representation.

Nor is there any requirement under the Act to provide people with information in relation to matters such as consent to treatment, the effects of medication, the right to confidentiality or complaints mechanisms; and there is no right to access medical records for any purpose.

It would seem that the only information given to patients is that contained on the ITO or CTO—in Samoan or English but in rather legalistic terms—and there are no general information brochures available in plain language. One interview respondent explains that emphasis is placed on verbal communication which is more appropriate to the predominantly oral culture of Samoans.[54]

Sections 20(5) and 21(6) render it an offence for a mental health care professional to fail to process an application for review of an ITO or a CTO without lawful or reasonable excuse.[55] It is suggested that, prior to the introduction of the Act, there was some reluctance to assist people with a challenge against a mental health worker's judgement in relation to an involuntary order. The inclusion of the penalty clauses was to remind health professionals they had dual roles—to treat the patient and to assist them with their rights.[56] One respondent claims that improved awareness and understanding since the introduction of the Act has minimised this problem.[57] Even so, the dual roles do create a conflict that is not easily resolved.

4. Challenges for the Future

Parkin concedes that there are some gaps in the legislation. For example, should Samoa ever have access to electro-convulsive therapy as a form of treatment, it would be necessary to establish statutory guidelines. Likewise, the prospect of ever needing to perform psychosurgery in Samoa is extremely remote and legislative provisions equally unnecessary. He further concedes that the issue of longer-term detention of mentally ill offenders may become a concern but the need to address it legislatively at this stage does not seem to be an imperative.[58]

It is not for this study to determine whether the community based mental health care model is working in Samoa. Even so, it is obvious there are relatively small numbers of consumers currently accessing formal mental health services. The treatment gap is significant

---

53 Ibid.

54 Email questionnaire from Dr Ian Parkin, Psychiatrist Samoa, to Helen Ménard, 15 April 2011.

55 *Mental Health Act 2007* (Samoa) ss 20(5), 21(6).

56 Email questionnaire from Dr Ian Parkin, Psychiatrist Samoa, to Helen Ménard, 15 April 2011.

57 Ibid.

58 Ibid.

and it is unlikely that current levels of service can sustain increasing populations or demands for formal mental health services. The test will be whether any increase in professional mental health resources will bring with it the demand for more medically based care and treatment—including more inpatient facilities—and whether the rights of mental health consumers will survive against more pressing and financially viable health options.

Although there is no longer any legislative framework for the role of official visitors or a lay patient advocates, Parkin supports the function as advancing the rights of mental health consumers in Samoa, particularly in accessing their rights of appeal. While this role could conceivably be filled by NGOs such as the Goshen Trust, with no inpatient beds currently in Samoa and no applications for appeal against CTOs, the question of access to justice under the legislation appears to be moot.

Nonetheless, at a broader level, the inability of Samoan mental health consumers to access their basic human rights to mental health care was highlighted by the events of 26 December 2012. Hans Dalton was 38 and had travelled from New Zealand to holiday with his family in Samoa. Previously diagnosed with a mental illness, he was taking medication but became unwell while in Samoa and was taken to the mental health unit by his sister. He was seen by the attendant psychiatrist and given additional medication. However, Hans became even more agitated and physically aggressive and—there being no inpatient mental health beds in Samoa since 2011—he was transferred to the local police station for protection and containment. Despite pleas from the family, the police then transferred Hans to Tafa'igata Prison because he was 'agitated and violent and could not be held at the police station as they were too busy.'[59]

Hans died the same day in Tafa'igata Prison although the cause of his death has been the subject of debate. He was placed in a prison cell without supervision and was later found head first in a one gallon container of water kept in the cells for the toilets. On subsequent examination at the hospital, Hans was found to have a fractured skull and other multiple injuries which may have been caused by him banging his head repeatedly on the concrete walls of his cell.[60]

Initially, prison authorities alleged Hans had committed suicide but, after an investigation into his death, another inmate, Jonathon Crichton, was charged with his murder. Crighton was found not guilty by the Supreme Court[61] and the verdict was upheld on appeal in 2014.[62] Two police officers, who were found to be negligent in their treatment of Hans, were subsequently terminated from the police force.[63] The series of events led to a Commission of Inquiry into the management and operation of Tafa'igata Prison; damming findings of widespread

59 Kolotita Talatalaga, 'Boxing Day Tragedy at Tafa'igata,' *Samoa Observer* (Apia, Samoa), 3 January 2013 <www.samoaobserver.ws/home/headlines/2710-boxing-day-tragedy-at-tafaigata (accessed 9 March 2013)>.

60 Ibid.

61 Lanuola Tupufia, 'Man Charged for Death of Hans Dalton,' *Samoa Observer* (Apia, Samoa), 18 January 2013 <www.samoaobserver.ws/local-news/police-and-prison/2956--man-charged-for-death-of-hans-dalton (accessed 9 March 2013)>.; Marj Moore, 'So Who Killed Hans Dalton?,' *Samao Observer* (Apia, Samoa), 10 February 2014 <http://www.samoaobserver.ws/editorial/9232-so-who-killed-hans-dalton (accessed 6 September 2015)>

62 *Attorney General v Crichton* [2014] WSCA 8.

63 *Samoan Police Officers Fired after New Zealander's Death* <www.3news.co.nz/Samoan-police-officers-fired-after-New-Zealanders-death/tabid/417/articleID/285936/Default.aspx (accessed 9 March 2013)>.

corruption and mistreatment of prisoners; the dismissal of the Commissioner of Police; and the resignation of the Assistant Commissioner for Prisons.[64]

Had there been suitable mental health treatment facilities available, Hans could have been detained and treated appropriately and his tragic death avoided. Sadly, the 'state of the art' mental health unit was too late for Hans. His family is now suing the Samoan government.[65]

[64] 'Commission Reports 'Below Standard Performance,' *Samoa Observer* (Apia, Samoa), 12 October 2014 <http://www.samoaobserver.ws/home/headlines/11856-commission-reports-below-standard-performance (accessed 6 September 2015)>

[65] Michael Field, 'Family Sues Samoa over Hans Dalton's Prison Death' (17 September 2014) <http://www.stuff.co.nz/world/south-pacific/61303199/family-sues-samoa-over-hans-daltons-prison-death (accessed 6 September 2015)>

Chapter 7

Fiji

This chapter on Fiji is the third and last chapter that explores the history of mental health legislation in a country with reformed mental health law. The chapter also traces the history of that reform and the anticipated future difficulties for Fiji. This exploration demonstrates that, following a long history of institutional mental health care, a stated commitment to community based mental health care policy and a range of international rights based principles has changed little in Fiji. The country has so far failed to establish any supporting funding or infrastructure to allow for effective transition to a community care model and most of the rights based provisions under the new Decree remain untested. There are a number of unexplained but notable deficiencies in the rights based platform of the Decree and the future of mental health service delivery in Fiji is as unpredictable as its political future.

1. The Law as It Was

Prior to 1874, Fiji (formerly Fiji then Fiji Islands)[1] was ruled by the local chiefs who ceded the islands to Britain as a colony under the Deed of Cession in 1874. It remained so until obtaining its independence as a sovereign democratic state in 1970.[2] At this time, the constitution in existence prior to independence was revoked and a new constitution introduced under the *Fiji Independence Order 1970* (UK). Section 5 of this Order also gave effect to all laws in existence at independence, including adopted English legislation. English statutes of general application in force as at 2 January 1875—referred to as the 'cut-off date'—were adopted in Fiji under the *Supreme Court Ordinance 1875*.[3] This 'cut-off date' preceded the enactment of any substantive mental health legislation in the United Kingdom.

---

1 Following independence in 1970, Fiji became the Sovereign Democratic State of Fiji. Under the 1990 Constitution and after two military coups in 1987, Fiji became the Republic of Fiji. This changed to the Republic of Fiji Islands under the amended Constitution in 1997. Following a policy decision by the interim government of Fiji, the name officially reverted back to the Republic of Fiji from 19 January 2011. (Adarshani Vikash (Ms), Legal Officer, Office of the Solicitor-General, Suva, Fiji email 14 March 2013). This has now been confirmed in the 2013 *Constitution of the Republic of Fiji*.

2 G Powles, 'The Legal Systems of the Region' in G Powles and M Pulea (eds), *Pacific Courts and Legal Systems* (University of the South Pacific and Faculty of Law Monash University, 1988) 291, 306.

3 These were then given effect after independence by s 5 of the *Fiji Independence Order 1970*.

This means that no English mental health legislation was adopted by Fiji under the Ordinance.

As with many other countries in the region, early mental health legislation in Fiji was based on the English statutes dating from around 1890 to 1930. The *Mental Treatment Act* [Cap 113] was enacted in 1940 and, as it did not purport to repeal any previous legislation and there was no equivalent English legislation already in force in Fiji, it is presumed to have been the first of its kind in Fiji. The Act underwent a number of minor amendments up to 1975 but there were no further amendments until the release of the *Mental Health Decree* in October 2010, which repealed the Act.[4]

1.1. Admission Criteria

In Fiji, the old legislation employed the term 'unsound mind' which was defined to 'include an idiot'. Neither of these terms has been considered in the context of mental health legislation or case law in Fiji.[5]

However, the meaning of the terms 'idiot' as it appeared in the *Crimes Ordinance 1961* (Samoa) did come before the Samoan Supreme Court in *Fono's* case.[6] There was no similar definition of 'unsound mind' in Samoa as including 'idiot' and as a result the term was never considered in the context of mental health legislation on Samoa. The Supreme Court adopted the definition of 'idiot' as laid down in the NSW Court of Appeal decision in *R v Colgan* as being 'persons [in whom] there exists mental defectiveness of such a degree that they are unable to guard themselves against common physical dangers.'[7] This decision might have been considered persuasive by Fijian courts had the occasion arisen.

There is little or no case law in the Pacific region that has dealt with the concept of 'unsound mind' in any detail and none in the context of a person detained under mental health legislation. However, in *Tangata's* case in 1997, the Cook Islands High Court, in the absence of any statutory definitions, was required to consider the term 'unsound mind' under the *Electoral Act 1966* in relation to the ability of a member of parliament to hold his seat.[8] The Chief Justice, in referring to two English decisions,[9] and after hearing evidence from several doctors, concluded:

4 The Decree came into operation on 1 July 2011. (LN 34, Fiji Gazette Supp.No.18, 13 May 2011). Following a military coup in Fiji Islands in December 2006, the Fiji Constitution was finally abrogated on 10 April 2009 and subsequently all laws in the country have been passed by Presidential Decree, most of which have repealed and replaced pre-existing legislation. See *Fiji Constitution Amendment Act 1997 Revocation Decree 2009* (Fiji Islands) and *Executive Authority of Fiji Decree 2009* (Fiji Islands). The latter decree appointed the Commander in Chief of the military forces as President of the Republic with the power to make decrees and by virtue of s 5 'No question as to the validity of this Decree or any other Decree shall be entertained by any Court of Law in Fiji.' Following democratic elections in Fiji in 2014, the *Constitution of the Republic of Fiji* came into force.

5 *Mental Treatment Act* [Cap 113] (Fiji Islands) s 2.

6 *Police v Fono* [1999] WSSC 51.

7 *R v Colgan* (1959) SR (NSW) 96.

8 *Tangata v Speaker of the Legislative Assembly* [1997] CKHC 1.

9 In *Buxton v Jayne* (1960) 2 All ER 697 the court stated 'It is enough to say that unsoundness of mind is plainly something more radical than an emotional disturbance requiring psychiatric treatment. The unsoundness of mind, whose presence is essential to justify a compulsory order, manifestly means something more than mental illness which qualifies a person to be a voluntary patient.' In *Kirby v Leather* (1965) 2 All ER 441 Denning L.J. stated 'It seems to me that the words ... must be construed in relation to the subject matter with which the status is dealing ... a person is of unsound mind when he is by reason of mental illness incapable of managing his affairs...as a reasonable man would do.'

> There really is no dispute as to the proper approach to the diagnosis of the condition of unsound mind. Each of the above doctors have [sic] expressed themselves in definition thereof in terms which are in accord with meaning of the term given by Lord Denning in Kirby v Leather (supra), and I am satisfied that the test to be applied to the plaintiff in considering whether he was of unsound mind within the provisions of section 7(1)(i) of the Electoral Act 1966 is whether he was by reason of a mental illness incapable of managing his affairs as a reasonable man would do.[10]

Gokal's case involved an application under the *Mental Treatment Act* to determine whether he was of unsound mind and incapable of managing his own affairs, thus necessitating the appointment of a 'committee of the person and/or estate' to manage his activities. The Fiji High Court, without discussing the legal definition of the term, found that a person who was suffering from confusion, disorientation as to time and place, dementia, irrational decision making and an inability to care for himself, satisfied the term 'unsound mind'.[11]

The criteria for involuntary detention in Fiji under the superceded legislation were as follows:

- that such a person is a person of unsound mind *and*
- was at large, *or*
- was dangerous to himself and others, *or*
- was not under proper care and control, *or*
- was cruelly treated or neglected by any relative or other person having the care or charge of him [12]

As only *one* of these conditions needed to be met, in conjunction with unsoundness of mind, the potential for abuse of individual human rights was significant.

1.2. The Rights to Appeal and Review

In Fiji, the medical superintendent was only required to make a general visit to the mental health facility three times a week.[13] If, at any time, an inpatient was examined and found to no longer meet the criteria for involuntary detention, he or she was to be discharged by the superintendent or on the recommendation of two members of the Board of Visitors. [14]

As with many jurisdictions, there was provision under the Act for a Board of Visitors appointed by the Minister[15] whose functions included visiting and inspecting the mental health facilities and its admission records[16] and reporting to the Minister.[17] The Act also required the Board—at least every three months—to 'see and examine every person of

10 *Tangata v Speaker of the Legislative Assembly* [1997] CKHC 1.
11 *In re Application under Part VI of the Mental Treatment Act, Gokal v Gokal* [2004] FJHC 28.
12 *Mental Treatment Act* [Cap 113] (Fiji Islands) s 9.
13 Ibid s 26.
14 Ibid ss 32–33.
15 Ibid s 4(2).
16 Ibid s 21.
17 Ibid s 22.

unsound mind' and to check their admission documents.[18] Visitors had the power to discharge a person—except anyone held under court order as being criminally insane—if two of them after two separate visits at least seven days apart considered any person was being detained without sufficient cause.[19] If, however, the superintendent disagreed, the consent of the Minister was needed to validate the discharge.[20]

There was no requirement under the legislation that the visitors have any particular qualifications or experience in mental health. One respondent suggests that, while these Boards were constituted and did produce reports for the Ministry of Health, 'they acted more to provide material goods to make patients' stay in hospital more pleasant. They did not review the admission status of patients.'[21] Furthermore, the Minister's approval was only ever sought for release or leave of patients under Governor or Presidential Orders.[22]

During the consultation for reform in 2006, there was general agreement that the Board of Visitors did not have the qualifications, capacity or skills to undertake legal reviews under the proposed legislation.[23] In fact, respondents maintain that, while some visitors were caregivers, most were appointed because of their connections in the business community and their ability to raise funds for the operation of the hospital.[24]

1.3. The Review Mechanism

There were no specific provisions in the legislation to enable an inpatient to apply for review of his or her detention or treatment, and no independent legal or quasi-legal oversight or review body for persons admitted and treated involuntarily.[25] However, the Supreme Court of Fiji (later the High Court)[26] could review an involuntary patient's status 'upon information on oath or otherwise' brought before it.[27] Respondents suggest that, in practice, these applications were never made.[28] However, this procedure was specifically *not* available to 'a criminal under sentence or a person legally detained during the pleasure of the Crown'.[29] This would not have prevented an application by way of writ of *habeas corpus* to the Supreme Court.

---

18 Ibid s 21.
19 Ibid s 33(1).
20 Ibid s 33(1).
21 Email questionnaire from AB, Fiji, to Helen Ménard, 22 March 2012
22 Ibid.
23 Fiji Law Reform Commission, 'Issue Paper No. 3 – Definition – Review Mechanisms' (2006) 2.
24 Email questionnaire from AB, Fiji, to Helen Ménard, 22 March 2012.
25 Fiji Law Reform Commission, 'Issue Paper No. 1 – Purpose, Principles and Definitions – Review of the Fiji Mental Treatment Act' (2006) 2.
26 The Supreme Court was the superior court with original jurisdiction until, following the abrogation in 1987 of the 1970 Constitution of Fiji and the passing of the *Constitution of the Sovereign Democratic Republic of Fiji 1990*, the jurisdiction of the Supreme Court was transferred to the High Court (see s 195(2)(g)) and the Supreme Court became a second level appellate court above the Court of Appeal. Despite subsequent coups, a new constitution in 1997, the abrogation of the *Constitution (Amendment) Act 1997* (Fiji Islands) in 2009 and a new Constitution in 2013, this judicial structure has essentially been preserved.
27 *Mental Treatment Act* [Cap 113] (Fiji Islands) s 38.
28 Email questionnaire from AB, Fiji, to Helen Ménard, 22 March 2012.
29 *Mental Treatment Act* [Cap 113] (Fiji Islands) s 38.

those exercising functions or providing services under Decree are all subject to a rider—*as far as practicable and subject to available resources*.[45]

In its discussion of review mechanisms, the FLRC considered the tribunal style model and the oversight model (for example, a Board of Visitors), accepting that each had a discrete function:

> In many countries these two mechanisms are independent of one another. They require members who have different skills and experience, and with unique powers and functions. In some countries, one mechanism might have the power to carry out both functions. There is no single right model; just the right model for each countries [sic] circumstance. Whatever is set up, being independent of mental health services is a very important principle.[46]

It has been suggested by respondents that the real impetus for legal change came when the interim military regime moved to implement a large amount of legislation that had been 'shelved' and was considered long overdue for review. However, this process was

> carried out with little public consultation or awareness—involving police, prisons, social welfare, employment, education and the judiciary—and without the implementation of any plans or infrastructure necessary to facilitate the operation of the Decree. Neither was any consideration given to the cost of employing many of the features outlined in the Decree.[47]

It may also be that such undue haste was responsible for many of the apparent legal inconsistencies and typographical errors in some sections of the Decree.

There appears to be little confidence that the new law—on paper a significant shift in social thinking—will change anything on the ground, as there are no additional resources to implement it and life will continue to be 'business as usual'.[48] This is epitomised by the comments of one interview respondent that 'with the new decree it has become rather chaotic as the judiciary are still using the old [law] and the hospital kind of shifts between the two documents depending on what is convenient.'[49]

In the end, this may be the significance of the rider—*as far as practicable and subject to available resources*. Nonetheless, it does not bode well for mental health consumers and their ability to access justice under the law.

3. The Law Now

The *Mental Treatment Act* [Cap 113] in Fiji was repealed by the *Mental Health Decree 2010* after a formal review process spanning more than ten years.[50]

---

45 *Mental Health Decree 2010* (Fiji Islands) s 4(1), (2); s 6(1)(2).
46 Fiji Law Reform Commission, above n 23, 1.
47 Email questionnaire from AB, Fiji, to Helen Ménard, 22 March 2012.
48 Ibid.
49 Ibid.
50 A Draft Bill was prepared by the Fiji Law Reform Commission in 2007 and, in essence, is reflected in the Decree passed on 15 October 2010, which came into force on 1 July 2011.

The objectives of the Decree, which appear to be based around the *WHO Ten Principles* and the *MI Principles*, are broad ranging and ambitious for a country with the resources of Fiji. They are outlined in s 5 as follows:

- to provide for the care, treatment, management, rehabilitation and protection of people with mental illness and other mental disorders;
- to regulate mental health care, treatment and rehabilitation services in a manner that makes mental health care, treatment and rehabilitation services available to the population equitably, efficiently and in the best interest of mental health care users within the limits of the available resources;
- to co-ordinate access to mental health care, treatment and rehabilitation services by various categories of mental health care users;
- to integrate the provision of mental health care services into the general and wider human services environment in the cultural context of Fiji;
- to promote the rehabilitation of persons with mental disorders and their integration into the community at the earliest appropriate time;
- to facilitate the development of community mental health services including the establishment of respite and halfway homes, residential facilities and group homes;
- to clarify the rights and obligations of mental health care users and the obligations of mental health care providers;
- to regulate the manner in which the property of persons with mental disorders may be dealt with.[51]

Yet, despite a stated commitment to the *Convention on the Rights of Persons with Disabilities* (CRPD), these objectives still pivot around a medical rather than social model and remain heavily predicated on protective care and treatment in an involuntary setting. While there is a requirement for persons and bodies under the Decree to aim to 'eliminate discrimination against, and abuse, mistreatment and neglect of, persons with a mental disorder,'[52] this is no more than the anti-discrimination provisions that appear in all human rights treaties and does not equate to the fundamental ideology of the CRPD, which disallows the detention and treatment of people based on disability. While the Decree appears to have attempted to be compliant with rights based principles, the inclusion of compliance with the CRPD would seem to have been an afterthought, as there is no indication that the Decree even obliquely contemplates social inclusion as a foundational framework.

3.1. Admission Criteria

Section 2(1) of the 2010 Decree defines both the terms 'mental disorder' and 'mental illness' and includes mental illness within the definition of 'mental disorder' together with personality disorders, dementia, intellectual disability and substance abuse.

---

[51] *Mental Health Decree 2010* (Fiji Islands) s 5.

[52] Ibid s 6(1)(i).

Mental disorder is defined as:

> a disturbance or defect, to a substantially disabling degree, of perceptual interpretation, comprehension, reasoning, learning, judgment or memory, motivation or emotion, whether or not the disturbance or defect is caused by –
>
> (a) mental illness;
> (b) personality disorder;
> (c) dementia;
> (d) intellectual disability; or
> (e) substance abuse.

Mental illness is defined, in almost identical terms to the NSW provisions, as follows:

> a condition that seriously impairs (either temporarily or permanently) the mental functioning of a person and is characterised by the presence in the person of any of the following symptoms:
>
> (a) delusions;
> (b) hallucinations;
> (c) serious disorder of thought form;
> (d) a severe disturbance of mood;
> (e) severe motivational deficit; or
> (f) sustained or repeated irrational behaviour indicating the presence of the symptoms referred to above.

Section 3(1) contains the standard list of exclusions found in the *MI Principles*[53] which outline various behaviours and beliefs that do *not* come within the definition of mental disorder as follows:

(a) the person expresses or refuses or fails to express, or has expressed or has refused or failed to express a particular political opinion or belief;
(b) the person expresses or refuses or fails to express, or has expressed or has refused or failed to express a particular religious opinion or belief;
(c) the person expresses or refuses or fails to express, or has expressed or has refused or failed to express a particular philosophy or cultural belief;
(d) the person expresses or refuses or fails to express, or has expressed or has refused or failed to express a particular sexual preference or sexual orientation;
(e) the person engages in or refuses or fails to engage in, or has engaged in or has refused or failed to engage in a particular political activity;
(f) the person engages in or refuses or fails to engage in, or has engaged in or has refused or failed to engage in a particular religious activity;
(g) the person engages in, or has engaged in sexual promiscuity;
(h) the person engages in, or has engaged in immoral conduct;
(i) the person engages in, or has engaged in criminal or other illegal conduct;
(j) the person engages in, or has engaged in antisocial or delinquent behaviour;

---

53 Office of the High Commissioner for Human Rights, *Principles for the Protection of Persons with Mental Illness and the Improvement of Mental Health Care*, GA Res 46/119, (17 December 1991) [4.3]

(k) the person takes or has taken alcohol or any other drug, volatile substance or other substance capable of inducing intoxication or altered state of mind; or
(l) any other behaviour involving a personally made decision or modus vivendi not amounting to a mental disorder.

(2) Subsection (1 (k) does not prevent the serious temporary or permanent physiological, biochemical or psychological effects of volatile substance taking from being regarded as an indication that a person has a mental disorder.

'Mentally disturbed' is defined as a 'psychological or behavioural pattern that occurs in an individual and is thought to cause distress or disability that is not expected as part of normal development or culture' and may warrant temporary detention.[54]

The adoption of a wider definition of 'mental disorder' was seen to be justified by underlying principles centred on community based care rather than institutionalised based treatment, which usually dictates more stringent human rights protection.[55] But this is only a valid approach if community prevention and treatment programs exist and are readily accessible. Otherwise, the default position is that if accessible care is only available within established institutional settings, the wider legislative definition runs the risk that less attention may be paid to restricting those who are caught in the net. One respondent (a senior mental health professional), in agreeing with this reservation, argues:

> It will only work if appropriate community prevention and treatment programs exist and are readily accessible. While there has been an attempt to develop community MH resources & facilities by the current Minister for Health, the evidence also suggests there has been a minimal shift in the philosophy & theoretical stance taken toward reconceptualising mental health.
>
> Despite some lip-service given to a less 'traditional' [view] (a less clinically based view of mental health - by acknowledging the role of social stress and environmental stressors), a basic contradiction remains [with respect] to conceptualisation and implementation of 'treatment' strategies. The approach taken so far is to set aside 'stress wards' within a traditional hospital setting to 'treat' stress patients! While some form of counselling has been mentioned in the press, what this treatment involves in practice and how it is delivered is still unclear.[56]

The same respondent's concerns in relation to the adoption of a new hypothesis in mental health thinking are further expressed as follows:

> The initiatives taken so far seem to involve the creation of 'different' and/or 'new' facilities without really changing the underlying philosophy and clinical assumptions and with only minor changes to treatment strategies. I believe that without change in these areas, substantive change in mental health in Fiji is unlikely to occur.
>
> Last year my concern with what I saw as a very superficial attempt to re-conceptualise mental health and update treatment strategies was communicated directly

[54] Section 2(1).
[55] Fiji Law Reform Commission, above n 25, 2.
[56] Email questionnaire from XY, Fiji, to Helen Ménard, 19 July 2012.

by letter to the Minister, along with an offer to meet with the Minister to discuss this concern – however, nothing transpired.

Coincidentally, the Ministry engaged a 'mental health expert' from Malaysia who was attached to the Fiji School of Medicine. I attended a major presentation by this gentleman: however, the views expressed by him were still essentially clinical and psychiatric in orientation and scope - reminiscent of a view of mental health that dominated psychiatric thinking roughly between 1960-80.[57]

Another respondent suggests that, regardless of the shift in philosophy underpinning the new definition, little is likely to change as there has been no specific allocation of resources to support the new community care model or promote community awareness.[58]

The requirements for detention and treatment in a mental health care facility under an Inpatient Treatment Order (ITO) in Fiji require that a person (a) has a mental disorder (b) is unwilling or unable to receive care on a voluntary basis; (c) requires care, treatment or protection in his or her interests or that of another person; and (d) cannot be treated in a less restrictive manner and such treatment is available.[59] Notably, there is no requirement in relation to the legal capacity of a person or his or her ability to provide informed consent, which is a critical element when considering the application of the CRPD.[60]

The criteria for detention under a Community Treatment Order (CTO) largely reflect those of an ITO and the order may be made by an authorised health care professional after certification by a medical practitioner.[61] A CTO may be issued for a period not exceeding twelve months and varied or renewed one month before expiry for a similar period.[62] A CTO requires a person to present at a nominated health centre and receive treatment; to refrain from taking drugs and alcohol; and to comply with any other specified conditions determined to be in his or her best interests.[63] The Mental Health Review Board (MHRB) must review a CTO every six months[64] at which time it may confirm, revoke or vary the condition of the CTO.[65] A person who fails to comply with the terms of a CTO may be required to undergo further assessment; and treatment and care must not be withdrawn simply because of a person's non-compliance.[66] As at 2013 few if any CTOs had been issued under these provisions and there were no measures in place to monitor compliance.[67] A couple of years on, it is estimated about 20 CTOs have been issued but none has come before the MHRB for review.[68]

---

57 Ibid; the 'mental health expert' referred to is M. Parameshvara Deva whose comments in relation to the provision of mental health care services in Fiji are discussed in Chapter 13.

58 Email questionnaire from AB, Fiji, to Helen Ménard, 22 March 2012.

59 *Mental Health Decree 2010* (Fiji Islands) s 61.

60 *Convention on the Rights of Persons with Disabilites*, opened for signature 13 December 2006, 2515 UNTS 3 (entered into force 3 May 2008) [12.2].

61 *Mental Health Decree 2010* (Fiji Islands) s 57(1), (2).

62 Ibid s 58(1)–(3).

63 Ibid s 57(3)–(4).

64 Ibid s 60(1).

65 Ibid s 99(3)–(4).

66 Ibid s 59(1)–(3).

67 Email questionnaire from AB, Fiji, to Helen Ménard, 10 April 2012; Email from EF, Fiji, to Helen Ménard, 16 January 2013.

68 Email questionnaire from IJ, Fiji, to Helen Ménard, 18 December 2015.

3.2. The Rights to Appeal and Review

If, at any time, an inpatient is examined and no longer meets the criteria for involuntary detention, he or she must be discharged by either an authorised health care professional and the treatment team or the MHRB.[69]

The status of a person who has been assessed and detained under an ITO must be initially reviewed by the MHRB[70] within three months and thereafter every three months[71] and those under a CTO within six months and thereafter every six months.[72] Compared with other jurisdictions—including Tonga and Samoa where the *initial* ITO reviews are to be conducted within seven days and six weeks respectively—three months is a long time for an initial review of an ITO in Fiji. It is argued that this is not consistent with the recommendation in the *MI Principles* that an *initial* review takes place within a 'short period'[73] and 'as soon as possible' after the decision to admit a person.[74] The recommendation in the *WHO Ten Principles* that a 'reasonable' period of time for a periodic review should not exceed six months, does not refer to an *initial* review and does not distinguish between ITOs and CTOs.[75] While the CRPD does not address the issue of timing of reviews, the implication is that any restrictions on a person should apply for the shortest time possible and be subject to regular review.[76]

In Fiji this means that within the first three months of admission, the onus is on the consumer to appeal against detention and activate the review process. While seven days might be considered too short a period—during which few severe psychotic symptoms would have subsided—three months does not reflect the practice of other jurisdictions and does not afford mental health consumers access to justice as advocated by the Decree. One may speculate that the initial review period may have been set to accommodate the average length of stay of inpatients in St Giles hospital at the time—being 110 days in 2010 and 102 days in 2009.[77] This is supported by the observations of respondents that procedures have been designed more to minimise administrative involvement and to control the process than to provide a genuine avenue for the exercise of consumer rights.[78]

As there is no central register within the Ministry of Health for people receiving treatment for mental illness, it is not possible to obtain accurate data in relation to the number of ITOs or CTOs in force at any one time. It is estimated by one respondent that 3-4 people a week are placed on ITOs and that the CTOs may now be being used more frequently.[79] It is

---

69 *Mental Health Decree 2010* (Fiji Islands) ss 66, 99.

70 Note: this section actually refers to review by the Tribunal with the powers as set out in s 100. There is no other use of the term 'tribunal' in the Decree; the term is not defined in s 2 and s 100 refers to powers of the Board. The Draft Mental Health Bill 2007 referred to a Tribunal as the statutory review mechanism and logically it must be assumed that the use of the term Tribunal in s 71 is a typographical error.

71 *Mental Health Decree 2010* (Fiji Islands) s 71.

72 Ibid s 60.

73 Office of the High Commissioner for Human Rights, *Principles for the Protection of Persons with Mental Illness and the Improvement of Mental Health Care*, GA Res 46/119, (17 December 1991) [16.2].

74 Ibid [17.2].

75 World Health Organisation, 'Mental Health Care Law: Ten Basic Principles' (1996).

76 *Convention on the Rights of Persons with Disabilites*, opened for signature 13 December 2006, 2515 UNTS 3 (entered into force 3 May 2008) [12.4].

77 Ministry of Health Fiji Islands, 'Ministry of Health, Annual Report 2010' (2010) 17.

78 Email questionnaire from XY, Fiji, to Helen Ménard, 19 July 2012.

79 Email questionnaire from AB, Fiji, to Helen Ménard, 10 April 2012; Email questionnaire from IJ, Fiji, to Helen Ménard, 18 December 2015.

also clear that, despite the fact that the provisions of the Decree were to have immediate effect from 1 July 2011, implementation has been slow to realise. This would appear to be consistent with one respondent's observations that the process in Fiji is wanting and

> one of the weaknesses is the lack of driving force within government's mental health team to push things forward. While we say no resources are available that is not entirely true as there are other avenues for funding available but someone has to take the initiative to progress it which is not so here in Fiji.[80]

As a general rule, an involuntary patient's care and treatment is controlled by the authorised psychiatrist or medical officer in charge and is rarely subject to monitoring. While there are mechanisms in some jurisdictions for a patient to appeal against involuntary detention to a tribunal, board or a magistrate, the appeal hearing is frequently designed to assess only the need for continued detention in accordance with specified criteria—*not* to review the appropriateness of treatment. There are some exceptions.

It is unclear, in the absence of a general power to review treatment—aside from electro convulsive therapy (ECT) and special medical treatment—whether the powers of the MHRB under s 99(3)(a) of the *Mental Health Decree 2010,* to review 'conditions' of a CTO made with regard to the criteria under s 57, are intended to extend to treatment. As one of the conditions of a CTO under s 57(3)(a) requires a person to 'receive treatment … determined by an authorised health care professional,' in reviewing the application of such a condition, the MHRB could review the appropriateness of treatment. One respondent is of the opinion that it was the intention of the legislative drafters to give the MHRB the power to review treatment in these circumstances.[81] However, to date no hearings in relation to CTOs have occurred.[82]

Section 99(5)(a) is a similarly worded provision to s 99(3)(a) but in relation to ITOs. However, it refers to the review of criteria under s 61—of which there are none. If it were accepted that the reference to s 61 is a drafting error and should refer to s 62, which requires a person under an ITO to receive treatment, s 99(5)(a) would have the same effect as that under s 99(3)(a) in relation to review of treatment.

Furthermore, before the administration of ECT to an involuntary patient, the MHRB must be satisfied that 'ECT is a reasonable and proper treatment and is necessary or desirable for the safety or welfare of the patient.'[83]

A person subject to an ITO or a CTO or the person's primary carer or any person with a bona fide interest may apply to the MHRB for review of the order, regardless of the MHRB's obligation to conduct a periodic review.[84]

In considering an application for review, the MHRB must take into account the number of applications already made and hearings already conducted during the currency of the order and may limit the hearings to one per order, unless exceptional circumstances exist.[85] There are no indications in the Decree as to what might be considered 'exceptional circumstances'.

---

80 Email questionnaire from AB, Fiji, to Helen Ménard, 22 March 2012.
81 Ibid.
82 Email questionnaire from IJ, Fiji, to Helen Ménard, 18 December 2015.
83 *Mental Health Decree 2010* (Fiji Islands) s 75(8).
84 Ibid s 98(1).
85 Ibid s 98(3), (5)–(6).

3.3. The Review Mechanism

Section 95 of the Decree establishes a Mental Health Review Board (MHRB) whose functions include:

- the hearing of applications for review of ITOs and CTOs;
- the periodic review of persons under voluntary status (every three months), involuntary status (every three months) and CTOs (every six months);
- the review of ECT consent and administration;
- the authorisation of surgical operations and special medical treatment;
- orders relating to the transfer and release of prisoners;
- review orders sought by mental health visitors and
- review of decisions to withhold access to personal records.[86]

The membership of the MHRB must include at least one man and one woman[87] and must be comprised of five persons—a judge of the High Court as President; one registered medical practitioner; two persons with psychiatric practice or nursing experience; and one person to represent the interests of mental health users and their families.[88] The reason for such a weightily constituted Board is not apparent from any of the founding documents and is a curious model not replicated in any other jurisdiction. None of the respondents was able to provide any rationale for the chosen model, but one speculated it might be 'a way of keeping greater control over the review process while giving the appearance of a genuine review.'[89] Although this view depicts a degree of cynicism, when read in the context of the prevailing political situation in Fiji at the time, it may also be a plausible assessment.

The first members of the MHRB were appointed in 2011 and included a High Court judge; a psychiatrist; two mental health nurses and the President of the community support group, Psychiatric Survivors Association. The inaugural meeting of the MHRB was held at the Ministry of Health offices in the capital, Suva, on 19 March 2012.[90] One respondent, then a member of the Board, commented that

> while all five members were present at the hearing no cases were heard. Literally only the names of persons who were for review of their Presidential Order were forwarded to the Board without any other information, so [the Board] could not deliberate on the cases.[91]

From March 2012 to January 2013 the MHRB only sat on a few occasions—sometimes by email only—and, in all but one instance, to review cases involving Presidential Orders. In two of these cases the MHRB discharged consumers, who were under Presidential Orders, into the community on CTOs. Initially, the Minister for Health deferred their discharge

86 Ibid ss 97, 40(4).
87 Ibid s 95(4).
88 Ibid s 95(2).
89 Email questionnaire from XY, Fiji, to Helen Ménard, 19 July 2012; Email from EF, Fiji, to Helen Ménard, 16 January 2013.
90 Email questionnaire from AB, Fiji, to Helen Ménard, 22 March 2012.
91 Email from EF, Fiji, to Helen Ménard, 16 January 2013.

pending advice from the Attorney-General's Office regarding the validity of the procedure. The MHRB then sought clarification from the Attorney General in relation to the role of the Minister in such circumstances and his or her power to overrule the MHRB.[92] Ultimately, and after a lengthy delay, the finality of the MHRB's decision was upheld and the CTOs were put into effect. In the interim, the MHRB President's contract expired, a new appointment was delayed and the MHRB did not resume hearings until 2014.[93]

Since then it would seem that systemic inertia has persisted. For a significant period of time the MHRB was unable to perform its functions due to delays appointing the health administrators responsible for activating the review process.[94] Health administrators do not appear to understand their functions under the Decree and little has been done to encourage them otherwise. The details of consumers due for review are not forwarded to the MRHB systematically and, frequently, matters that are scheduled for a hearing involve consumers who have already been discharged.[95] Poor organisation and communication between the Ministry, the MHRB and the treatment centres means that the MRHB is never fully constituted, is only able to meet irregularly, and consumers are unaware of scheduled hearing dates and unable to attend hearings.[96]

Thus far, there have been no periodic reviews of CTOs, only one appeal by a consumer against detention under an ITO, three reviews of Presidential Orders and a handful of periodic reviews of ITOs.[97] The one consumer appeal involved an inpatient who appealed against her detention after she was refused discharge from an ITO. The MHRB upheld the decision of the treating team but before her next review date the consumer had been discharged.[98] The small number of ITOs that have made it to the three month periodic review have all been extended by the MHRB—together with their treatment plans—for 'the further treatment and the safety of the individual'.[99]

Finally, according to one respondent, the function of the MHRB is a national one and involves a fulltime workload—a requirement none of the current Board members is able to meet as they are already engaged in fulltime professional positions. To compound the problem, none of the members has yet been paid any sitting fees in accordance with their statutory entitlement.[100]

It appears that no consideration has been given to how consumers will be transported to the hearings which are held away from the main psychiatric treatment centre at St Giles—and what arrangements will be made for consumers at regional centres. When posed with the question, one respondent stated:

92 Ibid
93 The Fijian Government, 'Heath Committed Towards Mental Health,' 7 November 2014 <http://www.fiji.gov.fj/Media-Center/Press-Releases/HEATH-COMMITTED-TOWARDS-MENTAL-HEALTH.aspx (accessed 21 December 2015)>
94 Email from EF, Fiji, to Helen Ménard, 16 January 2013.
95 Email questionnaire from IJ, Fiji, to Helen Ménard, 18 December 2015.
96 Ibid
97 Ibid
98 Ibid.
99 Email questionnaire from IJ, Fiji, to Helen Ménard, 18 December 2015.
100 Ibid

> This did not happen as no names were forwarded to the Board. But it would be the staff of the units who would accompany them from the facilities. It has not been discussed how those in the other cities (Lautoka and Labasa) would be managed or if video teleconferencing would be used for those.[101]

To date, the MHRB continues to convene at the Ministry's head office away from the main treatment centre and does not utilise video conferencing, again precluding consumers from being present at their reviews.[102]

The MHRB in carrying out its functions may confirm, reverse or vary orders subject to review[103] by majority decision[104] and, while not bound by the rules of evidence, it must act according to equity and good conscience and the rules of natural justice and may summon witnesses.[105] An applicant appearing before the MHRB may be legally represented,[106] and must be given access to his or her personal records[107] but evidence presented at a hearing cannot be used in any civil or criminal proceedings.[108] A member of the MHRB who has treated a person must not take part in the review of an assessment or order.[109]

In view of the fact that the MHRB has yet to become fully functional, there are no statistics to indicate patterns of operation including the extent of attendance by consumers or representation before the Board or requests for access to medical records. In any event, it seems that consumers rarely attend hearings and only one hearing, concerning the review of a Presidential Order, involved legal representation.[110]

In spite of a commitment under the Decree to 'respect of the rule of law and human rights in regard to mental health issues,'[111] there is no provision under the Decree for any application for review of involuntary detention to be heard within a given time frame; no requirement that records of hearings be kept or that written or oral reasons for decisions be given; nor is there any right to appeal a decision of the MHRB to a higher authority. These omissions are difficult to explain in the face of the requirement that the MHRB is bound by the rules of natural justice as outlined in s 100(6)(b).

If the reference in the Decree to 'the rule of law' is taken from the *WHO Ten Principles*, the omissions are even more confounding.[112] Principle 10 requires that 'the law applicable is the law in force at the time in question' and should be 'public, accessible and … understandable' and include the dissemination of relevant legal instruments.[113] The 'law in force' in Fiji still preserves the judicial system and the court hierarchy.[114] While none of the respondents was able to comment definitively on these anomalies, one suggested that:

---

[101] Email questionnaire from AB, Fiji, to Helen Ménard, 10 April 2012; Ibid
[102] Ibid
[103] *Mental Health Decree 2010* (Fiji Islands) s 99.
[104] Ibid s 100(3).
[105] Ibid s 100(6).
[106] Ibid s 100(6)(d).
[107] Ibid s 40(1).
[108] Ibid s 100(8).
[109] Ibid s 100(1).
[110] Email questionnaire from IJ, Fiji, to Helen Ménard, 18 December 2015.
[111] Ibid s 4(2)(j).
[112] World Health Organisation, above n 75, [10].
[113] Ibid.
[114] *Administration of Justice Decree 2009* (Fiji Islands).

> Although comment was solicited regarding the proposed legislation as a whole, and I seem to recall some reservation by a few about a lack of a review process and accountability relating to involuntary detention, I am not sure this issue was identified as clearly as indicated by your analysis.[115]

Despite reference to the UN and WHO principles on review and oversight mechanisms, no reference was made to any of these issues in the FLRC's discussion paper or in the draft legislation,[116] the reasons for which are not clear. These omissions mean that the Decree does not, in fact, comply with the provisions of the CRPD requiring equal access to justice for persons with disabilities.[117]

The absence of the right to appeal might partly be explained by the fact that, under s 95(2)(a), the President of the MHRB must be a qualified High Court judge.[118] Nonetheless, the quorum of the MHRB requires only four of the five nominated members and there is no requirement that the quorum must include the President. The President, when authorised, may sit alone[119] although there is no indication in the Decree when this might occur. It might be implied from ss 96(5) and 100(3) that the President must always sit on the Board, but the situation remains ambiguous. When filling a vacancy on the MHRB, s 96(5) permits the Board to proceed if there were a quorum 'subject to the temporary appointment of a President qualified'. Section 100(3) allows for majority decisions of the MHRB but, when only four members are able to vote, the President has an additional and casting vote.

Even so, a judge sitting in the capacity as President of the tribunal only assumes powers vested in that role, as confirmed by the Queensland Court of Appeal in *AG v B*:

> but although Chesterman J is a judge of the Supreme Court, he was not on this occasion sitting as the Court but as the Mental Health Tribunal, whose jurisdiction is confined to hearing and determining all proceedings 'duly instituted before it under the Act.'[120]

In the end, the answer may lie in the general right of appeal by way of judicial review but this can be a complex process and presumes ready access to good and, more likely than not, expensive legal representation. Regardless, the lack of a right to appeal is not consistent with the international principles that purportedly underpin the Decree and does not guarantee access to justice for mental health consumers.

Furthermore, these procedural factors are critical elements of natural justice and there is no justification in the FLRC's background to support such omissions. Even the WHO Resource Book, upon which the FLRC relied heavily, states 'as a basic human right, even in countries with fewer resources, … [that] appeals must be heard within a reasonable time'[121] and 'appeals against decisions of the review body must be allowed to go directly to the

115 Email questionnaire from XY, Fiji, to Helen Ménard, 19 July 2012.
116 Fiji Law Reform Commission, above n 23, 3.
117 *Convention on the Rights of Persons with Disabilites*, opened for signature 13 December 2006, 2515 UNTS 3 (entered into force 3 May 2008) [13.1].
118 The High Court in Fiji is a superior court with unlimited original jurisdiction and the power to hear appeals from the Magistrates' Courts.
119 *Mental Health Decree 2010* (Fiji Islands) s 100(2).
120 *AG v B* [2001] QCA 169 (McPherson JA).
121 Freeman, above n 39, 68.

courts'.[122] This militates against the use of the progressive realisation rider—'as far as practicable and subject to available resources'—to justify the exclusion of fundamental rights of review and appeal.

While the FLRC conceded that there was 'widespread interest in establishing an independent review mechanism in Fiji', it also noted there was concern that 'existing resources, infrastructure opportunities and the expertise and skill base in psychiatry' might impact on the ideal.[123] In any event, given that tribunal style forums in other jurisdictions usually include only three members, the need for a five member board in Fiji seems unclear and, if nothing else, unnecessarily costly. Respondents were unable to explain the choice of this particular model.

In addition to the MHRB, Fiji has retained a general oversight body—the Board of Mental Health Visitors (BMHV)—whose functions include conducting inspections of the physical facilities; reviewing unusual incident reports and deaths; responding to complaints from patients or family members; and ensuring the rights of patients are enforced.[124] The BMHV also has the power to refer a matter to the MHRB if it considers a person has been wrongfully detained or subjected to an inappropriate treatment order.[125]

3.4. Specific Rights

Despite its precarious political situation, Fiji is the only country in the region to have attempted openly to incorporate international human rights norms into its mental health agenda. In fact, it has gone to great lengths to integrate a comprehensive rights based platform throughout the Decree—albeit with some unexplained omissions.

Some of the stated rights include:

- provision of information to patients in relation to admission, treatment and legal rights (ss 35, 44)
- provision of information to primary carers in relation to admission, treatment and legal rights (ss 41-42, 46)
- use of interpreters (s 38)
- access to legal representation (s 100(5)(d))
- right to confidentiality (s 39)
- provision of information regarding medication and different forms of treatment (ss 43-45)
- right to make advance directives (s 55)
- prohibition of certain types of treatment and
- over use of medication (ss 52-53)

---

122 Ibid 68–9.
123 Fiji Law Reform Commission, above n 25, 2.
124 *Mental Health Decree 2010* (Fiji Islands) s 102(2).
125 Ibid s 102(4).

While it is not within the ambit of this study to explore in depth the legal capacity of mental health consumers, the provisions in relation to advance directives merit comment as they are unique in the region. Even though capacity to consent is not one of the criteria for involuntary detention in Fiji, legal capacity and a person's right to accept or refuse treatment is a central feature of the CRPD and has the potential to impact on a person's ability to access justice. Section 55(1) provides that every person has the right to make an advance directive, irrespective of whether he or she is receiving treatment, specifying:

> (a) the ways the person wishes to be cared for and treated for a mental disorder;
> (b) the ways the person wishes not to be so cared for and treated,
>
> in the event of his or her becoming affected by a mental disorder and his or her ability to make decisions about the matters referred to in paragraphs (a) and (b) being, because of that, significantly impaired.
>
> (2) An advance directive may be made by a person whether or not he or she has suffered from a mental disorder in the past and whether or not he or she has received treatment for a mental disorder in the past.

One distinguishing feature of this provision is that the directive is not binding on the health care professional.[126] Although there is provision for the Minister to make regulations regarding the circumstances and extent to which health care professionals may disregard a directive, no such regulations have yet been formulated.[127] Based on similar models in Scotland, it may be that a refusal to accept treatment that puts another person's safety at risk might be what was contemplated.[128] In any event, the ability to disregard the directive would appear to undermine the effect of the section. Unlike Fiji, in some jurisdictions any decision to override an advance directive can be appealed to a review body.[129]

On the assumption that the person has capacity to execute the directive as a legal document, and applying the 'equality' principle of CRPD, a mental health directive should be no different to a directive that stipulates any other form of medical treatment when the person is incapable of giving instructions or informed consent. In the case of *Malette v Shulman,* the Supreme Court of Canada held that the medical practitioner—in ignoring the patient's clear directive *not* to be treated with blood products and treating her under emergency conditions with a blood transfusion, thereby saving her life—violated her right to autonomy and was liable for battery.[130] This case indicates that the failure of a health care professional to follow an advance directive may otherwise give rise to liability in some circumstances.

There is no requirement under the Decree for a person to have legal capacity to execute the directive—although it may be implied from the wording of s 55(1), as outlined above. The FLRC's discussion paper defined an advance treatment statement as 'a written statement drawn up and signed when a person is mentally well' and also as a 'form of informed consent which could help meet the requirements of human rights conventions'.[131] This might indicate

---

126 Ibid s 55(3).

127 Ibid s 56(3).

128 J M Atkinson et al. 'Issues in the Development of Advance Directives in Mental Health Care' (2003) 12(5) *Journal of Mental Health* 463.

129 For example Scotland; see Fiji Law Reform Commission, 'Review of the Fiji Mental Treatment Act, Issue Paper No. 5 – Advanced Treatment Statement' (2006) 2.

130 *Malette v Shulman* (1990) 67 DLR (4th) 321.

131 Fiji Law Reform Commission, above n 129, 1.

an intention to comply with the terms of the CRPD, but the intention has been somewhat lost in translation.

One of the customary arguments against the automatic enforcement of general heath advance directives is that, when there is a significant delay between the execution and application of the directive, there is a prospect that the person's views on treatment may have changed. This is based on the premise that most directives relate to withholding or withdrawing treatment in 'end of life' situations.[132] Most often, when a directive is formulated the person is making a decision based on a hypothetical scenario but, when faced with reality, the same person may view the treatment options quite differently.

This argument is less compelling in the case of mental illness. Particularly in relation to chronic illness and the recurring need for treatment—the person is not dealing with a hypothetical situation because the circumstances have been well and truly tested on previous occasions. Presumably, this is what is envisaged by s 55(2) of the Decree, which deals with the ability to make a directive regardless of past illness and treatment. Atkinson also argues that for mental health law to be consistent with general medicine, where a competent person may refuse lifesaving treatment for reasons seemingly irrational to others, a similarly competent person must be allowed to refuse psychiatric treatment (for example ECT) for equally irrational reasons.[133] This approach is essential to comply with the CRPD. Aside from the issue of public safety, the rationale for the health care professional's ability to ignore the directive is harder to explain. The argument is even less persuasive when the Decree requires that any advance directive must be made in writing to the person's current treating practitioner and must be reviewed and amended after each admission to a mental health facility.[134]

The other issue for consideration is whether the reference to being 'cared for' in s 55(1) in addition to being 'treated' could be construed to mean actual detention. This raises the question previously discussed by Dawson that substituted decision making should apply to both detention and treatment and that there should not be separate criteria for detention for mental illness compared to any other illness.[135]

Whether these provisions will have any practical force is a question for the future and there is no evidence yet to suggest that any person has invoked this right.[136] If international experience is any yardstick, the forecast is not encouraging.

Weller asserts that

> [w]here psychiatric advance directives have been introduced as an adjunct to a rights based model their impact has been disappointing… [f]rom a rights perspective, psychiatric advance directives are supposed to give substance to the autonomy rights of persons with mental illness by enabling them to retain control over their medical treatment during periods of anticipated incapacity. However, they intrude uncomfortably upon a legal framework that allocates the authority for medical decision making to the clinician… [in] the legal framework of rights based legalism, where the obligation falls

132 I Kerridge, M Lowe and C Stewart, *Ethics and Law for the Health Professionals* (3rd ed, 2009) 269.

133 Atkinson et al. above n 128, 468.

134 *Mental Health Decree 2010* (Fiji Islands) s 56(1).

135 J Dawson and G Szmukler, 'Why Distinguish "Mental" and "Physical" Illness in Involuntary Treatment?' in M Freeman and O Goodenough (eds), *Law, Mind and Brain* (Ashgate, 2009) 173.

136 Email questionnaire from AB, Fiji, to Helen Ménard, 22 March 2012.

on the clinicians to act in the person's 'best interests,' the legal ramifications of following a psychiatric advance directive are far from clear.[137]

Young people[138] are given special consideration under the Fijian Decree in relation to voluntary admission. This includes:

- prohibition against the admission of a child under the age of 12;[139]
- nomination of a primary carer not being a parent;[140]
- informed consent to treatment;[141] and
- accommodation rights in an inpatient facility.[142]

Sections 5, 6 and 7 outline, in some detail, the objectives of the Decree; responsibilities of various persons and bodies in dealing with mental health issues; and anti-discrimination polices—with particular reference to workplace discrimination—all of which appear to be consistent with the cited principles and UN conventions. Section 34 prescribes principles for care and treatment of people with a mental disorder.

These sections, excepting those relating to workplace discrimination, are subject to the proviso being '*as far as practicable and subject to available resources.*'[143] With the limited availability of resources being a significant factor in the region, the uncertain breadth of the rider, and the current policies of the government in Fiji, the impact of the 'practicability' qualification remains to be seen.[144] As discussed in Chapter 3, the doctrine of progressive realisation does not apply to fundamental rights and freedoms and not in relation to the CRPD in Fiji, as Fiji is only a signatory and not a State Party.[145] While Weller argues that the enforcement of human rights on the basis of non-discrimination under the CRPD carries an obligation of immediate application and is not subject to resource availability,[146] this does not necessarily recognise the political and economic reality of many countries.

It remains to ask why a country such as Fiji would include a commitment to the principles of the CRPD and other like instruments, in the full knowledge that realising them would be highly improbable. One might speculate that the answer has more to do with ensuring the flow of foreign aid by being seen to 'play the game' rather than any genuine

---

137 P Weller, 'Lost in Translation: Human Rights and Mental Health Law' in B McSherry and P Weller (eds), *Rethinking Rights Based Mental Health Laws* (Hart Publishing, 2010) 51, 63.

138 Those aged 14–18; *Mental Health Decree 2010* (Fiji Islands) s 2.

139 Ibid s 17(5).

140 Ibid s 42.

141 Ibid ss 83–84.

142 Ibid s 83(3)–(7).

143 Ibid ss 5–7, 34.

144 Interestingly, no specific reference is made to the *UNHCR Principles for the protection of persons with mental illness and the improvement of mental health care* (although this document was cited in the Law Reform Commission's Issue Paper No. 1 which preceded the legislation). The legislation also refers to persons with a mental illness having access to rights recognised under other conventions including *International Covenant on Economic, Social and Cultural Rights, International Covenant on Civil and Political Rights* and *Body of Principles for the Protection of All Persons under Any Form of Detention or Imprisonment.* The *UNHCR Principles* are, of course, quite distinct from the *WHO principles*.

145 See Table 12.1, Chapter 12.

146 P Weller, 'Supported Decision Making and the Achievement of Non Discrimination: The Promise and Paradox of the Disabilities Convention' (2008) 26(2) *Law in Context Special Issue: International Trends in Mental Health Laws* 85, 94.

intention to fulfil the obligations under the Convention—hence the rider. In answering the question, one respondent poses that:

> It depends on how cynical one might be. However, in the Fiji and Pacific context, the notion of 'window dressing' does come to mind, especially since this does occur [with respect] to other matters. It is difficult not to draw the conclusion that the rider permits inclusion of positive declarative statements of principle without real or genuine obligation/commitment.[147]

4. CHALLENGES FOR THE FUTURE

The future holds many challenges for Fiji, not least of which is maintaining a stable democratic platform of government. According to a recent situational analysis of health services in Fiji, 'recent political, economic and social developments have adversely affected Fiji's stability and prosperity. Military coups in 1987, 2000 and 2006 have polarised Fijian society, isolated the country internationally and hastened the migration of skilled workers.'[148] These political tensions have also 'slowed economic growth resulting in an estimated 35 percent of the population below the poverty line and a high proportion of the employed earning below the taxation threshold.'[149] This is particularly significant as the health sector is almost entirely funded through taxation revenue and low levels of tax collection have severely limited the ability to achieve targets for improved health care.[150]

The emigration of health workers to developed countries is seen as a critical issue that will require 'innovation in terms of career structures, other incentives for health professionals and greater investment in training.'[151] From 1999-2001 the number of trained nurse resignations from the public health sector—for reasons of retirement, migration or private employment—exceeded the number of graduates. In 2008 there were 84 graduates and 78 resignations, which induced the government to increase the number of graduate entrants to 200 per annum for three years in an attempt to meet the demand for services.[152]

If political, social and economic stability is restored, then the country's resolve to implement its stated mental health objectives might be properly tested. At this point in time, the legislative framework exists to facilitate the move to a community based care and a rights based model, but there is little evidence of any practical transition to a new mental health paradigm.

As one respondent observes:

> legislation alone is not sufficient – neither is legal training … my sense of it is the need for a broader educative process designed to inform and explain why various principles and positions might/should be valued over others.

---

147 Email questionnaire from XY, Fiji, to Helen Ménard, 19 July 2012.

148 College of Medicine and Nursing and Health Sciences, 'Situational Analysis of Specialised Clinical Services in the Republic of Fiji 2010-12, Strengthening Specialised Clinical Services Program' (2012) [4.1.2].

149 Roberts G et al. 'The Fiji Islands Health System Review' (World Health Organisation & Asia Pacific Observatory on Health Systems and Policies, 2011) 10.

150 Ibid.

151 Ibid 9.

152 Ibid 76.

> In my experience, without appropriate understanding, valuing plus informed commitment, legislative changes tend to be implemented superficially and 'mechanically' especially by health practitioners and the legal system: a situation that is prone to generate bizarre applications: i.e., a tendency to 'go through the motions' without really understanding why something is supposed to be carried out. While this might 'work' where fairly routine situations are involved, it falls apart when a situation or case requires problem solving.[153]

One of the few initiatives that appears to have been implemented under the Decree is the establishment of three 'stress management' wards in the main regional general hospitals. According to Deva this is intended to reflect the reportedly increasing numbers of people suffering from emotional stress disorders associated with the physical sequelae of lifestyle diseases and who are not recognised as part of the mentally ill population because they have never been admitted to a psychiatric facility.[154] At least one respondent, however, sees this development as merely 'lip-service given to a less "traditional" view of mental health'.[155] Nonetheless, the Ministry of Health has attributed the significant reduction in the bed occupancy rate at St Giles in 2013, in part, to the existence of these wards.[156]

For the present, it seems as though the 'available resources' rider will continue to provide an escape valve for the administration against any criticism for failure to meet its objectives under the Decree. One respondent maintains that 'whatever changes are occurring, they are very much constrained by limited resources – evidence of a more profound change (apart from indicators of some superficial change), suggests the "subject to...." rider is being applied.'[157]

The progress of implementation to date under the new Decree in Fiji has been less than visible. Perhaps the answer for Fiji will come from experiences of countries such as Chile which embarked on a comprehensive reform package of mental health policies in 1993. On returning to democracy after 17 years of military dictatorship, the population was very sensitive about social issues and human rights violations although not specifically aware of human rights of people with mental disorders.[158]

---

153 Email questionnaire from XY, Fiji, to Helen Ménard, 19 July 2012.

154 MP Deva, 'Matters of the Mind,' *The Fiji Times ONLINE* (Online), 28 August 2012 <www.fijitimes.com/story.aspx?id=210296 (accessed 4 October 2012)>.

155 Email questionnaire from XY, Fiji, to Helen Ménard, 19 July 2012

156 Ministry of Health Fiji, 'Ministry of Health Annual Report 2013' (2014) <http://www.health.gov.fj/PDFs/Annual%20Report/Annual%20Report%202013.pdf (accessed 7 September 2015)> 17.

157 Email questionnaire from XY, Fiji, to Helen Ménard, 19 July 2012.

158 Freeman, above n 39, 101.

Chapter 8

VANUATU

This chapter on Vanuatu is the last in the comparative series examining the history of mental health legislation in the Pacific. Unlike the previous three countries, Vanuatu's mental health law—unchanged for almost 50 years—is still a long way from reform. There are only two recently trained mental health professionals in the country and no inpatient or supported community mental health services. Vanuatu struggles to achieve even basic levels of general health care and mental health care is far from a priority on any political agenda.

1. THE LAW AS IT IS

Prior to gaining its independence as a sovereign democratic republic in 1980, Vanuatu was jointly governed from the 1900s by the English and French as the British and French condominium of New Hebrides. The legislative position in relation to introduced law in Vanuatu is complex. As outlined in Chapter 4, theoretically the provisions of the *Mental Health Act 1959* (UK) could still apply in Vanuatu.

As a general proposition, s 15 of the *Western Pacific (Courts) Order 1961* (UK) provided a framework for the adoption and application of English law in Pacific dependencies by 'statutes of general application in force in England … so far only as the circumstances of any particular territory and its inhabitants ... permit and subject to such qualifications as local circumstances render necessary.'[1] The phrase 'statutes of general application' was not defined in the legislation nor did the Order provide for these statutes to be in force unconditionally. There was very little judicial discussion of this issue until 1989 when the matter was brought before the High Court of Tuvalu which, in an advisory opinion of the Chief Justice, found that imperial enactments received under s 15 of the Order would only become part of the law of Tuvalu if they were specifically adopted as law by the parliament or the High Court of Tuvalu.[2] It was not until 2012 that this decision was overturned, when a differently constituted High Court did not consider itself bound by an advisory opinion and found that all laws in existence by virtue of s 15 of the Order were already part of the laws of Tuvalu; the

---

1 *Western Pacific (Courts) Order 1961* (UK).

2 *In the Matter of the Constitution and the Laws of Tuvalu Act 1987*, No.4 /1989 (unreported, High Court of Tuvalu, Donne CJ).

provisions of s 15 merely allowed them to be modified to suit local conditions.[3] This later decision is more consistent with the approach taken by the courts in Vanuatu.

It had always been uncertain to what extent local legislation replaced 'applied' or 'adopted' legislation—in particular statutes of general application in force in England at a specified date. However, in the case of Vanuatu, the position was clarified by the Court of Appeal in its decision in *Joli v Joli*.[4] The Court held that applied or adopted English legislation served to 'fill the gaps' in the law, provided such legislation met the requirements of s 95 of the Constitution of Vanuatu.[5] The Court of Appeal held as follows:

> The central issue ... is whether the passing of Cap 192 rendered all of the provisions of the 1973 English Act no longer applicable in Vanuatu or ... only rendered inapplicable those provisions that dealt specifically with the aspects of matrimonial law covered by Cap 192 ... In our opinion Cap 192 does not operate as a comprehensive code ... we consider the 1973 English Act has a residual operation ... the 1973 English Act, save in so far as its application has been overtaken by the provision of Cap 192, is law which applies in Vanuatu in accordance with the provisions of Article 95(2) and will continue to do so until Parliament otherwise provides.[6]

In relation to mental health law in Vanuatu this means that, subject to provisions of the Constitution of Vanuatu and any ruling of the courts, the *Mental Health Act 1959* (UK) could operate in Vanuatu to the extent there are gaps in the local legislation. However, as far as the records reveal, and at least since independence in 1980, the English provisions have never been invoked[7] and will not be discussed further.

The only local mental health legislation in Vanuatu is the *Mental Hospital Act* [Cap 38] enacted by way of joint regulation in 1965.[8] It has not been amended since that time and no rules or regulations have been made pursuant to the statute. Nor is there any delegated power under the Act for the Minister to make subsidiary legislation. The purpose of the Act is stated as being to 'provide for the reception and detention of persons of unsound mind in the mental hospital at Port Vila.' As there does not appear to have been a designated mental hospital or any inpatient facility for the mentally ill in Vanuatu, at least for the 35 years since independence,[9] the Act has effectively been non-operational. In fact, in practice, it seems that

---

3 *Iosefa v Tuvalu Red Cross* [2012] TVHC 9.

4 *Joli v Joli* [2003] VUCA 27.

5 Namely, that it has not been otherwise provided for by parliament; has not been revoked; is not incompatible with independence and wherever possible takes into account custom.

6 *Joli v Joli* [2003] VUCA 27. Note that this judgment is in contrast to the decision in *In the Matter of the Constitution and the Laws of Tuvalu Act 1987* where the High Court of Tuvalu held that statutes of general application in force in England were not part of Tuvalu unless they had been held by the High Court to apply to that country or unless they had been adopted by the Parliament of Tuvalu.

7 Email questionnaire from John Obed Alilee, Supreme Court Registrar, Vanuatu, to Helen Ménard, 15 July 2013.

8 Prior to independence in 1980, Vanuatu (formerly the New Hebrides) was governed as a joint condominium between Britain and France pursuant to Article 8 of the *1914 Protocol relating to the New Hebrides between Britain and France*. The *New Hebrides Orders in Council* (1922-1970) gave effect to Protocol and gave powers to High Commissioner to make Joint Regulations or Queens Regulations. Laws were a combination of Joint Regulations made by the High Commissioner (UK) and High Commissioner (France) and Queens Regulations made by the High Commissioner (UK) or the High Commissioner (France). All such regulations were given the force of law at independence by virtue of s 95 of the Constitution.

9 Email questionnaire from John Obed Alilee, Supreme Court Registrar, Vanuatu, to Helen Ménard, 15 July 2013.

cases involving persons with mental illness rarely come before the courts in Vanuatu and then only in the context of a criminal offence.[10]

There are no specific provisions for community-based mental health care in Vanuatu but a person may be discharged into 'domiciliary custody' with the consent of two medical practitioners, provided that he or she is not deemed to be dangerous to him or herself or others.[11] In reality, given the lack of mental health services, this means discharge into the care of the person's family or the village community—typically without treatment.

1.1. Admission Criteria

There is no statutory definition of the term 'unsound mind' as it appears in the *Mental Hospital Act*[12] or in any other relevant legislation in Vanuatu; nor has there been any local case law that has considered the issue. The only criteria for involuntary detention under the Act are that the person be suspected of being

- of unsound mind *and*
- either dangerous to himself or others; *or*
- wandering at large *or* not receiving proper care and attention.[13]

Nonetheless, the certificate of detention does require the certifying medical practitioner to state 'facts indicating insanity' in support of any certification for detention.[14]

1.2. The Rights to Appeal and Review

Following compulsory admission a person must be visited and examined by the superintendent within 24 hours of admission and thereafter at least once a week.[15] If, at any time, an inpatient is examined and is found to no longer meet the criteria for involuntary detention, he or she must be discharged by the superintendent and one other medical officer.[16]

1.3. The Review Mechanism

There are no provisions in the legislation to enable an inpatient to apply for review of his or her detention. The Act simply refers to 'the Board' as 'the Board appointed to visit and

---

10 Ibid; see, e.g, *Public Prosecutor v Nicholls* [2003] VUSC 8. In this case the defendant who had been diagnosed with manic depression and prescribed lithium, which he took erratically, was charged with several counts of threat to kill and malicious damage to property. He pleaded not guilty on the grounds of insanity, which was supported by his treating general practitioner. The court upheld his plea.

11 *Mental Hospital Act* [Cap 38] (Vanuatu) s 10.

12 Ibid s 3.

13 Ibid s 3(2).

14 Ibid Schedule.

15 Ibid s 5(1).

16 Ibid s 6(1).

inspect the mental hospital'[17] and, apart from being appointed by the Minister,[18] makes no reference to its constitution or functions. The Board's only powers are to examine any inpatient and all records and, after consultation with the superintendent, to forward its recommendations regarding any patient or the general conditions in the hospital to the Minister.[19] The Act is silent on any powers the Minister may have on receipt of such a report.

This would not limit a person's right to challenge his or her detention via a writ of *habeas corpus* in the Supreme Court but such an action usually presupposes ready access to legal representation and no such application has ever been made.[20]

2. Challenges for the Future

In practice, mental health legislation is not applied in Vanuatu. While there are notional facilities at the general hospital, there are few if any trained mental health professionals to care for or treat those with a mental illness. A separate concrete walled room occasionally used for 'seclusion' of patients has no artificial lighting, one small window and a thin mattress on the floor. Food is usually provided but patients are often left locked in the room for days at a time without care or attention from anyone.[21] One mental health consumer, who is 'known' to the police and the hospital for displaying antisocial behaviour, is regularly brought to the hospital in handcuffs and given the 'standard treatment'. This consists of an injection of anti-psychotic medication and seclusion for three days—all without any initial assessment by a medical practitioner or subsequent review.[22] While this may not *prima facie* constitute a breach of the Act—which has very broad admission criteria and no provisions regarding seclusion and treatment—it is, at a minimum, a gross violation of human rights including the *Convention on the Rights of Persons with Disabilities* (CRPD), to which Vanuatu is a State Party.

Currently, no information in relation to mental health care is provided to the community in Vanuatu. The Ministry of Health has been developing educational health information as part of general community awareness programs but has been openly resistant to incorporating material on mental health, particularly issues surrounding youth suicide.[23] There is no separate budget line for mental health, and mental health services come within the auspices of public health where they continue to compete for funds with high profile service needs including HIV/AIDS and other communicable and non-communicable diseases.

Vanuatu has had law reform enabling legislation on its books for over 30 years.[24] No formal law reform body was established until 2010, when it was staffed by an overseas youth volunteer for one year. Permanent staff were not recruited until the end of 2012 when the first

[17] Ibid s 1.

[18] Ibid s 2(2).

[19] Ibid s 12.

[20] Email questionnaire from John Obed Alilee, Supreme Court Registrar, Vanuatu, to Helen Ménard, 15 July 2013.

[21] Interview with Carlie Dodds, Clinical Psychologist, Vanuatu (Port Vila, 28 June 2012).

[22] Ibid.

[23] Ibid.

[24] *Law Commission Act* [Cap115] (Vanuatu).

public submissions for reform were sought.[25] The Commission released its first report on the review of public health legislation in February 2013. Despite a muted suggestion that mental health legislation might have been incorporated into the revised public health legislation,[26] there is no reference at all to mental health in this report.[27]

It has also been suggested that the Ministry of Health, as part of the Vanuatu Mental Health Policy and Plan (2009-2014),[28] considered a submission to reform mental health legislation in Vanuatu—although, according to the Plan, the legislation was supposed to have been in draft form by 2010.[29] This project appears not to have progressed and no reference has yet been made to the Law Commission for review. As Powles describes law reform processes in the Pacific, it may be a case of culturally sensitive issues often being dealt with out of the public domain or simply placed in the 'too hard basket'.[30]

The approval for one nurse to undergo post graduate mental health training in Fiji in 2012 and one medical practitioner in 2013[31] provides a glimmer of light on a dark horizon—the evolution of other objectives under the Plan is far less encouraging.

The biggest challenge for Vanuatu lies within the overall health administration—recently some donor agencies have been forced to re-evaluate their programs and withdraw funding. The Ministry of Health has not published an annual report since 2011 and the Minister for Health in February 2013 described a lengthy accumulation of administrative crises as follows:

> The misuse of Ministry and Department of Health vehicles and assets are worse than any other Vanuatu Government Ministries and departments… [there are] huge problems [that] relate to lack of control of vehicles and assets as well as donor funds gone or spent on things not intended for…this has been going on for years.[32]

In essence, the future of health care in Vanuatu—let alone mental health care—remains bleak.

---

25 Vanuatu Law Commission, <www.lawcommission.gov.vu/index.php?option=com_content&view=article&id=19&Itemid=3 (accessed 14 June 2012)>.

26 Interview with Carlie Dodds, Clinical Psychologist, Vanuatu (Port Vila, 28 June 2012).

27 Vanuatu Law Commission, 'Public Health Act Legislative Review 2013' (2013) <www.lawcommission.gov.vu/images/stories/public%20health%20act-%20report.pdf (accessed 5 April 2013)>.

28 Government of the Republic of Vanuatu Ministry of Health, 'Vanuatu Mental Health Policy and Plan (2009-2014)' (2009) 8.

29 Ibid 13.

30 G Powles, 'Law Reform in Pacific Island States' in B Opeskin and D Weisbrot (eds), *The Promise of Law Reform* (Federation Press, 2005) 404, 419.

31 P Kaloris, '2012 Vanuatu Mental Health Annual Report' (Ministry of Health (Vanuatu), 2012).

32 G Ligo, 'Problems in Health is Huge: Ken,' *Vanuatu Daily Post* (Port Vila, Vanuatu), 27 February 2013.

Part III: Access to Justice and its Challenges in the Pacific

Chapter 9

Access to Justice

1. Overview

Access to justice exists at many levels in society and takes many forms. Justice itself can mean different things in different settings. Creating pathways to justice can be challenging. For mental health consumers, involuntary detention involves significant deprivation of liberty and, more often than not, invasive treatment without consent. In these circumstances, accessing justice via the law and the legal system is critical; both at the time of admission and subsequently throughout continuing confinement. This section merely introduces the core concepts of access to justice—a more detailed examination of the concept appears in Chapter 10. The major issues that are considered to impede access to justice in the region including culture and customary practice, policy development, resource allocation and service provision are all discussed in depth in Chapters 11, 12 and 13.

2. Literature

Formal works on access to justice in the Pacific are few and far between—indeed, there appears to be no relevant literature with respect to access to justice for mental health consumers. Intermittent media articles have appeared in the region and only occasional reference is made to improving access to justice in government reports.[1]

In 2009, the Asia Pacific Judicial Reform Forum published a compilation of case studies from the Asia Pacific region, one of which included a discussion by Jowitt on barriers to accessing justice in Vanuatu.[2] The author identified a number of factors impeding access to justice including legal pluralism and the effects of introduced legal systems; customary law; geography; language and low literacy levels; and inconsistent economic development. The writer then analysed two case studies—the operation of the island land courts and domestic

---

1 See, e.g., Government of Samoa Office of the Attorney General, 'Samoa Law and Justice Sector Plan 2008-2012: Justice for a Safe and Stable Samoa' (2008); G Shing, 'Access to Justice Has Failed Considerably: Salwai,' *Vanuatu Daily Post* (Port Vila, Vanuatu), 28 August 2012 <www.dailypost.vu/print/8377>.

2 A Jowitt, 'Barriers to Accessing Justice: The Vanuatu Experience' in Asia Pacific Judicial Reform Forum (ed), *Searching for Success in Judicial Reform: Voices from the Asia Pacific Experience* (Oxford University Press, 2009) 137.

violence protection legislation—where access to justice challenges were identified, actions developed and implemented were scrutinised, and outcomes assessed. The study appears to have been a retrospective evaluation of two select processes and did not involve original quantitative or qualitative research. Nonetheless, a number of extrapolations were drawn from the case studies including the essential—but not novel—observation that community involvement is critical in any successful reform process—especially when addressing inequality in marginalised groups.

A needs evaluation survey by the South Pacific Lawyers Association in 2011 reported on legal services and regulation of the legal profession across 13 Pacific island countries including Fiji, Samoa, Tonga and Vanuatu.[3] The object of the survey—the first of its kind undertaken in the region—was primary data collection with a longer term view of improving the quality of legal services throughout the South Pacific. The report made a number of general recommendations—acknowledged as being only a starting point for future engagement—including a comprehensive review of legal assistance funding as a means to improving access to justice.[4]

Powles describes some of the obstacles to law reform in the Pacific and the challenges to long term policy development.[5] These factors—which in effect also deny access to justice—largely reflect the issues discussed in Chapters 11, 12 and 13 concerning resources, culture, language, sources of law, lack of policy making capacity and international relationships.

3. What Does It Mean?

Justice as a concept invokes notions of fairness, equality and integrity. Access to justice, therefore, in its broadest form may be extended to encompass access to social and community services; political representation; expression of human rights; and systemic advocacy at any level of society. In mental health it might specifically include access to quality mental health care services. Equally, the concept might be confined to access to information, representation and effective participation in the legal system in the resolution of disputes.

Justice is more easily defined when discussions are taking place within the structured framework of Western common law legal systems and is generally understood to mean justice according to written law. However, if law as a concept is considered to be something other than Western style written law, then access to justice may take on a completely different meaning.

A detailed excursion into law and justice and legal pluralism is outside the scope of this work, but the observations of the late Bernard Narokobi in Papua New Guinea are equally applicable to other Melanesian cultures in Fiji and Vanuatu and parts of Polynesia. He posed the notion that:

> In the classical Melanesian context law is not an independent science or discipline, nor a highly specialised discipline restricted to an initiated few. It is an aspect of the total and cosmic way of life, an integral part of the whole way in which people go about

[3] South Pacific Lawyers Association, 'Needs Evaluation Survey for South Pacific Lawyer Associations: Final Report' (2011).

[4] Ibid 9.

[5] G Powles, 'Law Reform in Pacific Island States' in B Opeskin and D Weisbrot (eds), *The Promise of Law Reform* (Federation Press, 2005) 404.

undertaking various tasks in the community. Many languages in Melanesia lack any concept of the 'rule of law.'[6]

That is not to say that Melanesian societies were in any way lawless—they simply existed without any independent concept of the rule of law. Narokobi suggests 'it is difficult for modern states to imagine human communities without any formal notion of law or justice'[7] and that where tension exists between social groups in Melanesia social order still exists within that tension.[8] The concept of law in Melanesia presents an uncomfortable blend of natural or customary law. At the same time, introduced Western laws—while forming the basis of the legal system in all countries in the region—often struggle to achieve social understanding and acceptance. The assumption that justice must be done according to the body of written law automatically excludes sets of principles and beliefs that have been an integral part of custom and culture for many centuries.[9]

Traditional views on accessing justice have evolved from strict interpretations of equality of access to legal services; to correcting structural inequalities within legal systems; to focusing on informal justice and alternative dispute resolution; to improving access by implementing competition policy in the allocation of resources to access to justice and lowering the cost of legal services; and finally to a broader concept of community or 'everyday justice' that is not dependent on the mechanics of legal institutions.[10]

In measuring access to justice for mental health consumers in the Pacific in the context of involuntary detention and treatment under the mental health legislation, this study will concentrate on the provision of readily understandable *information* about the law and legal services; *representation* and effective *participation* in the legal process; judicial fairness and procedural transparency. These are the critical factors that facilitate access to justice for mental health consumers under detention—albeit in an inpatient facility or the community. The study will also focus on those legislative mechanisms that create pathways to justice—or a legal solution—for mental health consumers with particular reference to criteria for involuntary detention; mechanisms for appeal against, and periodic review of, involuntary detention; and some related rights based provisions.

The fundamental elements of *information*, *representation* and *participation* are considered in detail in Chapter 10. The discussion centres around the availability of easily understandable information about the legal process including information in different languages where appropriate; impartial advocacy—either legal or non-legal—with the assistance of interpreters if necessary; hearings conducted in an informal environment free from intimidation and which facilitate communication; and a cost effective, impartial, timely, responsive and transparent review process that is subject to appeal.

The meaning of access to justice and its application in the context of this study is set out in the concept map below. It is argued that the legislative process—which provides for

---

6 B Narokobi, *Lo Bilong Yumi Yet – Law and Custom in Melanesia* (Institute of Pacific Studies of the University of the South Pacific and The Melanesian Institute for Pastoral and Socio Economic Service, 1989) 4.

7 Ibid 15.

8 Ibid 15.

9 *Acting Public Prosecutor v Uname Aumane* [1980] PNGLR 510; [1980] PGSC 5.

9 Narokobi, above n 6.

10 Australian Government Attorney General's Department, 'A Strategic Framework for Access to Justice in the Federal Civil Justice System, Report by the Access to Justice Taskforce Attorney General's Department' (2009) 3.

periodic review of or appeals against involuntary detention and treatment without consent—is the lynchpin of justice within the mental health system. The statutory criteria that determine detention, the existence of the right to review detention and the review mechanism itself are critical elements of this process. The ability to access the process is created by pathways of *information, representation, participation* and specific legislative rights.

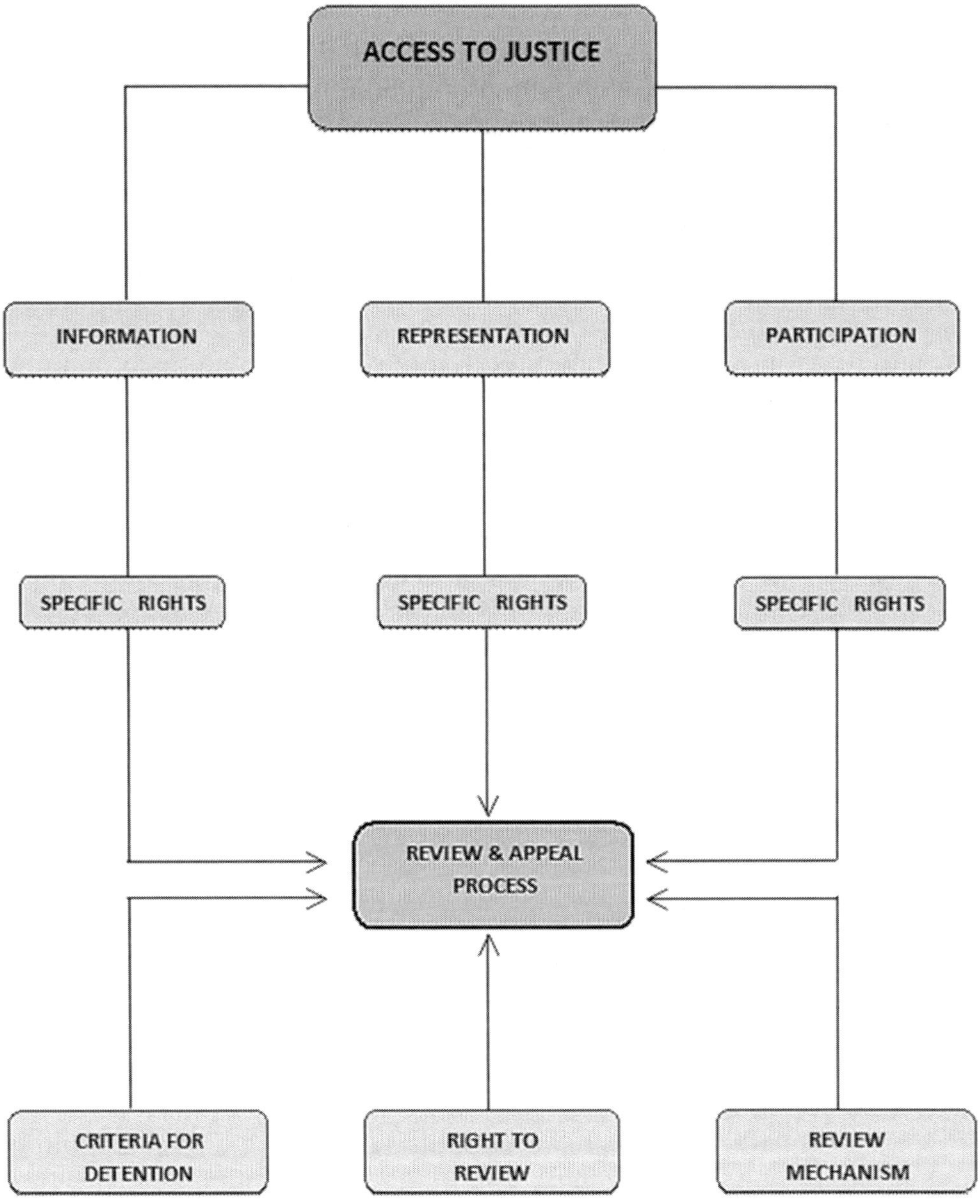

Figure 3. Concept Map – Pathways to Justice.

4. Pacific Views on Access to Justice

There has been very little written on access to justice as a general concept in the Pacific, even less on disability, and nothing at all in the context of mental health. A selected review of access to justice, as understood in some recent civil justice reforms outside the region, follows.

4.1. Vanuatu

Charlot Salwai, Vanuatu's then Minister of Justice and Community Services—in addressing members of the public and the legal profession during Law Week in August 2012—stated that 'access to justice in Vanuatu has failed considerably and in some parts of Vanuatu people lack total justice.'[11] He considered some of the contributing factors to be expensive legal fees; the prioritisation by lawyers of money over the provision of legal services; and a failure by lawyers to recognise the constitutional roles of custom and religion in the law.[12]

In outlining the Ministry's objective in 2014 to 'develop and implement appropriate and evidence based collaborative strategies that address barriers to access' it stated that

> Access to justice services is [sic] currently restricted to citizens in all provinces. These limitations occur because of geographic isolation, funding the cost of service delivery to isolated locations, knowledge/skill issues, gender considerations and the effectiveness and efficiency of service delivery. The strategy is designed to ensure that in the future all citizens are provided with the same opportunity to access justice services that are perceived as fair, efficient, effective and appropriately coordinated.[13]

In a 2009 paper, Jowitt identified a range of issues that impede access to justice in the state legal system in Vanuatu, but not specifically in relation to persons with disabilities or mental disorders.[14] Nonetheless, different combinations of these issues are common throughout the Pacific and impact to varying degrees on the ability of mental health consumers to access justice.

4.2. Samoa

While the courts in Samoa are generally regarded as independent and fair, severe and chronic backlogs of cases exist—up to ten years in the Supreme Court. Barriers to community access to justice are identified as including cumbersome legal procedures and poor case

---

11 G Shing, 'Access to Justice Has Failed Considerably: Salwai,' *Vanuatu Daily Post* (Port Vila, Vanuatu), 28 August 2012 <www.dailypost.vu/print/8377>.

12 Ibid.

13 Government of the Republic of Vanuatu, 'Strategy for the Justice and Community Services Sector 2014 - 2017, Ministry for Justice and Community Services' (2014) 14.

14 A Jowitt, 'Barriers to Accessing Justice: The Vanuatu Experience' in Asia Pacific Judicial Reform Forum (ed), *Searching for Success in Judicial Reform: Voices from the Asia Pacific Experience* (Oxford University Press, 2009) 137, 142.

management; out of date colonial era laws; low public awareness of legal rights and laws only published in English; inability to afford private lawyers and limited legal aid; longstanding staff shortages and lack of in-service training; and dilapidated court buildings.[15]

Samoa's Law & Justice Sector Plan 2008-2012 identified one of its objectives being access to justice.[16] The primary strategy aligned with the access to justice objective was '[to] improve access to justice, law and legal services – including establishing the Law Reform Commission and community legal centres, expanded legal aid and community empowerment, and the Human Rights Commission.'[17] Other proposed activities include the creation of a Public Defender's Office and a Disabled People's Rights Unit.

The same plan for 2012-2016 expressed disappointment that some of these objectives had not been met.

> A Community Law Centre, while agreed as a priority and a valuable mechanism for improving Access to Justice for our Communities, it is still yet to be established and as reported in a Review Report of the previous Samoa Law and Justice Sector Plan, "it reflected poorly on the Sector" and should be afforded key priority project status if the Sector is to deliver on access issues, that impact some of the most vulnerable members of our society.[18]

Both reports acknowledge the challenge of 'marrying' the relationship between formal and customary or traditional domains of law and justice and recognises the 'quality and dimensions in this relationship lie at the heart of *Fa'a-Samoa* (the Samoan Way) and are profound, complex and sensitive in nature.'[19] Cleary, this philosophy must be factored into any reform that concerns legal processes or access to justice—in whatever form—in Samoa.

On the other hand,

> many [Samoans] are concerned by the erosion of the traditional authority structure and standing of village councils and Pulenu'u [village mayor] by courts whose jurisdiction are increasingly being invoked by villagers dissatisfied with those decisions exercising their 'legal' rights and possibly reaching contrary decisions that disregard and/or override that authority.[20]

In some cases, the government has developed initiatives to counter this problem such as introducing traditional mediation procedures and legislation for community based supervision.[21]

---

15 Government of Samoa Office of the Attorney General, 'Samoa Law & Justice Sector Plan 2008-2012: Justice for a Safe and Stable Samoa' (2008) 27–9.

16 Ibid iv.

17 Ibid 11.

18 Government of Samoa Office of the Attorney General, 'Samoa Law & Justice Sector Plan 2012-2016: Justice for a Safe and Stable Samoa' (2012) <http://www.samoaljs.ws/english/images/stories/uploads/SLJS_Plan_2012-2016_English.pdf (accessed 5 September 2015)> 16.

19 Government of Samoa Office of the Attorney General, 'Samoa Law & Justice Sector Plan 2008-2012: Justice for a Safe and Stable Samoa' (2008) 23.

20 Ibid 23.

21 Ibid 23.

4.3. South Pacific Lawyers Association

A report in 2011 by the South Pacific Lawyers Association recommended that 'governments in the South Pacific countries should conduct a comprehensive review of the funding of legal aid/assistance and the improvement of coordination of legal aid and assistance services in partnership with the legal profession to improve access to justice.'[22] This was on the basis that, apart from Fiji, no formal legal aid services are routinely available in the Pacific. In fact, there is no community legal centre or government legal aid at all in Tonga; the Samoan Law Society provides limited legal aid for serious criminal cases and is in the process of establishing a community legal centre; and in Vanuatu very limited free representation is provided by the Public Solicitor's Office and through a community legal centre operated under the auspices of the University of the South Pacific School of Law.[23]

5. International Views on Access to Justice

There have been many reports written on accessing justice in both the criminal and civil legal systems. It is not the intention to review all those reports but to look at select jurisdictions to see if they have specifically dealt with mental health consumers.

5.1. United Kingdom

Lord Woolf, in his seminal review of the civil justice system in the United Kingdom in 1996

> identified a number of principles which the civil justice system should meet in order to ensure access to justice. The system should: (a) be just in the results it delivers; (b) be fair in the way it treats litigants; (c) offer appropriate procedures at a reasonable cost; (d) deal with cases with reasonable speed; (e) be understandable to those who use it; (f) be responsive to the needs of those who use it; (g) provide as much certainty as the nature of the particular cases allow; and (h) be effective: adequately resourced and organised.[24]

The major defects Lord Woolf exposed in the civil justice system included disproportionate costs of claims; slow resolution of cases; unequal treatment of litigants; uncertainty of outcomes; lack of understanding of the legal process; overuse of the adversarial approach to litigation; as well as a lack of adherence to and enforcement of procedural rules.[25] In focusing on case management and cost issues in the civil system, the report made no reference to disadvantaged groups, although all the issues identified would have equal application to mental health consumers attempting to access the legal system.

---

22 South Pacific Lawyers Association, 'Needs Evaluation Survey for South Pacific Lawyer Associations: Final Report' (2011) [rec. 3].

23 Ibid Ch 6.

24 H Woolf, 'Access to Justice: Final Report (UK)' (1996) <www.justice.gov.uk (accessed 5 March 2012)> [1].

25 Ibid.

Clearly, access to justice for disadvantaged groups, such as mental health consumers, requires a higher standard of care when applying the general principles on account of the reduced levels of comprehension and increased anxiety levels associated with the symptomology of particular illnesses and the effects of medication taken to treat them.

5.2. New Zealand

The New Zealand Human Rights Commission has produced two reports in the last ten years neither of which has referred specifically to the rights of mental health consumers.[26] The earlier report in 2004 deals with the right to justice in the context of human rights and international law and assessed the status of access to justice against key indicators including 'clear laws that incorporate human rights standards; an independent and impartial legal system; legal processes that ensure equality and fairness; and laws that are known and openly made.' [27] The report considered that equal and fair access to justice necessitated the provision of private legal services, government funded legal aid and community legal services.[28] Unfortunately, in the broader Pacific, legal aid and community legal services are rarely available and would be unable to meet these criteria. In its final assessment the report concluded that

> research suggests that there are significant variations in the realisation of the right to justice among different New Zealanders, including disabled people, Maori and Pacific peoples, and children and young people. There are no clear human rights measures to assess progress in the realisation of the right.[29]

However, this report predated the *Convention on the Rights of Persons with Disabilities* (CRPD) which New Zealand has now ratified. The report also found that there was a general lack of knowledge of human rights in the community which reflects the position in the countries under examination and as outlined in Chapter 12.

The later report in 2010 which, when dealing with accessing justice, focuses on the criminal justice system and concedes that significant issues remain unresolved.[30] Mental health consumers are not given separate consideration but when considering the right to physical and mental health, the report recognises the need to amend mental health legislation to comply with the CRPD especially in relation to the concept of capacity.[31] There are several minority groups identified in the report, none of which includes mental health consumers. While there are oblique references to mental health in the section on the 'rights of disabled people,' the imperatives center around the needs of those with physical disabilities.[32]

---

[26] Human Rights Commission Te Kahui Tika Tangata, 'Human Rights in New Zealand 2010, Nga Tika Tangata o Aotearoa 2010' (2010) <www.hrc.co.nz>; Human Rights Commission Te Kahui Tika Tangata, 'Human Rights in New Zealand Today, Nga Tika Tangata o Aotearoa i Tenei Ra' (2004) <www.hrc.co.nz/report/chapters/chapter10./justice01/.html>.

[27] Human Rights Commission Te Kahui Tika Tangata, above n 26 [10].

[28] Ibid.

[29] Ibid.

[30] Human Rights Commission Te Kahui Tika Tangata, above n 26, Summary 33.

[31] Ibid Summary 47.

[32] Ibid Summary 72-6.

5.3. New South Wales, Australia

There have been several major reports on access to justice in Australia, but the only one that has targeted mental health issues is the New South Wales Law and Justice Foundation's report on access to justice and the legal needs of the mentally ill.[33] This report identifies the barriers to accessing legal assistance by the mentally ill as a lack of awareness of their legal rights; disorganised and sometimes difficult behaviour; being overwhelmed and frightened; lack of trust in legal service providers; communication problems; lack of mental health care; limited availability of affordable services; time constraints on legal services; lack of services in rural and remote areas; perceived lack of credibility of mentally ill clients; and intimidating aspects of the physical environments in which legal services are provided.[34]

This report also identifies obstacles preventing people from participating effectively in the legal system including stress; cognitive impairment; time management and communication problems associated with the symptoms of mental illness; the formality of courtrooms; lack of legal representation; and the failure to identify or recognise a person's mental illness.[35] Some of the primary strategies posed by the report to address these barriers consist of a more flexible approach to legal service delivery—such as allowing for breaks in proceedings and taking time to explain procedures—to overcome stress and communication problems; implementation of a less adversarial approach within the courtroom; and mental illness awareness training for lawyers, judges, court staff and other legal service providers.[36]

While legislative reform in the target countries of the Pacific has created a range of rights based frameworks based largely on Western style models, these rights are mostly unrealised. A detailed consideration of the more significant barriers to effective realisation, in the context of mental health, appears in the following chapters. It is not practical to attempt to rank these factors in terms of their impact on the realisation of rights, as they are all interconnected and often assume varying significance in different societies. They are dealt with throughout simply in an order that suits the relevant discussion.

---

33 M Karras, 'Access to Justice and Legal Needs Vol. 4: On the Edge of Justice: The Legal Needs of People with a Mental Illness' (Law and Justice Foundation of New South Wales, 2006).

34 Ibid xviii-xx.

35 Ibid xx-xxi.

36 Ibid xxii.

Chapter 10

Accessing Justice in Mental Health

1. Access to Justice in Context

As indicated at the outset, access to justice in this context has been conceptualised as the provision of *information*, *representation* and effective *participation* within the legal mechanisms established under the relevant mental health laws. The focus, thus far, has been on a comparative analysis of past and present statutes which provide access to justice, or a legal solution, for mental health consumers subject to involuntary detention in the Pacific. This analysis of whether legislative pathways to justice have been created or improved by mental health law reform, has primarily been measured against benchmarks of the criteria for involuntary detention; mechanisms for review of and appeal against involuntary detention; and explicit legislative rights that facilitate information, representation and participation.

In creating pathways to justice, *information* is a key component in understanding and successfully participating in any process, be it for mental health consumers or their advocates. *Representation*, though not indispensable, often serves to enhance the outcome of participation in the process. *Participation* by the consumer in a process that determines his or her liberty and quality of treatment is the ultimate embodiment of justice, equality and respect for the human rights and dignity of individuals.

This first half of this chapter considers each of these features individually and examines their general operation in some non-Pacific jurisdictions. The second half reviews their specific application in the Pacific jurisdictions under discussion. The examination takes place in the context of statutory devices enabling access justice for mental health consumers—principally, the criteria for involuntary detention and mechanisms for review of and appeal against detention.

1.1. Therapeutic Jurisprudence

A detailed excursion into the concept of therapeutic jurisprudence is not within the scope of this work even though it did have its origins in mental health law in the 1980s.[1] In essence, the concept

1 D B Wexler, *International Network on Therapeutic Jurisprudence, Therapeutic Jurisprudence: An Overview* <www.law.arizona.edu/depts/upr-intj/ (accessed 25 May 2013)>.

> concentrates on the law's impact on emotional life and psychological well-being. It is a perspective that regards the law (rules of law, legal procedures, and roles of legal actors) itself as a social force that often produces therapeutic or anti-therapeutic consequences. It does not suggest that therapeutic concerns are more important than other consequences or factors, but it does suggest that the law's role as a potential therapeutic agent should be recognised and systematically studied.[2]

It also involves looking at studies in psychology, psychiatry, clinical behavioural sciences, criminology and social work to see whether those insights can be incorporated or brought into the legal system with the aim of 'humanising the law and concerning itself with the human, emotional, psychological side of law and the legal process.'[3]

While not always identified as such, much of the following analysis and discussion of the elements needed to access justice takes place in a therapeutic framework. It is the existence of these factors—information, representation and participation—in a setting that facilitates access to justice that, in turn, enables a therapeutic legal outcome.

1.2. Information

Information and the opportunity to respond to adverse information are integral to the administration of procedural fairness.[4] No decision made without appropriate and accurate information can be either informed or effective.

An important report entitled 'Lacking Insight' detailing consumer experiences before the Mental Health Review Board in Victoria (Australia), expressed several concerns about the lack of access to personal and procedural information by mental health consumers.[5] In the context of the principles of natural justice or procedural fairness, some consumers stated 'they had no knowledge of their right to access their files ... they were not provided with enough time to understand the file's contents ... or were disturbed that the file had documents missing.'[6] In some cases, the difficulties of accessing files also extended to the consumer's legal representative.[7]

The timing of access to information in preparation for a hearing can be as critical as access itself, as described by these consumers:

> It didn't give me enough time and I'm intellectually with it ... just think of other people that [sic] are not and partly unwell who would not have a hope of understanding those reports on the morning [of the hearing].[8]
>
> It's always a shock when I read my file because it's always full of exaggerations and I always make sure I get that the day before because if I get that right – a couple of times I've had it right before the Review Board hearing and I'm so upset from reading it that

2 Ibid.

3 Ibid.

4 N Rees, 'International Human Rights Obligations and Mental Health Review Tribunals' (2003) 10(1) *Psychiatry, Psychology and Law* 33, 39.

5 V Topp, M Thomas and M Ingvarson, 'Lacking Insight: Involuntary Patient Experience of the Victorian Mental Health Review Board' (2008) 42.

6 Ibid.

7 Ibid 43.

8 Ibid 44.

> I'm a bit speechless during the Review Board hearing, so I try to make it that I had read that the day before.[9]

The report noted that lack of effective information about the hearing process created confusion, frustration and anxiety among many consumers. This extended to the different roles of the Board and its members and the way in which the person's clinical condition was evaluated against the various legal criteria.[10]

Many consumers stressed the fact that information alone was unproductive unless they were given assistance to understand its application, especially where their comprehension was affected by their symptoms or medication.[11]

1.3. Representation

The critical factors in this area are the right to choose representation, the competence of the representative and the cost of representation. Opinion seems to be divided about the positive effects of representation—legal or non-legal—at a periodic review or appeal hearing. Family members and carers might pursue their own agendas, which are not necessarily aligned with the mental health consumer's viewpoint.[12] On the other hand, family members are often the ones who can provide supportive behavioural evidence outside a hospital setting. Legal advocates may be inexperienced in dealing with the complexities of mental illness and adopt an overly adversarial approach towards clinicians and other witnesses.[13] Conversely, they can provide the only effective 'voice' that a consumer has in the face of an intimidating tribunal and an oppositional clinical team. Clinicians often view legal advocates as potentially counterproductive to the patient–practitioner relationship, and lawyers see clinicians as operating in an excessively paternalistic manner and infringing individual rights.

Some argue that the ideal course for advocacy is the middle ground between representing the client's views at the same time as ensuring the best health outcome—but this is by no means a universally held view.[14]

In the end, it depends on how one defines advocacy—for whom and why. Lawyers who advocate—in the true sense of the word—for their clients within the mental health arena will frequently fall foul of those who subscribe to the 'best interests' philosophy regardless of how non adversarial their approach might be. The treatment team and, more often than not, family and carers are primarily motivated by the patient's 'best interests'. It falls to the lawyer to promote the patient's view despite any irrationality—but it is often simply about 'being heard'. In the final analysis, it is the tribunal or court, as the decision maker, that is tasked with arriving at a balanced outcome.

---

9 Ibid 44.

10 Ibid 44–6.

11 Ibid 47.

12 T Carney et al. *Mental Health Tribunals: Balancing fairness, freedom, protection and right to treatment?* (Themis Press, 2011) 291; see also F Clair and S Fisher, 'Powering - and Empowering - Through Change: The Queensland Tribunal's Experience of Transition from Old Systems to New' (2003) 10(1) *Psychiatry, Psychology and Law* 184, 187.

13 Carney et al. above n 12, 252.

14 T Carney et al. 'Advocacy and Participation in Mental Health Cases: Realisable Rights or Pipe- dreams?' (2008) 26(2) *Law in Context Special Issue: International Trends in Mental Health Laws* 125, 131.

As Donnelly points out in her discussion of the process of judicial review of treatment decisions in the United Kingdom:

> While judicial review of treatment decisions attracts procedural entitlements to a full hearing with cross examination and legal representation, the English experience reminds us that this formality is not always facilitative of accessibility, openness and participation ...[a] number of commentators have argued that effective legal representation is the key to the protection of patient rights. However legal representation may also serve as a barrier, preventing the person affected by the decision from engaging with the process.[15]

This is illustrated by the comments of the High Court of England and Wales in *R's* case, where upon refusing a request by counsel that the claimant be allowed to give oral evidence, Collins J stated 'it did not seem to me that his evidence would conceivably assist me in reaching a decision.'[16] And as Donnelly puts it 'this approach clearly fails to deliver a process which is either fair to, or likely to be trusted by the person affected by it.'[17]

The various Australian states deal differently with the right to representation ranging from a general right to representation by any person (Victoria) to mandatory representation by a legal practitioner where the person elects to be represented (South Australia).[18] In contrast to other states, for a time the Northern Territory statute guaranteed free legal representation to all persons appearing before the tribunal.[19] As Williams argued these provisions effectively imposed legal representation on all persons and disempowered mental health consumers by taking away their right to choose and was in conflict with the *MI Principles*.[20] The legislation has now been amended and allows mental health consumers the right to choose unless the Tribunal 'thinks representation is necessary' and regardless of any objections by the consumer.[21]

1.3.1. Representation Rates and Results

A recent study of the operation of the Mental Health Review Tribunal in New South Wales (Australia), conducted over a four year period, found that while 64 percent of tribunal hearings on substantive matters involved applications for CTOs,[22] only one percent of these orders were declined by the tribunal. The attendance of a support person—usually a nuclear family member or carer—at any type of hearing was uncommon, at approximately 20 percent for inpatient hearings and 33 percent for CTOs.[23] Only one percent of all CTO hearings involved a legal representative and those who did appear were always publically funded

---

15 M Donnelly, 'Review of Treatment Decisions: Legalism, Process and the Protection of Rights' in B McSherry and P Weller (eds), *Rethinking Rights Based Mental Health Laws* (Hart Publishing, 2010) 275, 282.

16 *R (on the application of JB) v RMO, Dr Haddock* [2005] EWHC 921 (Admin) [14].

17 Donnelly, above n 15, 282–3.

18 V Williams, 'The Challenge for Australian Jurisdictions to Guarantee Free Qualified Representation Before Mental Health Tribunals and Boards of Review: Learning from the Tasmanian Experience' (2009) 16(1) *Psychiatry, Psychology and Law* 108, 117; see also *Mental Health Act 1986* (Vic)s 6(3); *Mental Health Act 1993* (SA) s 27.

19 *Mental Health Act 1998* (NT) ss 41(1), 131.

20 Williams, above n 18, 114.

21 *Mental Health and Related Services Amendment Act 2007* (NT) s 83.

22 M Cain et al. 'The NSW Mental Health Review Tribunal: An Analysis of Clients, Matter and Determinations' (2011) 24.

23 Ibid 27.

lawyers.[24] While the overall legal representation rate for all hearings was 21 percent, inpatient orders only made up around 17 percent of the tribunal hearings and of these 79 percent involved legal representation.[25] Despite this seemingly high level of representation, less than two percent of applications for inpatient orders were declined.[26] Even with overall representation rates as high as 70 percent in New Zealand this did not increase the patients' chances of a successful discharge.[27] Another study revealed that the overall legal representation rate in Victoria was only 13 percent but of these 16 percent were private lawyers compared to only 4.7 percent in New South Wales.[28]

This is a different experience to that outlined in 'Lacking Insight'. This report suggests that, while the rate of discharge from involuntary status in Victoria by the Mental Health Review Board is approximately 3.4 percent,[29] 'the chances of such an outcome are markedly increased when legal representation is engaged ... people with legal representation were discharged at a rate more than three times greater than unrepresented consumers.'[30]

The same report maintains that 'perceptions of a predetermined decision by a consumer may result in consumer non-attendance at Board hearings' and that the level of non-attendance at hearings is in the vicinity of 48 percent.[31] This perception is epitomised by one consumer's comment: 'I did know I could have legal representation but I didn't see the point.'[32]

Consumers' reasons for non-attendance also included the view that hearings merely 'rubber stamped' the decision of treating clinicians or the person was simply too unwell to participate. They also expressed the view that a person was more likely to attend a hearing if he or she had legal representation.[33]

On balance, it seems that a person's experience before a mental health tribunal hearing is enhanced by representation—either by a support person whose views are aligned to the consumer's or an experienced legal advocate—if only for the reason that representation improves the prospects of the person attending the hearing and understanding the decisions that are made. The fact that in many jurisdictions representation does not seem to improve the chances of release is not so much the point—it is the sense of meaningful *participation* in the process that is empowering.

1.3.2. Limitations

In most Pacific jurisdictions, the reality is that the legislative right to legal representation is a hollow promise—there are very few, if any, lawyers with mental health expertise in the region and even fewer clients who seek it.

---

24 Ibid 48.

25 Ibid 26. Note: this is more a reflection of the legal aid policy in NSW of extending assistance to all inpatient reviews in the first 12 months of detention and not extending aid to those on CTOs.

26 Ibid 24.

27 T Carney, 'Mental Health Tribunals – Rights, Protection or Treatment? Lessons from the ARC Linkage Grant Study?' (Paper presented at the Rights Responsibilities Rhetoric - Unpacking the Policy and Practice Issues in Mental Health Law, Guardianship and Trusteeship, Adelaide, October 2009) 16.

28 Ibid 7.

29 Topp, Thomas and Ingvarson, above n 5, 22.

30 Ibid 41.

31 Ibid.

32 Ibid.

33 Carney et al. above n 12, 170.

On the other hand, difficulty accessing legal representation is not peculiar to poorly resourced countries. Zuckerberg, in describing some of the shortcomings of the Canadian system, states:

> The limited availability of legal representation stems from a number of factors including lack of expertise in mental health law, unavailability of legal aid for patients appearing before the MHT, unwillingness to take legally aided clients ... in some cases an unwillingness to work with mentally ill clients ... and short time-frames for scheduling MHT hearings.[34]

Carney et al. describe the situation across three Australian states as 'problematic' due largely to short lead in times to arrange legal representation; the scarcity of available legal resources, particularly for CTO clients; and the limited time clients are able to spend with advocates.[35] They suggest that some of the gaps could be filled by expanding the role of community visitors; the use of volunteer independent person programs or trained lay advocates.[36] Similar suggestions have been made by Parkin in relation to Samoa but the lack of a formal review mechanisms and the lack of review hearings in that country make this less of an imperative.

1.4. Participation and Review Mechanisms

An integral part of the overall process must be the operation of the mechanism through which mental health consumers access justice—the periodic review of or appeal against involuntary detention. The options, in reality, are few.

They range, at one end, from no review at all, whereby the patient is reliant solely on the unregulated review and recommendations of the clinician; to multi member independent legalistic tribunals at the other end. In between are a number of variations on the theme. These range from visiting boards comprised of non-professionals with limited and rarely used review powers; the seldom accessed right of review through the superior court system; multi member panels comprising treating clinicians of questionable impartiality; single member panels making decisions 'on the papers'; video conference and telephone hearings; limited right of judicial review of treatment decisions; and second opinion professional review of treatment decisions.

1.4.1. The Tribunal – To Be or Not to Be

In situations where the tribunal model is in operation, the options can vary from the clinical model—where the psychiatrists have substantial determinative powers—to the legal model—where the emphasis is more about the application of legal criteria by a legal body—to those of a more hybrid nature.[37]

---

34 J Zuckerberg, 'Mental Health Law and its Discontents: A Reappraisal of the Canadian Experience' in B McSherry and P Weller (eds), *Rethinking Rights Based Mental Health Laws* (Hart Publishing, 2010) 299, 323.

35 Carney et al. above n 12, 287.

36 Ibid 291.

37 T Carney, D Tait and F Beaupert, 'Pushing the Boundaries: Realising Rights Through Mental Health Tribunal Processes?' (2008) 30 *Sydney Law Review* 329, 340–41.

There has been much discussion among writers about the ideal composition of these tribunals—whether they should be single member or multi member bodies—and the mix of professional expertise. Invariably, single member bodies involve a lawyer, magistrate or judge without the benefit of comprehensive medical advice. Those who assert that the decision to detain and treat a person should be a clinical one argue that the legal approach over simplifies the end result. It can also overlook the fact that a person's social circumstances might be critical in interpreting clinical information.[38]

Despite the fact that Carney et al. concluded that 'it is vital that genuinely interdisciplinary and multi member hearings be retained' and that they 'run genuinely inquisitorial hearings,'[39] the style of the review model adopted will be governed by local policy and resources—referred to by some as the 'pragmatic' approach.[40] This is the case in the Pacific, where the major determinative issues are resources—both economic and professional. Indeed, South Australia, over strong objections from the Public Advocate, has recently moved to single member hearings—ostensibly as a cost-saving measure.

With some models, the consumer has the right to mandatory initial and periodic reviews of detention—with others, for example Samoa, the person is simply given the right to request a review at any time during the currency of the order, although the number of reviews is limited to one per order.

At one end of the spectrum, the underlying procedural philosophy revolves around medical paternalism and the 'best interests' of the consumer where the principal purpose is to protect the consumer from the community. The philosophy then graduates from legalism to rights based legalism, at the other end, where detention is more often centred on protecting the community from the consumer.

The difficulty remains that in order to give sufficient weight and integrity to the important issue at hand—the deprivation of personal liberty—some degree of formality of process is warranted. Yet, in many cases, it is this very formality that seems to be counterproductive. While de facto inquisitorial in nature and not bound by the rules of evidence, tribunals still allow adversarial representation and purport to apply the rules of natural justice. And so a conundrum arises. If it is accepted that a quasi-legal mechanism is the best option—if only to create a *perception* of fairness and independence—then the crux of the matter becomes not the existence of the mechanism but its method of operation.

Most writers agree that legal process alone will not facilitate justice—the process itself needs to be impartial, transparent and (in the context of mental health) guarantee an experience and outcome that is therapeutic and satisfying for the consumer. This relies on the ability and willingness of panel members to refrain from passively applying the law in a manner that prefers medical paternalism over individual human rights.[41]

---

38 Carney et al. above n 12, 96–7.

39 Ibid 99.

40 Ibid 308.

41 J Peay, *Tribunals on Trial: A Study of Decision-Making under the Mental Health Act 1983* (Clarendon Press, 1989) 202.

1.4.2. Shortcomings of the Tribunal Model

When discussing the optimum environment in which tribunals should function, Freckelton asserts 'an empowered witness is likely to be a more articulate and confident communicator as well as later a more satisfied consumer of the review tribunal process.'[42]

The same author identifies some of the factors which militate against consumers' confidence in the operation of such bodies hence reducing their ability to participate effectively:

- A sense of clinical opposition and resultant intimidation in that if the clinician agreed with the patient there would be no need for a hearing;
- The intimidating aspect of appearing, often unrepresented, before a multi-party professional panel;
- The perception of bias arising from the location of the hearings frequently in the hospital buildings owned by health service providers from whom the patient is seeking release;
- Failure by panel members to explain in unthreatening terms the operation and independence of the panel and the limits on its powers;
- Failure by panel members to explain the patient's right to ask questions of the panel or clinicians either directly or through a representative;
- Failure by panel members to focus on the patient at the hearing and facilitate the flow of information from the patient in a non-patronising environment;
- Any perception of bias arising from a patient's failure to be heard or taken seriously or that panel members have a preconceived view of the outcome;
- Failure to provide equal access to medical records when it is obvious that panel members have read the patient's file;
- Failure by panel members to allocate sufficient time to hearings to enable appropriate canvassing of the issues;
- Failure by panel members to ensure all participants are treated with dignity—this includes treating thought disordered, overly anxious or heavily medicated patients with fairness and patience and attenuating the adversarial nature of the process where necessary.[43]

Freckleton maintains that some of these factors can be ameliorated by taking appropriate breaks during hearings; avoiding hostile cross examination of patients or clinicians; eliminating complex methods of questioning; minimising the discussion of sensitive or embarrassing symptomatology; reducing unhelpful conflict and unduly lengthy hearings; limiting the use of inaccurate or unsubstantiated hearsay evidence; exploring reasons for non-compliance with treatment or medication; avoiding undue deference to other tribunal members; and basing decisions on proven facts and appropriate application of the legislative criteria.[44]

---

[42] I Freckelton, 'Mental Health Review Tribunal Decision-Making: A Therapeutic Jurisprudence Lens' (2003) 10 *Psychiatry, Psychology and Law* 44, 46.

[43] Ibid 44–63.

[44] Ibid 49–59.

While the resolution of many of these issues simply amounts to the application of common sense and sensitivity, lamentably, several consumer-based surveys have found otherwise.[45]

The New South Wales Law and Justice Foundation's report on access to justice[46] did not raise specific issues in relation to the operation of the Mental Health Review Tribunal in NSW, leaving this to be dealt with (as one of the participating industry partners), under the separate collaborative research study resulting in the 2011 monograph by Carney et al. However, general mention was made of the legal issues facing people with a mental illness who had been hospitalised '[including] confusion about when they are to be discharged from hospital; confusion about when they move from voluntary to involuntary status; [and] not understanding their rights in relation to medical treatment.'[47]

A number of recently released investigative reports into mental health tribunals in Australia have provided valuable insights into the operation and effectiveness of the tribunal system. Yet, none has suggested that the model be discarded. Instead, each has found that there is significant room for improvement in the protection of consumer rights, the communication of information to consumers, and the delivery of therapeutic jurisprudence.[48] One report submitted that, while there is no agreed 'best practice' benchmark within Australia or internationally,[49] there were 'strong and opposing views about what is considered to be "effective" and "appropriate" practice ... in particular the legal model and the medical model.'[50]

Where video conference or telephone hearings were conducted for consumers in regional, remote or rural areas of New South Wales the feedback was mixed. In general, it was a negative experience for consumers. While accepting that the 'gold standard' for hearings is 'face to face' mode, cost was an issue in more remote areas. Efforts have since been made to reduce the number of non-face to face hearings in light of technology difficulties and the fact that this method was considered to simply 'provide another level of disadvantage to consumers who are already significantly disadvantaged.'[51]

As mentioned earlier in this chapter, the furthest Carney et al. go in terms of alternatives is to suggest that some situations may lend themselves to expanding the role of community visitors or the use of independent volunteers or trained lay advocates.[52] In supporting the retention of the tribunal model, the authors argue that to achieve best practice (in Australia) emphasis needs to be placed on the allocation of more time to individual hearings; improved access to alternate professional opinions; independence and accountability of the review body; more therapeutic physical surroundings; and greater access to legal representation for consumers.[53]

---

45 See, e.g., Peay, above n 41 and D Mohan, 'Mental Health Review Tribunal Decisions in Restricted Hospital Order Cases at One Medium Secure Unit, 1992-1996' (1998) 8 *Criminal Behaviour and Mental Health* 57.

46 M Karras, 'Access to Justice and Legal Needs Vol. 4: On the Edge of Justice: The Legal Needs of People with a Mental Illness' (Law and Justice Foundation of New South Wales, 2006).

47 Ibid 48.

48 MHDAO NSW Ministry of Health, 'Communio Final Report: Evaluation of Efficacy and Cost of the Mental Health Inquiry System' (2012) 8–10; Carney et al. above n 12, 276–281.

49 MHDAO NSW Ministry of Health, above n 48, 7.

50 Ibid 7.

51 Ibid 38.

52 Carney et al. above n 12, 287–291.

53 Ibid 309–315.

However, all these aspects, aside from the physical surroundings, are contingent on adequate legal and medical professional resources. This presents a major stumbling block for the Pacific. As such, it should be a reason to motivate policy makers to educate their communities about the nature and treatment of mental illness and human rights based principles, so the community can assist mental health consumers to access justice by providing lay advocacy and representation.

Shah, in a recent review of mental health tribunal decisions in the United Kingdom, argues there is a range of evidence suggesting potential bias or perceived bias in the MHRT system[54] and listed a series of factors that could create a perception of bias among participants:

- The MHRT being too reliant on the opinion of the RMO (Responsible Medical Officer);
- Funding of the MHRT by the department of health which also funds hospitals which in turn detain patients;
- Approximately 90 percent of cases brought before tribunals did not result in a change of the patients' status;
- The majority of tribunal members regarded issues of public safety as paramount even in cases where evidence of mental disorder was doubtful;
- Lack of adversarial nature of hearings in that medical evidence was rarely challenged particularly when it was subjective opinion unsupported by facts;
- Undue influence exerted by the medical member of the tribunal;
- Increased numbers of cases resulting in delays or cancellations in hearings;
- Inadequate legal representation.[55]

In addition, a major socio-legal study by Peay found that mental health tribunals in the United Kingdom frequently:

- Interpreted evidence in a way that ensured a more cautious or protective outcome;
- Lacked the impetus to seek additional information in order to properly address the need for continued detention;
- Gave inadequate weight to consultant clinicians who might be in disagreement with treating clinicians;
- Were conflicted between their role as an impartial, formal decision maker and the informal collation and presentation of evidence allowing for subjective and protective decisions based on flimsy evidence.[56]

Shah further poses that discontent with the tribunal system has been found at all levels including the medical profession who 'found the adversarial attitude of the legal representatives stressful and potentially detrimental to the doctor-patient relationship.'[57] Tribunal members expressed dissatisfaction with inadequate levels of training and the limited

---

54 A Shah, 'Is the Mental Health Review Tribunal Inherently Unfair to Patients?' (2010) 17(1) *Psychiatry, Psychology and Law* 25, 27.

55 Ibid 25–31.

56 Peay, above n 41, 209–218.

57 Shah, above n 54, 26.

powers of the MHRT to enforce its recommendations or make orders in relation to treatment. Many patients expressed significant levels of misunderstanding about the tribunal procedure and their rights within the process. More than half the patients surveyed could not understand the booklet explaining their rights under the system.[58]

Peay, while not advocating the abolition of tribunals in the UK, suggests that 'quality of the safeguards that tribunals represent undoubtedly depends both on the substance of the law and the abilities and inclinations of those who apply it.'[59] She argues the system could be improved by more structured and regular training for tribunal members especially in relation to the application of non-medical criteria; greater procedural regulation and guidelines particularly in relation to concepts of dangerousness; appropriate allocation of resources to provide real alternatives to compulsory impatient care; and greater powers for tribunals to carry through their recommendations.[60]

1.4.3. Treatment Reviews

Donnelley asserts that *treatment* reviews have been described as 'a high water mark of legalism' but the notion does not attract universal support.[61] When analysing the new experience of judicial review of treatment decisions in England, Wales and Ireland, on the basis of the formality and inflexibility of the legal process and the inability of patients to participate in the process, Donnelley concludes that 'for most involuntary patients, judicial review is simply not a realistic option'[62] and that 'judicial review falls short of providing an open, accessible, inclusive and trustworthy approach to decision-making.'[63]

The review of *treatment* decisions by mental health review tribunals in Victoria was incorporated into the legislation in 2003[64] with the rider that the tribunal could only approve a treatment plan that is 'capable of being implemented by the approved mental health service.'[65] This obviously places limits on the scope of treatment decisions made by tribunals and may even serve to negate the effect of review especially when the treating team's plan already incorporates the maximum options available under the system. Nonetheless, as Donnelly points out, when compared to judicial review 'the tribunal model provides a chance to escape the confines of legal formality and to craft a more accessible process.'[66]

While both the Tongan and Fijian legislation anticipate the review of treatment plans, the relevant provisions are rarely applied in Tonga and, in the few cases that have been reviewed in Fiji, existing treatment plans have been approved.

1.4.4. Second Opinion Appointed Doctors

The other review model examined by Donnelly is the option under the United Kingdom and Irish legislation for the second opinion of an appointed doctor (SOAD) for the review of treatment.[67] Patients' views of the SOAD have been mixed[68] and the courts, as demonstrated

58 Ibid 26.
59 Peay, above n 41, 230.
60 Ibid 231.
61 Donnelly, above n 15, 275.
62 Ibid 282–3.
63 Ibid 283.
64 *Mental Health Act 1986* (Vic) s 35A.
65 Ibid.
66 Donnelly, above n 15, 287.
67 Ibid 291.

in *R's* case, have taken a limited view of the role in only requiring the professional to satisfy the ordinary standards of medical care and ignoring any obligation to ensure the protection of the patient's human rights.[69] As Donnelly deduces, following the English Court of Appeal's decision in *R's* case, 'unless a person seeks judicial review [of treatment], English law provides no mechanism to protect his or her [European Convention on Human Rights] rights'[70] and while

> [r]eviews by judges and tribunals may be criticised for their excessive deference to medical professionals ... tribunal reviews would seem to have the greatest potential to provide a package which protects substantive rights, ensures the most appropriate treatment and provides an accessible, fair and participative process.[71]

This model has received support from other quarters including Carney.[72] However, regardless of the merits of this scheme, the critical shortage of mental health professionals in the Pacific could not currently support such an arrangement.

1.4.5. Single Member Tribunals

While conceding that 'hearings are a stressful experience for all concerned no matter how sensitive tribunal members may be to the needs of the participant' and that there might well be situations where 'a formal hearing may be therapeutically undesirable,' Rees argues that mental health review tribunals should continue to operate with multi member panels because lawyers, psychiatrists and community members each bring their own particular skills and insights to the decision making process.[73]

He recommends that, in more difficult circumstances, 'one member of the tribunal may speak with a patient away from the hearing room, but in the presence of a legal representative and clinical staff, and then report back to the other members of the tribunal.'[74] And in poorly resourced situations 'limited funds might be more wisely expended by the tribunal being comprised of one member in the first instance with the option to refer the case to a multi member tribunal if required by the circumstances of the case.'[75]

Rees also proposes that tribunals be given the power to issue legally binding guidelines to clarify complex statutory provisions and improve ready accessibility to the law for all participants in the process.[76] This would have the added benefit of providing more consistent decision making and a higher degree of consumer confidence in the overall process.

Samoa has, in effect, implemented this model by designating that all appeals under the Act be heard before a District Court judge.

---

68 Ibid 294.

69 *R (on the application of JB) v RMO, Dr Haddock* [2006] EWCA Civ 961.

70 Donnelly, above n 15, 292.

71 Ibid 294–5.

72 T Carney, 'Australian Mental Health Tribunals: 'Space' for Rights, Protection, Treatment and Governance?' (2012) 35(1) *International Journal of Law and Psychiatry* 1.

73 Rees, above n 4, 40.

74 Ibid.

75 Ibid.

76 Ibid.

1.4.6. Independence and Impartiality

Rees also asserts that to comply with the *MI Principles* a review must be 'external' and this means it

> must possess an appropriate degree of independence from the executive branch of government which employs, and ultimately directs, those people who make clinical decisions. It is highly questionable whether most mental health review tribunals have achieved an appropriate degree of independence. Whilst concerns about independence may be of little regard in most cases, from time to time mental health review tribunals are called upon to make decisions which are politically contentious and which have ramifications that extend far beyond individual involuntary patents.[77]

In the Lord High Chancellor's Special Report to the United Kingdom Parliament in 2000, the Council on Tribunals reiterated the need for independence and integrity of tribunals and, of equal importance, the perception of independence. The Report recommended that tribunals adopt the presidential model of tribunal organisation—the head being a member of the judiciary—to overcome the difficulties associated with regional tribunals and the equal status of regional chairpersons. This model was considered to promote a greater degree of judicial independence and separation from the sponsoring government department.[78] The Report further recommended that 'the tribunal hearing an application for variation of a compulsory order [for treatment and detention] should not have the same membership as the tribunal making the initial order.'[79] Furthermore, the Report 'opposed in principle the single member tribunals and the move towards paper based hearings' as working against the principle of natural justice and giving sufficient weight to issues concerning the deprivation of liberty. [80]

Other recommendations in this Report included the adoption of proper rules of procedure; high quality appointment of members; proper training for members; appropriate standards of judicial performance; and appropriate hearing facilities independent of the sponsoring health department.[81]

As has been demonstrated in previous chapters, independence and impartiality are serious challenges for the Pacific in the context of the review process. The shortage of mental health professionals almost guarantees that those involved as treating practitioners will be those acting as decision makers. As this is a problem without a short term solution, it means that access to justice for those seeking review under the legislation is equally constrained.

1.5. Consumers' Views

What do mental health consumers think of the tribunal style model?

Review hearings by the Mental Health Review Board in Victoria are conducted by a three member tribunal comprising a lawyer, a psychiatrist and a community representative. In a

---

77 Ibid 38.

78 Council on Tribunals, 'Special Report: Mental Health Review Tribunals' (2000) <www.council-on–tribunals.gov.uk/publications/184.htm (accessed 30 November 2010)>.

79 Ibid 11.

80 Ibid.

81 Ibid 4.

comprehensive review of consumers' experiences before the Board in Victoria,[82] the reported findings were principally negative and included comments such as:

> [I felt] disempowered, absolutely disempowered, hijacked and totally wilfully misrepresented.[83]
>
> it appeared to me that the hearings had a predetermined outcome… [the] decision was made before I had gone in. There was no testing of the evidence, there was no probing of the evidence, it was just whatever the psychiatrist said.[84]
>
> you open the door and walk in and all of a sudden you are in the hands of people asking you a heap of questions. [Then] they send you on your way, you know, you feel totally frustrated.[85]

Conversely, one legal representative commented that 'if the person feels they've been given an opportunity to be heard and understood during the course of the Board's hearing, that's probably the only opportunity they've had during their entire stay [in hospital].'[86]

Comprehensive recommendations by consumers and other stakeholders included recommendations on the following topics:

- the adversarial nature of Board proceedings;
- the tendency of the Board to accept without question the medical view;
- consumer participation in review hearings; consumers' access to information about the review process;
- consumers' level of understanding of their rights and the review process;
- consumers' access to medical files;
- hearing practices and procedures and interaction with consumers; legal or advocate representation;
- the role of community members;
- the availability of alternate psychiatric opinions; the timeliness of reviews;
- treatment plans; reasons for decisions; and
- the training of board members, mental health workers and advocates.[87]

While the report made voluminous proposals for improving the operation of the Board, in order to enhance consumer experience, it did not propose an alternative review model. Even so, the report did ask the question whether the existing structure was the best model for review.[88] This question was later considered in a study carried out over a four year period from 2005–2008 comparing the operation of mental health tribunals in New South Wales, Victoria and the Australian Capital Territory.[89] The report found that the Australian tribunals were unduly constrained by underfunding and by the absence of routine second medical opinions or the advocacy and legal representation schemes which are becoming the 'gold

---

82 Topp, Thomas and Ingvarson, above n 5.
83 Ibid 8.
84 Ibid 39.
85 Ibid 49.
86 Ibid 9.
87 Ibid 9–17.
88 Ibid 18.
89 Carney et al. above n 12.

standard internationally.'[90] Furthermore, the level of tribunal performance, leaving aside many of the operational difficulties, 'still falls short of what is expected under human rights principles.'[91] Even so, this later study was not a consumer based project and although there was considerable consumer consultation throughout the research, the final report was prepared by a panel of academics and professionals with a broader mandate than consumers' views.

Yet again, there was no recommendation that the tribunal model be abandoned.

An earlier study in Queensland in 2000, prior to the establishment of the MHRT and the implementation of the new *Mental Health Act*[92] in 2002, canvassed the views of mental health consumers. Consumers were concerned about the timeliness and quality of reviews and 'needed assurance that the decision of the tribunal would be clearly independent of the treating practitioner.'[93] They also expressed the need for hearings to be 'more accessible to consumer though creating an atmosphere that is less intimidating and more user friendly' and that they have access to legal representation, interpreters and advocates of their own 'culture or language group'.[94]

An extensive consumer study in New Zealand in 2005, surveying the attitudes of mental health consumers to CTOs, did not examine their views on the role of the review tribunals or consumers' ability to access justice.[95]

1.5.1. In the Pacific

There has been no analogous consumer research in the Pacific countries under discussion where a similar tribunal style model is in use—but there is no reason to believe that the Pacific consumer experience would be significantly different.

In the final analysis, it would appear that it is not the existence of a quasi-legal body as the preferred review mechanism that is the issue; it is its ability to operate impartially, independently, sensitively and with integrity when determining the most basic of human rights—individual liberty. There will always be consumers who find the least formal hearings intimidating and stressful, and those for whom the lack of formality deprives them of a sense of legal redress. Yet, on balance, it seems that the tribunal model remains the most effective solution for creating the perception and the actuality of fairness and justice—albeit not the perfect solution for all of the people all of the time. In the Pacific, however, the added complexity of appropriate cultural interaction needs to be considered.

1.6. The Rest versus the West

This leads us to the 'non Western' world—specifically, the Pacific.

Dawson contends that while compulsory treatment of the mentally ill by way of community treatment orders cuts across the edges of human rights concerns, especially in

90 Ibid 315.
91 Ibid 115.
92 *Mental Health Act 2000* (Qld).
93 Clair and Fisher, above n 12, 185.
94 Ibid.
95 A Gibbs et al. 'How Patients in New Zealand View Community Treatment Orders' (2005) 14(4) *Journal of Mental Health* 357.

jurisdictions with constitutionalised human rights provisions, it still provides a preferable alternative to institutionalised care.[96] He maintains, as is pertinent in the context of this work, that

> when mental health laws are designed, the structure and availability of the local psychiatric services must be taken into account so a proper fit can be established between those services and the local legal regime. If no comprehensive network of community based psychiatric services were available, for instance, that would prevent any effective use of a CTO regime.[97]

This, however, has not prevented many affluent countries from subscribing to the community care model without first assembling adequate supporting infrastructures and then forever struggling to catch up with increasing demands for services.

More developed countries, when assessing their rights based compliance, might ask 'have we done enough' or 'how far can we push this human rights barrow'. Bartlett poses that, in resource-poor countries, the question is more likely to be whether rights based legalism is even the solution.[98] This is certainly the case in some Pacific jurisdictions where resistance to human rights based initiatives is apparent. This feature is explored in more depth in Chapter 12. Bartlett stresses that any form of legalism on its own is not enough and that provision of infrastructure for services is required concurrently with legislative reform.[99] The same author also argues, in the context of Africa where 'legislative provision tends toward the rudimentary',[100] that law has value in its ability to 'create advocacy bodies … to foster development of the programmatic agenda … [and] to ensure that the relevant reforms do not slip off the political agenda.'[101] These sentiments apply equally to the Pacific. However, in Pacific island countries where vastly different cultural imperatives exist and resources at all levels—including trained health professionals—are seriously challenged, the support needed to ensure that rights based legalism works is unlikely to be available.

Is there an alternative? Bartlett contends that apart from abandoning the rule of law completely in relation to the rights of the mentally disabled and conceding that 'rights often do not exist in a meaningful way outside economically advantaged countries,'[102] law and culture needs to play a role in setting an appropriate standard of care and, ultimately, should involve some form of engagement with consumers—even though engagement without enforcement is worthless.[103] In the same way that Bartlett contends local culture may prove relevant in designing successful mental health programs in Africa,[104] so too should local culture be part of similar programs in the Pacific.

---

96 J Dawson, 'Community Treatment Orders and Human Rights' (2008) 26(2) *Law in Context, Special Issue: International Trends in Mental Health Laws* 148, 148.

97 Ibid 149.

98 P Bartlett, 'Thinking About the Rest of the World: Mental Health and Right Outside the First World' in B McSherry and P Weller (eds), *Rethinking Rights Based Mental Health Laws* (2010) 397; P Bartlett and V Hamzic, 'Reforming Mental Disability Law in Africa: Practical Tips and Suggestions' (Human Rights Law Centre, The University of Nottingham, 2010) 11.

99 Bartlett, above n 98, 397.

100 P Bartlett, R Jenkins and D Kilma, 'Mental Health Law in the Community: Thinking about Africa' (2011) 5(21) *International Journal of Mental Health Systems* 1 <www.ijmhs.com/content/5/1/21 (accessed 5 June 2013)>.

101 Ibid.

102 Bartlett, above n 98, 412.

103 Ibid 411.

104 Bartlett and Hamzic, above n 98, 13.

In the end, it simply comes down to 'do what you can do'—allow the richer countries to set the ideals to which others can aspire. If the best a country can achieve, within the confines of its socio-cultural and legal setting, is a lesser version of the optimum, then that must be better than nothing. There will always be varying levels of development and political commitment. As long as everyone is encouraged to improve as best they can within their means and development is seen as a work in progress, any progress must be viewed as positive. Those in the position of least advantage should not be made to feel lesser citizens or that they have failed. One size does not fit all—in relation to culture, religion, community, family, law, education, health, fiscal development or natural resources—and never will. This, however, assumes that countries are making genuine efforts within their means to advance the human rights of their citizens.

When attempting to measure whether Australian mental health legislation complied with international conventions and the UN Principles on human rights, the federal Attorney General's department developed a rights analysis instrument, which attributed numerical scores to sets of targeted questions and answers or indicators. This resulted in a compliance rating of 'substantial,' 'significant,' 'partial' or 'minimal'.[105] While this might be a useful threshold tool in the Pacific to benchmark legislation on its face, the reality on the ground is likely to be vastly different.

The instrument itself has not been without criticism. Rees asserts the *MI Principles* are not an effective measurement tool in view of some of the deficiencies in the instrument, specifically the focus on detention and treatment in institutional settings and the fact that 'the instrument seeks to measure quantitatively much that can only be measured qualitatively.'[106] Furthermore, Rees contends the *MI Principles* are interpreted in isolation from other mental health laws and there is inadequate explanation to support the ranking of rights used within the analysis document.[107] In any event, as the document predates the introduction of the CRPD, its value will be limited until such time as it is revised in the context of the CRPD.

A better instrument is the 'QualityRights Tool Kit' released by the WHO in 2012,[108] which aims to help countries assess and improve the quality of their mental health care facilities.[109] The Kit—designed to be used by a variety of organisations and government bodies—provides practical strategies for evaluating and benchmarking care and facilities against the CRPD, with particular reference to standards of living and health care; legal capacity and personal liberty; and freedom from cruel and degrading treatment.[110]

While not dealing directly with article 13 of the CRPD in terms of access to justice, the document sets a range of standards and criteria by which those standards can be measured in relation to involuntary detention, informed consent, the provision of information and access to medical records. The Kit suggests that appropriate benchmarking would be reached where people who are detained and treated without consent are informed about procedures for appealing their detention and treatment; are supported to access those procedures and legal representation; are provided with clear and comprehensive information about their rights and

105 H Watchirs and G Heesom, 'Report on Right Analysis Instrument for Use in Evaluating Mental Health Legislation' (Attorney General's Department, 1996).

106 Rees, above n 4, 36.

107 Ibid.

108 M Funk and N Drew, *WHO QualityRights Tool Kit: Assessing and Improving Quality and Human Rights in Mental Health and Social Care Facilities* (World Health Organisation, 2012).

109 Ibid 3.

110 Ibid 4–6.

treatment options; and are able to freely nominate support persons to assist with supported, rather than substituted decision making.[111] These, along with other criteria in the document, champion the underlying principles of the CRPD in promoting equality, respect and dignity for those with mental health disabilities.

How then does the Pacific fit into this rights based landscape? The answer is somewhat of a potpourri.

2. Reviewing Pathways to Justice in the Pacific

There are a number of critical factors that unlock the pathways to justice—thereby enabling mental health consumers to exercise their rights under mental health legislation and to access justice. Without effective operation and interaction of these factors justice is denied or hindered. These features involve the initial criteria for detention; the existence of the right to review of detention; the character of the review mechanism; the provision of *information* about the process; the right to *representation* during the process; and other dynamics and legal rights that facilitate a person's ability to *participate* in the review process. It is now opportune to examine each of these elements and how they present in the Pacific.

While the new regional provisions have many similarities, there is by no means a wholly consistent approach. Table 10.1 below sets out, in summary form, the extent to which the elements of justice under discussion existed under old legislation in the target countries and, by comparison, under the revised legislation. The table simply indicates whether the legislation addresses the matters listed—not whether, in practice, the factors did or do now exist.[112] Examples of brochures and printed materials provided by various mental health facilities can be found in Annexures 1-11.

Although there appear to be significant advances in most areas, the reality is a different issue. For example, while the legislation may incorporate a right to legal representation, appropriate counsel may not be available in a particular jurisdiction. Tonga appears to have the most comprehensive rights based legislative framework but little capacity for realisation. The absence of some rights in the Samoan statute may be more a reflection of the limited means of implementation, for example, the lack of a review body, the need for written decisions and the use of interpreters. The lack of a right of consumers to access their medical records is less easily explained.

The absence of certain rights in the Fiji Decree is of more concern. There is no right to representation before the MHRB by a family member or a carer. This means that the only representation allowed is by way of legal counsel which, given the number of experienced counsel prepared to act pro bono,[113] may be limiting. In addition, there are no requirements that MHRB hearings be heard within a reasonable timeframe, that written reasons be provided by the MHRB, or that the decisions of the MHRB be subject to appeal. The reasons for these

---

[111] Ibid 80–82.

[112] In the case of *information*, if the legislation did not require that people be provided with information but there is evidence information was provided, the column is indicated with an asterisk (*). Similarly, if the legislation provides for a particular right but it is doubtful the right can be realised in practice, the column is indicated with a question mark (?).

[113] The Legal Aid Commission in Fiji has yet to determine whether or not MHRB hearings will come within its guidelines.

omissions are unknown but they throw a dim light on the ability of mental health consumers in Fiji to effectively access justice under the Decree.

As there has been no reform to mental health legislation in Vanuatu, and the existing statute makes no reference to any of the features under discussion, Vanuatu will not be dealt with separately in the following paragraphs.

Table 10.1. Evaluation of the key elements of justice under old and new mental health legislation in the Pacific

ELEMENTS OF JUSTICE	TONGA			SAMOA		FIJI	
	1948	1992	2001	1961	2007	1940-1975	2010
INFORMATION							
Available	x	x	√	x	√	x *	√
Easy to read	x	x	√	x	x	x	√
Accurate	x	x	√	x	√	x	√
Multilingual	x	x	√	x	√	x	√
Culture sensitive	x	x	x	x	x	x	√
REPRESENTATION							
Available under the Act	x	x	√	x	√	x	√
Legal	x	x	√	x	√	x	√
Family/carers/others	x	x	√	x	√	x	x
Interpreters	x	x	√	x	x	x	√
PARTICIPATION							
Structured review mechanism	x	x	√	x	?	x	√
Right to periodic review	x	x	√	x	√	√	√
Right to review/appeal	x	√	√	√	√	√	√
Competent/impartial decision makers	x	√	√?	√	√	√	√
Access to medical records	x	x	√	x	x	x	√
Informal, uncomplicated hearings	x	x	√	x	√	x	√
Stress free environment	x	x	√	x	√	x	√?
Timely processes and responses	x	x	√	x	x √	x	x
Written reasons	x	x	√	x	x	x	x
Cost appropriate for consumers	x	x	x	x	√	x	√
Right of further appeal	x	√	√	√	√	x	x
Training for legal/mental health service providers	x	x	x	x	√	x	√

2.1. Criteria for Involuntary Detention

At a conceptual level under earlier legislation, all countries used the undefined term 'unsound mind.' All persons who fell within that term could be detained if they were 'at large' (for example in Fiji), or if they required care and protection for their own safety or the safety of others. In 1992, Tonga moved to the term 'mental disorder' which was defined so broadly as to incorporate any possible form of mental condition. Under these circumstances, a wide range of people could potentially be detained regardless of any actual illness or disability simply on the grounds of appearing to need care or accommodation or exhibiting 'unacceptable' behaviour.

Reformed legislation in Samoa and Fiji now includes mental illness in the definition of mental disorder, while Tonga does not. Tonga separates the definitions of mental disorder and mental illness, each with different criteria for detention. Fiji and Tonga define mental illness—Samoa does not. Fiji and Samoa, in seeming compliance with the *MI Principles*, exclude a range of beliefs and behaviours that do not constitute either a mental disorder or mental illness—Tonga does not. *Prima facie* it would seem easier to detain a person under mental health legislation in Tonga than either Fiji or Samoa.

Furthermore, Tonga does not appear to address the issue of personality disorders at all, leaving the scope for detention at a much broader level. Samoa separates 'antisocial personalities' from mental illness but makes no specific reference to personality disorders. Fiji, on the other hand, includes personality disorders in the definition of mental disorder but excludes 'antisocial behaviour.' This tends to point to a clear distinction between the concepts of behaviour and disorder, the application of which is unclear but possibly implied in the Samoan provisions.

Finally, while Tonga makes no specific reference to intellectual disability, the condition is clearly considered to be a mental disorder in Fiji—though not a mental illness. Samoa also excludes intellectual disability as a mental illness but makes no direct reference under the term mental disorder. Presumably, unless the person satisfied the remainder of the definition of mental disorder, being 'a medical condition that is characterized by a significant disturbance of thought, mood, perception or memory,'[114] the Act would not apply to an intellectually disabled person in Samoa.

The variations in definitions are intended to control who does and who does not meet the criteria for admission under involuntary status and, therefore, who is subject to treatment without consent. The broader the definition, the easier it is for people to be caught in the net and the greater the need for protective mechanisms. Some jurisdictions opt for separate legislation for persons with intellectual disabilities but this is not the case in the Pacific. On the other hand, narrower definitions, which define mental illness or mental disorder in medical terms, perpetuate the 'medical model' and potentially leave a class of persons without access to services in poorly resourced countries—itself an abuse of human rights.

Aside from satisfying the statutory definitions of mental illness or mental disorder, other criteria for detention in Tonga necessitate that the mental illness must require treatment that is available at the inpatient facility; the person is likely to cause imminent harm to himself or others or be likely to suffer serious mental or physical deterioration without detention and treatment; the person lacks capacity to give informed consent or has unreasonably refused treatment; and there is no less restrictive form of treatment available.[115]

In Samoa and Fiji, the person must be unwilling or unable to receive care, support, treatment or protection on a voluntary basis; and as a result of the mental disorder the person requires care, support, treatment or protection in his or her own interests or those of another person; and the care, support, treatment or protection required is available and cannot be provided in a less restrictive manner.[116]

---

[114] *Mental Health Act 2007* (Samoa) s 2.
[115] *Mental Health Act 2001* (Tonga) s 18.
[116] *Mental Health Act 2007* (Samoa) s 13; *Mental Health Decree 2010* (Fiji Islands) s 61.

2.1.1. Community Treatment Orders

Tonga, Samoa and Fiji all have legislative provisions allowing for compulsory mental health care and treatment in a community setting, requiring a person to comply with specific treatment and rehabilitation programs. Aside from the requirement to be treated in the least restrictive way, the criteria for detaining a person under an inpatient treatment order (ITO) are the same as for a community treatment order (CTO).[117] CTOs can only be made by the MHRT in Tonga.[118] A health care professional may make a CTO in Samoa, as can an authorised health care professional in Fiji but only after certification by a medical practitioner.[119]

Dawson argues that to place a person on a CTO may constitute a breach of human rights unless the person poses a serious threat or harm to themselves or others (essentially for preventive purposes)[120] —and therefore it is important who actually makes the order. The questions become to what extent any such breach can be justified, what if any protection applies, and the real effectiveness of CTOs. Dawson asserts that the rights most directly affected by CTOs are those relating to the 'negative liberty' interest or the right to be 'left alone' by community health care teams and to be free from interference in one's private life—including the right to refuse medical treatment.[121] Of course, this presupposes both the actual existence of community mental health care teams and with the capacity to 'interfere'—issues of particular significance in the Pacific.

So far CTOs have not been problematic in the Pacific—simply because relatively few are in use. The question for most jurisdictions, but much more so for the Pacific, is whether it is a greater breach of human rights to detain a person under an ITO with access to care and treatment than to transfer the person into the community where there are inadequate mental health support services. Fiji has only implemented a handful of CTOs under the Decree and none has yet come before the MHRB by way of periodic review or appeal. As there are no records available it is unknown whether the reviews have not occurred for administrative reasons, the CTOs had not reached their review dates or they had been cancelled prior to first the review date. While Samoa has focussed on community mental health care only small numbers of CTOs are utilised at any one time and none has been the subject of an appeal under the *Mental Health Act*. Following Dawson's human rights versus harm argument, there is also no indication as to how many of these CTOs in Samoa meet the 'harm' criteria—imminent or otherwise—especially as the legislation only refers to 'treatment or protection in his or her own *interests* or those of another person' rather than imminent harm.[122] On the other hand, Tonga's concentration on inpatient care has come about primarily because the country lacks the resources to establish community support services needed for the wider use of CTOs. Accurate data in relation to the numbers of CTOs in Tonga is not available but one

---

117 *Mental Health Act 2001* (Tonga) s 44; *Mental Health Act 2007* (Samoa) s 10; *Mental Health Decree 2010* (Fiji Islands) s 57(1).

118 *Mental Health Act 2001* (Tonga) s 45.

119 *Mental Health Act 2007* (Samoa) s 11; *Mental Health Decree 2010* (Fiji Islands) s 57(2).

120 J Dawson, 'Compulsory Outpatient Treatment and the Calculus of Human Rights' in B McSherry and P Weller (eds), *Rethinking Rights-Based Mental Health Laws* (Hart Publishing, 2010) 327, 328.

121 Ibid 329.

122 At least one CTO in Samoa in 2010 involved a 42 year old man convicted of grievous bodily harm who was sentenced to a two year suspended term of imprisonment on the condition that he submit to a CTO. See *Police v Auvailiili* [2010] WSSC 88.

respondent estimated that about 20 orders were made per year.[123] It is unclear whether this means 20 people or 20 orders, some of which may be renewals of existing orders. Due to the overcrowding in the inpatient mental health unit in Tonga, it is also unclear whether those who are 'home on trial leave'[124] at any one time are released on CTOs or simply discharged on a de facto equivalent by way of release 'on leave' under their ITO. Appeals to the MHRT in Tonga against CTOs are rare and successful appeals even rarer.

2.2. The Rights to Appeal and Review

The 1948 Act in Tonga provided no legal recourse for inpatients; but under the 1992 Act observation and treatment orders could be appealed to the Supreme Court or the Court of Appeal, respectively.[125] There is no evidence to suggest these provisions were ever used. Samoan legislation provided a right to apply to the Supreme Court to vary, cancel or review a court order for detention but, again, for reasons largely associated with delays and procedural complexity, these were not utilised. While there was a limited right to review under the old statute through the superior court system in Fiji, it was rarely, if ever, used.

Under amended legislation, all three countries now grant mental health consumers under involuntary detention the *right to review* or appeal the order for detention and all provide a *process* by which a mentally ill person can seek review of or appeal against his or her involuntary detention. Tonga and Fiji have both established statutory review tribunals largely based on overseas models and whose primary functions are to conduct periodic reviews of, and hear appeals from, persons detained involuntarily in an inpatient facility or the community.

2.3. The Review Mechanism

Previously, none of the countries under discussion had a discrete formal mechanism through which mental health consumers could seek review of their involuntary status.

2.3.1. Tonga

Tonga's MHRT has been operational since 2004 but seldom hears appeals against detention—the majority of hearings being periodic review of orders either within the initial seven days following admission or renewal after six months. Almost all initial review cases result in orders for continued detention but many patients are discharged prior to the six-month review period. All persons under detention orders in Tonga have the right to appeal against the order[126] but successful appeals are few and usually only occur where there is a treating doctor's recommendation or the person can be adequately supported in the community.[127]

---

[123] Loupua Sefokuli, Interview with Ilaivatu Mafi, Sister in Charge MHU (Tonga,13 June 2012).

[124] Ibid.

[125] *Mental Health Act 1992* (Tonga) ss 10(5), 11(5).

[126] *Mental Health Act 2001* (Tonga) ss 53, 140.

[127] Email questionnaire from Salesi Mafi, Senior Magistrate Tonga, to Helen Ménard,16 September 2011.

The challenge for Tonga, in terms of operating a watertight rights oriented review mechanism, is the dearth of medical practitioners with any psychiatric experience and the even more limited number of qualified legal personnel available to sit on the MHRT. This brings into question the impartiality of the process. The remaining quandary is whether a process that cannot guarantee impartiality, and hence fairness and justice, is better than no process at all. This work contends that it is. While not perfect, some faith must be placed in those individuals who administer the process and there is no evidence to suggest that this faith is misplaced.

2.3.2. Samoa

The Samoan Act, while not providing for periodic reviews, does afford a person the right to apply for review of an order to the District Court—albeit limited to one review per order and only with the Court's leave.[128] Samoa elected not to create a statutory body for the hearing of periodic reviews or appeals—presumably as a reflection of the non-availability of professional resources and the strong preference for community based care and treatment. There is no statutory process by which a person other than a mental health professional can conduct periodic reviews of inpatient or community based orders. All orders are either renewed after the required statutory intervals or the person is released from the order before it expires. In any event, it seems that, in practice these orders are used sparingly and inpatient orders are seldom renewed past the initial six week period.

The Act requires that 'the Court' consist of a District Court judge and a mental health care professional acting as 'advisor' to the Court. The Court can exercise all powers in relation to civil proceedings and is mandated to operate on a Western style natural justice model.[129] This presents a hybrid solution and is akin to the single member tribunal model—a legal or judicial member hearing the matter informally, at any suitable venue and with all powers in relation to civil proceedings, yet not constrained by the rules of evidence or legal technicalities.

Since the commencement of the Act in 2007, there has only been *one* such hearing before the Court. This involved an unsuccessful appeal against an ITO within the initial six week certification period. While there is no reason to suggest that a District Court judge would be anything less than competent and impartial in such a hearing, it is the infrequency of these hearings in Samoa that makes the objectivity of the decision maker less of an issue. There are, however, the concerns of sufficient consideration being afforded to clinical and social factors when employing a single legal decision maker.

2.3.3. Fiji

All persons subject to involuntary detention orders in Fiji have the right to review regardless of any periodic statutory review.[130] However, initial reviews are not required to be conducted inside three months of admission for an ITO or six months for a CTO. These time frames are not reflected in any other jurisdiction and could be seen to support administrative convenience rather than the recognition of human rights. Although Fiji has established a statutory MHRB, lack of resources and administrative commitment have meant it sits

[128] *Mental Health Act 2007* (Samoa) ss 20–21.
[129] Ibid s 22.
[130] *Mental Health Decree 2010* (Fiji Islands) s 98(1).

infrequently and, in the five years since the passing of the Decree, there have been no periodic reviews of CTOs, one appeal against detention under an ITO, three reviews of Presidential Orders and a small number of periodic reviews of ITOs.[131] It would seem too early to evaluate the effective operation of this body. However, in terms of its impartiality, the larger number of available mental health and legal professionals in Fiji means it may have a better chance of safeguarding the process, especially as a member of the MHRB who has treated a person must not take part in the review of an assessment or order.[132] The reality remains to be seen.

2.3.4. The Right to Higher Appeal

Under the superceded laws, as all orders for detention in Tonga and Samoa were made by the superior courts, although not expressly stated in the statutes, access to the appellate jurisdiction would have existed. While orders for detention were made by a magistrate in Fiji, the stated right of review to the Supreme Court—now the High Court—would itself have been appealable to the Court of Appeal.

Tonga now specifically provides for the appeal of MHRT decisions to the Supreme Court of Tonga.[133]

It is presumed—although not stated in the legislation—that any decision of the District Court of Samoa regarding mental health orders is appealable to the Supreme Court of Samoa.

One of the outstanding concerns in Fiji is the lack of any provision in the new Decree for any right to appeal a decision of the MHRB to a higher authority—despite a commitment under the Decree to 'respect of the rule of law and human rights in regard to mental health issues.'[134] The solution may lie in the general right of review by way of judicial review but this is often a complex process and presumes ready access to good legal representation.

2.4. Accessing the Review Process

In exploring the pathways to justice for mental health consumers in the Pacific, this study has looked at the nature of a person's right to review or appeal and the various review mechanisms available. It will now examine some of the preconditions critical for engaging the right to review and accessing those review mechanisms and hence accessing justice. These involve the provision of comprehensible information, advocate representation and effective participation in the review process.

2.4.1. Information

None of the earlier statutes in Tonga, Samoa or Fiji contained any requirements for the provision of information of any kind to mental health consumers. Despite this, it is evident that, in Fiji at least, some material was produced by the Ministry of Health about the services provided at St Giles Psychiatric Hospital and the general symptoms and treatment of mental illness.[135]

---

[131] Email questionnaire from IJ, Fiji, to Helen Ménard, 18 December 2015.

[132] *Mental Health Decree 2010* (Fiji Islands) s 100(1).

[133] *Mental Health Act 2001* (Tonga) s 141(1).

[134] *Mental Health Decree 2010* (Fiji Islands) s 4(2)(j).

[135] See, e.g., Annexures 8–11.

Current legislation in all three countries now requires that consumers be supplied with information regarding their rights under the various laws, including the right to apply for review and the right to representation in multilingual format (Samoa);[136] an explanation of rights under the Act in a comprehensible form (Tonga);[137] an explanation in 'a language, style and manner the person is readily able to understand' (orally or in writing) of the order and the reasons for the order, the person's rights generally including the right to review and the right to legal representation (Fiji).[138]

In Fiji the provision of information also extends to assessment procedures, treatment, treatment alternatives and the effects of treatment;[139] types and dosages of medication;[140] confidentiality and advance directives;[141] change of status; and the administration of ECT, psychosurgery or special medical treatment.[142]

Tonga provides separate written information in relation to the operation of the mental health unit and various forms of mental illness and their symptoms—both prepared by the resident psychiatrist Dr Puloka—and also a Tongan translation of ss 89-99 of the *Mental Health Act 2001* which relate to patients' rights and complaint mechanisms.[143] This information is only available in the Tongan language and is purportedly given to patients and their families on admission.[144]

The written information currently provided by the Ministry of Health in Samoa—while available in both English and Samoan—is minimal, only relates to the review process which is rarely utilised, is rather legalistic and simply uses the terminology of the Act.[145] Interview respondents suggest that more emphasis is placed on verbal information being given to mental health consumers.

It would seem that the Ministry in Fiji has yet to produce any new material covering consumer rights as required under the *Mental Health Decree 2010*.

2.4.2. Representation

Previous legislation in the region did not contain any right to any form of representation other than the fact that an application to the Supreme Court to review an inpatient order could be made by a relative in Tonga.[146]

The present-day situation is that all three countries allow for mental health consumers to be represented at review hearings by lawyers; or health professionals (Samoa); or family members, friends or other interested persons (Tonga).[147]

However, there are very few lawyers with mental health expertise in the region and most consumers do not seek legal representation. The evidence in Tonga suggests that less than 30 percent of hearings include representation for the patient and rarely does this involve legal

---

136 *Mental Health Act 2007* (Samoa) s 19; see also Annexures 4–7.
137 *Mental Health Act 2001* (Tonga) s 89; see also Annexure 1.
138 *Mental Health Decree 2010* (Fiji Islands) ss 34(j), 35(1), 44(1)–(3).
139 Ibid ss 34(g), 35.
140 Ibid s 43(1).
141 Ibid s 43(3)(c), (d).
142 Ibid s 45.
143 See Annexures 1–3.
144 Email questionnaire from Loupua Sefokuli, Lawyer Tonga, to Helen Ménard, 10 March 2012.
145 See Annexures 4–7.
146 *Mental Health Act 1992* (Tonga) ss 10(5), 11(5).
147 *Mental Health Act 2001* (Tonga) ss 3, 134.

representation.[148] The sole case to be heard in Samoa thus far did not involve consumer representation—legal or otherwise.

This means that advocacy, when it exists, will usually be by family members or carers where their representational motives may be ambivalent. There are limited community support groups in the region and none that currently actively fills this role.

The Psychiatric Survivors Association in Fiji—formed in 2004 as part of the Fiji Disabled Peoples Association—purports to advocate for 'the rights of people with mental illness and for government support' on what would appear to be a systemic basis.[149] In its Strategic Plan June 2011–June 2014, the association's stated objective in relation to advocacy is 'to provide specialist advocacy service ... to serve people with mental disorders throughout Fiji to include individual advocacy and advocacy on issues and concerns that affect all survivors.'[150] The action supporting the objective is stated as:

> Advocacy training to PSA members, volunteers and staff on CRPD mental health protections, complaints and review processes. Support to people with complaints and those appearing before the Mental Health Review Board. Liaise with Fiji legal aid to ensure representation before the Board and the courts for people on Presidential orders and action on complaints and abuse.[151]

This objective may well be overly ambitious and the extent to which the organisation will be able to provide representation before the newly formed MHRB in Fiji will undoubtedly be determined by its available resources. It is still uncertain whether legal aid services will be available for MHRB hearings in Fiji.

Goshen Trust Mental Health Services is a non-profit organisation in Samoa established with the support of the Samoan Ministry of Health. The Trust also conducts 'mental health advocacy training' but which is aimed primarily at diagnosing mental illness, developing care plans, and 'writing advocacy skills plan relevant to developing community awareness about stigmatisation in Samoa',[152] rather than individual advocacy.

It would seem, therefore, in the Pacific that if representation is to play a significant role in the future, support will need to be drawn from alternate options as suggested in other jurisdictions—the likes of trained lay advocates, an extended role for community visitors, and community support groups where they exist.[153]

The difficulty is that any scheme—even if it uses the services of volunteers—needs to be sufficiently funded to cover basic administrative costs and elementary training of its advocates. To provide effective representation at a review hearing, an advocate needs to have some understanding of the consumer's rights under the legislation and the application of the statute. Advocacy Tasmania was established as an NGO in Tasmania, Australia, in 1990 to provide advocacy services for people with disabilities, using the services of trained

---

148 Email questionnaire from Salesi Mafi, Senior Magistrate Tonga, to Helen Ménard,16 September 2011.

149 Psychiatric Survivors Association, <www.fdpa.org.fj/Psychiatric_Survivors_Association.aspx (accessed 3 April 2012)>.

150 Psychiatric Survivors Association, 'Strategic Plan June 2011–June 2014' (2011) 2.

151 Ibid 5.

152 Goshen Trust Mental Health Services Samoa, <www.sungo.ws/index.php?option=com_content&view=article&id=83&Itemid=156 (accessed 28 May 2012)>.

153 Carney, above n 27, 20.

volunteers.[154] The organisation provides a range of advocacy services for mental health consumers and, following a successful and innovative pilot project in 2003, now provides state wide free representation before the Mental Health Tribunal under the Mental Health Tribunal Representation Scheme.[155] The scheme utilises volunteers who are predominantly undergraduate or post graduate law students from the University of Tasmania who undergo a period of compulsory specialist training. The scheme aims to provide competent and free representation for those who choose to be represented and to improve mental health awareness and training for professionals new to mental health practice.[156] Nonetheless, the project does receive financial support from the state government to fund its activities, which undoubtedly costs the government less than if representation were provided under the Legal Aid scheme.

Such a scheme in the Pacific, it is argued, would struggle to attract adequate support to allow its effective operation. The only likely candidate for such an arrangement in the future might be Psychiatric Survivors Association in Fiji but this would depend entirely on funding—which it currently does not have—and its ability to adequately train volunteers.

2.4.3. Participation

There has been much discussion about the myriad of factors that best facilitate therapeutic jurisprudential outcomes in the environment of mental health law, and how best to maximise a mental health consumer's participation in the review process. For the purpose of this study, a number of key elements have been identified as being integral to accessing justice for these people in the context of periodic reviews of and appeals against involuntary detention.

The roles information and representation play in opening the pathways to justice in the region have already been examined. Some of the other features linked to the review process—which are critical in shaping the quality of a person's participation in the process—include access to medical records; the formality of the hearing process; the hearing environment; the timing of the process; the cost of the process; and the provision of written reasons for the decision.

None of the earlier legislation in any of the target countries addressed any of these factors.

The legislation in Samoa and Fiji specifically requires that the review body be bound by the rules of natural justice but neither jurisdiction requires that the body provide reasons for its decisions.[157] On the other hand, the Tongan statute requires that reasons for any decision be provided[158] but there is no duty on the review body to be bound by the rules of natural justice. Still, given the obligations of the review body under the Tongan legislation, procedural fairness may well be implied. While the question of whether the failure to provide reasons for a decision constitutes a breach of the rules of natural justice or procedural fairness

---

154 Advocacy Tasmania Inc, <www.advocacytasmania.org.au/mentalhealth.htm (accessed 11 April 2013)>.

155 Williams, above n 18, 111.

156 Ibid 118.

157 *Mental Health Act 2007* (Samoa) s 22(1)(c); *Mental Health Decree 2010* (Fiji Islands) s 100(6)(b).

158 *Mental Health Act 2001* (Tonga) s 132(k).

has not been the subject of judicial consideration in the Pacific, the *MI Principles* certainly include written reasons as part of its recommended procedural safeguards.[159]

In the absence of a statutory requirement to provide reasons, the common law position had been divided as to whether reasons constitute part of the right to a fair hearing.[160] Nonetheless, the High Court of Australia, in overturning a decision of the NSW Supreme Court, held that there was 'no rule of common law and no principle of natural justice' that required a tribunal to give reasons.[161] Even so, the High Court did acknowledge the case for change stating:

> [M]ost people would agree that it is desirable that bodies exercising discretionary powers ... should as a general rule give reasons for their decisions ... the giving of reasons is required by the ordinary man's sense of justice and is also a healthy discipline for all who exercise power over others.[162]

If ever there were grounds to make a case by way of exception, tribunals dealing with the most basic of human rights—personal liberty and medical treatment without consent—should be a case in point. In terms of *participation* in the review process and the promotion of access to justice for mental health consumers, the case is aptly stated by Forbes:

> Without reasons, how can a party be confident that the case was understood and properly considered? ... a person wishing to appeal is much better placed if a tribunal provides a clear statement of the facts found, the interferences drawn from them, its view of the law and the intellectual path to its decision.[163]

Of course this decision may well be distinguishable depending on the type of legislation in question,[164] and is not binding precedent in the Pacific.

The Act in Tonga now provides: for access to medical records;[165] for reviews to be conducted expeditiously and 'with little formality and technicality';[166] that reviews not be adjourned for more than seven days;[167] and that written statements for decision be provided within 21 days or three days if requested by the person or the person's representative.[168]

The actuality is somewhat different. According to respondents, all review hearings are held in private in a room at the mental health unit and the proceedings are not tape-recorded—as required under the Act. In ten years of operation, only two patients have asked for access to their medical records to assist at a hearing and none has sought access to the court files or asked for a tribunal decision in writing.[169] According to the President, the

---

159 Office of the High Commissioner for Human Rights, *Principles for the Protection of Persons with Mental Illness and the Improvement of Mental Health Care*, GA Res 46/119, (17 December 1991) [18.8].

160 J R S Forbes, *Justice in Tribunals* (Federation Press, 3rd ed, 2010) 250.

161 *Public Service Board of NSW v Osmond* (1986) 159 CLR 656, 662.

162 Ibid 668.

163 Forbes, above n 160, 249.

164 Ibid 252.

165 *Mental Health Act 2001* (Tonga) s 135.

166 Ibid s 133.

167 Ibid s 133.

168 Ibid s 132(k), (l).

169 Email questionnaire from Ma'afu Sefokuli, Court Clerk Tonga, to Helen Ménard, 20 June 2011.

MHRT's practice is not to give written reasons for its decisions but only to make orders in relation to continuing detention and treatment.

In Samoa the Act states that review hearings should be conducted 'in the least formal manner possible in the circumstances' and 'in any suitable place or venue'. There is no provision for the person to access his or her medical records, nor is the court required to provide written reasons for its decision, though it is bound by the rules of natural justice.[170] While there is a time limit for the court to hear the review of an inpatient order—within 14 days of leave being granted—there is no equivalent time limit for the review of a community treatment order.[171]

The sole review hearing, to date, in Samoa was heard within a few days of application and, even though it was held in the court precinct, the proceedings were conducted in a 'round table' informal arrangement. The judge, assisted by a mental health nurse, aided the unrepresented patient but it is unclear whether the patient had access to the medical file.[172] In this instance, while the court is bound by the rules of natural justice, there are clearly gaps in the legislation in terms of promoting the rights of the mental health consumer and his or her access to justice. Still, it is hard to see how natural justice can be met if a person appears before the court without having had an opportunity to review the material to be presented in relation to him or her.[173]

The Decree in Fiji allows a person to access his or her medical records[174] and requires that MHRB hearings be carried out 'in the least formal manner possible in the circumstances' and 'in any suitable place or venue' and that the Board act without regard to technicalities or legal forms.[175]

However, the composition of the MHRB by five members is not the best way to facilitate informality. In fact, the 2007 draft bill required the MHRB to comprise a *minimum of six* persons.[176] Assuming that the person under review is not represented but that at least one member of the treating team is present—probably two—this is a total of at least six—possibly seven—people in a room, all focused on the unwell and vulnerable consumer. Given the frequently negative experiences of consumers with tribunal style forums in other countries—where the models involve a *maximum of three* members—this has potential to be extremely intimidating and counterproductive for the person under review. One respondent argues that this is particularly so 'in the socio-cultural context that is Fiji.'[177] As discussed further in Chapter 11, this context is one that is strongly patriarchal and hierarchical in which identity is tied to the inherited chiefly system.[178]

There is no available information as to why this formulation was adopted in Fiji. There have been insufficient hearings to date to assess the situation, so how it will play out and whether specific measures will be employed to counterbalance the numbers and to ameliorate the potential for intimidation is unknown.

170 *Mental Health Act 2007* (Samoa) s 22.
171 Ibid ss 20–21.
172 Email questionnaire from Dr Ian Parkin, Psychiatrist Samoa, to Helen Ménard, 15 April 2011.
173 See, e.g., Topp, Thomas and Ingvarson, above n 5; Carney et al. above n 12; Peay, above n 41.
174 *Mental Health Decree 2010* (Fiji Islands) s 40(1).
175 Ibid s 100(6).
176 Consultation Draft, *Mental Health Bill 2007* (Fiji Islands) s 15(1).
177 Email questionnaire from XY, Fiji, to Helen Ménard, 19 July 2012.
178 P Imrana Jalal, 'Pacific Culture and Human Rights: Why Pacific Island Countries Should Ratify International Human Rights Treaties' (2006) <www.rrrt.org/images/pacificcultureandhumanrights.pdf (accessed 5 April 2013)> 5–6.

Moreover, in the face of a stated commitment to 'respect of the rule of law and human rights in regard to mental health issues',[179] and to pay due regard to 'international agreements and standards concerning the care and treatment of the mentally disordered,'[180] there is no provision for any application for review of involuntary detention to be heard within a given time frame; no requirement that records of MHRB hearings be kept or that written or oral reasons for decisions be supplied; nor is there any right to appeal a decision of the MHRB to a higher jurisdiction.[181]

As the model has yet to become effectively operational in Fiji, it may be premature to predict a result. Still it is difficult not to be skeptical. For all the stated objectives, principles and responsibilities in relation to the delivery of optimum mental health care services; the promotion of rights of self-determination; the elimination of stigma and discrimination against the mentally ill; and commitments to international human rights instruments—all *as far as practicable and subject to available resources*—the unexplained omission of some of the more fundamental conditions necessary to access justice is difficult to justify.

The *Mental Health Bill 2007* (Fiji Islands)—a consultation draft prepared by the FLRC—was released for comment in 2006. The country subsequently underwent a major political crisis involving a military coup d'état in December 2006, and Fiji's constitution was eventually abrogated in 2009. The FLRC was dissolved and non-essential legislative reform dissipated. Over time and under international pressure to return to democracy, the law reform process was reactivated and resulted in the emergence of the *Mental Health Decree* in 2010. None of the rights relating to access to records; privacy; confidentiality; timeframes for hearings; written reasons; or the right to appeal a decision of the MHRB appeared in the draft bill. Some attention must therefore have been given to including those rights that *did* emerge in the ultimate Decree in 2010.

Was a conscious decision made to exclude the missing rights or was it drafting oversight under pressure of time? One respondent suggests that the excluded provisions might have been an oversight under pressure rather than a deliberate strategy.[182] The answer is not readily apparent but may lie in another respondent's observations that the interim regime's decision to implement overdue legislative reform regarding mental health was carried out with little or no public consultation and without the implementation of any plans or infrastructure necessary to facilitate its operation.[183] Another respondent comments:

> at the time (early 2006), I was a member of an Advisory Panel tasked to comment on proposed changes. The issues you refer to were raised in discussion with the two [overseas] consultants engaged to redraft and/or completely rewrite the legislation. At that time the view expressed by the two consultants was that the existing legislation was beyond amendment and repair and that a completely new Act was required. However, as you mention, as a consequence of the military coup in late 2006, non-essential legislative reform slipped off the agenda.

---

179 *Mental Health Decree 2010* (Fiji Islands) s 4(2)(j).

180 Ibid s 4(1)(b).

181 All of these provisions are covered under Office of the High Commissioner for Human Rights, *Principles for the Protection of Persons with Mental Illness and the Improvement of Mental Health Care*, GA Res 46/119, (17 December 1991) [18].

182 Email questionnaire from XY, Fiji, to Helen Ménard, 19 July 2012.

183 Email questionnaire from AB, Fiji, to Helen Ménard, 22 March 2012.

> Although during 2008 I made inquiries as to what was occurring with the MH legislation, no-one I spoke to seemed to know. Nothing occurred as far as I am aware until a draft of proposed legislation emerged late 2009/early in 2010 for 'community comment.' At that time I ... did not read the draft ... I am unable to say what comments were made at that time. [184]

Finally, while there is no mention of procedural costs in the Tongan Act, Samoa relieves any party of bearing costs of an application[185] and Fiji states that the cost of any review application must *not* be borne by the patient or the patient's parent or primary carer.[186]

3. Conclusion

This chapter has explored access to justice under mental health legislation for mental health consumers, both within and outside the Pacific region. In examining each of the features central to accessing justice—information, representation and participation—it is apparent that a significant void lies between the written law in the Pacific and its application. The question is whether the void can be filled.

In drafting any legislation in the Pacific, an overriding challenge is the ability to realise objectives in a poorly resourced environment. The challenge is whether broadly drafted legislation with little foreseeable prospect of implementation—as may be the case in Tonga and Fiji—is preferable to a less ambitious model that simply reflects contemporary reality—as may be the case in Samoa.

Tonga has the most comprehensive raft of rights in its revised legislation without any qualification in the Act that the exercise of these rights is subject to available resources or practicality. Even so, resources of every kind are acutely limited and consequently many of the provisions are not utilised. The MHRT in Tonga is based on the multi-member tribunal model which appears to operate within the statutory boundaries but its impartiality may be compromised by the critical shortage of legal and mental health professionals. On the other hand, while its discharge rates on review are very low they are not significantly different to those in jurisdictions without similar resource restrictions. The best information available suggests that the MHRT conducts approximately 150 hearings per year, of which at most ten percent are appeals. Few are successful. On balance, the process appears to be working as best as it can given the existing constraints, but most respondents agree the current state of affairs is far from ideal. Nevertheless, some pathway to justice is better than none at all.

Statutory reform in *Samoa* was driven by an overriding commitment to community based care and treatment. While still providing a statutory framework aimed at protecting the rights of mental health consumers, it is a model that anticipates minimal interaction with formal legal systems. Samoa does not provide for external or independent periodic review of detention orders and opted for a single member review body operating on a natural justice model but located within the judicial system. With only one hearing to its record in the history of its operation, any assessment of the effectiveness or appropriateness of this forum

---

184 Email questionnaire from XY, Fiji, to Helen Ménard, 19 July 2012.
185 *Mental Health Act 2007* (Samoa) s 31.
186 *Mental Health Decree 2010* (Fiji Islands) s 99(2).

seems meaningless. There are some gaps in the legislative suite of rights but, given the infrequent use of compulsory detention orders and the even less frequent appeals against them, the impact of these shortcomings may be marginal. Even so, the question stands to be answered—if only one or two people access the process, is that good reason to compromise the quality of the product? The answer must be no.

Fiji has also adopted the multi-member tribunal model, which has yet to be really tested in its legislative form. The structure and functions of the MHRB appear to have many of the features of impartiality and independence and, while there is a shortage of mental health professionals in Fiji relative to developed countries in the Pacific Rim, there may be a better prospect of procedural independence than in Tonga. Unfortunately, there are no reliable statistics in Fiji regarding the number of registered mental health consumers or those subject to current inpatient orders. However, if the use of CTO's significantly increases the number of orders in existence, the ability of the MHRB to accommodate all the statutory reviews and appeals in an independent and impartial manner may be undermined. Even so, unlike Tonga, the initial mandatory review in Fiji Islands is after three months for inpatient orders and six months for community orders; hence it might be that many patients will have been discharged from those orders before the initial review arises and will never be subject to external review.

However the Pacific is not alone in this regard. In 1993, Victoria increased the time for initial reviews of inpatient orders from four to eight weeks by which time Rees contends that most people have been discharged from hospital.[187] He suggests that 'interference with busy clinical schedules and costs' were part of the motivation for reform[188] yet the Victorian situation provides a stark contrast with New South Wales where all inpatient orders must be reviewed by an external body within seven days.[189]

As with Samoa, the legislative rights platform in Fiji is missing some key features with reference to the review process. The reasons for these omissions are unclear. However, the country has included many other rights based provisions that do not appear in either Tonga or Samoa—for example, those pertaining to advance directives, confidentiality, information about medication and various forms of treatment, and the prohibition of certain types of treatment. Fiji's ability or motivation to deliver on its promises is unproven—its enthusiasm to date is not evident and, with the overarching rider in the Decree—*as far as practicable and subject to available resources*—there may frequently be other priorities.

In the end, the best that can be said is that without mental health legislation there will be no motivation at all to address the issues. If rights based legislation can create some avenues for securing better services and access to justice for mental health consumers, then that represents its value. Ultimately, statutory objectives for optimum mental health care and human rights should be viewed as goals to be achieved over time. The inability to deliver the optimum immediately should not be seen as a reason to restrict the rights and protections under the legislation or as a failure on the part of current day service providers.

---

187 N Rees, 'Learning from the Past, Looking to the Future: Is Victorian Mental Health Law Ripe for Reform?' (2009) 16(1) *Psychiatry, Psychology and Law* 69, 82.

188 Ibid 83.

189 Ibid 82.

Chapter 11

IMPEDIMENTS TO ACCESSING JUSTICE THROUGH MENTAL HEALTH LAW REFORM — SOCIETY AND CULTURE

A number of factors have hampered the development and implementation of mental health legislation and policy throughout the region. It is problematic to attempt to rank the importance of these issues—they interact in different jurisdictions in different ways. In essence, underlying cultural views on mental health and human rights principles, combined with inadequate financial and professional resources, culminate in reduced political motivation to elevate mental health policy and services on the domestic agenda. This, in turn, hinders the realisation of human rights based principles underpinning reformed mental health legislation in the region and, in the end, access to justice for mental health consumers.

This chapter explores the socio-cultural notions that play the most significant roles in impeding access to justice under rights based mental health legislation and policy in the Pacific. Issues in relation to human rights and economic policy and professional resources will be discussed in the following chapters.

1. INTRODUCTION

An international survey conducted by the WHO in low and middle income countries, involving experts in government, civil society, mental health consultancies and academia, attempted to identify barriers to the implementation of existing mental health knowledge into mental health services.[1] The survey confirmed that, regardless of the nature of the agencies involved, 'mental health is typically low on the agenda in most Ministries of Health.'[2] This was most commonly attributed to the lack of funding priority even from major international donors; inadequately coordinated mental health policy and advocacy plans; poor mental health leadership and shortages of professional resources; and widespread low levels of awareness of mental health issues at all levels of government and across the community.[3]

---

1 World Health Organisation, 'Expert Opinion on Barriers and Facilitating Factors for the Implementation of Existing Mental Health Knowledge in Mental Health Services' (2007).

2 Ibid 48.

3 Ibid 6–7.

By way of illustration of the lack of political standing of mental health in the region, the Pacific Islands Ministers of Health meeting in Tonga in March 2003—the fifth since its inception in 1995—included mental health on its agenda for the *first* time.[4] Its eventual inclusion most probably occurred as a result of the impact of the WHO Regional Strategy for Mental Health in 2002. However, despite a unanimous decision at the 2003 meeting to prioritise national mental health agendas, mental health did not rate a mention in the eighth meeting of health ministers in Papua New Guinea in 2009.[5] On a more positive note, subsequent meetings in Solomon Islands in 2011 and Samoa in 2013, while acknowledging the limited progress in mental health in the Pacific and existing barriers, placed the issue at the forefront of emerging health issues to be given priority.[6]

Furthermore, poor levels of education within the region compound the proper understanding of the aetiology of mental illness and different methods of treatment. Traditional healers, who often play a major role in health delivery in the region, have widely variant views to western-trained psychiatric personnel concerning the causation, diagnosis and treatment of mental illness. This restricts the way in which communities are able to respond to the mental health needs of their members.

2. LITERATURE

While it is important to discuss the roles of Pacific society and culture in mental health in order to understand the socio-demographics of mental illness in the region, this context does not permit an in depth exposition of the interaction of these factors in mental illness. Similarly, this is not primarily sociological research and any review of this category of literature must be viewed within that context. Nonetheless, a wider-ranging literature review of socio-cultural and health issues surrounding mental health in the Pacific has been undertaken in an attempt to understand the concept of mental health within its appropriate cultural setting. From that base, it is argued that cultural imperatives should play a significant role in determining the most suitable and effective *legal* framework in which to place issues arising from mental health law.

2.1. Overview

Although much has been written on health generally in the Pacific—including the interrelationship between traditional healing and Western style medicine—the greater part of academic literature on *mental health* in the Pacific has only emerged since 2005. An early

4 G Roberts, M Cruz and E S Puamau, 'A Proposed Future for the Care, Treatment and Rehabilitation of Mentally Ill People in Fiji' (2007) 14(2) *Health Promotion in the Pacific* 107.

5 World Health Organisation and Secretariat of the Pacific Community, 'Eighth Meeting of Ministers of Health for Pacific Island Countries' (2010).

6 World Health Organisation and Secretariat of the Pacific Community, 'Ninth Meeting of Ministers of Health for the Pacific Island Countries,' (July 2011) <http://www.wpro.who.int/southpacific/pic_meeting/reports/honiarareport.pdf?ua=1 (accessed 7 September 2015)>; World Health Organisation and Secretariat of the Pacific Community, 'Apia Outcome Tenth Pacific Health Ministers Meeting,' (July 2013) <http://www.wpro.who.int/southpacific/pic_meeting/reports/apia_outcomefull3.pdf?ua=1 (acessed 7 September 2015)>

exception was the *Pacific Health Dialog—Journal of Community Health and Clinical Medicine for the Pacific*—which carried a short article on suicide in its first issue in 1994.[7]

Two regions of the Pacific—Papua New Guinea and Micronesia—appear to be an exception to this rule. In Papua New Guinea studies on the epidemiology of mental illness and transcultural psychiatry in preliterate societies appeared as early as the 1960s.[8] Most of the studies in Micronesia, which appeared in the 1980s, examined the incidence of adolescent suicide within selected communities.[9]

There have also been a number of studies on suicide in the wider region dating back to the 1980s.[10] Despite the fact that suicidal ideation may be a feature of some forms of mental illness, it is by no means definitive of mental illness and commonly exists outside the mentally ill population. As such, the aetiology and incidence of suicide within the region will not be the focus of this research. It is a complex area of study in itself and is not central to the question of access to justice.

The earliest comprehensive study of the prevalence and aetiology of mental illness in the Pacific appears to have been carried out in the late 1970s by Murphy—a Canadian Professor of psychiatry attached by way of consultancy to the South Pacific Commission (now the Secretariat of the Pacific Community) in New Caledonia.[11] There appears to have been no work of equivalent scope since. The research project covered 13 territories including Fiji, Tonga, Western Samoa (now Samoa) and the New Hebrides (now Vanuatu) over a six month period. It was motivated by the fact that 'around 1964 it was recognised by those governing the SPC that as island societies became more technologically developed, their mental health problems were likely to increase, approaching the considerably higher level found in countries on which they were tending to model themselves.'

The author remarked that in 1977 'it was decided to take a further look at the subject, particularly with the view to assessing what problems might arise and what resources might be exploitable over the next ten years.'[12]

Prior to this period Murphy observed that:

> In the medical services of the territories covered by the South Pacific Commission, mental health has traditionally received low priority. That low priority was justified, since mental health was generally good, there were many other health problems with greater social impact and psychiatric care is a complex matter rarely yielding quick results. The care of the mentally ill was thus left to the patients' own families and to traditional

---

7 F Hezel, 'What Can We Do to Prevent Suicide in the Pacific?' (1994) 1(1) *Pacific Health Dialog* 59.

8 See, e.g., B Ross, 'Mental Health in Papua New Guinea' (1965) 1 *Medical Journal of Australia* 478; BG Burton-Bradley, 'Papua and New Guinea Transcultural Psychiatry: The First One Thousand Referrals' (1969) 3 *Australian and New Zealand Journal of Psychiatry* 383.

9 See, e.g., DH Rubenstein, 'An Investigative Study of Adolescent Suicides in Micronesia' (1982) 15 *Pacific Health* 2; FX Hezel, 'Cultural Patterns in Trukese Suicide' (1984) 23 *Ethnology* 193.

10 See P Vivili, S Finau and E Finau, 'Suicide in Tonga, 1982-1997' (1999) 6(2) *Pacific Health Dialog* 211; J Tiatia, 'Young Pacifican Suicide Attempts: A Review of Emergency Department Medical Records, Auckland, New Zealand' (2001) 8(1) *Pacific Health Dialog* 124; T Bourke, 'Suicide in Samoa' (2001) 8(1) *Pacific Health Dialog* 213; RH Haynes, 'Suicide in Fiji: A Preliminary Study' (1984) 145 *British Journal of Psychiatry* 433; RH Haynes, 'Suicide and Social Response in Fiji: A Historical Survey' (1987) 151 *British Journal of Psychiatry* 21; G Roberts et al. 'Attempted Suicide in Western Viti Levu, Fiji' (2007) 14(2) *Health Promotion in the Pacific* 29.

11 HBM Murphy, *Mental Health Trends in the Pacific Islands: A Report on a Tour of Pacific Territories* (South Pacific Commission, 1978), 8.

12 Ibid 1.

healers, with only the most socially disruptive being hospitalised, and in the whole Pacific region very few medical personnel were given any special training in this work.[13]

While the project was forward-looking in its objectives and utilised both quantitative and qualitative methodology, very little of the raw data gathered by the researcher formed part of the report—with the exception of some admission statistics[14]—the author preferring to draw generalised conclusions from the data. This makes any independent assessment of the weight of such information difficult. Interviews were conducted across a broad spectrum of community members and visits made to a wide selection of locations including urban and remote island villages. Even with the logistical difficulties at the time—not the least of which must include restricted travel options and technology together with limited hard data and poor record keeping—the results are undeniably of historical significance. The contents of this report are discussed in more detail later in this chapter.

At a more general level, a number of writers have observed the interface between culture and spirituality and mental health in the Pacific. Mila-Schaaf and Hudson's 2009 theoretical paper introduces the concept of the 'negotiated space' as the intersection between Pacific indigenous references and the dominant Western mental health paradigm of the bio-psycho-social. The 'negotiated space' allows the exploration of relationships between different, and often conflicting, understandings of mental health and illness.[15] In searching for culturally appropriate models of care and rejecting the notion that acculturation '[implies] one-way traffic from indigenous to Western',[16] the authors propose that intercultural negotiations enable cultural innovation which promotes individual as well as community identities.[17]

The authors theorise about *va*—a Pacific concept that refers to 'space that relates' between people guided by principles of balance, reciprocity and respect—and the fact that it 'provides a larger landscape of different ways of tending, resolving, negotiating and mediating a *relationship* between cultures and knowledge traditions.'[18] However, they do not suggest ways to implement the theory in a practical setting. While proposing that those with different cultures and knowledge need to share and understand each other's experiences and that effective health care models need to be diverse and innovative, the discussion stops short of developing any practical recommendations that might have any implications for mental health care.

Samu and Suaalii-Sauni looked at attributes—'cultural competencies'—that enable systems and individuals to respond respectfully to all peoples' cultural needs. The authors maintain that in mental health, Pacific cultural competencies are a blend of ethnic, cultural and clinical beliefs and practices. The New Zealand study explored five key themes (language, family, *tapu* relationships, skill and organisation policy) through workshop discussions with a combination of mental health service providers, mental health consumers, family members and community representatives from five selected migrant communities—

---

13 Ibid 1.

14 Ibid 4–5.

15 K Mila-Schaaf and M Hudson, 'The Interface Between Cultural Understandings: Negotiating New Spaces for Pacific Mental Health' (2009) 15(1) *Pacific Health Dialog* 113.

16 Ibid 117.

17 Ibid 118.

18 Ibid 116.

Cook Islands, Niue, Samoa, Tonga and Fiji.[19] In recognising that mental health services in New Zealand focus on the medical model, it was anticipated that the findings would increase awareness and sensitivity in relation to the impact of culture and lead to the creation of more culturally appropriate services.[20]

In another study, Suaalii-Sauni et al. sought to obtain in depth qualitative data on Pacific perceptions and experience of the theory, practice and utilisation of Pacific mental health services in New Zealand. Their findings indicated that among other things 'access to culturally competent health staff contributes towards consumer recovery and assisting families.'[21]

2.2. Tonga

One of the earliest studies of significance was that of Murphy who used Tonga to explore Tuke's nineteenth century theory that mental disorder was rare in stable, traditional, rural societies.[22] While conceding that more research was warranted regarding the 'social mechanisms that protect mental health in some societies,'[23] Murphy concluded that Tongans—as a result of their more traditional and communal lifestyles—experienced lower rates of serious mental illness when compared with more individualistic and competitive societies such as Australia.[24] The implications of this study are discussed later in this chapter.

Occasional articles on traditional medicine and mental health appeared in Tonga in the 1990s, including a paper by Puloka who describes the different types of *'avanga'*—a psychiatric condition believed to be caused by spirits. He defines their folk explanations, physical symptoms and precipitating factors, relating them as far as possible to psychiatric disorders. Puloka maintains some types of *avanga* are best treated by folk healers and others warrant medical and psychiatric assessment and treatment. He describes the plants used by traditional healers and asserts traditional and modern approaches to mental health must work together to produce a service relevant to Tonga.[25]

Foliaki examined the effects of migration on the mental health of Tongans, suggesting that social support and cultural integration, rather than acculturation, are protective factors for Tongans migrating to other communities.[26]

In a qualitative study in 2001, Toafa et al. investigated the role of traditional Tongan healers in New Zealand by conducting in depth interviews with 29 adult healers working within Tongan communities in New Zealand.[27] The results found that the use of traditional

---

19 K Seataoai Samu and T Suaalii-Sauni, 'Exploring the 'Cultural' in Cultural Competencies in Pacific Mental Health' (2009) 15(1) *Pacific Health Dialog* 120.

20 Ibid 120–130, 124.

21 T Suaalii-Sauni et al. 'Exploration of Pacific Perspectives of Pacific Models of Mental Health Service Delivery in New Zealand' (2009) 15(1) *Pacific Health Dialog* 18.

22 H Murphy and B Taumoepeau, 'Traditionalism and Mental Health in the South Pacific: A Re-examination of an Old Hypothesis' (1980) 10 *Psychological Medicine* 471.

23 Ibid 482.

24 Ibid 480.

25 See M Puloka, 'A Commonsense Perspective on Tongan Folk Healing' (1997) 2 *Int J Ment Health Nurs* 69.

26 See S Foliaki, 'Migration and Mental Health: The Tongan Experience' (1997) 26(3) *International Journal of Mental Health* 36.

27 V Toafa, R Moata'ane and B Guthrie, 'Traditional Tongan Medicine and the Role of Traditional Tongan Healers in New Zealand' (2001) 8 *Pacific Health Dialog* 78,79.

medicine by Tongans living in New Zealand was widespread and the aliments treated were similar to those of Tongans in their home country.[28] There was no universally accepted system of classification of healers or the ailments they treated,[29] but the efficacy of healing was seen more as being connected to the individual healer than the treatment used.[30] Healers expressed concern about the lack of understanding of their role by the Western health system and the need for an increased understanding of the cultural basis of health care.[31]

In a later study, Vaka et al. explored the mental health related beliefs and practices of Tongan traditional healers and Tongan workers in the Western style mental health services and found that both groups use very different explanatory models and treatment methods.[32] The authors discussed the connection between culture based and Western style concepts of illness and concluded that Tongan traditional healers—who had a rather negative view of the Western style system—attributed mental health problems to spiritual or social causes rather than physical illness.[33] By contrast, Western trained staff were generally more accepting of traditional healing and incorporated aspects of Tongan culture into their practices.[34] This qualitative study involved equal numbers of traditional healers and medical staff from the mental health unit—eight in each group—who were subject to semi-structured interviews in Tongan over several hours.[35] Although fewer people were interviewed by Vaka than in Toafa's earlier study, the information elicited by Vaka and the fact that all respondents were in practice in Tonga, could be seen to have more significance and practical application within the Tongan community.

Vaka, however, did find that the approach of traditional healers in Tonga was less inclusive of biological and Western perspectives than their Samoan counterparts.[36]

2.3. Samoa

Apart from Murphy's previously mentioned study of the Pacific, early writings on mental health in Samoa are uncommon. Allen noted that 'published studies on major mental illness in Samoa seem to be rare which is unfortunate given that much work has been done in other areas [public health, migration] that would allow such research to be put into a proper cultural context' and 'unlike other Pacific communities, Samoan ethno-medical practices and beliefs have been researched in some detail.'[37] Furthermore, the bulk of the later literature on Samoan mental health tends to focus on the experiences of Samoan populations in New Zealand rather than in their home country, which raises a different set of issues.

Cluny and La'avasa Macpherson's lengthy sociological dissertation on medical belief and practice in Samoa deals with a range of concepts, including the interaction between illness,

28 Ibid 81.

29 Ibid.

30 Ibid 80.

31 Ibid 81.

32 V Sione et al. 'Walking Apart Towards the Same Goal? The View and Practices of Tongan Traditional Healers and Western Trained Tongan Mental Health Staff' (2009) 15(1) *Pacific Health Dialog* 89.

33 Ibid 90–91.

34 Ibid 92.

35 Ibid 91.

36 Ibid 93.

37 J Allen and J Laycock, 'Major Mental Illness in the Pacific: A Review' (1997) 4(2) *Pacific Health Dialog* 105, 112.

culture and society; the historical development of indigenous Samoan medicine; the role of traditional healers; beliefs about health, illness and the human body; and the co-existence and relationship between indigenous and introduced health systems.[38] They argue a strong and inextricable connection between illness, society and culture and that a 'failure to appreciate the importance of indigenous belief and practice lies behind the limited success of various Western health interventions in the Third World.'[39]

In recognising that each process had its limitations, in this research the authors combined the anthropological case study method and random sampling survey methodology. They gathered data from a variety of sources but primarily from a group of 22 selected traditional healers consisting of twelve women and ten men aged from 30-93 years. Their education levels ranged from none to completed secondary school and some paramedical training; they trained in rural and peri-urban areas and were from a mixture of Christian based religious denominations.[40] Interviews ranged from formal to observation of medical consultations and informal discussions; covered training, belief and practice; and all were tape recorded.

As with some other studies, none of the raw data gathered by the researchers formed part of the final paper, even though excerpts from interviews and clinical observations were peppered throughout the text to support particular arguments. Although the work deals in depth with each part of the body in terms of the interaction between belief, culture, illness, diagnosis and treatment, only scant reference is made to mental illness or psychological conditions—even though the Samoan psyche is an integral component of the diagnosis and treatment of any physical condition. Nonetheless, the breadth of this work renders it highly significant within its sphere of learning.

In 2005 Tamasese et al—in what appears to be the first research of its kind—authored a paper outlining their findings after setting out to develop a culturally appropriate research method designed to investigate Samoan perspectives on mental health issues. The writers also aimed to apply these values to the care and treatment of Samoans with mental health problems.[41] The culturally derived method—referred to as *Fa'afaletui*—used gender specific focus groups consisting of Samoan elders and service providers—44 participants in total—facilitated by Samoan researchers in the Samoan language. Systematic analysis of transcripts, adapted to the cultural context, were conducted in Samoan and later translated into English.

The Samoan 'self' was identified as an essential concept for understanding Samoan views on mental health and participants identified the need for a culturally based mental health service for Samoans to address key cultural factors.[42] The study concluded that *Fa'afaletui,* as a new research method, was methodologically rigorous while at the same time sensitive and responsive to Samoan cultural norms. The Samoan concept of self provides a theoretical foundation for understanding mental health needs of Samoans and a basis for developing appropriate services.[43] Even though this study was conducted within the Samoan population in New Zealand, the findings are original and are probably applicable within any Samoan setting, especially as the authors found that 'research methods traditionally used in the mental

---

38 C Macpherson and L Macpherson, *Samoan Medical Belief and Practice* (University of Hawai'i Press, 1990).

39 Ibid 4.

40 Ibid 11.

41 K Tamasese et al. 'Ole Taiao Afua, the New Morning: A Qualitative Investigation into Samoan Perspectives on Mental Health and Culturally Appropriate Services' (2005) 39 *Australian and New Zealand Journal of Psychiatry* 300.

42 Ibid 300.

43 Ibid 300.

health field have not been well accepted by Pacific Island groups.'[44] The significance of this research is discussed later in this chapter.

Lui in a paper discussing the impact of spirituality on mental health in Samoa, asserts that a greater understanding of traditional beliefs is necessary if Western approaches to psychiatric treatment are to be successful.[45] The author argues that modern health systems based on Western medical paradigms and scientific models fail to acknowledge the spiritual element and traditional beliefs, resulting in inappropriate diagnosis and treatment of traditional, spiritual illnesses.[46] Lui also contends that a person's beliefs and perception of their illness determines their responses and the treatment they will undertake.[47] This discussion with case study illustrations—unlike several others—provides a practical demonstration of how different paradigms can come together in a cross cultural setting to maximise the outcome for the affected party.

Turner-Tupou, another Samoan writer, also uses some of her own case studies as a counselor to argue that, for a person diagnosed with a mental illness, relief and restoration to a sense of wholeness was realised when the person

> was able to engage in a counseling relationship with another woman of the same culture, who spoke the same language and used the same cultural protocols. These reflected the *mea-alofa*, the traditional cultural and spiritual values and beliefs, integrated effectively within a holistic model of practice.[48]

Tiatia, a New Zealand-born Samoan, studied the interplay between suicidal behaviour and spirituality in New Zealand-born Samoan youth and found that 'spirituality is often ignored in a public health approach to suicide prevention despite research concluding that the spiritual world is considered a positive feature and should not be ignored as a potential suicide prevention resource.'[49]

2.4. Fiji

One of the earliest studies on mental health in Fiji was that by Wilson who examined psychiatric inpatient admission statistics by race and gender from 1941-1963 and then compared them with a similar cohort in New Zealand.[50] Raw data was taken from Fijian census information and selected Fijian and New Zealand government reports. As there is no reference to accessing individual clinical files—for the purposes of differential diagnoses—

---

44 Ibid 306.

45 D Lui, 'Spiritual Injury: A Samoan Perspective on Spirituality's Impact in Mental Health' in P Culbertson, M N Agee and C Makasiale (eds), *Penina Uliuli: Contemporary Challenges in Mental Health for Pacific Peoples* (University of Hawaii Press, 2007) 66, 66.

46 Ibid 72.

47 Ibid 72.

48 F Turner-Tupou, 'Using Mea-alofa in a Holistic Model for Pasifica Clients: A Case Study' in P Culbertson, M N Agee and C Makasiale (eds), *Penina Uliuli: Contemporary Challenges in Mental Health for Pacific Peoples* (University of Hawai'i Press, 2007) 149,158.

49 T Tiatia, 'New Zealand-born Samoan Young People, Suicidal Behaviours and the Positive Impact of Spirituality' in P Culbertson, M N Agee and C Makasiale (eds), *Penina Uliuli: Contemporary Challenges in Mental Health for Pacific Peoples* (University of Hawai'i Press, 2007) 94,100.

50 G Wilson, "Europeanisation' and Admission to a Mental Hospital in the Fiji Islands' (1965) 64 *New Zealand Medical Journal* 364.

this study appears to be purely quantitative in nature. The overall findings, which are discussed in more detail in Chapter 2, were that the indigenous Fijian rate of hospitalisation was half that of the Fijian Indian population. Comparative New Zealand admission rates were found to have more than doubled during the period under study and those rates were between five and nine times greater than Fijian admissions.[51] The author hypothesised that this reflected the degree of Europeanisation rather than a 'tendency to generate "disturbed" individuals.'[52]

Price and Karim published two studies in the 1970s, one examining *matiruku* as a form of hypomania amongst the Fijian population[53] and the other evaluating community based care for people following admission to a psychiatric facility for an acute mental illness. The latter study found that there was minimal expertise within the community to provide such care and urged those responsible to establish requisite services.[54]

Murphy's 1970s study in Fiji found that specialist psychiatric resources were minimal—being one psychiatrist and one psychiatric trained nurse for a 200 bed hospital—and as such the only dedicated psychiatric facility in Fiji provided no more than custodial care with no available outpatient or community care for the mentally ill.[55]

Roberts explored the effects of violence and masculinity on the mental health of youth in Fiji and other parts of Melanesia concluding that 'cultural explanations for mental illness in the Pacific are largely inconsistent with modern explanations' limiting effective community responses.[56] The Fijian component of this study used a combination of qualitative and quantitative methods including surveying a number of youth focus groups. The report presented a substantial amount of data and discussed findings from the various focus groups regarding cultural transition; parenting; education; unemployment; human rights; counselling; communication; ethnicity; social roles; squatter settlement issues; drugs and alcohol; inter racial tension; social justice and crime.[57] It also made a variety of recommendations in relation to public policy; community action; developing personal skills; creation of supportive environments; reorienting services mediation and advocacy[58] and is an important baseline study for setting benchmarks for youth and current mental health issues.

In the face of reportedly increasing levels of mental disorders in Fiji, Seru-Puamau examined mental health services provided by St Giles Psychiatric Hospital through a retrospective case series review of first time admissions in 2002. The aim was to establish if any of those patients may have benefitted from community based care and thus avoided the stigma of a psychiatric admission.[59] While acknowledging limitations with the validity of some of the available material from both medical records and inpatient files, a substantial

---

51 Ibid 366.

52 Ibid 367.

53 J Price and I Karim, 'Matiruku, a Fijian Madness: An Initial Assessment' (1978) 133 *British Journal of Psychiatry* 228.

54 J Price and I Karim, 'An Evaluation of Psychiatric After-care in a Developing Country (Fiji)' (1976) 129 *British Journal of Psychiatry* 155.

55 Murphy, above n 11, 67.

56 G Roberts, 'Masculinity, Mental Health and Violence in Papua New Guinea, Vanuatu, Fiji and Kiribati' (2007) 14(2) *Health Promotion in the Pacific* 35, 35.

57 Partners in Community Development-Fiji, 'Youth Mental Stress & Violence in Fiji: Situation Analysis' (2005) 34–41.

58 Ibid 64–71.

59 E Seru-Puamau, 'Utilisation Review of First Admissions in 2002: St Giles Psychiatric Hospital, Suva, Fiji' (2006) 13(2) *Pacific Public Health* 79.

amount of quantitative data was collated regarding length of admission, gender, age, ethnicity, marital status and diagnosis. The author concluded that 'a significant proportion of first admissions to hospital appear to be for valid psychiatric diagnoses, some of which are difficult to manage in the community.'[60]

However, the author also found there was potential to provide treatment in a less restrictive environment for many first time young people admitted for a variety of 'nonspecific diagnoses suggestive of situational stress reactions and minor rather than major disorders.'[61] The study also found that research on the appropriate use of the hospital's services and alternative treatment options had not been adequately addressed and these issues were in urgent need of reform.[62]

Roberts et al. in a short paper in 2007—which did not present any empirical data but reviewed existing services at St Giles Hospital in Fiji—urged the Ministry of Health to devote adequate resources to the long awaited development of alternative treatment models to hospitalisation and to integrate mental health services into general health care.[63]

In an editorial in 2007, Chang—the former medical superintendent of St Giles Psychiatric Hospital—also urged a commitment to improve mental health care delivery through integration with primary health care.[64] As co-author of a review of the Fiji health system in 2011, she again described the physical and personnel resources in mental health, indicating that some progress had been made in terms of community awareness programs through mental health advocacy groups and the establishment of some outreach clinics in regional hospitals.[65] However, the report was principally descriptive in nature and did not take the opportunity to make specific recommendations in relation to future mental health care or policy.

2.5. Vanuatu

As with many countries in the region, Allen found that published reports on major mental illness in Vanuatu were rare and that Murphy's Pacific study in this country did not reveal exceptional trends in terms of the prevalence of mental illness.[66] The first in-depth studies in Vanuatu were WHO sponsored projects, the earliest of which was that of Wilton in 1997 which 'reviewed patterns and current treatment of mental health problems and mental disorders, along with rehabilitation strategies and existing policies in Vanuatu.'[67] In finding mental health services to be 'rudimentary', the author made a number of recommendations including the development of mental health policy; training of mental health professionals;

60 Ibid 84.
61 Ibid 84.
62 Ibid 85.
63 Roberts, Cruz and Puamau, above n 4, 107.
64 Ibid; O Chang, 'Mental Health Services in Fiji and the Way Forward' (2007) 15(2) *General Practitioner* 4.
65 O Chang, 'Mental Health Care in Fiji' (2011) 3(2) *Asia Pacific Psychiatry* 73.
66 Allen and Laycock, above n 37, 105–118, 144.
67 D Hughes and Foundation of the Peoples of the South Pacific International, 'Masculinity, Mental Health and Violence in Vanuatu: Situation Analysis' (2004) 18, citing NM Wilton, 'Mental Health in the Republic of Vanuatu' (WHO Regional Office for the Western Pacific, 1997).

suicide prevention strategies; the provision of inpatient facilities; strategies for increased community awareness of mental health issues; and accurate data collection.[68]

Dupré-Wheeler's study of suicide in Vanuatu in 2001—purportedly the first of its kind in the country—sampled groups of people in urban, rural and remote areas and surveyed over 35,000 people with the assistance of volunteers with limited training. While she found the overall suicide rate to be comparatively high, data collection for the study was limited by poor infrastructure and low project funding.[69] Furthermore, as discussing black magic and its perceived relationship to suicide are 'tabu', one village, renowned for suicides, denied researchers entrance—reportedly because of traditional secrets related to suicide.[70]

Hughes' later study on masculinity, mental health and violence reviewed existing literature, collected information from relevant stakeholders—police, prisons, hospitals, courts, and government departments—and conducted comprehensive interviews and focus groups among approximately 1500 young males aged 18-25, taking into account a combination of anecdotal and observational information.[71] The study concluded that 'youth in Vanuatu are at risk of facing depression, suicide and violence because of lack of support and understanding from family, community and government ministries. In many cases these problems are preventable with program support for youth.'[72] The study made a number of recommendations addressed at family, community and government levels, including community mental health education, youth counselling and support programs, trained mental health professionals and inpatient mental health facilities.[73]

Two Australian general medical practitioners, Benson and Pond, discussed the outcomes of a project—jointly funded by the WHO and NZAID—to provide culturally appropriate basic mental health training to health professionals and community leaders in selected communities—urban, rural and remote—throughout Vanuatu in 2009 and 2010.[74] In accepting that 'one-off Western style training has not been found to be successful' and that 'it is both efficient and cost effective to train primary care workers in a culturally appropriate manner',[75] the aim of the project appeared to be to facilitate the integration of mental health into primary health care. While the participants' evaluation of their skills development during the project was reported as positive and enthusiastic, it is probable that without ongoing training and government support its effectiveness is likely to be short lived. The authors' comment that 'Vanuatu is now well on the way to addressing inequity of access to mental health care with a culturally-appropriate and self-sustaining mental health workforce',[76] seems unduly optimistic given the lack of momentum and commitment to mental health care currently displayed by the Vanuatu government.

---

68 Hughes and Foundation of the Peoples of the South Pacific International, above n 67, 18, citing Wilton, above n 67.

69 D Dupre-Wheeler, 'Bali Hai Cries for Help: World Health Organisation Regional Office of the Western Pacific Health Survey Report–Vanuatu Suicide and Related Issues Baseline Survey' (2002) <www.inspq.qc.ca/pdf/publications/129_Trauma2002/%28J%29PreventionSuicide.pdf (accessed 13 September 2012)>.

70 Ibid.

71 Hughes and Foundation of the Peoples of the South Pacific International, above n 67.

72 Ibid 34.

73 Ibid 35–6.

74 J Benson et al. 'A New Era in Mental Health Care in Vanuatu' (2011) 2011 *International Journal of Family Medicine* 1.

75 Ibid 3.

76 Ibid 1.

In 2010 George, an Australian medical practitioner and an academic, surveyed mental health and the role of the church in Vanuatu.[77] Questionnaires were distributed to 80 adult members of four different Christian churches and included approximately the same number of females as males. As there is a paucity of mental health research in Vanuatu, it is regrettable that work of this nature has become part of the literature landscape and is quoted with authority. The value of George's research is, at best, anecdotal and merely involved a short series of leading and judgement-laden questions seeking a 'yes' or 'no' answer from the respondents—aimed, it could certainly be argued, at eliciting pre-determined answers. For example, 'Do you think mental illness is due to sin?' and 'Is it wrong to feel sad or depressed?' Given the low adult literacy levels in Vanuatu, and the fact that these questions were presented in English and not the local language (Bislama), the comprehension rate must be questioned. Limited demographic data in the paper was simply drawn from the *Air Vanuatu* inflight magazine.

3. Cultural Views on Mental Health and Illness

It is evident from the above examination of the literature in the region, the interaction between culture and concepts of health and illness remains an ever present and powerful dynamic in many Pacific communities. While this is not a sociological study, some conceptual analysis is necessary to view the notion of mental health and illness through a cultural lens. Many of the Pacific writers discussed in this chapter assert that *effective* mental health care must incorporate local cultural values and practices. It will be argued that the significance of these cultural imperatives is such that they should also play a role in determining the most suitable and effective *legal* framework in which to place issues arising from mental health law. Only then can the realisation of rights based initiatives—as integrated into mental health legislation—be successfully achieved and access to justice accomplished.

Murphy, in his ground breaking study, noted that while the primary care of the mentally ill in the Pacific rests within families and communities, some of those traditional community structures were already in the process of breaking down. He forecast that this would probably lead to a greater demand for public psychiatric services.[78] Murphy argued against 'defending tradition for its own sake' as it could 'perpetuate the custom of families locking up their patients in cramped cages or darkened huts' but that, in the face of inevitable change, new and alternative means of community support needed to be explored either within the community or special facilities.[79] He observed, with concern, that attitudes respecting mutuality and support for the weak were also changing at both family and community levels, including the decline in authority of chiefs and community elders with a commensurate reduction in community activities.[80] Family structures were moving more to 'nuclearisation' and becoming more economically self-sufficient with a lesser ability to provide extended support to a wider range of family members.[81]

---

[77] See K George, 'Vanuatu: Happiest Nation on Earth, Mental Health and the Church' (2010) 18(1) *Australian Psychiatry* 63.

[78] Murphy, above n 11, 29.

[79] Ibid 29.

[80] Ibid 32.

[81] Ibid 33.

3.1. Pacific Belief Systems

Several writers have described the notion that illness in Pacific cultures is seen as either tied to their local culture or introduced by foreigners.[82] This classification can ultimately determine how an illness is diagnosed and treated. Language also plays an important part in the portrayal of mental illness—most commonly used terms being derogatory in nature despite their etymology. For example, when describing people with mental illness, the Samoan word *valea* means 'stupid' or 'crazy' and *cavuka* in Fijian means 'broken' or 'snapped'.[83]

Perceptions of mental health in the Pacific might be best summarised as follows:

> Politicians and the general public are only partly aware of the fact that effective treatment of most mental disorders is possible. The image of mental illness is contaminated with images of violence, sin and laziness. Most health workers are not conversant with modern methods of treatment of mental illness and often do not possess the necessary skills to deal with it. Among them there are many who believe that the only way of dealing with mental illness is long term hospital care. In the majority of countries, including developed ones, there is no parity of care for mental and physical illnesses. Stigma of mental illness gains strength from these misconceptions and reinforces them.[84]

However, much of this is true only if one views mental health service delivery in a Western paradigm. The dichotomy is clearly described by David Lui who, along with other Pacific writers,[85] is firmly of the view that in relation to the Samoan people

> [t]here is an increasing acceptance of spirituality as an important part of health care among consumers, service users, community health workers and health professionals. Even some clinicians, health care providers and policy makers have recognised that spirituality is an important part of at least some consumers' healing and recovery process.[86]
>
> My experience working in the Pacific Islands mental health is that Pacific consumers have a different view of and a higher need for, the spiritual realm in their healing and recovery processes … even some consumers who may not appear to be religious or spiritual express a desire to explore or include spirituality in their care plan.[87]
>
> Furthermore, Lui contends:
>
> In fact, psychiatry is often hostile to religious and spiritual beliefs, or worse, such beliefs are considered by psychiatrists to be symptoms of mental illness itself.[88]
>
> Spiritual experiences such as seeing or hearing deceased ancestors or other spirits are natural and uplifting. The Western psychiatrist, on the other hand, often discounts such

82 S Vaka et al. 'Walking Apart Towards the Same Goal? The View and Practices of Tongan Traditional Healers and Western Trained Tongan Mental Health Staff' (2009) 15(1) *Pacific Health Dialog*, 90.

83 Seataoai Samu and Suaalii-Sauni, above n 19, 122.

84 World Health Organisation, *Mental Health Advocacy* <www.who.int/mental_health/advocacy/en/ (accessed 11 June 2012)>.

85 See also Tiatia, above n 49, 97;Turner-Tupou, above n 48, 149.

86 Lui, above n 45, 67.

87 Ibid.

88 Ibid 73.

experiences, or worse, may consider such experiences to be delusions or hallucinations and a sign the patient is 'off his head.'[89]

In a study of mental illness across four Melanesian countries, including Vanuatu and Fiji, Roberts observed that the widespread misunderstandings of the nature and causes of mental illness in Pacific communities seriously limits their ability to respond. He argues that

> cultural explanations for mental illness in the Pacific are largely inconsistent with modern explanations. They tend to demonise the phenomena (black magic and/or demonic possession) or attribute some moral failing to the sufferer (poor peer group relationships, religious failing or drug use). [90]

3.1.1. Tonga

In Tonga there are two systems of medicine: *mahaki faka-Tonga* based on sickness and traditional Tongan medicine and *mahaki faka-Palangi* based on disease (thought to be introduced by Europeans) and Western medicine.[91] A belief system exists in Tonga whereby *avanga* and *te'ia* refer to a person under possession of spirits of the dead or 'spooks,' while *mala* refers to a person considered to be cursed due to the breaking down of cultural norms and values.[92]

Puloka contends that psychosocial and ecological factors are often involved in the occurrence of *avanga* wherein sufferers are compelled to obey the orders of a ghost and to follow the ghost to a more peaceful, secluded place away from the psychosocial stressors—maybe the family. Such a place would typically be the beach, the bush or a burial place—places believed to be frequented by the spirits of the dead.[93] There are many types of *avanga* but commonly an episode is 'characterised by acute onset of cognitive, emotional, perceptual and behavioral disturbances but not physical symptoms per se'[94] and may be of 'short duration, several days or even a week depending on its response to traditional medicine.'[95] The author also maintains that it is a 'Culture Bound Syndrome which is specific to the cultural system in Tonga and does not conform to western nosologic entities.'[96]

3.1.2. Samoa

Similarly, in Samoa there are two types of illness: *ma'i samoa*—illnesses traditional to Samoa and often caused by gods—and *ma'i palagi*—illnesses brought to Samoa by others, usually Europeans.[97]

Lui claims that traditional Samoan belief incorporates two essential elements—the physical and the spiritual—the body (*tino*) and the spirit or soul (*loto*). The spirit includes the

89 Ibid 72.
90 Roberts, above n 56, 40.
91 Toafa, Moata'ane and Guthrie, above n 27, 78.
92 Puloka, above n 25, 69.
93 M Puloka, 'Avanga: Tongan Concepts of Mental Illness' (1999) 6(2) *Pacific Health Dialog* 268, 269.
94 Ibid 270.
95 Ibid.
96 Ibid 268–74.
97 Macpherson and Macpherson, above n 38, 151.

soul and the mind, and both the body and soul are 'integral to the whole person and cannot be separated.'[98]

> The spiritual part includes a person's mental dimension. Spirituality may be described as our sense of connectedness to our *Atua* [God] to the *laufanua* [land and environment] and to our ancestors who have passed on. Samoans also believe in the existence of *aitu* (spirits) and *sauali'i* (ghosts).[99]
>
> A person's beliefs and their understanding and perception of their health and illness determine their response, their practice and the treatment and intervention they will undertake.[100]

Highlighting a different challenge, Turner Tupou writes that

> the *pálagi* [foreign or western] concept of counselling is still foreign to most Pasifica people. In our cultures, conversations about one's wellbeing normally take place in the home where the family members gather and share stories or problems, for traditionally, these are to be solved within the family. Therefore Pasifica people do not readily attend counselling even when referred. In addition, because we live communally, confidentiality is an unfamiliar concept.[101]

3.1.3. Fiji

Roberts' study, when referring to Fijians, asserts that 'both [indigenous] Fijian and Indo-Fijians predominantly attribute the cultural explanations for aberrant behaviour or psychotic thinking to demonic possession, sorcery and/or excessive cannabis use… these views also exist among some health professionals.'[102]

Schultz contends that 'if one considers Fijian notions that equate with mental health, one finds concepts like being in harmony with one's physical environment, spirits, ancestors and family, [*vanua*] and achieving a balance between one's physical, emotional and spiritual self.'[103]

3.1.4. Vanuatu

Similar spiritual based belief systems are prevalent in Vanuatu and graphic illustrations of the inherent misunderstanding of the aetiology of many mental disorders are not hard to find.

> Livan died in 2007.
> She was twelve years old.
> Livan was severely intellectually disabled with a history of epilepsy.
> She was in need of constant care and attention, yet, Livan died alone locked in a tin hut.

---

98 Lui, above n 45.
99 Ibid 71.
100 Ibid 72.
101 Turner-Tupou, above n 48, 153.
102 Partners in Community Development-Fiji, 'Youth Mental Stress & Violence in Fiji: Situation Analysis' (2005) 21.
103 R Schultz, 'Community Mental Health: Avoided by Some, Neglected by Others' (2001) 8(1) *Pacific Health Dialog* 200.

> Her parents kept her in the hut, deprived her of food and clothing and forced her to sleep in the dirt and eat her own faeces.
> When Livan was hungry and angry at not being fed, she would chew on the wood around the one small window frame in the hut.
> The only medication Livan ever received in her short life was Panadol.[104]

Livan's story is not only a reflection of the way mental disorders are still viewed in Vanuatu society today but an illustration of the direct consequences of extremely poor mental health care services.

At a more anecdotal level:

> Johnson was probably in his thirties.
> He lived on the island of Tanna in Vanuatu.
> No one really knew whose family he belonged to but the people in the village had always ostracised him.
> Johnson was 'not quite right.'
> Every few months Johnson would appear in the village and 'do bad things' such as breaking into huts and stealing chickens and food to eat.
> The men of the village would throw stones at him, beat him with sticks and chase him into the bush.
> In the end Johnson would run away.
> Eventually he never returned. [105]

3.2. Youth, Culture and Mental Illness

Youth in the Pacific—defined as those under 24 years of age—represent a considerable majority of the population—between 47 percent in Fiji and 58 percent in Samoa, Tonga and Vanuatu.[106] In countries such as Vanuatu, this is further compounded by high population growth rates and zero emigration rates. Youth face formidable challenges throughout the region, not the least of which include poor education opportunities, high unemployment and deteriorating levels of social and economic stability. These factors increase their susceptibility to mental stress and, in some cases, mental illness. How youth identify and react to such stressors are critical factors; how they view mental illness and its causes will determine whether they have any chance of receiving appropriate support and treatment.

3.2.1. Tonga

The common perception among youth in Tonga is that people with mental illness are *'born like that'*, have been disabled by an accident, or their illness is a result of cultural or spiritual forces.[107] In a study on youth and mental health in Tonga, Puloka noted the tendency for parents and caregivers to identify 'strange' behaviour of their children's mental illness

---

[104] *Public Prosecutor v Kalon* [2008] VUSC 9.

[105] Story told by ST who as a child lived in the same village. Johnson is an assumed name.

[106] Secretariat of the Pacific Community, *Statistics for Development Program, Pacific Islands Populations Estimates, May 2011* <www.spc.int/sdp (accessed 28 December 2011)>.

[107] O Guttenbeil-Likiliki and Foundation of the Peoples of the South Pacific International, 'Youth and Mental Health in Tonga: A Situational Analysis' (2009) 7.

with *'puke faka-tevolo'* (spiritual and cultural dimensions), rather than illnesses as a result of chemical imbalance.[108]

In the same report, 53 percent of young respondents thought that people with mental health problems should be kept separately from the rest of society and that mentally ill persons have more criminal and violent tendencies.[109]

3.2.2. Samoa

Alefaoi, in a study of the ethnic identity of Samoan youth, examined the role family plays in shaping their values and beliefs and the impacts of acculturation. He highlights the glaring difference between the concepts of family in the Western world and the Pacific as follows:

> The 'ideal family' in the Western world is often perceived as one which thrives on goals for independent living, self-sufficiency and eventually retirement in a retirement village on one's own. This is far removed from the picture or real life illustrations of lives lived in nations of the Pacific. In Samoa, for example, village life is the epicenter of the nation ... the systemic goals of life are for fostering interdependence, living to support the whole aiga/family, sufficiency for the whole aiga/family and eventually growing old and being cared for by the aiga/family.[110]

3.2.3. Fiji

One study on youth and mental stress in Fiji asserts that mental illness is rarely recognised for what it is, largely due to the general lack of understanding by medical professionals of mental processes in Pacific cultures.[111] The same study explains that:

> In the village setting, it is unlikely that schizophrenia or depression will be diagnosed early, so the sufferer may undergo a protracted period of distressing symptoms without adequate social support or medical response. An unmanageable burden of care falls on families who have no understanding of mental illness. Even in the urban setting a psychotic youth may be undetected and go through a period of rejection by family and friends for inappropriate behaviour before coming to the attention of services. Some may never receive treatment and will attempt to alleviate their inner tensions through some form of substance abuse or abuse of others.[112]

3.2.4. Vanuatu

The majority of young participants in a 2004 study on masculinity and mental health in Vanuatu, had not heard of the English words 'mental health,' 'depression,' 'suicide' or 'violence'—nor were there any equivalent words in the local language (Bislama).[113]

---

108 Ibid 20.

109 Ibid 26.

110 S Alefaoi, 'Reflections of a Practitioner: Purely a Journey of the Heart' (2009) 15(1) *Pacific Health Dialog* 169, 172.

111 Partners in Community Development-Fiji, above n102, 21.

112 Ibid 22.

113 D Hughes and Foundation of the Peoples of the South Pacific International, 'Masculinity, Mental Health and Violence in Vanuatu: Situation Analysis' (2004) 23.

3.3. Integrating Culture and Tradition into Modern Mental Health Care

Mila-Schaaf, in exploring cultural understandings of mental illness in the Pacific, asserts that:

> A colonial legacy has meant that Pacific indigenous knowledge systems have been actively rejected by dominant western paradigms (i.e., theological, philosophical, scientific) from initial cross cultural contact. This experience of colonisation has meant that indigenous knowledge is not always easily accessed in contemporary settings.[114]

Moreover 'in contrast to being under-documented and difficult to access, the dominant western paradigms of mental health are well documented and well recorded.'[115]

When exploring the concept of cultural competencies in mental illness, Seataoai Samu contends that 'working with Pacific people in mental health requires working through the cultural nuances of their perceptions of illness, treatment and wellbeing'[116] which includes 'understanding the spiritual aspects of Pacific mental illnesses and health belief systems.'[117] The author also argues that 'Pacific culture in mental health is about ethnic culture and so cultural competencies are defined by ethnic markers, issues of language, family and *tapu*' [the sacred].[118] The writer's study of five ethnic groups in New Zealand, including Samoans, Tongans and Fijians, emphasised the continuing significance of cultural and ethnic values even among these immigrant communities. Each group:

> implicitly and explicitly suggested a relationship between mental illness and breaches of *tapu* … to talk of *tapu* relations is to talk about the sacred bonds between people. For Pacific people these bonds stem from their stories of creation and the cosmic and spiritual relationships between them, their environment and their god(s) … to breach *tapu* relationship is arguably to invoke the wrath of the god(s) ancient and/or Christian. In most cases this is the wrath of ancient gods … [which] is often manifested in, among other things, the sudden occurrence of mental illness.[119]

In the same study, when addressing the issue of the competency of mental health workers, all groups considered that a combination of clinical, spiritual and/or traditional healing practices were necessary to address mental health problems.[120]

3.3.1. Tonga

In examining the different approaches of traditional healers and western-trained psychiatric personnel to the treatment of mental illness, Vaka found that:

> Traditional Healers universally defined mental health difficulties from a traditional perspective using the Tongan terms *avanga, te'ia* and *mala*. These conditions were seen

[114] Mila-Schaaf and Hudson, above n 15.
[115] Ibid.
[116] Seataoai Samu and Suaalii-Sauni, above n 19, 121.
[117] Ibid.
[118] Ibid.
[119] Ibid 123.
[120] Ibid 124.

as covering most, if not all, people who presented with what would be considered mental illness in the west. They attributed these conditions to spiritual or social causes rather than physical illness.[121]

On the other hand, the western-trained psychiatric staff were more inclined to explain mental health problems as an illness of the brain or abnormal thinking and behaviour—consistent with their western training and beliefs.[122]

There was, however, little difference between the two groups in relation to their perceptions of the signs and symptoms of mental illness.[123]

Vaka's study also found that:

> Tongan Traditional Healers were drawing on Christian and on other traditional Tongan spiritual beliefs and incorporated elements of a psychosocial and family-systems approaches consistent with western thinking in their treatment modalities but there was in general little recognition or acceptance of the biological component of the western model.[124]

As the only indigenous western trained psychiatrist in Tonga, Dr Puloka has been accredited with pioneering the concept of transcultural psychiatry in the country. This involves developing methods to bridge the gaps between traditional beliefs and practices and formal psychiatric medicine in order to achieve optimum treatment outcomes for mental health consumers. Between 1996 and 1998, he organised a series of workshops with traditional healers and mental health workers. The workshops were designed to create interaction between the groups, to elicit information from the healers, and to give mental health workers greater access to ways in which consumers were being treated in their villages before they reached formal mental health services.[125]

Puloka found that the healers had little in common with one another apart from a belief in 'sickness cause by spirit', and they utilised a wide spectrum of treatment from 'beneficial to outright dangerous'.[126] An illustration of such cooperation follows:

> In New Zealand P received 'traditional' healing for unusual violent behaviour. This didn't work so the family sent him to Tonga. Dr Puloka was invited to treat him in the family home to avoid wider awareness of his condition. The negative reactions of the family were confirmed in the way they looked at him.
>
> On taking a history he realised it was a clear case of bipolar disorder, despite no family history of the condition. The family had gone from healer to healer and yet the patient became more dangerous, often smashing things. Dr Puloka treated him under section 9 of the mental health act. He responded well to treatment and the episodes stopped, allowing him to enrol in a tertiary institution.

---

121 Vaka et al. above n 82, 91.
122 Ibid.
123 Ibid.
124 Ibid.
125 M Poltorak, 'Traditional Healers, Speaking and Motivation in Vava'u, Tonga: Explaining Syncretism and Addressing Health Policy' (2010) 80(1) *Oceania* 1.
126 Ibid.

During one of the first workshops a particularly famous healer claimed that the family had acknowledged his remedies as having cured the patient. Dr Puloka said nothing, recognising this as both a strategy of the healer to bolster his reputation and the family to avoid the stigmatisation that would result from wider recognition that the patient had a psychiatric disorder. This same healer was many years later discovered to have started adding small amounts of an anti-psychotic medication into his remedies in the year after the workshops.[127]

3.3.2. Samoa

In their seminal work on medical belief and practice in Samoa, the Macphersons contend that in 'developing' societies such as Samoa 'Western medicine must compete for support with established indigenous medical systems which enjoy the support of significant parts of the population and effectively control the power to heal.'[128] In probing the link between culture and illness, the authors define culture as:

> a set of shared beliefs and ideas about the way things are. It is a body of knowledge which adherents draw on for explanation of the natural and social worlds in which they live. It establishes connections between various phenomena and becomes a guide to conduct for those who share it … there are bodies of ideas about illness and its management which constitute a medical culture. The connections which cultures establish between phenomena may not stand 'objective scientific' scrutiny and in cases can be shown to be incorrect. But culture does not have to establish connections which can stand such scrutiny to be successful. It only has to allow adherents to make sense of their world … if people believe something to be true and act as if it is true, then it makes little difference to them that it is not.[129]

The writers explore each part of the human body in great detail and the ways in which traditional beliefs, diagnosis and treatment impact on illnesses seen to result from biological, social or supernatural disturbances.[130] However, when referring to the head or brain, little or no consideration is given to psychological illnesses; except to say that psychological and physical disorders are considered quite different categories. Psychological disorders are described as those that are congenital, associated with old age, caused by temporary excesses of emotion and lapses of judgement or those caused by various forms of spirit possession.[131] There is no further discussion on this point, leading one to conclude that most of the more serious psychotic illness—as known to Western psychiatry and unlinked to any physical cause—must be attributed to spirit possession. Moreover, the authors suggest that the significance of the supernatural in Samoan life does *not* appear to have declined despite growing European influence and the increase of modern formal education.[132]

In balancing the intersection between traditional and modern views on mental illness in Samoa, the Macphersons maintain:

---

[127] Ibid.
[128] Macpherson and Macpherson, above n 38, 9.
[129] Ibid 19 fn 4.
[130] Ibid 159.
[131] Ibid 176.
[132] Ibid 239.

> If more and more Samoans are exposed to introduced medicine and come to have a basis for comparison of the speed and efficacy of alternative treatments, beliefs about the power of Samoan [traditional] medicine are more likely to be contested. However, this presumes that people will put themselves in positions in which they accept non-Samoan medicine for Samoan illnesses. Given the development of a health system based on a central hospital and the constraints on the growth of the system, this is unlikely to happen in Western Samoa in the foreseeable future.[133]

Lui supports the Macphersons' overall analysis of the interaction between culture and illness. He argues that the successful treatment of mental illness calls for a greater recognition of traditional beliefs and understandings, without which Western approaches to psychiatric treatment cannot begin to address the cause of the problem, regardless of the provision of symptomatic relief.[134]

Lui further asserts that modern health systems based on Western medical paradigms and scientific models fail to acknowledge the spiritual element and traditional beliefs, resulting in inappropriate diagnosis and treatment of what can be 'essentially a traditional spiritual illness or condition.'[135] The author describes two case studies, both involving women who had emigrated from Samoa to New Zealand in their youth and who later displayed symptoms of mental illness for which they were both hospitalised.[136] One of the women, Mele, presented with episodes of uncontrolled aggression and violence, hallucinations and disorientation followed by amnesia. The family believed her condition was due to a curse—placed on her family after an incident involving her father many years before—but took her to the hospital for safety reasons. A negotiated plan of management between the medical staff and a traditional healer—which involved withholding medical diagnosis and treatment until Mele had the opportunity to receive traditional healing—resulted in a complete recovery. Lui argues that Mele's condition was not medical and, while medical intervention with medication might have provided short term relief—as well as the stigma of a psychiatric diagnosis—it would not have dealt with the underlying cause of her illness.[137]

This approach is supported by Tamasese's research which maintained that research methods traditionally used in mental health have not been well accepted by Pacific island groups.[138] His study developed an authentic Samoan methodology for exploring mental health issues known as *Fa'afaletui*. The *Fa'afaletui* process describes a method that facilitates the gathering and validation of important knowledge within the culture and weaving together all the different expressions of knowledge from within the various focus groups.[139] When the process was applied to examining issues surrounding mental health, the participants considered that 'it was not possible to understand concepts of mental health and ill health without first understanding the Samoan concept of self.'[140]

In essence, this means that there is no such thing as a Samoan person independent of others and that each person is a relational being and part of a collective context. In addition,

---

[133] Ibid 243.
[134] Lui, above n 45, 66–76.
[135] Ibid 72.
[136] Ibid 73–6.
[137] Ibid 74.
[138] Tamasese et al. above n 41, 306.
[139] Ibid 302.
[140] Ibid.

each person has physical, mental and spiritual aspects that cannot be divided.[141] Mental illness is seen as being caused by 'breaches of forbidden or sacred relationships' that involve grave transgressions of family, village or district relational boundaries resulting in curses being placed on the offending person.[142] Healing is achieved by establishing why there is a curse on the person and seeking reconciliation through appropriate processes. Spirituality must be addressed in the process if the mental health care is to be effective.[143] Tamasese maintains that

> The results of this study challenge a number of prevalent presuppositions about the nature of self in modern psychiatry and raise questions about the assumptions that dominant western views of *self* are applicable across cultures. In particular the Western notions of the self as being primarily individuated rather than relational and secular/scientific rather than spiritual, differ substantially from those identified by participants in this study.[144]

In reinforcing the significance of cultural values, the Samoan Mental Health Policy emphasises that:

> (a) Mental well-being is grounded in the *aiga* [extended family] and the community. The Samoan understanding of dignity and self-esteem is collective and relational in nature. What is achieved or lost by the individual is felt by the *aiga*. In this context the *aiga* is the natural and appropriate health care setting for the promotion of mental health and the management of mental disorders with the exception of some severe disorders requiring hospitalisation or seclusion.
> (b) …
> (c) …
> (d) Recognition that mental, physical social and spiritual health is indivisible and [an] holistic approach best addresses this.[145]

3.3.3. Vanuatu

In a study by two Australian general practitioners—a WHO funded project to teach mental health skills to primary care health professionals in Vanuatu—a number of factors tied to culture and custom were seen as causing mental health issues including:

- the use of kava [a social drug] causing social disruption in families;
- the role of religion in the culture;
- the role of chiefs in the resolution of family and community disputes;
- stress arising from [culturally] arranged marriages; and
- the importance of certain cultural traditions.[146]

141 Ibid 303.
142 Ibid 303–4.
143 Ibid 307.
144 Ibid.
145 Government of Samoa Ministry of Health, 'Samoa Mental Health Policy' (2006) 3–4.
146 Benson et al. above n 74, 8–9.

In a different study in the same country, most people who were identified as having mental disorders similar to those found in patients in Australia, were found to have been untreated—except with custom medication—and had a traditional understanding of the cause of the problem.[147]

3.3.4. Pacific Islanders overseas

The impact of migration and acculturation on the prevalence of mental illness in migrant Pacific populations has been discussed in Chapter 2.

However, Toafa and Vaka's studies of the role of traditional healers in mental health in Tongan communities—in New Zealand and Tonga respectively—both had similar findings, especially concerning the lack of understanding of their role by the Western health system and the need for an increased understanding of the cultural basis of health care.[148]

Tamasese found that psychiatric treatment based on Western medical beliefs, and the inability to speak the local language and understand the significance of cultural issues were major impediments in the treatment of mentally ill Samoans in New Zealand. He argues that to deliver effective mental health care more 'culturally appropriate' services necessitated the provision of services based on a traditional model of care, targeted counselling for families, community based services and the use of traditional healers.[149]

4. Conclusion

In the final analysis, a culture specific approach to understanding and improving mental health care needs to be adopted, but not in a way that assumes homogeneity across cultures and ignores individual differences.[150]

While an examination of the different philosophies underpinning models of mental health care delivery is beyond the scope of this work, the rationale must have some bearing on the operation of legal mechanisms under mental health legislation if it is to provide jurisprudence in a therapeutic environment.

One Western jurisdiction that *has* factored this into the equation is New Zealand. Section 5 of the *Mental Health (Compulsory Assessment and Treatment) Act 1992,* via an amendment in 2000, now directs that any court, tribunal or person exercising power under the Act must do so with proper recognition of the person's ties with his or her family, whanau [extended family], hapu [clan or sub tribe], iwi [tribe] and family group and the contribution those ties make to the person's wellbeing; and with proper respect for the person's cultural and ethnic identity, language, and religious or ethical beliefs.[151] Fiji is the only country in the region to have followed suit with a similar provision—however its application has yet to be tested.[152]

There are compelling arguments for and against the role of indigenous medicine within society. According to Macpherson, those committed to indigenous medicine argue that its

---

147 Ibid.

148 Toafa, Moata'ane and Guthrie, above n 27; Vaka et al. above n 82.

149 Tamasese et al. above n 41, 306.

150 Department of Mental Health and Substance Abuse in Collaboration with the Victorian Health Promotion Foundation and the University of Melbourne, 'Promoting Mental Health: Concepts, Emerging Evidence, Practice. Summary Report – A Report of the World Health Organisation' (WHO, 2004) 22.

151 *Mental Health (Compulsory Assessment and Treatment) Act 1992* (NZ) s 5(1), (2).

152 *Mental Health Decree 2010* (Fiji Islands) s 6(1)(c).

'success' rests on its efficacy; those opposed to the idea argue that its apparent 'success' is very largely psychological and/or incidental.[153] The reality is far more complex than these mono causal theories suggest. The authors also maintain that Samoans, in particular, are intensely pragmatic and will try various forms of treatment in the search for an effective result. However, despite significant social change and external demographic and economic influences, kinship remains a central feature of social organisation in countries such as Samoa.[154]

It is apparent that, despite the alleged weakening of cultural norms and the effects of globalisation in many Pacific communities, there remain strong imperatives to retain and nurture indigenous culture. The links between culture and mental health and illness in the Pacific appear to be irrefutable, regardless of the reasons why any particular form of treatment may be effective. Several writers have argued that Western medicine has frequently been ineffective in non-Western countries when applied in a cultural vacuum. To achieve optimum results, cultural sensitivity must be part of any formula that is applied to mental health services—either in a therapeutic or legal setting.

---

153 Macpherson and Macpherson, above n 38, 237.
154 Ibid 238–9.

Chapter 12

IMPEDIMENTS TO ACCESSING JUSTICE THROUGH MENTAL HEALTH LAW REFORM — HUMAN RIGHTS

This chapter explores the human rights themes that play the most significant roles in impeding access to justice under rights based mental health legislation and policy in the Pacific. Issues in relation to economic policy and professional resources follow in Chapter 13.

1. OVERVIEW

The resistance throughout Pacific countries to the unqualified acceptance of human rights principles is clearly evident. One of the primary reasons for the Pacific's reluctance to embrace human rights treaties is the alleged conflict between Pacific cultural values based on communal rights and the doctrines of individualism that underpin human rights instruments. As the former Vice President of Fiji and human rights proponent, Ratu Joni Madraiwiwi, observed:

> In the Asia/Pacific region there is some resentment about the concept of human rights. Some of our leaders are fond of decrying them as a western or alien concept at odds with our values. Human rights are universal in nature. They are about fairness and decency …it is not the downtrodden, the oppressed or the marginalised who make the criticism. It is those of us who are part of the established power structures that query the applicability of those rights.[1]

A related concern is that human rights protagonists place too much emphasis on 'rights' and too little on 'duties' or responsibilities—being the duty of the state to ensure the rights of individual as opposed to the duties of individuals to exercise their rights responsibly and fulfil their obligations to others and their communities.[2] A more polarised view of the dilemma has been expressed as 'human rights discourse is simply another foreign imposition which works

---

[1] Law Commission New Zealand, 'Converging Currents: Custom and Human Rights in the Pacific, Study Paper 17' (2006)15.

[2] Ibid 21.

to undermine customary ways, to the detriment of both national identity and community identity.'[3]

2. LITERATURE

When compared with health, little has been written about human rights in the Pacific. Even less so on human rights in the Pacific in the context of disability. Academic literature in relation to the human rights of mental health consumers—as a sub set of the disability community—is even harder to locate.

Wilson and Hunt edited a series of papers in 2000 on various aspects of the application of cultural rights in the Pacific.[4] Within the collection, Polu and Taufe'ulugaki examine the significance of cultural rights in Samoa and Tonga and the effects of globalisation and changes in social order on traditional practices.[5] Hunt, on the other hand, outlines cultural rights, their genesis in various international treaties, and how the divide between individualism and collectivism might be reconciled.[6] All writers recognise the importance of culture in society and suggest ways to minimise the erosion of tradition by non-Pacific influences.

The New Zealand Law Commission published a comprehensive report in 2006, following a recommendation from the Pacific Islands Human Rights Consultation that an in depth study of the relationship between custom and human rights be undertaken in the Pacific.[7] The focus of the study was an overview directed at the practical operation of justice mechanisms in the courts and a wide range of community justice bodies—it was not intended as 'a model for future management of custom and human rights across the Pacific region.'[8] The study highlighted problems associated with women and children's rights; freedom of speech, religion and movement; minority and migrant communities; courts, community justice and court access to custom law; legislation, public review bodies and regional relationships.[9] There was neither particular reference to persons with disabilities or mental health consumers as part of a minority group nor any reference to human rights concerns experienced by these people.

The Commission saw one of its primary challenges as being the perceived conflict between custom and human rights in the Pacific—namely that while human rights are seen by some as a threat to custom, conversely custom is seen as a threat to individual freedom and justice.[10] In proposing that custom and human rights *could* be harmonised in Pacific legal

---

3 Ibid.

4 M Wilson and P Hunt (eds), *Culture, Rights, and Cultural Rights: Perspectives from the South Pacific* (Huia Publishers, 2000).

5 L Polu, 'Cultural Rights and the Individual in the Samoan Context' in M Wilson and P Hunt (eds), *Culture, Rights, and Cultural Rights: Perspectives from the South Pacific* (Huia Publishers, 2000) 57; A Taufe'ulugaki, 'Cultural Rights in the Tongan Context: Some Issues' in M Wilson and P Hunt (eds), *Culture, Rights, and Cultural Rights: Perspectives from the South Pacific* (Huia Publishers, 2000) 91.

6 P Hunt, 'Reflections on International Human Rights Law and Cultural Rights' in M Wilson and P Hunt (eds), *Culture, Rights, and Cultural Rights: Perspectives from the South Pacific* (Huia Publishers, 2000) 25

7 Law Commission New Zealand, above n 1.

8 Ibid 11, 28.

9 Ibid 240–45.

10 Ibid 11.

systems 'by looking to the shared underlying values of both',[11] the Commission made a number of practical suggestions as to how the proposition might be achieved. The comparative study across 25 countries was primarily based on existing literature sourced from a wide range of published and unpublished material. While it did not involve independent empirical research—acknowledged as a major limitation—the expectation was that the work would provide impetus for further research.[12] Nonetheless, the report provides a comprehensive and widely researched discussion of relevant issues and a solid platform for future study and development in the region.

Madraiwiwi, in a short unreferenced paper, discusses one of the major obstacles in relation to the acceptance of human rights ideology it the Pacific—its perceived conflict with and threat to the collectivism of traditional indigenous values. The author contends that the conflict is not irreconcilable but that a non-confrontational approach needs to be taken if human rights philosophies are to be accepted and incorporated effectively with custom.[13] This paper provides an important insight into indigenous views of human rights principles in the region.

One of the leading human rights organisations in the region—Pacific Regional Rights Resource Team (RRRT)—which now operates under the auspices of the Secretariat of the Pacific Community (SPC), has published a series of annotated case law throughout the region dealing with constitutional and international treaty based human rights issues. A selection of relevant cases is discussed later in the chapter. Although some courts have made decisions consistent with the principles of the CRPD in relation to mental disabilty, courts in the region are yet to address the CRPD directly.[14]

Jalal, one of the leading writers on human rights in the Pacific and formerly associated with RRRT, has published a number of articles on the role of culture and human rights in the region. In a paper in 2005, outlining the organisational background and field work principles of RRRT, she identifies a series of human rights challenges in Pacific island countries. These include the alleged conflict between human rights and Pacific culture, identity, patriarchy and religious fundamentalism; democracy and human rights as obstacles to economic growth; the lack of regional human rights bodies; poor legal frameworks for NGOs; interruptions to democracy; poverty, instability and poor governance; and globalisation.[15]

Jalal also notes the resistance by countries in the region to embracing a human rights culture—including the ratification of international treaties—matters she explores in more detail in a subsequent article in 2006. The bulk of the 2005 article examines the principles used by RRRT in its endeavour to progress the acceptance of human rights in the region by working within existing cultural and religious frameworks, using several case studies as illustrations of the application of those principles. RRRT's methodology essentially involves an 'infiltration' style approach whereby personnel identified at three levels—legal and

---

[11] Ibid 12.

[12] Ibid 26.

[13] J Madraiwiwi Ratu, 'Navigating Passage Between Human Rights and Culture in Fijian Waters' in M Powles (ed), *Pacific Futures* (Pandanus Books,The Australian National University, 2006).

[14] P Imrana Jalal and J Madraiwiwi (eds), *Pacific Human Rights Law Digest* (RRRT, 2005); P Imrana Jalal and J Madraiwiwi (eds), *Pacific Human Rights Law Digest* (RRRT, 2008). After RRRT was subsumed into SPC in 2008, three further volumes where produced under the authorship of SPC in 2011, 2013 and 2015. See, for example, *Regina v Belo* [2012] SBHC 88.

[15] P Imrana Jalal, 'Using Rights-Based Programming Principles to Claim Rights: The Regional Rights Resource Team (RRRT) Project in the Pacific Islands' (May 2005) <www.rrrt.org/images/usingrightsbased programmingprinciples.pdf (accesssed 5 April 2013)>5–6.

policymaking, government and the community—are trained in 'rights based philosophy' and then continue to network, lobby and advocate within those sectors for change within a human rights framework sensitive to social and cultural values.[16] Although the author contends that this approach has been criticised by some as being 'too soft', she upholds the view that incremental change through building networks is more sustainable in the long term and this is evidenced by the organisation's success on a range of projects in countries throughout the region.[17]

In an insightful discussion of issues in a later paper in 2006, Jalal explores the reasons for the low levels of ratification of international treaties in the Pacific. In summary, these are identified as constraints on financial and human resources; cultural, economic, legal and political imperatives; the role of NGOs and the UN; and the lack of regional human rights bodies.[18] The writer analyses the history of ratification in the region and the challenges faced by most Pacific island countries. Particular consideration is given to a number of treaties but—as the article predates the introduction of the *Convention on the Rights of Persons with Disabilities* (CRPD)—there is no specific discussion of disability or mental disorders. Nonetheless, many of the arguments raised are equally applicable to disability in the context of human rights. While much of Jalal's work is self-referenced to RRRT projects and research, the organisation has been instrumental in regional human rights reform and—in the face of a dearth of published literature—is an important contribution.

Rantala et al. in their paper in 2010, seek to clarify the synergy between health and human rights and the role of the WHO in spearheading reform on global health matters.[19] The authors emphasise the importance of education, awareness and understanding of the impact of human rights conventions—without which measures such as legislative intervention are futile.[20] The paper describes a WHO funded project which introduced the International Diploma in Mental Health Law and Human Rights in 2008 at the University of Pune, India. The initiative followed the WHO publication—WHO Resource Book on Mental Health Human Rights and Legislation—released as a guide for countries in the process of developing mental health legislation to promote the rights of people with mental disabilities. However, 'while many countries found the Resource Book a useful guide for this purpose, the lack of trained professionals was a significant barrier to effectively converting guidance into action.'[21]

One study that explores the operation of the CRPD in the Pacific is that of Harpur and Bales.[22] The first country in the Pacific to ratify the CRPD was Vanuatu in 2008. The paper discusses the general history and application of the CRPD and then examines the operation of the treaty in the region, in particular the effect of ratification of the CRPD in Vanuatu. The authors contend that 'to meet the level of protection anticipated by the CRPD Pacific Island

---

16 Ibid 9–10.

17 Ibid 30.

18 P Imrana Jalal, 'Pacific Culture and Human Rights: Why Pacific Island Countries Should Ratify International Human Rights Treaties' (April 2006) <www.rrrt.org/images/pacificcultureandhumanrights.pdf (accessed 5 April 2013)>7.

19 R E Rantala et al. 'Right to Health through Education: Mental Health and Human Rights' (2010) 1 *Human Rights Education in Asia–Pacific* 188, 189.

20 Ibid 190.

21 Ibid 193.

22 P Harpur and R Bales, 'The Positive Impact of the Convention on the Rights of Persons with Disabilities: A Case Study on the South Pacific and Lessons from the U.S. Experience' (2010) 37(4) *Northern Kentucky Law Review* 362.

States must at least have robust domestic anti-discrimination laws that are enforced.'[23] The paper poses the question whether laws in Pacific Island States adequately protect persons with disabilities. In answering the question, the authors purport to examine the laws of relevant Pacific jurisdictions. While there is no indication when this paper was written, it was published in 2010 and it might have been more persuasive if, at the time of publication, the material was more accurate. For example, when discussing Fiji as the 'only South Pacific Island State to expressly protect the rights of persons with disabilities',[24] reference is made to the Bill of Rights contained in the 1997 Fiji Constitution and enforced through the Fiji Human Rights Commission. Yet, the 1997 Constitution, along with its Bill of Rights, was abrogated by Presidential Decree on 10 April 2009.[25] The paper also cites the *Human Rights Commission Act 1999* as the relevant legislation. This statute was repealed by the *Human Rights Commission Decree 2009*, which established a new Human Rights Commission in Fiji, albeit with significantly reduced powers.[26]

Harpur and Bales assert that the CRPD is having a positive impact on Vanuatu by virtue of the fact that the country has adopted a national disability plan[27]—notwithstanding the fact that the plan has yet to be implemented—and they examine the policy in terms of how it aims to ensure the rights of disabled persons to employment.[28] There is a reference to a *National Disability Act* in Vanuatu which must be assumed to be an erroneous reference to the disability plan, as no such statute has been enacted in Vanuatu.[29] Finally, as with the Vanuatu disability plan itself, the paper makes no mention of mental health consumers as part of any group of disabled persons.[30]

The only other regional publication specifically to address human rights in the context of mental health, is the study on Youth Mental Stress & Violence in Fiji discussed previously in this chapter.[31] In its qualitative findings on human rights, the study describes a series of tensions, including the role of human rights in the breakdown of traditional chiefly authority; the conflict of human rights as a set of individual rights with the collective rights of custom; the preference of human rights over indigenous rights; and specific complexities in relation to the rights of women and children within traditional society.[32] The report made a number of suggestions as to how these problems could be approached, but the study was released in 2005 not long before the military coup d'état in Fiji in 2006 that brought with it the abolition of the Human Rights Commission, and the abrogation of the Fiji Constitution and its Bill of Rights in 2009.[33]

In a Commonwealth Foundation funded project in 2013, Pathare and Sagade reviewed the mental health legislation in Commonwealth member states to determine how legislation

23 Ibid 371.
24 Ibid 372.
25 *Fiji Constitution Amendment Act 1997 Revocation Decree 2009* (Fiji Islands).
26 *Human Rights Commission Decree 2009* (Fiji Islands).
27 Government of the Republic of Vanuatu Ministry of Justice & Social Welfare and The National Disability Committee, 'National Disability Policy and Plan of Action 2008-2018' (2009).
28 Harpur and Bales, above n 22, 377.
29 Ibid 388.
30 Mental health is dealt with separately under the *Vanuatu Mental Health Policy and Plan (2009-2015)*.
31 Partners in Community Development-Fiji, 'Youth Mental Stress & Violence in Fiji: Situation Analysis' (2005)
32 Ibid 36.
33 The new *Constitution of the Republic of Fiji* came into force after democratic elections in 2014 and the Fiji Human Rights and Anti-Discrimination Commission was established under section 45. The Commisison's roles and functions are supplemented by the *Human Rights Commission Decree 2009* (Fiji Islands)

complied with the CPRD in adopting a rights based framework.[34] The results were presented in a statistical format with selected illustrations from particular countries mapped against various provisions of the CRPD. There was no individual examination of country by country legislation in the report nor did the report consider the impact of subsidiary legislation or related health or social rights statutes. Current legislative reform projects and whether existing or new laws reflected actual practice were also excluded.[35] The report's overall findings, that mental health legislation in the vast majority of member states was outdated and did not comply with rights based obligations under the CRPD, were not surprising.[36]

3. Application of Human Rights Instruments in the Pacific

All the Pacific countries under examination are members of the United Nations and, as such, have implicitly, through their membership, accepted the principles enshrined in the UN Charter and the UDHR.[37]

An extensive consideration of the extent and operation of human rights legislation in the region is well beyond the ambit of this project. All the same, the signature or ratification of international conventions in the region in relation to human rights—particularly those impacting directly on mental health issues—is patchy at best. While Tonga, Samoa, Fiji and Vanuatu have all acceded to or ratified the *Convention on the Rights of the Child* (CRC),[38] only a few countries in the region including Tonga, Samoa Vanuatu and Fiji have signed or ratified the CRPD.[39] Of the four countries, Vanuatu is the sole signatory to the *Convention against Torture and other Cruel, Inhuman or Degrading Treatment or Punishment* (CAC)[40] and Fiji the sole signatory to the *Optional Protocol to the* CRPD.[41] Samoa and Vanuatu have respectively acceded to and ratified the ICCPR[42] and none of the countries under discussion is even a signatory to the ICESCR.[43] While this could be explained from a resource perspective,

---

34 Pathare S and J Sagade, 'Mental Health: A Legislative Framework to Empower, Protect and Care. A Review of Mental Health Legislation in Commonwealth Member States.' (2013).

35 Ibid 33.

36 Ibid 2, 33.

37 *Member States of the United Nations* <www.un.org/en/members/index.shtml (accessed 31 December 2012)> (Samoa in 1976; Tonga in 1999; Fiji in 1970 and Vanuatu in 1981).

38 Samoa 29 November 1994; Fiji Islands 13 August 1993; Tonga 6 December 1995; Vanuatu 7 July 1993; Domesticated by *Convention On The Rights Of the Child (Ratification) Act* [Cap 219] (Vanuatu), date of commencement 3 May 1993; www.paclii.org/pits (accessed 5 August 2011)

39 Samoa 24 September 2014, Fiji 2 June 2010; Tonga 15 November 2007; Vanuatu 17 May 2007 *United Nations Treaty Collection*<http://treaties.un.org/Pages/ViewDetails.aspx? src=TREATY&mtdsg_no=IV-4&chapter=4&lang=en (accessed 5 September 2015)> and domesticated by *Convention On The Rights Of Persons With Disabilities (Ratification) 2008* (Vanuatu), date of commencement 23 June 2008.

40 Domesticated by *Convention Against Torture And Other Cruel, Inhuman Or Degrading Treatment Or Punishment (Ratification) 2010* (Vanuatu), date of commencement 14 March 2011; *Fiji Disabled Peoples Association* <www.fdpa.org.fj/ProjectsAndServices.aspx (accessed 3 April 2012)>.

41 Fiji 2 June 2010; above n 39.

42 Samoa: 15 February 2008; Vanuatu: 29 November 2007; Nauru: 12 November 2001; www.paclii.org/pits (accessed 5 August 2011).

43 Vanuatu has plans to undertake community consultations in 2015 with a view to eventual ratification of the ICESCR. See Government of the Republic of Vanuatu, 'Universal Periodic Review (UPR) Recommendations Vanuatu, *A National Implementation Plan (2014-2018),* Ministry of Justice & Community Services' (2014)

it remains a significant omission in light of the ICESCR's right 'to the enjoyment of the highest attainable standard of physical and mental health'.

Jalal asserts that the Pacific region has by far the lowest ratification rates worldwide of the core international human right treaties.[44] The author further claims that Pacific countries often do not see the need for ratification of the ICCPR as most civil and political rights are already incorporated in their constitutions and ratification would only burden them with onerous reporting responsibilities.[45] Furthermore, most countries have limited financial and human resources and lack the technical expertise to fulfill treaty obligations. Those treaties least likely to upset the powerful stakeholders such as religious bodies and customary chiefs are more likely to be ratified.[46]

Compliance with the State reporting requirements under the conventions is even more sporadic. United Nations Human Rights records indicate that neither Vanuatu nor Samoa has met its State reporting obligations under the ICCPR—namely, initially within a year and thereafter as required.[47] Vanuatu is yet to report under the CRPD and has never submitted a State report under the CAC. Tonga and Fiji—being only signatories to the CRPD—are under no State reporting obligations. Initial individual State reports under the CRC were due in 1995—Fiji reported in 1996 and Vanuatu in 1997. Samoa did not submit its initial report until 2006, despite having ratified the convention in 1994. Tonga, having acceded to the CRC in 1995, has never reported to the UN as a State party.[48] A summary of the relevant provisions appears in Table 12.1 below.

Table 12.1. Signature [S], Accession [A], Ratification [R] of Treaties[49]

Treaty	**Tonga**	**Samoa**	**Fiji**	**Vanuatu**
ICCPR (1966)	x	2008 [A]	x	2007 [S] 2008 [R]
Last state report (initial report due within 1 year)	n/a	nil	n/a	nil
ICESCR (1966)	x	x	x	x
Last state report	n/a	n/a	n/a	n/a
Torture (CAC) (1984)	x	x	x	2011 [A]
Last state report (initial report due within 1 year)	n/a	n/a	n/a	nil
Rights of the Child (CRC) (1989)	1995 [A]	1990 [S] 1994 [R]	1993 [S/R]	1990 [S] 1993 [R]
Last state report (initial report due within 2 years)	nil	2006	1996	1997
Persons with Disabilities (CRPD) (2006)	2007 [S]	2014 [S]	2010 [S]	2007 [S] 2008 [R]
Last state report (initial report due within 2 years)	n/a	nil	n/a	nil

<http://www.mjcs.gov.vu/images/news/disability_desk/UPR/UPR_National_Action_Plan_20142018_.pdf (Accessed 3 September 2015)> 7.

44 Imrana Jalal, above n 18.

45 P Imrana Jalal, 'Using Rights-Based Programming Principles to Claim Rights: The Regional Rights Resource Team (RRRT) Project in the Pacific Islands' (2005) <www.rrrt.org/images/usingrightsbased programmingprinciples.pdf (accesssed 5 April 2013)> 7.

46 Imrana Jalal, above n 18, 6.

47 *International Covenant on Civil and Political Rights*, opened for signature 16 December 1966, 999 UNTS 171 (entered into force 23 March 1976) art 40.

48 *United Nations Treaty Collection, State Reports* <http://www.ohchr.org/EN/HRBodies/CRC/Pages/ CRCIndex.aspx (accessed 17 December 2015)>

49 *United Nations Treaty Collection, Participant Search* <http://treaties.un.org/pages/Treaty ParticipantSearch.aspx?tab=UN (accessed 9 Nov 2012)>; *United Nations Treaty Collection, State Reports* <http://tb.ohchr.org/default.aspx (accessed 5 September 2015)>.

3.1. The Effects of 'State Party' Status

The question then becomes, to what extent ratification impacts on whether international instruments become part of the law of a country. And even when they *do* become law in a country, what observance is given to that law. In the context of mental health law, this is relevant to countries such as Samoa and Vanuatu as State Parties to the ICCPR and Vanuatu which is the only country to have ratified the CRPD.

International law is not directly enforceable in the courts of common law countries although, as a matter of statutory interpretation, domestic legislation is interpreted consistently with international obligations wherever it is possible to do so.[50] This doctrine of non-enforceability has been inherited from Britain, which has no written constitution with an entrenched Bill of Rights.[51] Most constitutions in the Pacific region contain an assortment of fundamental human rights and freedoms to be applied without discrimination, generally modelled on the International Covenants. In Samoa and Vanuatu these include life, liberty, freedom from inhumane treatment and the right to due process and a fair trial.[52] A general right to freedom exists under section 1 of the Constitution of Tonga along with general rights to due legal process.[53] Fiji adopted a new constitution, in 2014 following the abrogation of its previous constitution by the interim military regime in April 2009. Chapter 2 of the new Fijian Constitution contains an extensive raft of freedoms and rights including the right to freedom from discrimination on the grounds of health and disability, the right to health and specific rights directed to children and persons with disabilities.[54] Some countries in the region apply the doctrine of non-enforceability strictly—to a lesser extent Tonga—while others regard international law as a legitimate part of domestic law, often irrespective of signature or ratification—such as Fiji (under the previous constitution) and Samoa.[55]

Several Pacific countries have specific constitutional provisions allowing the application of international conventions by the courts without the need for ratification.[56] Despite not being a signatory to the ICCPR, Fiji under its then constitution—which required the court to have regard to public international law as an interpretative aid—upheld the rights of privacy and equality for sexual minorities prosecuted under the former Penal Code for illegal acts of homosexuality. In *Nadan & McCoskar,* the High Court of Fiji recognised the strong opposition from the churches and much of the community to the decriminalisation of homosexuality, but held there must be serious reasons before the State or community could interfere with individual rights of privacy including sexual conduct by consenting adults.[57]

---

50 See *Polites v Commonwealth* (1945) 70 CLR 60.

51 Imrana Jalal and Madraiwiwi, above n 14, ix.

52 *Constitution of the Republic of Vanuatu* s 5; *Constitution of the Independent State of Western Samoa 1960* ss 5–7.

53 Substantive amendments to the Tongan Constitution in 2010 did not affect the declaration of rights per se except in relation to the constitution of parliament; election procedures; and the power of the King and Cabinet. See *Act of Constitution (Amendment) Act 2010 (Tonga); Act of Constitution (Amendment) (No. 2) Act 2010 (Tonga); Act of Constitution (Amendment) (No. 3) Act 2010 (Tonga).*

54 *Constitution of the Republic of Fiji* Chapter 2.

55 Imrana Jalal and Madraiwiwi, above n 14, ix.

56 For example, Constitution of Tuvalu, art 15(5)(c).

57 *Nadan & McCoskar v State* [2005] FJHC 252. This decision was premised on the fact that, at the time, Fiji had ratified the ICCPR (which includes the right to privacy).Winter J stated 'Fiji has ratified the International Convention on Civil and Political Rights. The appellants are entitled to expect that I will interpret these rights in accordance with its provisions.' However, no United Nations or PITS records support this assertion and the

Under the current constitution in Fiji, when interpreting and applying Chapter 2 Bill of Rights, 'a court, tribunal or other authority ... may, if relevant, consider international law, applicable to the protection of rights and freedoms in this Chapter.'[58]

Even without empowering constitutional provisions and without having signed or ratified the convention, Samoa applied the principles of the *Hague Convention on the Civil Aspects of International Child Abduction*[59] in the case of *Wagner v Radke* and ordered the return of a child to his mother in Germany after the father had abducted his son—contrary to a German court order—and taken him to live with him in Samoa.[60] Conversely, the Supreme Court of Tonga refused to apply the same convention in a similar fact scenario, on the grounds that Tonga had not ratified the convention and it was therefore unenforceable.[61]

However, some later cases in Tonga have taken a more flexible view. In *Tone v Police*—while conceding that the *Convention on the Rights of the Child* was unenforceable unless domesticated—the Supreme Court held it was, nonetheless, appropriate to refer to the terms of the CRC as a guide as to what was acceptable treatment for children.[62] In considering the effect of Tonga's accession to the convention, Ward C. J held that 'whilst the accession by a State to a convention indicates its willingness to be bound by the terms of the convention, it will only be enforced by the enactment of necessary domestic legislation.'[63]

The same court went a step further and applied the CRC in the case of *Fa'aoso v Paongo* when it awarded damages against the state for injuries inflicted on a child after he was assaulted by police officers while in custody.[64]

In *R v Vola* the Supreme Court of Tonga—in the country's first case involving the application of the principles of the ICCPR—when deciding whether to impose the death penalty for a convicted murderer, did *not* consider itself constrained by the fact that Tonga was neither a State party nor a signatory to the convention.[65] The Court considered the principles underlying the right to life in the ICCPR—specifically the arbitrary deprivation of life—as 'important' to its decision. Jalal and Madraiwiwi maintain this case illustrates a clear departure from the traditional approach of non-enforceability of international law.[66] However, it is consistent with the increasing tendency of courts to have regard to international human rights norms when applying and interpreting domestic law.

3.2. Human Rights Principles versus Pacific Culture

Ratu Madraiwiwi contends that 'throughout Pacific societies there is profound skepticism, even suspicion, about the compatibility of traditional and cultural values with the concept of human rights' and 'many traditional leaders and nationalists make little effort to

case did not go further on appeal. The relevant provisions the Penal Code have since been repealed by *Crimes Decree 2009* (Fiji Islands).

58 *Constitution of the Republic of Fiji* s7(1)(b).

59 *Hague Convention on the Civil Aspects of International Child Abduction*, opened for signature 25 October 1980, 1343 UNTS (entered into force 1 December 1983).

60 *Wagner v Radke* [1997] WSSC 6.

61 *Gorce v Miller* [2003] TOSC 46.

62 *Tone v Police* [2004] TOSC 36.

63 Ibid.

64 *Fa'aoso v Paongo* [2006] TOSC 37.

65 *R v Vola* [2005] TOSC 31.

66 Imrana Jalal and Madraiwiwi, above n 14, 69.

understand it.'[67] The author also asserts that, in the Fijian context, human rights—particularly when promoted by economically advanced societies and aid donors—are seen as a threat to traditional indigenous values, which hold the rights of the individual subject to those of the collective.[68] Even so, Madraiwiwi claims that the two are not irreconcilable as both philosophies have an ultimate interest in 'peace, order and good government'. [69]

In a number of papers outlining the field work principles and research findings of Regional Rights Resource Team (RRRT), Jalal, a respected human rights activist, identifies a series of human rights challenges in Pacific island countries. These include the alleged conflict between human rights and Pacific culture, identity, patriarchy and religious fundamentalism; democracy and human rights as obstacles to economic growth; the lack of regional human rights bodies; periodic interruptions to democracy; and poverty, poor governance and globalisation.[70] Jalal asserts that, while governments of most Pacific countries *officially* support human rights principles, the culture is intensely impervious. Indigenous traditional power structures are patriarchal and hierarchical, and identity is tied to the inherited chiefly system. It is this system that is 'strongly resistant to human rights intervention as it is seen as a "Western imposition" on culture and identity.'[71]

To add to the complexity of the situation, Jalal argues that the small populations in many Pacific island countries make it socially difficult for human rights activists to take an unpopular stand against the State or the village chiefs. Such behaviour is seen as a betrayal of one's culture.[72] Furthermore, Christian churches are very powerful in the Pacific and many view human rights as a threat to their existence. For example, the movement of Samoans from established churches to new fringe churches has been blamed on the human right to religious freedom rather than the prospect that it might simply be a case of more educated Samoans exercising more available choices.[73]

Jalal gives particular consideration to a number of treaties but—as these writings precede the introduction of the CRPD—there is no specific discussion of disability or mental disorders. Nonetheless, many of the arguments raised are equally applicable to disability and mental health in the context of human rights.

Globalisation and the increasing reliance on donor aid in developing countries in the Pacific contributes to the tension between rights based ideology and culture. While economic and development imperatives are seen as high priority in the region, increasing urbanisation continues to create environmental pressures that are reaching breaking point.[74] Conversely, customary values and practices underpin everyday life in the rural areas and are often seen as jeopardising the protection and promotion of human rights. The dependence on donor aid often brings with it a nominal commitment to good governance and human rights initiatives[75]—requirements that are frequently equated to a denial of political sovereignty. In fact, Jalal goes so far as to suggest that many Pacific countries 'resist ratification as an

67 Madraiwiwi Ratu, above n 13, 50–52.
68 Ibid.
69 Ibid.
70 Imrana Jalal, above n 15, 5–6.
71 Ibid 7.
72 Ibid.
73 Imrana Jalal, above n 18, 7.
74 Law Commission New Zealand, above n 1, 22.
75 Ibid 22.

expression of hostility against what they consider to be forced ratification by superpowers and the hegemonic attitudes of the UN.'[76]

Other justifications for this ideological tension include the perceived costs of compliance with State party obligations and the limited resources—both professional and financial—that developing countries are prepared to allocate to such tasks. In some cases, countries may be averse to international scrutiny in relation to their domestic human rights practices.[77] Furthermore, where constitutional rights are part of the law of the state—for example in Samoa and Vanuatu—expenditure of additional resources on the adoption of international standards is seen as unnecessary.[78]

The individualism versus collectivism conflict exists despite the fact that the protection of individual rights is enshrined in many Pacific constitutions. However, the synthesis between constitutional rights and domestic legislation in the region is somewhat erratic. The conundrum, therefore, lies in the practical application of those rights. As the Law Commission of New Zealand suggests in its comprehensive analysis of custom and human rights in the Pacific:

> Custom provides Pacific nations with much of their sense of identity and with vital governance and dispute resolution mechanisms. Human rights provide Pacific people (especially the most vulnerable) with protection and support for realising their aspirations. A harmonising approach will strengthen legal systems and the development of jurisprudence unique to Pacific states[79].
>
> [C]ustom and human rights can be harmonised by looking to the shared, underlying values of both. Harmonisation will enhance custom by bringing it more into line with changing social conditions and ensuring that it continues to reflect the underlying values of Pacific communities. Far from threatening custom, human rights can help it to develop and therefore survive in a modern world. Harmonisation will also assist the legitimisation of human rights by presenting them in a way that reflects the values of Pacific societies.[80]

Taufe'ulungaki, when discussing cultural rights in Tonga, argues that 'Pacific cultures, if they are to survive, must be lived by the peoples of the Pacific'[81] and that Pacific countries in their pursuit of modernity and development are 'willingly conniving in the destruction ... of their cultural heritages by adopting alien and inappropriate education, social, cultural, political and economic systems.'[82] The author claims that globalisation has had a significant negative impact on social order and available wealth in Tonga and, in a situation where cultural identity is now ambiguous, youth—who make up more than half the population—are bearing the brunt of cultural change.[83] One of the 'knock on' effects of this is likely to be an increase in risk taking behaviour and substance abuse and thus the incidence of mental illness. As discussed in Chapter 5, the demand for psychiatric services in Tonga is on the increase

---

76 Imrana Jalal, above n 18, 16.
77 Law Commission New Zealand, above n 1.
78 Ibid 69.
79 Ibid 11.
80 Ibid 12.
81 A Taufe'ulugaki, 'Cultural Rights in the Tongan Context: Some Issues' in M Wilson and P Hunt (eds), *Culture, Rights, and Cultural Rights: Perspectives from the South Pacific* (Huia Publishers, 2000) 91, 93.
82 Ibid 99.
83 Ibid 97.

and, for those who are subjected to involuntary detention, access to justice becomes a critical issue.

3.3. Human Rights Instruments and Mental Health Laws

To date, no court in the region has had cause to consider the application of international law with particular regard to the rights of mental health consumers. Even so, the trend in Samoa and Tonga—to apply international law irrespective of treaty signature or ratification—is encouraging should the rights of mental health consumers ever come before the courts. The prediction for Fiji is less clear. Before the abrogation of its constitution in 2009, Fiji had demonstrated a willingness to apply international principles, where appropriate, regardless of ratification. The fact that Fiji's 2010 *Mental Health Decree* includes reference to several international conventions and principles should be taken as a positive sign as should the expansive nature of the Bill of Rights in Fiji's new constitution. The reality or otherwise of this is a matter for the future.

While the constitutional provisions of the countries under discussion make some reference to fundamental human rights and freedoms, none deals directly with rights in relation to mental health, medical treatment or involuntary medical detention or freedom from discrimination on the grounds of disability.

3.3.1. Tonga

Apart from s 17 of the *Mental Health Act 2001* (Tonga), which requires that the determination of mental illness be made in accordance with 'internationally accepted medical standards'—presumably based on Principle 4 of the *MI Principles*—the legislation makes no reference to compliance with international instruments regarding the treatment of mental health consumers. However, it is more than likely that some or all of these instruments were considered when the legislation was being drafted. The provision of verbal and written information; informed consent and independent review mechanisms illustrate some of the international principles that have found their way into the legislation.

3.3.2. Samoa

Similarly, Samoan mental health legislation makes no specific reference to international instruments concerning the care and treatment of mental health consumers. However, it is clear that culturally appropriate mental health care[84] was a paramount consideration in Samoa with the adoption of the community care model. The exclusion of non-clinical criteria from the assessment of mental disorders[85] and review of detention are examples of some of the basic principles that have been transposed into the Samoan statute.

In foreshadowing protection of the rights of disadvantaged minorities, section 15 of the Samoan Constitution guarantees equality of all before the law and under section 15(3)(b) provides that 'nothing shall prevent the making of any provision for the protection or

---

84 Office of the High Commissioner for Human Rights, *Principles for the Protection of Persons with Mental Illness and the Improvement of Mental Health Care*, GA Res 46/119, (17 December 1991) [2].

85 *Mental Health Act 2007* (Samoa) s 2.

advancement of women or children or of any socially or educationally retarded class of persons.'

The Samoan National Policy on Disability has as one of its primary objectives to 'empower people with disabilities to promote and advocate for their human rights'[86] and that 'all stakeholders conduct awareness programmes and consultations on the *Convention on the Rights of Persons with Disabilities*, relevant national Acts and the Constitution.'[87] It seems that little progress has been made towards the fulfilment of these objectives.

3.3.3. Fiji

The only country in the region to have made direct reference to any of these human rights instruments in its mental health law is Fiji. The *Mental Health Decree 2010* requires that

> due regard be given to the WHO principles[88] and other international agreements and standards concerning the care and treatment of the mentally disordered—including the *International Covenant on Human Rights*, the *United Nations Convention on Rights of the Child* and the *Convention on the Rights of People with a Disability* [sic].[89]

The Decree makes no specific mention of the *MI Principles* but these principles—which formed the basis of the *WHO Ten Principles* in 1996—were referred to in the Fiji Law Reform Commission (FLRC) report, which preceded the new legislation.[90] It may have been a deliberate omission given that many writers consider the CRPD to have superseded the *MI Principles.* Or it may be that the reference to 'other international agreements and standards' imports the *MI Principles* by implication as the wording suggests the list is not intended to be exhaustive.

The FLRC, in drafting the *Mental Health Bill 2007*—which ultimately formed the basis for the *Mental Health Decree 2010*—relied heavily on the WHO Resource Book.[91] While the stated objectives of the Decree appear to be consistent with the cited principles and conventions, most of the provisions are subject to the rider 'as a far as practicable and subject to available resources'.[92] The extent of rights incorporated in this Decree has been discussed previously in Chapter 7.

3.3.4. Vanuatu

A case that clearly illustrates the void between the law and the reality of life, albeit outside the mental health context, occurred in 2011 in Vanuatu—a country that has ratified and domesticated more rights based conventions than any other in the region, including the CRC. A healthy six-year-old boy was offered by his parents—as the rarest and ultimate form

86 Government of Samoa Ministry of Women Community and Social Development, 'Samoa National Policy on Disability' (2009) [1.1].

87 Ibid 24.

88 *Mental Health Decree 2010* (Fiji Islands) s 4(a). It is assumed this is a reference to the *WHO, Mental Health Care Law: Ten Basic Principles (1996).*

89 Ibid s 4(b). The drafting errors seen here in relation to the titles of these conventions are typical of the Decree and give some indication of the haste with which it was implemented.

90 Fiji Law Reform Commission, 'Issue Paper No. 1 – Purpose, Principles and Definitions – Review of the Fiji Mental Treatment Act' (2006) 1.

91 M Freeman, *WHO Resource Book on Mental Health, Human Rights and Legislation* (World Health Organisation, 2005).

92 *Mental Health Decree 2010* (Fiji Islands) ss 5–7, 34.

of traditional reconciliation and 'a symbol of peace'—to a family in another village in an attempt to resolve a 27-year-old land dispute between the two waring families. The quarrels between the families had involved extensive property damage to gardens and livestock, the destruction of ten houses and various threats on the lives of family members.[93]

The rationale of the reconciliation was described as follows:

> The main reason for handing over a child instead of reconciling in the usual way is that all the suffering they have been going through as a result of the dispute must come to an end. If any conflict should arise in the future, the presence of the boy would immediately remind both parties of the importance of peace to prevail at all times.[94]

Such a traditional arrangement—which can only be described as 'trading' a child—unmistakably offends both international and domestic law. At the very least, the legislation in Vanuatu that domesticated the CRC,[95] prohibits punishment on the basis of beliefs held by the child's parents (art.2); treatment other than that in the best interests of the child (art. 5); separation from the child's parents or family except by court order (art. 9, 20); exploitation of the child (art. 19, 36); traditional practices prejudicial to the child's health (art. 24); the abduction, sale or trafficking of children (art. 35); and degrading treatment or punishment (art. 37). In this instance, neither the ratification of the CRC nor its domestication served to protect this child.

The legislation, which has been in force now for almost 20 years, requires the state to 'recognise the right of the child to the enjoyment of the highest attainable standard of health and to facilities for the treatment of illness and rehabilitation of health.'[96] While there is no specific reference to mental health, a mentally ill child in Vanuatu could not realistically expect that his or her rights would be protected any more than those of the young child discussed above.

While the Vanuatu Constitution guarantees a raft of fundamental rights and freedoms to all persons without discrimination, there is no reference to disability as a ground of discrimination.[97] Still, as Jowitt writes, 'legally women are granted equality under art. 5 of the Constitution and Vanuatu has ratified CEDAW but in reality the majority of women in Vanuatu do not experience equality with the gravest injustice being the high levels of violence against women.'[98] Jowitt viewed the legal system as denying justice to women and made recommendations to improve access to justice, including in camera proceedings conducted in the local language to reduce the intimidation associated with attending court, as well as reductions in court fees.[99]

In recognising the substantial conflict with custom law and the roles of women within that framework, awareness training by itself was seen as inadequate protection for women who access the justice system, and it was recommended that customary dispute resolution be

[93] L Garae, 'Family Offers Boy as Reconciliation,' *Vanuatu Daily Post* (Port Vila, Vanuatu), 20 August 2011, 9.

[94] Ibid.

[95] *Convention On The Rights Of the Child (Ratification) Act* [Cap 219] (Vanuatu).

[96] Ibid art 24.

[97] *Constitution of the Republic of Vanuatu* s 5.

[98] A Jowitt, 'Barriers to Accessing Justice: The Vanuatu Experience' in Asia Pacific Judicial Reform Forum (ed), *Searching for Success in Judicial Reform: Voices from the Asia Pacific Experience* (Oxford University Press, 2009) 137, 151.

[99] Ibid 156.

incorporated into the state legal system.[100] This scenario has parallels for equally marginalised groups such as mental health consumers where similar degrees of sensitivity are appropriate. It is self-evident in Vanuatu, as Jowitt maintains, that 'despite the widespread paper commitment to rights, a law or a signature on an international document is only a symbolic commitment. In reality many people suffer injustice on a daily basis.'[101]

After conducting a basic mental health care training program in Vanuatu in 2009, Benson writes

> [h]uman rights issues for people with severe psychosis depended on the support of the community, the family, how dangerous they were, and what contact they had had with the criminal justice system. People with severe untreated schizophrenia, bipolar disorder and brief psychotic disorder have been given traditional medication and religious exorcism and cared for by their family and community.[102]

To say that law without enforcement is not law, is trite. Yet, this represents the status of much of the law in Vanuatu. Harpur and Bales, in their study of the operation of the CRPD in the Pacific, assert that the CRPD is having a positive impact on Vanuatu by virtue of the fact that the country has adopted a national disability plan.[103] This assertion is debatable given the fact that the plan has yet to be implemented. In fact, in setting up a workshop in 2012 to develop Vanuatu's initial report to the UN under the CRPD—which was due in 2010—the then Minister of Justice and Community Services admitted that 'the government had not really committed itself ... to the implementation of the Convention which is an obligation for a state party.'[104] To date only a draft report has been prepared and has yet to receive endorsement from the Council of Ministers.[105]

In promoting its strategic objective to develop a national framework for implementation of treaties and constitutional provisions, the situation was succinctly outlined in 2014 by the responsible ministry as follows

> Currently International Conventions are poorly understood, obligations are not met, and are not owned. Insufficient consultation has contributed to lack of understanding. The consequence is that vulnerable groups, such as the disabled and the aged, are not adequately catered for through law and support services, or worse, are discriminated against. The strategy is intended to result in greater respect and protection for citizens through legislation, greater awareness by individuals about their rights and improvement to Vanuatu's international standing.[106]

---

100 Ibid 157.

101 Ibid 137.

102 J Benson et al. 'A New Era in Mental Health Care in Vanuatu' (2011) 2011 *International Journal of Family Medicine* 3.

103 Government of the Republic of Vanuatu Ministry of Justice & Social Welfare and The National Disability Committee, above n 27.

104 G Ligo, 'Initial Report on Disability in Vanuatu Released,' *Vanuatu Daily Post* (Port Vila, Vanuatu), 15 November 2012, 3.

105 Government of the Republic of Vanuatu, 'Annual Report 2013 Ministry of Justice & Community Services' (2013) <http://www.mjcs.gov.vu/images/research_database/Annual_Report_2013__05JUN14.pdf (Accessed 3 September 2015)> 18.

106 Government of the Republic of Vanuatu, 'Strategy for the Justice and Community Services Sector 2014 - 2017, Ministry for Justice and Community Services' (2014) 12.

3.4. National Human Rights Institutions

There is no independent human rights commission in Tonga.

An interim National Human Rights Committee, which has yet to be formalised, was established in Vanuatu 2013. It was envisioned that this would take place in 2014 and the National Human Rights Committee would assist the ministry in establishing the Human Rights Commission.[107] To date neither the Committee nor the Commission has been formed. The Vanuatu Law Commission released an issues paper in March 2015 asking whether Vanuatu needed a Human Rights Commission and if such functions and responsibilities should be assumed by the Office of the Ombudsman.[108] The Commission has yet to report on this matter.

Following the abrogation of the Constitution of Fiji in 2009, along with its Bill of Rights, there was no constitutional framework for human rights in Fiji.[109] In the same year the *Human Rights Commission Act 1999*—which enshrined the Fiji Human Rights Commission—was repealed by the *Human Rights Commission Decree 2009.* A new Human Rights Commission was established under the Decree but with considerably reduced powers[110] and resources and operated with neither a chairperson nor commissioners from 2009, inhibiting its independence and effectiveness.[111] The Commission was not authorised to investigate complaints against the abrogation, other actions of the government, or the 2006 coup, a prohibition which continues with its replacement body.[112] No reported cases have been heard by the Commission, in either of its forms, since 2004 and the body has produced limited publications for public dissemination, the last of which was December 2009.[113] The then Commission produced two inspection reports in 2011 and 2012 describing conditions in prisons and police holding cells and making limited recommendations.[114] A new Fiji Human Rights and Anti-Discrimination Commission was established under section 45 of the new Fijian Constitution and the roles and functions of the Commission, as stipulated in Chapter 2 of the Constitution, are supplemented by the *Human Rights Commission Decree 2009.*[115] In May 2015, a High Court judge, Mohammed Ajmeer, was appointed as the Chairperson of the Commission and the commissioners' positions were to be advertised.[116] The current website and public interface for the Commission is undeveloped and outdated.[117] While disability remains a 'prohibited ground of discrimination' under the Decree and the Constitution, until

[107] Ibid 16.

[108] Vanuatu Law Commission, 'Ombudsman Act - Issues Paper No 1 2015 ' (2015)

[109] *Fiji Constitution Amendment Act 1997 Revocation Decree 2009* (Fiji Islands).

[110] *Human Rights Commission Decree 2009* (Fiji Islands).

[111] United States Department of State Bureau of Democracy Human Rights and Labor, 'Country Reports on Human Rights Practices for 2013 - Fiji' (2013) 3.

[112] Ibid 19.

[113] Fiji Human Rights Commission, (December 2009) 8(4) *Rights Quarterly*

[114] Fiji Human Rights Commission, 'Correctional Centre Inspection Report 2011' (2011) <http://www.fhrc.org.fj/index.php?option=com_docman&task=cat_view&gid=40&Itemid=11 (accessed 20 december 2015)>; Fiji Human Rights Commission, 'Police Holding Cells Inspection Report 2012' (2012) <http://www.fhrc.org.fj/index.php?option=com_docman&task=cat_view&gid=40&Itemid=11 (accessed 20 December 2015)>

[115] Fiji Human Rights and Anti - Discrimination Commission, <http://www.fhrc.org.fj/ (accessed 18 December 2015)>

[116] Sofaia Koroitanoa, 'President Made Appointments to PSC and Human Rights and Anti Discriminatory Commission,' *FijiOne* (Suva, Fiji), 8 May 2015 <http://fijione.tv/president-made-appointments-to-psc-and-human-rights-and-anti-discriminatory-commission/ (accessed 18 December 2015)>

[117] Fiji Human Rights and Anti - Discrimination Commission, above n 115.

the Commission is functional access to any supervisory mechanisms under the Decree is denied.

Samoa's Law & Justice Sector Plan 2012-2016 has one of its key objectives as improving access to justice, law and legal services, and includes the establishment of an independent Human Rights Commission.[118] While there is still no legislative human rights platform in Samoa, the mandate of the Ombudsman was expanded in 2013 to establish a national human rights institute and to promote awareness of human rights, engage and cooperate with civil society, business and academia, monitor compliance with international and domestic human rights law, and report to Parliament annually on the status of human rights in Samoa.[119]

The Australian Human Rights Commission has recommended ongoing capacity building support for the development of human rights mechanisms in the Pacific,[120] but some countries still oppose the concept given the ongoing costs of maintaining such bodies.[121] In making its recommendations, the Commission appeared to be cognisant of the challenges facing human rights mechanism in the region, including the lack of knowledge and approval of human rights and the need to support societies to improve awareness and acceptance.[122]

In the end, however packaged, such programs still come in the form of donor aid—with all the contingent obligations—and, unless they are carried out in a way that is sympathetic to regional cultural imperatives, will fail to achieve their objectives.

4. Conclusion

Cultural views on mental health and international human rights principles play a major role in discouraging the acceptance of human rights based initiatives in the region. Many of these initiatives are the foundation of reformed mental health legislation and hold the key to unlocking pathways to justice for mental health consumers. Yet, the mere existence of legislative rights is not enough. Despite the impact of globalisation, cultural beliefs and traditional practices remain an integral part of life in Pacific island countries. Legislative based rights in mental health law that do not take into account these beliefs and practices and do not operate in a culturally sensitive setting will only serve to frustrate access to justice. Tonga and Samoa are good illustrations of jurisdictions where individual mental health care professionals have made important inroads into researching and developing transcultural mental health care in order to optimise outcomes for mental health consumers. Some of these methodologies could be applied in a legal setting so as to facilitate access to justice for those detained under mental health legislation—or even to circumvent detention in the first place. Undoubtedly, this is what the New Zealand legislation contemplated by its requirement that

---

118 Government of Samoa Office of the Attorney General, 'Samoa Law & Justice Sector Plan 2012-2016: Justice for a Safe and Stable Samoa' (2012) <http://www.samoaljs.ws/english/images/stories/uploads/SLJS_Plan_2012-2016_English.pdf (accessed 5 September 2015)> 16,19.

119 *Ombudsman (Komesina o Sulufaiga) Act 2013* (Samoa) s33.

120 Australian Human Rights Commission, 'Human Rights Mechanisms and the Asia-Pacific Region: Submission to the Human Rights Sub-Committee of the Joint Standing Committee on Foreign Affairs, Defence and Trade' (2008) 5.

121 Ibid 22.

122 Ibid 20–21.

powers be exercised and proceedings conducted with 'proper respect for the person's cultural and ethnic identity'.[123]

As Jalal properly maintains, while culture should not take precedence over basic human rights, rights based interventions should take place in a culturally appropriate manner.[124] Jalal argues that

> engaging in dialogue is more likely to achieve a sustainable outcome than engaging in the 'naming, blaming and shaming' approach favoured by most human rights organisations. This is particularly important in small countries where people are closely connected in various ways through their social and land owning, clans, *wantok* or *mataqali* groups.[125]

Some other problems concerning the acceptance of human rights principles in the Pacific are less easy to resolve. The individualism versus communalism debate requires community education at all levels and government policy commitment for any prospect of resolution—despite the existence of domestic constitutional rights. As long as resources are limited and compliance with human rights treaties is seen as undermining sovereignty and a 'price to pay' for continued international aid, genuine commitment to realisation of those rights will continue to elude priority on political agendas.

A discussion of how other factors such as the availability and distribution of resources and the implementation of government policy have also served to frustrate the development of mental health care and access to justice in the Pacific follows in the next chapter.

---

123 *Mental Health (Compulsory Assessment and Treatment) Act 1992* (NZ) s 5(2)(c).
124 Imrana Jalal, above n 15, 28.
125 Ibid.

Chapter 13

Impediments to Accessing Justice through Mental Health Law Reform - Resources and Policy

This chapter examines the demographic, economic and policy themes that are instrumental in obstructing access to justice under rights based mental health legislation in the region. These aspects—combined with the cultural and human rights issues canvassed in the previous chapters—are largely responsible for the inability of mental health consumers to access justice effectively under rights based mental health laws.

1. Introduction

The delivery of general health services in the Pacific is characterised for the most part by a lack of universal access to health services, a focus on public—as opposed to private—health care providers; and a lack of specialist expertise. In many Pacific island countries, those living in outlying remote islands are unable to access qualified health professionals except by travelling—in many cases long distances—to larger centres. It is often the case that people requiring specialist medical care are flown to Australia, New Zealand, Fiji or New Caledonia for treatment, although rarely does this include treatment for any form of mental health disorder.[1] Traditional healers, village elders and family members often play a role in the care of the mentally ill when transport problems compromise the operation of the outreach mental health teams.

The WHO, in its 2002 Western Pacific strategy, identified a number of challenges for the region, most of which are common to the region.[2] Some countries continue to experience an emigration of trained health professionals to other countries in the region. In most countries where national revenue is limited, government funds are frequently diverted from essential services such as health, education and infrastructure for political expediency. Mental health services, for the most part, are not integrated into general health services and—where finance is available for health services—mental health services are not seen as necessitating a discrete

---

1 P MacFarlane and H Ménard, *Medical Law in the South Pacific* (Kluwer Law International, 2014) 29.

2 World Health Organisation, 'Regional Strategy for Mental Health' (WHO, Western Pacific Region, 2002) 13.

source of funding and is even less of a priority.[3] Funding is frequently not available for the supply of appropriate medicines and other resources. Where financial assistance is provided by non-government agencies there is limited coordination with governments in the use of these resources.[4] Regrettably, little progress has been made since.

Social and economic conditions also have a critical impact on mental health. In the context of the Western Pacific, the WHO paints a graphic picture when describing rapid social change; social and economic instability; globalisation; poverty and poor education; armed conflict and violence; urbanisation; migration; unemployment; family disruption and social isolation as some of the stress factors contributing to the increasing prevalence of mental health disorders.[5]

> The social fabric of society is weakening and failing to help those who are ill and to transmit moral guidance to its members. This is reflected by more dissatisfaction, more crime, more intolerance and more discrimination against those who are different ... the world and its tasks are becoming more complex; people with marginal capacity cannot function in it.[6]

Mental health is unquestionably a growing concern for Pacific communities, particularly so for youth who often comprise over half the population and for whom there are reduced employment opportunities; weakened cultural connections through urban migration; and increased incidence of substance abuse, youth suicide and mental illness. As is the global experience, stigmatisation of mental illness is a major obstacle to identifying and treating those in need. Yet, despite repeated commitments by regional governments over the years to develop and improve mental health service delivery, few have delivered on their promises.

2. Professional Resources

In many of the smaller countries in the region, the availability of specialised skills and resources is a major limitation when it comes to the provision of mental health services and, indeed, health services in general. In the WHO situational analysis conducted throughout the Pacific in 2005, neither Samoa nor Vanuatu had the services of a resident specialist psychiatrist; Tonga had one; and Fiji two, with three undergoing post graduate training.[7] Ten years on little has changed—Samoa now has the services of one part time expatriate psychiatrist and, while up until 2013 Fiji had four registered psychiatrists, only two were employed in the public health system,[8] which supports a large inpatient facility of 136 beds.

---

3 Ibid.

4 Ibid 14.

5 Ibid 11.

6 Ibid 11.

7 World Health Organisation, 'Situational Analysis of Mental Health Needs and Resources in Pacific Island Countries' (WHO, Centre for Mental Health Research, Policy & Service Development, 2005) 83–118.

8 College of Medicine and Nursing and Health Sciences, 'Situational Analysis of Specialised Clinical Services in the Republic of Fiji 2010-12, Strengthening Specialised Clinical Services Program' (2012) [4.4.1]

Fiji has now been reduced to three registered psychiatrists with only one employed full time in the public health system.[9]

The number of mental health trained nurses in the region varies from approximately thirty in Fiji to none in Tonga.[10] There are no resident trained clinical psychologists in Samoa, Tonga or Vanuatu.[11]

Roberts' 2007 study on masculinity and mental health across Melanesia revealed a common need for professional counselling services, which were not a feature of public sector workforce planning. Community based mental health follow-up or rehabilitation services were virtually non-existent or were seriously limited in scope and professional expertise.[12] There is no evidence that the situation is significantly different some years later.

Apart from the University of Papua New Guinea, which has not been the institution of choice for the countries under discussion, there are no postgraduate training opportunities in psychiatry for medical practitioners in the region. Those who wish to undertake such study travel to New Zealand, Australia or beyond and many never return.[13] There are no post graduate specialist courses in mental health—for psychologists or nurses—in Tonga or Vanuatu. The National University of Samoa and the Fiji National University both provide specialist training in mental health nursing, although the courses are not offered on a regular basis and the course in Fiji was suspended from 2008 to 2013 due to staff shortages.[14] In 2012 Fiji National University introduced a 12 month Post Graduate Diploma in Mental Health for mental health professionals.[15]

2.1. Demographic Overview

The population of Pacific island countries—including Melanesia, Micronesia and Polynesia—was estimated to have reached 10.5 million in 2013.[16] Nonetheless, this is a relatively small population given the large geographical area of land and sea territory. Thirty seven percent of this population was projected to be under 14 years and only 5.2 percent over 60 years.[17] In all the countries under examination, between 46 and 58 percent of this population is under 24 years of age. Clearly, the major challenges in the region lie within the younger population—and no less so for health and mental health. This has a significant impact on resources when unemployment levels are high, new employment opportunities are low and—in cases such as Vanuatu—the annual population growth rate is high and the net migration rate is zero.

9 S Singh et al. 'WHO Profile on Mental Health in Development (WHO proMIND): Fiji.' (World Health Organisation, 2013) <http://www.who.int/mental_health/policy/country/countrysummary/en/index.html (accessed 2 January 2016)>34.

10 See Table 13.5.

11 World Health Organisation, above n 2.

12 G Roberts, 'Masculinity, Mental Health and Violence in Papua New Guinea, Vanuatu, Fiji and Kiribati' (2007) 14(2) *Health Promotion in the Pacific* 35, 36.

13 WHO, 'Report on the Workshop on Human Resource Development for Mental Health in Pacific Island Countries' (WHO, Regional Office for the Western Pacific, 2003) 10.

14 For example: College of Medicine and Nursing and Health Sciences, above n 8 [4.4.1] see also Singh et al. above n 9, 38.

15 Email from Dr Odille Chang, Fiji National University, to Helen Ménard, 12 June 2013.

16 Secretariat of the Pacific Community, *Statistics for Development Program, Pacific Islands Populations Estimates, Mid-year 2013* <http://www.spc.int/ (accessed 13 May 2013)>.

17 Ibid 24.

In addition, poor education systems and low literacy levels in countries such as Vanuatu, together with the high number of indigenous languages, have a bearing on the effectiveness of educational initiatives—community awareness programs on mental health or legal rights, for example.

Specific population statistics are summarised in the following tables.

Table 13.1. Population statistics for Pacific countries[18]

Country	Last population census	Population	Urban population %	Annual growth rate %	Net annual migration rate %
Tonga	2011	103,252	23	0.1	-19.3
Samoa	2011	187,820	20	0.0	-24.1
Fiji	2007	837,271	51	0.5	-6.1
Vanuatu[19]	2009	234,023	24	2.5	0.0

Table 13.2. Estimated population statistics for Pacific countries[20]

Country	Estimated population to mid-2013			
	Total	Males	Females	0-24 yrs %
Tonga	103,300	52,100	51,200	56.7
Samoa	187,400	97,000	90,400	57.7
Fiji	859,200	438,100	421,100	46.0
Vanuatu	264,700	135,200	129,500	57.3

2.2. Tonga

While almost 70 percent of Tongans live on the main island of Tongatapu,[21] it is estimated that as many as 100, 000 Tongans live overseas—most of them in Australia, New Zealand and the United States.[22] Tonga's net migration rate in 2011 was a negative 19.3 percent (compared to a negative 6.1 percent in Fiji)[23] and is a major concern when it comes to the availability of trained health professionals in the country. This is especially so given there

18 Ibid.

19 Vanuatu National Statistics Office Ministry of Finance and Economic Management, *National Census of Population and Housing Summary Release* <www.vnso.gov.vu/images/stories/2009_Census_Summary_release_final.pdf (accessed 1 April 2013)>.

20 Secretariat of the Pacific Community, above n 16. Projected estimates for 2015 were unchanged for Samoa and Tonga while Fiji was 867,00 and Vanuatu 277,600. Secretariat of the Pacific Community, *Statistics for Development Division, Pacific Islands Populations Estimates, Mid-year 2015* <http://www.spc.int/nmdi/population (accessed 2 January 2016)>

21 O Guttenbeil-Likiliki and Foundation of the Peoples of the South Pacific International, 'Youth and Mental Health in Tonga: A Situational Analysis' (2009) 25, 13.

22 *WHO, Western Pacific Region, 2010, Tonga* <www.wpro.who.int/countries/ton/2010/TON.htm (accessed 14 March 2011)>.

23 Secretariat of the Pacific Community, above n 16 (accessed 13 December 2013).

is a very low reliance on expatriates in the health profession and none amongst mental health professionals.[24]

Youth unemployment is said to exceed 50 percent.[25] Yet, despite this, the literacy rate is very high in Tonga and, while most primary schools teach in Tongan, secondary education is mainly conducted in English. The education rate is similar for both genders but Tonga has yet to sign the *Convention on the Elimination of all forms of Discrimination against Women*[26] and women continue to be discriminated against in legislation, including land ownership rights, child support rights and inheritance laws.[27]

The standard of living has improved dramatically over the last 50 years and there is now little absolute poverty. The country has the highest ranking on the United Nations Development Programme's Human Development Index of any Pacific island state at 85 out of 182 indicating higher overall educational and health standards than other Pacific countries.[28]

2.2.1. The Professional Workforce

There are currently 12 general trained nurses working in the mental health unit in Tonga, none of whom has mental health training. There are *no* nurses working in mental health in the community. There are approximately six mental health assistants employed in the unit—with an acute need for many more—none of whom has any formal training at all. There is one psychiatric social worker who no longer works in the mental health field.[29] Some in service training has been conducted for nurses and psychiatric assistants.[30] The draft Mental Health Corporate Plan for 2015-2020 has one of its objectives as providing appropriate training for mental health staff and to grant approval for two clinical nurses to undergo the post graduate diploma in mental health at FNU.[31] The plan also proposes to secure funding to recruit for a number of mental health positions including three welfare officers, a clinical psychologist, a social worker, an occupational therapist, a psychotherapist and a specialist medical officer.[32]

There is only one registered full time psychiatrist in Tonga, Dr Puloka, who has been the sole practitioner in the country for almost thirty years. He also provides mental health consultancy services to the Republic of Nauru. However, China AID did provide a psychiatrist for the mental health unit on a two year part time contract that expired in July 2012.[33] One medical practitioner completed the Post Graduate Diploma in Mental Health at FNU in 2014[34] and it is proposed to seek funding for one other to undergo a three month

24 World Health Organisation, 'Human Resources for Health, Country Profiles: Tonga,' (2014) <http://www.wpro.who.int/hrh/documents/publications/wpr_hrh_country_profiles_tonga_upload.pdf (accessed 2 January 2016)> 6.

25 Guttenbeil-Likiliki and Foundation of the Peoples of the South Pacific International, above n 21, 13.

26 *Convention on the Elimination of all Forms of Discrimination Against Women*, opened for signature 1 March 1980, 1249 UNTS 13 (entered into force 3 September 1981).

27 World Health Organisation Western Pacific Region, 'Tonga Country Profile' (2011) <www.wpro.who.int/countries/ton/33TONpro2011_finaldraft.pdf (accessed 2 June 2013)>.

28 Ibid.

29 Loupua Sefokuli, Interview with Ilaivatu Mafi, Sister in Charge MHU (Tonga,13 June 2012).

30 WHO, above n 13, 9.

31 Government of Tonga, 'Ministry of Health Corporate Plan 2015/16-2019/20: Mental Health (Draft), ' (2015) 2,3,8.

32 Ibid 3.

33 Government of Tonga, 'Report of the Minister of Health for the Year 2010' (2010) <www.health.gov.to/sites/default/files/AR2010.pdf> 60.

34 Email from Dr Odille Chang, Fiji National University, to Helen Ménard, 10 January 2016.

psychiatric attachment in New Zealand and another to complete a graduate certificate in suicidology.[35]

In 2000, the Tongan Ministry of Health identified 'the development and maintenance of an appropriate skill base as one of the greatest challenges facing the Ministry.'[36] Yet, at that time, there was still no plan for the local training of healthcare professionals and there seemed to be a well-founded reluctance to send clinicians for training overseas as they frequently failed return to Tonga to practise.[37] For the first time, the draft Corporate Plan for Mental Health for 2015-2020 appears to be addressing some of the workforce issues although all initiatives are subject to procuring external funding. There is still no accreditation process for registering professional counsellors in Tonga,[38] which could be a less costly way of meeting the shortfall in professional services within the community.

2.3. Samoa

Seventy five percent of the Samoan population lives on Upolu—the smaller of the two main islands. Samoa's net migration rate in 2011 was a negative 24.1 percent—compared to a negative 6.1 percent in Fiji.[39]

Democratic traditions and a strong social system based on village communities and extended family ties continue to play a major role in maintaining peace in Samoan society. More than 80 percent of the population live under the *matai*—customary chief—system, which is particularly strong in the rural areas.[40] Samoa attained its independence from New Zealand in 1962 under a constitution that enshrined the *matai* titles and customary land ownership 'in accordance with Samoan custom and usage.'[41]

Gender issues, such as the promotion and protection of women's rights, gender equity and women are of high importance in Samoan society and women's access to education and achievement in the formal educational system is virtually equal to men. Samoa has one of the highest rankings in the Pacific on the United Nations Development Programme's Human Development Index at 94 out of 182[42] and the country is no longer classified as a Least Developed Country (LDC).[43]

---

35 Government of Tonga, above n 31, 8-9.

36 World Health Organisation, above n 2, 112.

37 Ibid.

38 Guttenbeil-Likiliki and Foundation of the Peoples of the South Pacific International, above n 21, 29.

39 Secretariat of the Pacific Community, above n 16 (accessed 24 June 2012).

40 World Health Organisation Western Pacific Region, 'Samoa Country Profile' (2011) <www.wpro.who.int/countries/wsm/29SMApro2011_finaldraft.pdf (accessed 2 June 2013)>.

41 *Constitution of the Independent State of Western Samoa 1960* ss 100–101. Note: All references to Western Samoa were amended to Samoa in accordance with the provisions of *Constitution Amendment Act (No. 2) 1997* (Samoa).

42 World Health Organisation Western Pacific Region, above n 40.

43 F Hope Eseta and Foundation of the Peoples of the South Pacific International, 'Youth and Mental Health in Samoa: A Situational Analysis' (2009) 14, citing the Asian Development Bank 2007.

2.3.1. The Professional Workforce

While mental health policy in Samoa includes provision for multi-disciplinary teams, there are few para health professionals and a desperate shortage of trained nurses. The first appointment of a psychiatrist as Acting Head of the Mental Health Unit in Samoa occurred in 2007.[44] As at 2016 Samoans still only have access to the services of one part time expatriate psychiatrist, Dr Ian Parkin.[45] Five nurses completed post graduate training in mental health in 2004 at the National University of Samoa but only three are presently employed in the mental health unit.[46] There is currently one indigenous Samoan doctor undergoing post graduate training in psychiatry in New Zealand and working in the mental health unit.[47] Another who completed her psychiatric training in 2013 remains in full time practice in New Zealand.[48]

Parkin concedes that:

> We are a resource poor country. With more resources we could provide much better service. We could educate the population and this would result in us treating more people and optimising their outcomes. The nature of the family in Samoa provides a lot of the 'safety' aspects that need to be legislated in western countries.'[49]

2.4. Fiji

In 1966 Indo-Fijians comprised 50.5 percent of the total Fijian population, with indigenous Fijians only 42.4 percent. In 1996, for the first time, the Indo-Fijian population fell below that of the indigenous Fijians. This reversal in trends has largely been attributed to the high emigration rate of Indo-Fijians—especially since the military coup d'état in 1987.[50] At the last population census in 2007, the Fijian ethnic population consisted of 57 percent iTaukei (indigenous Fijian),[51] 37 percent Indian (Indo-Fijian) and 6 percent others—including Rotuman,[52] Chinese, Europeans and other Pacific Islanders.[53] It was estimated that, by 2012, iTaukei would represent 59 percent of the population compared to 33 percent of Indian descent.[54]

The main languages spoken in Fiji are Fijian (iTaukei), Hindustani and English.[55]

---

44 Ibid 17.

45 Email questionnaire from Dr Ian Parkin, Psychiatrist Samoa, to Helen Ménard, 10 January 2016.

46 Government of Samoa Ministry of Health, 'Samoa Mental Health Policy' (2006) 5.

47 Email questionnaire from Dr Ian Parkin, Psychiatrist Samoa, to Helen Ménard, 15 April 2011.

48 Email from Dr Ian Parkin to Helen Ménard, 22 January 2013; Email questionnaire from Dr Ian Parkin, Psychiatrist Samoa, to Helen Ménard, 10 January 2016.

49 Email questionnaire from Dr Ian Parkin, Psychiatrist Samoa, to Helen Ménard, 15 April 2011.

50 Fiji Islands Bureau of Statistics, <www.statsfiji.gov.fj/Census2007/Release%201%20-%20Population%20 Size.pdf (accessed 3 September 2012)>.

51 *Fijian Affairs (Amendment) Decree 2010* (Fiji Islands).

52 Rotuma is a volcanic island north of Fiji. Although the island has been politically part of Fiji since 1881, Rotuman culture more closely resembles that of the Polynesian islands to the east, most noticeably Tonga, Samoa, Futuna and Uvea. Because of their Polynesian appearance and distinctive language, Rotumans now constitute a recognisable minority group within the Republic of Fiji http://www.rotuma.net/.

53 Fiji Bureau of Statistics, <www.statsfiji.gov.fj/ (accessed 31 August 2012)>.

54 Ibid.

55 Ibid.

Indigenous iTaukeis own 87.9 percent of the land in Fiji while 3.9 percent is state owned, 7.9 percent freehold and 0.3 percent Rotuman.[56]

Ethnicity and land ownership have played major roles in the history and political instability of Fiji and, consequently, its legislative reform programs. Although Fiji is one of the most developed of the Pacific island economies, the volatile political situation has had an adverse impact on the country's economy—particularly with the suspension of foreign aid by the European Union and other aid donors from 2006 until democratic elections were held in 2014.[57]

2.4.1. The Professional Workforce

The Fiji National University (FNU) provides post graduate masters programs for medical practitioners in anaesthesia, internal medicine, surgery, obstetrics and gyneacology, paediatrics and ophthalmology,[58] but, despite a high demand for psychiatric services,[59] not psychiatry.[60] This means that potential candidates are removed from the health system for three to five years while they study overseas and many do not return. The government is then forced to fill the vacancies with expatriates—frequently from countries with lower professional standards and who have no proficiency in the local languages.[61] The significance of language in effective mental health care is self-evident and impacts on appropriate diagnosis and treatment. Up until 2013 there were still only four registered psychiatrists in Fiji, only two of whom worked fulltime in the public health system and two of whom were expatriates.[62] This number subsequently reduced to three[63] when one psychiatrist employed in the public health sector relocated to American Samoa.

In January 2012 FNU introduced a 12 month Post Graduate Diploma in Mental Health the graduates of which are summarised in Table 13.3. The initial intake had an enrolment of six Fijian candidates—three nurses and three doctors. Only three doctors and one nurse completed the program. The 2013 intake had eight candidates all of whom were doctors—five from Fiji and three from the region including Vanuatu, Kiribati, and Palau [64] only six of whom graduated. In each of 2014 and 2015 there were two doctors enrolled, all of whom graduated.[65] It has been suggested that there are plans to establish a post graduate masters program in psychiatry at FNU.[66]

---

56 Ibid.

57 World Health Organisation Western Pacific Region, 'Fiji Country Profile' (2011) <www.wpro.who.int/countries/fji/7FIJpro2011_finaldraft.pdf (accessed 2 June 2013)>.

58 College of Medicine and Nursing and Health Sciences, above n 8 [4.4.2].

59 Ibid.

60 Roberts G et al. 'The Fiji Islands Health System Review' (2011) 1(1) *Health Systems in Transition* 78.

61 Ibid.

62 College of Medicine and Nursing and Health Sciences, above n 8 [4.4.1].

63 Singh et al. above n 9, 34.

64 Email from Dr Odille Chang, Fiji National University, to Helen Ménard, 12 June 2013. Despite being published in April 2012, the report by College of Medicine and Nursing and Health Sciences, above n 8 makes no reference to the new Post Graduate Diploma in Mental Health commencing January 2012.

65 Email from Dr Odille Chang, Fiji National University, to Helen Ménard, 10 January 2016.

66 Singh et al. above n 9, 34.

Table 13.3. Post Graduate Diploma Mental Health FNU[67]

Year	Graduates Post Graduate Diploma Mental Health (FNU)			
	Country	Doctors Enrolled	Nurses Enrolled	Graduates
2012	Fiji	3	3	4 (3 doctors & 1 nurse)
2013	Fiji	5	-	3
	Vanuatu	1	-	1
	Kiribati	1	-	1 (2015)
	Palau	1		1
2014	Fiji	1	-	1
	Tonga	1	-	1
2015	Fiji	1	-	1
	FSM	1	-	1

The majority of Fiji's medical workforce is concentrated in the urban hospitals—of which St Giles is one—leaving an acute shortage of services in rural areas.[68] This is of particular significance to service provision since 49 percent of Fijians live in rural areas.[69]

With the only dedicated psychiatric inpatient facility in the region, Fiji is in a unique position to provide training opportunities for post graduate students while, at the same time, relieving some of the pressure on the few existing trained professionals. With appropriate supervision, graduates could also be used to support and develop more regional mental health services. Such training programs could also provide additional public revenue by offering places to regional graduates. The newly introduced Post Graduate Diploma in Mental Health at FNU is a positive step in this direction.

The Fiji School of Nursing, now part of FNU, commenced its first post basic mental health nursing program in 2006.[70] The course was thereafter postponed for several years pending its evaluation and was scheduled to recommence in 2013.[71]Although reliable and specific statistics are hard to confirm and much of the available data is contradictory, it seems that around 33 nurses received the Postgraduate Diploma in Mental Health Nursing from 2007-2010,[72] 15 of those in 2010.[73] In addition, the Fiji School of Nursing—in association with James Cook University, Australia—graduated 51 nurses with Postgraduate Certificates in Mental Health Nursing in 2010.[74] As at 2013, some data suggests that of the 32 registered nurses working at St Giles only 9 or 10 had completed post basic training in mental health.[75]

67 Email from Dr Odille Chang, Fiji National University, to Helen Ménard, 10 January 2016.
68 Roberts G et al. above n 60, 61.
69 Ibid 10.
70 O Chang, 'Mental Health Services in Fiji and the Way Forward' (2007) 15(2) *General Practitioner* 44.
71 Singh et al. above n 9, 38.
72 College of Medicine and Nursing and Health Sciences, above n 8 [4.4.3].
73 Ministry of Health Fiji Islands, 'Ministry of Health, Annual Report 2010' (2010) 23, 50.
74 Roberts G et al. above n 60, 79.
75 Singh et al. above n 9, 34, 39. This same report states that as at 2013 there were only 4 qualified psychiatric nurses working at St Giles (see p 45)

There are no trained psychiatric social workers, occupational therapists or psychologists working in the public health system in Fiji.[76]

2.5. Vanuatu

Vanuatu's annual population growth rate, at 2.5 percent, is one of the highest in the region. This compares with between zero percent and 0.1 percent in Samoa and Tonga and 0.5 percent in Fiji.[77] The economy is based primarily on subsistence or small-scale agriculture—which provides employment for 76 percent of the population—but is moving towards complete dependence on the tourism industry.[78]

Very few new jobs are created annually across all sectors of the economy—especially for returned trainees and graduates.[79] Yet, the net annual migration rate of zero percent is the lowest in the region. Literacy levels are some of the lowest in the Pacific at 34 percent in the adult population compared with 99 percent in both Samoa and Tonga and 93 percent in Fiji.[80] Research conducted by the Vanuatu Education Policy Advocacy Coalition in 2011, found that 72.4 percent of people between the ages of 15 and 60 were illiterate. Furthermore, 64.8 percent of people who completed primary school were illiterate compared to 45 percent who completed secondary school.[81] The same survey found that less than 20 percent of those surveyed between the ages of 15 and 60 had completed secondary school up to year 10 and only 5 percent up to years 12-13.[82] Apart from the official languages of English, French and Bislama, over 155 local languages are spoken throughout the country.[83] This is compounded by the fact that the education system is poor, the attrition rate in primary schools is high, and 40 percent of the population is under the age of 15.[84] All this creates monumental challenges for any community educational initiatives that might be aimed at promoting human rights principles in a mental health context with the hope of creating access to justice.

2.5.1. The Professional Workforce

Vanuatu's relationship with mental health is probably the saddest of all. With the fourth largest population in the island Pacific region, it has equal to the least mental health services of any country in the region—namely, until 2013, no trained mental health professionals of any kind. This is despite there being 29 medical practitioners, 37 nurse practitioners, 52 midwives and 423 general trained nurses in the country.[85] The other countries in the region in

---

76 Roberts G et al. above n 60, 109; see also Singh et al. above n 9, 34.

77 Secretariat of the Pacific Community, above n 16; Vanuatu National Statistics Office Ministry of Finance and Economic Management, above n 19.

78 World Health Organisation Western Pacific Region, 'Vanuatu Country Profile' (2011) <www.wpro.who.int/countries/vut/35VANpro2011_finaldraft.pdf (accessed 2 June 2013)>.

79 Ibid.

80 Commonwealth of Australia, 'Pacific 2020, Challenges and Opportunities for Growth' (2006) 18.

81 Vanuatu Education Policy Advocacy Coalition Asia and South Pacific Association for Basic and Adult Education Australia, 'Education Experience Survey and Literacy Assessment: Shefa Province Vanuatu' (April 2011) vii-viii.

82 Ibid.

83 *Vanuatu* <www.mapsofworld.com/country-profile/vanuatu-information-geography-history.html (accessed 30 June 2012)>.

84 Vanuatu National Statistics Office Ministry of Finance and Economic Management, above n 19.

85 Government of the Republic of Vanuatu, *Ministry of Health Annual Report 2009* (2011) <https://gov.vu/health.html (Accessed 3 September 2015)> 12.

the same category in terms of mental health personnel—Niue, Nauru and Tokelau—all have populations under 15,000—less than one-twentieth of Vanuatu's population.[86]

Prior to 1980, there were some trained mental health personnel in Vanuatu including a psychiatrist who staffed the mental health ward in the former French Georges Pompidou Hospital.[87] Following independence in 1980 the hospital was closed.

Wilton's study in 1997 proposed the development of a mental health policy which would include training of professional mental health staff, the provision of inpatient facilities, community awareness programs and data collection.[88] Almost twenty years later little has come to pass despite a series of further reports making similar recommendations.[89]

There is a heavy reliance on traditional or religious approaches to mental health care at the village level and no NGO in the community dedicated to mental health. While there are periodic services provided from overseas in specialties such as orthopaedics, ENT and plastic surgery, no such services are available in the field of mental health.[90] The Vanuatu College of Nursing Education qualifies general nurses to diploma level and the curriculum does include several mental health modules. However, there are no specialist training courses in mental health and no post basic nursing courses that deal with mental health.[91]

In 2009, the Vanuatu Mental Health Policy and Plan (2009-2015) was approved and an Australian volunteer psychologist was recruited and based in the community to assist with mental health issues in several rural villages.[92] In 2009, and in line with this policy, two Australian general medical practitioners were engaged as WHO consultants to conduct outreach mental health awareness and diagnostic training sessions for health professionals throughout the country particularly in the outer islands.[93]

Progress since then has been slow. Despite the Ministry of Health's admission in 2009 that 'at present it is likely that the majority of the population with mental illness are left untreated',[94] successive governments have appeared to lack any real commitment to address the problem at a more formal level.

Finally, in March 2012, an acting part time Mental Health Coordinator was appointed within the Non Communicable Disease Unit of the Public Health Directorate whose function was to implement the objectives of the National Mental Health Policy.[95] This contract expired in August 2013.[96] Funding was approved in 2012 for one nurse to attend FNU to complete the

86 World Health Organisation, above n 2, 83–118.

87 D Hughes and Foundation of the Peoples of the South Pacific International, 'Masculinity, Mental Health and Violence in Vanuatu: Situation Analysis' (2004) 18.

88 NM Wilton, 'Mental Health in the Republic of Vanuatu' (WHO Regional Office for the Western Pacific, 1997) 6–7.

89 D Dupre-Wheeler, 'Vanuatu Suicide Baseline Survey' (WHO Regional Office for the Western Pacific, 2001); MP Deva, 'Mission Report Executive Summary' (WHO Regional Office for the Western Pacific, 2003); Hughes and Foundation of the Peoples of the South Pacific International, above n 87; World Health Organisation, above n 2.

90 Republic of Vanuatu Ministry of Health, 'Vanuatu Mental Health Policy and Plan (2009-2014)' (2009) 23.

91 L Tarivonda et al. 'WHO Profile on Mental Health in Development (WHO ProMIND); Vanuatu' (World Health Organisation, 2012) 34; Interview with Jane Laycock, Clinical Nurse Educator, Vanuatu (Port Vila, 22 August 2013).

92 J Benson et al. 'A New Era in Mental Health Care in Vanuatu' (2011) 2011 *International Journal of Family Medicine* 1, 61.

93 J Benson, 'Mental Health in Vanuatu' (2009) July *GPReview* 27.

94 Republic of Vanuatu Ministry of Health, above n 90, 4.

95 P Kaloris, '2012 Vanuatu Mental Health Annual Report' (Ministry of Health (Vanuatu), 2012) 3; Interview with Peter Kaloris, Mental Health Cordinator, Vanuatu (Port Vila, 24 June 2013).

96 Kaloris, above n 95.

Diploma in Mental Health Nursing but no further funding has been made available since 2013. In 2013, the Public Service Commission approved leave for the first local doctor to attend FNU to undertake the Post Graduate Diploma in Mental Health[97] and he graduated and returned to Vanuatu in the same year.[98]

3. Government Policy and Action

When it comes to the provision of essential services in Pacific island countries—namely health, education and transport—the geographical spread of islands within a particular country is a significant factor in determining the allocation of resources. For countries such as Vanuatu, where the provinces are spread across 2,500 kilometres, the provision of even basic services to the more remote and less populated locations is poor. In general, the distribution of resources is prioritised within the central urban areas, and transport services to outer islands are erratic, expensive and in some cases non existent. This has a serious impact on the provision of services in those areas, not the least of which are health and mental health services. Similar factors affect the northernmost and southernmost island groups in Tonga and Fiji. Remoteness is far less of an issue in Samoa where there are fewer islands spread over a much smaller area, and the population is concentrated on two main islands separated by only a few kilometres.

3.1. Distribution of Financial Resources

Globally, spending on mental health care is less than two US dollars per person per year and less than 25 cents per person per year in low income countries. Almost half of the world's population lives in a country where, on average, there is one psychiatrist or less to serve 200,000 people. Outpatient mental health facilities are 58 times more prevalent in high income compared to low income countries and consumer organisations are only present in 49 percent of low income countries.[99]

There is no question that financial resources continue to be in desperately short supply throughout the entire Pacific region.

The WHO regional strategy on health financing in 2009 recommended that total health expenditure (THE) as a percentage of gross domestic product (GDP) in the Western Pacific region should range between four and five percent.[100] Consistent, current and comparative figures on health expenditure in any of the target countries are difficult to find and none of the data identifies mental health expenditure as a separate line item.[101] As such, the table below is based on the WHO estimates for 2008 and is only intended as a guide for comparing the different countries in the region.

97 Ibid; Interview with Peter Kaloris, Mental Health Cordinator, Vanuatu (Port Vila, 24 June 2013).

98 See Table 13.3

99 World Health Organisation, 'WHO Mental Health Atlas 2011' (2011) 10.

100 College of Medicine and Nursing and Health Sciences, above n 8, 47.

101 In relation to Fiji and Samoa, there are variations between the National Health Account figures and the WHO estimates for 2008; equivalent national figures for the same period are not available for all countries. Ibid 46; THE for 2010 in Fiji was reported in the NHA at 4.8 percent of GDP; Ibid 54; THE for 2009 in Samoa was reported in the NHA at 6.3%; see below n 103.

As demonstrated by Table 13.4, Fiji, as one of the more developed countries in the region, had THE in 2008 below the WHO recommended level, while Samoa's THE was at the upper end of the recommended range. Tonga and Vanuatu had the lowest THE per capita of the target countries. When comparing government health expenditure (GHE) as a percentage of THE, Fiji and Tonga recorded the lowest rate and Samoa the highest, with Vanuatu in the mid-range. This suggests that a more substantial portion of the healthcare budget in Fiji and Tonga is supplemented by the private sector and overseas aid than, for example, in Samoa.

Table 13.4. Total health expenditure (THE) and government health expenditure (GHE) 2008[102]

Country	THE as percentage of GDP	GHE as percentage of THE	ANNUAL total health expenditure per capita ($US)
Tonga	4.0	68.7	152
Samoa	5.1	84.8	234
Fiji	3.8	68.4	166
Vanuatu	4.1	79.2	155
Australia	8.8	68.0	3,448
New Zealand	9.0	78.7	2,465

Even though the above figures suggest that Samoa presents the strongest position in terms of health spending in the region, up until the latest figures available for the period 2008- 2009, there was no line item in the health budget for mental health and no available data on the cost of mental health services in primary health care.[103] Despite a statement in Samoa's Mental Health Policy that 'financial estimates shall meet the need and reflect the planning and budgeting for mental health',[104] it is not possible to establish from published information whether this has occurred. The National Health Accounts published in 2012 relate to the period 2008/2009 and contain no information at all in relation to expenditure on mental health.[105] Similarly, the Ministry of Health Annual Report for 2010/2011 contains minimal budgetary information—none linked to mental health. [106]

The WHO Pacific report in 2005 indicated that 1.7 percent of the health budget in Fiji and 0.5 percent of the health budget in Tonga was allocated to mental health and there was no corresponding allocation in Samoa or Vanuatu.[107] While this assertion is consistent with the lack of available information in Vanuatu and Samoa, there is no published material with readily discernible information on mental health care spending that would support the alleged expenditure in Tonga or Fiji.

---

102 Ibid 47–55.

103 Government of Samoa Ministry of Health, 'Samoa National Health Accounts FY 2008/2009' (2012) <http://www.health.gov.ws/Portals/189/News/NHA2008-09/Final%20Draft%20NHA2008-09%20-_Copy.pdf (accessed 6 September 2015)>

104 Government of Samoa Ministry of Health, 'Samoa Mental Health Policy' (2006) 17.

105 Government of Samoa Ministry of Health, above n 103.

106 Government of Samoa Ministry of Health, 'Annual Report Financial Year 2010-2011,' (2011) <http://www.health.gov.ws/Portals/189/Master%20Copy%20-%20Annual%20Report%20FY10-11.pdf (accessed 30 August 2015)>

107 World Health Organisation, above n 7, 21–2.

3.2. Existing Mental Health Services

In the context of rapid development in the Pacific, mental health services have not developed at the same pace as other health services; funding for mental health services is low; and mental health promotion and service delivery are not seen as priorities for the governments of Pacific Island countries.[108]

In 1978 Murphy observed that there was no available care for those suffering from mental disorders in Pacific countries other than community care—commonly involving traditional healers and religious leaders—or inpatient psychiatric facilities; and the inpatient centres could provide little more than institutionalised custodial care due to the critical lack of trained staff, inadequate financial resources, absence of appropriate medication; lack of regional training facilities for psychiatric staff and mental health prevention strategies.[109] Murphy also predicted that the lower rates of hospitalisation of the mentally ill in the Pacific compared to more affluent Western countries would not continue 'unless steps are taken to reinforce the community care tradition.'[110]

At that time Murphy also forecast the need for new community leaders to replace or supplement the more traditional but disappearing roles; greater community awareness of the needs of the mentally ill; community care structures in preference to institutional settings; regionalisation of mental health services; increases in the number of trained mental health personnel; and appropriate research into suitable local solutions for mental health care treatment.[111] Regrettably, for the most part, Murphy's 'wish list' is a long way from being fulfilled.

A sketch of mental health service providers and facilities in the Pacific countries under discussion appears in Table 13.5 below. While there are currently no inpatient beds for mental health consumers in Vanuatu, there are inadequate inpatient facilities in Fiji and Tonga. As at 2013, there were no mental health professionals at all in Vanuatu, only 4.5 psychiatrists throughout the countries under discussion—three of whom were in Fiji—and less than 50 trained mental health nurses, almost all of whom were in Fiji. Of the six mental health trained nurses in Samoa, only three work in the mental health unit.[112] There are no trained mental health nurses in Tonga and few allied health professionals in the region. Some services, where they do exist, are often limited as a result of geography and transport, particularly in rural areas.[113]

---

108 F Hughes, 'Mental Health in the Pacific: The Role of the Pacific Island Mental Health Network' (2009) 15(1) *Pacific Health Dialog* 177.

109 HBM Murphy, *Mental Health Trends in the Pacific Islands: A Report on a Tour of Pacific Territories* (South Pacific Commission, 1978) 20–27.

110 Ibid 36.

111 Ibid 49–59.

112 Hope Eseta and Foundation of the Peoples of the South Pacific International, above n 39, 17.

113 Hughes, above n 108, 178.

Table 13.5. Mental health service provision in Pacific countries[114]

Country	Mental Health Service Providers				
	Population (Table 13.2)	**Inpatient Beds**	**Psychiatrists**	**Trained Mental Health Nurses**	**Psychologists/ Social Workers**
Tonga	103,682	22	1.0	0 (7-12 *general* nurses working in inpatient mental health)	1(left public health in 2013)
Samoa	183,617	2 (closed from 2011 - 2015 for renovation)[115]	0.5	6 (3 working in the mental health unit)	0
Fiji[116]	851,745	136	3 (1 in government service)[117]	30 (could be as high as 80)[118]	0
Vanuatu	251,784	0-1	0	1[119]	0

3.2.1. Tonga

Prior to the 1940s, health services for the mentally ill in Tonga were non-existent and those presenting with mental illnesses were almost always diagnosed with other illnesses. In 1948, the Ministry of Health started to isolate particular patients from the main hospital wards to the national Hu'atolitoli prison,[120] thereby reinforcing a criminal justice stigma, rather than a treatment-oriented medical paradigm. Frequently, these patients had been identified as verbally and physically abusive and the prison was seen as providing protection for them and others. It was thirty years before a psychiatric unit was established at the Ministry of Health's Vaiola Hospital in the capital Nuku'alofa, at which time all patients were transferred from the prison to the mental health unit.[121]

The mental health unit contained a total of 16 beds with six designated security beds.[122] The unit was extended in 2005 and was almost immediately inadequate. In September 2010 this 22 bed unit had 50 current admissions, 18 of whom were home on 'trial leave' and four were voluntary patients.[123] This means there were 32 inpatients being accommodated in a unit designed for 22. One respondent, not surprisingly, contends that 'overcrowding and non-gender segregation frequently creates sexual tension in the unit.'[124]

---

114 World Health Organisation, above n 2, 28–9, 83–118.

115 The new mental health unit opened in 2015 with two secure beds and an additional four beds subject to staffing and demand. Email questionnaire from Dr Ian Parkin, Psychiatrist Samoa, to Helen Ménard, 10 January 2016.

116 College of Medicine and Nursing and Health Sciences, above n 8, 109.

117 Singh et al. above n 9, 34.

118 While the WHO figures in 2005 maintain there were 32 trained mental health nurses this is unlikely to be accurate as other literature suggests that prior to the introduction of the post basic mental health nursing programs in 2006 there were no certificate trained mental health nurses in Fiji: see G Roberts, M Cruz and E S Puamau, 'A Proposed Future for the Care, Treatment and Rehabilitation of Mentally Ill People in Fiji' (2007) 14(2) *Health Promotion in the Pacific* 107, 108. Other sources say there were only 12 in 2008 (see above n 53); the MOH Annual Report 2010 states that 60 nurses were trained in mental health in 2009 and 15 in 2010. The most likely current figure is approximately 80 if one includes both diploma and certificate trained mental health nurses, although there is no indication how many of those trained are actually working throughout the public health system. See also para 2.4.1 above.

119 Kaloris, above n 95, 10.

120 Guttenbeil-Likiliki and Foundation of the Peoples of the South Pacific International, above n 21, 21–2.

121 Ibid.

122 Ibid 23.

123 Interview with Loupua Sefokuli, Law Graduate, (Port Vila, November 2010).

124 Loupua Sefokuli, Interview with Dr Yang Yangpin, Psychiatrist (Tonga,13 June 2012).

In 2005, the WHO reported that churches, community leaders and traditional healers played important roles at the primary health care level in Tonga and there was an emphasis on managing mental health at the primary health care level and promoting deinstitutionalisation.[125] However, while there is ample evidence of the ongoing role of traditional healers in mental health in Tonga, there is little evidence to support the fact that community based mental health care is replacing inpatient care. This is despite the Health Ministry's statement in 2010 that the mental health section is responsible for 'the continuation of the process of deinstitutionalisation for all psychiatric cases.'[126]

The Tongan Mental Health and Disabilities Association was established in 2010 as the first NGO for mental health in Tonga but there is little indication that it is widely operational.

3.2.2. Samoa

Samoa consciously moved away from institution-based care in the early 1990s to a system in which families and nurses share responsibility for the care and treatment of people with mental disorders—within their families and communities.[127] According to the Samoan Nurses Association, the move has been beneficial to people with mental illness and is evidenced by improved medication compliance; earlier recovery due to communication with families; less disruption to interpersonal relationships by hospitalisation; fewer introduced methods of Western style care; and greater chances of the ill person's care being tailored to specific needs within a family setting.[128] They argued that regimented sleeping, eating, exercise and medication programs, stigmatising green and blue uniforms and solitary confinement practices, were compelling reasons to depart from the institutionalised care model.[129]

There is now no dedicated inpatient facility for mental health consumers in Samoa and—as a last resort—when the mentally ill need medical attention they are referred to the general hospital—which has no allocated mental health beds—or, in more serious cases, police cells.[130] A four-bed ward was built at Tupua Tamasese Meaole General Hospital in the capital Apia, to enable treatment of inpatients but the beds were never officially opened and the building has been used mainly as a day care centre.[131]

Samoa currently has a small mental health unit employing mental health nurses who provide outreach services to the mentally ill within a community setting.[132] There is limited access to psychological treatment or rehabilitation[133] and, even though it was estimated that 16 percent of patients in 2006 presented with drug induced psychosis, there are no substance abuse services available.[134] Where at all possible mental health consumers are treated as a day patients at the mental health unit and returned to their family with community support. However, the limited available resources and the difficulties providing outreach services hamper the effectiveness of this support.

---

[125] World Health Organisation, above n 2, 33.
[126] Government of Tonga, above n 31, 60.
[127] Hope Eseta and Foundation of the Peoples of the South Pacific International, above n 39, 11.
[128] Ibid 12.
[129] Ibid 11.
[130] Ibid 17.
[131] Government of Samoa Ministry of Health, above n 42, 12.
[132] Hope Eseta and Foundation of the Peoples of the South Pacific International, above n 39, 11.
[133] Government of Samoa Ministry of Health, above n 42, 9.
[134] Ibid 9.

For example, the unit only has one vehicle which is frequently out of service; at these times no outreach services are available.[135]

The only two secure beds in the mental health unit were closed in 2011 while a new mental health unit was being developed as part of a hospital renovation program. It is anticipated that the new facilities will be 'state of the art' and provide safe and humane containment and treatment and reduce the need for any patients to be treated in prison.[136] As at the beginning of 2013, building had yet to commence [137] but was finally completed in 2015. The new unit contains two secure beds, an outpatient office facility and a day hospital area with the potential for up to four inpatients subject to demand and adequate staffing.[138]

In 2014, with the support of the National Health Services, a specialist taskforce was put together to 'strengthen Samoa's capacity to deal with mental health issues.'[139]

There are no official statistics in Samoa on the number or people presenting with mental illness nor those treated within the community on community treatment orders.

Traditional healers—of which there an estimated 900 in Samoa[140]—village elders and family members play a crucial role in the care and treatment of the mentally ill in Samoa, especially when transport problems compromise the operation of the outreach mental health teams.[141]

3.2.3. Fiji

Fiji has the only dedicated psychiatric facility in the region—St Giles Psychiatric Hospital in the capital Suva. The Lunatic Asylum, as it was then known, was built in 1884 and began as a single ward catering to the mentally ill expatriate population who were cared for by lay wardens who, in turn, were supervised by a Board of Visitors. [142] The Board—the Attorney General, the Chief Medical Officer and a prominent member of society—scrutinised committal orders and decided who should be discharged. It was not until the 1960s that a psychiatrist was appointed as a full time medical superintendent.[143]

St Giles is now a 136-bed psychiatric facility and caters for those with mental illness, substance abuse issues, developmental disabilities and the 'abandoned'.[144] It has been the sole provider of psychiatric services in the country, including outpatient, day care, occupational therapy and some limited community nursing services.[145] Many of its buildings are now decrepit and desperately in need of serious repair and maintenance, despite repeated promises from successive governments to address the problems.[146]

---

135 Government of Samoa Ministry of Health, 'Health Sector Strategic Plan 2008-2018' (2008) 55.

136 Email questionnaire from Dr Ian Parkin, Psychiatrist Samoa, to Helen Ménard, 15 April 2011; Email from Dr Ian Parkin to Helen Ménard, 22 January 2013.

137 'Health Looks into New Mental Clinic,' *Samoa Observer* (Apia, Samoa), 24 January 2013, <http://www.samoaobserver.ws/local-news/28-health-/3063-health-looks-into-new-mental-clinic (accessed 6 September 2015)>

138 Email questionnaire from Dr Ian Parkin, Psychiatrist Samoa, to Helen Ménard, 10 January 2016.

139 'Taskforce Looks at Mental Health,' *Samoa Observer* (Apia, Samoa), 19 January 2014 <http://www.samoaobserver.ws/local-news/28-health-/8915-taskforce-looks-at-mental-health (accessed 6 Septemeber 2015)>

140 Government of Samoa Ministry of Health, above n 135, 55.

141 World Health Organisation, above n 2, 35.

142 Roberts, Cruz and Puamau, above n 118, 107.

143 Ibid 107.

144 Chang, above n 66, 3.

145 World Health Organisation, above n 2, 30.

146 Chang, above n 66, 3.

In the face of repeated calls from mental health professionals, over the years, to recognise the importance of community based mental health care,[147] the decentralisaation of psychiatric services was rejected by all governments in Fiji.[148]

In 2009, the Health Minister, Dr Neil Sharma, admitted that the current infrastructure was outdated and that there was a lack of allied mental health workers, psychiatric nurses and psychiatrists. He promised that St Giles Hospital would soon be developed into a regional mental health institute with the capacity to provide specialised clinical psychiatric services, training and research.[149] The Minister also conceded that, while the number of patients seen at the hospital was increasing, rehabilitative services were limited to occupational therapy for inpatients. Daycare services for outpatients in the greater Suva area had been non-operational due to lack of resources.[150] Little has changed.

In 2011, the same Minister, in committing to the regionalisation of psychiatric services,[151] again admitted that there was a treatment gap of about 90 percent for adults with a mental illness—largely contributed to by the difficulty in accessing mental health services the urban areas and the stigma associated with mental illness and St. Giles Hospital.[152] In referring to the new mental health legislation in Fiji,[153] the Minister agreed with the 'need to develop a better understanding of the new mental health decree and improve our psychiatry service delivery.'[154]

A graphic illustration of the lack of reach of services into rural areas involves 49-year-old Nur Nisha, a Fijian woman who had been locked in a tin hut for 30 years. After the case was highlighted in the New Zealand media in June 2013, Fiji Ministry of Health officials confirmed Nur was being prepared for admission to hospital to be treated for her mental illness. The Ministry also stated that, contrary to media reports, she had been receiving regular treatment from visiting doctors and nurses.[155] Given the description that follows it is hard to imagine that any health professional could 'treat' a person in these circumstances without seeking care for her in more humane conditions. When a representative from the Nadi Disabled Persons Foundation, Filimone Waqanisau, visited Nur's 'home' he said:

> [Nur] was found naked and squatting on the concrete floor of a two square-metre shed that served as her sleeping quarters, dining room, toilet and shower. She was covered in a blanket ... the decrepit condition of what had become her home ... was almost impossible to believe ... a plastic pipe on the floor served as makeshift toilet, from which emitted the overpowering stench of raw sewage. The roofing iron shed had no

---

147 J Price and I Karim, 'An Evaluation of Psychiatric After-care in a Developing Country (Fiji)' (1976) 129 *British Journal of Psychiatry* 155; R Schultz, 'Community Mental Health: Avoided by Some, Neglected by Others' (2001) 8(1) *Pacific Health Dialog* 200;Roberts, above n 12.

148 M Karan, 'Hospital Lack Psychiatry Services,' *Fiji Times ONLINE* (Online), 8 March 2011 <www.fijitimes.com/story.aspx?id=167763 (accessed 29 March 2011)>.

149 TemoL, *St Giles Hospital to Be Turned into a Regional Mental Health Institute* (Fri, 23/10/2009,0936) <www.connectme.com.fj/news/national/St-Giles-Hospital-to-be-turned-into-a-regional-mental-health-institute (accessed 29 March 2011)>.

150 Ibid.

151 Karan, above n 148.

152 TemoL, above n 149.

153 *Mental Health Decree 2010* (Fiji Islands).

154 Karan, above n 148.

155 Fiji Times, 'Woman Locked for 30 Years,' *Vanuatu Daily Post* (Port Vila), 15 June 2013.

ventilation or windows … there was no bedding … her elder sister is the only one who looks after her by washing her down with a hose-pipe and feeding her.[156]

Despite all this, Fiji still lacks data on the national incidence and prevalence of mental disorders,[157] and mental health services remain essentially centralised at St. Giles in the capital, Suva. While general adult psychiatric services are available, there are no sub-specialist psychiatric services available for women, children and adolescents, geriatrics, refugees, forensics patients or those suffering from substance abuse illnesses. There are no community facilities such as residential facilities, respite care, day care, crisis intervention, psychosocial rehabilitation or vocational facilities.[158] St Giles also operates monthly psychiatric clinics at the Suva Women's Prison and Naboro Prison and is responsible for conducting forensic assessments and evaluations at the request of the judiciary.[159]

As previously mentioned, three 'stress management' units opened in 2012 in each of the divisional general hospitals with a total of 22 beds.[160] One mental health clinic was established at Samabula in the central region in 2011 and, while some outpatient clinics operate from the general hospitals, there is no liaison psychiatry available at any of these hospitals.[161] This decentralisation was held to be partly responsible for the reduction in the bed occupancy rate at St Giles from 104.12 percent in 2012 to 42.48 percent in 2013.[162] There is no other statistical data that would support this contention.

Limited community outreach services are provided in some communities but the only community mental health service available in Fiji is based at St Giles and therefore only services consumers living in the greater Suva area.[163] In regional areas where there are no allocated psychiatric beds people who require containment are usually held at the local police station while they await transfer to a divisional hospital or directly to St. Giles.[164]

Government services are supplemented by NGOs and faith based organisations—such as Pacific Counselling and Social Services and Fiji Women's Crisis centre—which provide counselling and support services as well as some education awareness and advocacy programs provided by Psychiatric Survivors Association and Fiji Association for Mental Health.[165]

Despite the fact that people often access traditional healers before conventional services, traditional healers are not a formal part of mental health service delivery in Fiji.[166]

3.2.4. Vanuatu

Effectively, there have been no formal mental health services in Vanuatu since before independence—and none at all for ni-Vanuatu (indigenous people of Vanuatu). Prior to

---

156 Ibid.
157 O Chang, 'Mental Health Care in Fiji' (2011) 3(2) *Asia Pacific Psychiatry* 73.
158 Roberts G et al. above n 60, 109.
159 Singh et al. above n 9, 45.
160 MP Deva, 'Matters of the Mind,' *The Fiji Times ONLINE* (Online), 28 August 2012 <www.fijitimes.com/story.aspx?id=210296 (accessed 4 October 2012)>
161 Singh et al. above n 9,45.
162 Ministry of Health Fiji, 'Ministry of Health Annual Report 2013' (2014) <http://www.health.gov.fj/PDFs/Annual%20Report/Annual%20Report%202013.pdf (accessed 7 September 2015)> 17.
163 Singh et al. above n 9, 46.
164 Ibid
165 Roberts G et al. above n 60, 109-110.
166 Singh et al. above n 9, 47.

independence in 1980, the mental health ward in the French hospital was used almost exclusively for the treatment of expatriates.[167]

A new two bed secure psychiatric unit that was built in the Port Vila Central Hospital (PVCH) has rarely been used for this purpose due to lack of trained staff.[168] When it is used to accommodate a seriously mentally ill person, family members are required to care for the patient and sleep in the corridor.[169] Even though the unit has a secure 'safe room,'[170] the room is most often used to quarantine tuberculosis patients.[171] Information published by the Ministry of Health in 2009 suggests there are four mental health beds—two in PVCH and two in the northern region which are described as 'mental health beds in the general medical ward.'[172]

In reality, one respondent claims that there are no specific beds in the regional hospital and the 'old TB ward' at PVCH is only used

> when we have patients who require seclusion or need a space away from other people. I don't know how it would function as a 2 bed ward as there is only one physical bed. There has never been more than one inpatient at any given time while I have been here. Otherwise patients who need admission but do not need/want to be separated can and sometimes do stay on the general ward. We also use this space [the TB ward] to see outpatients.[173]

Following the WHO sponsored mental health awareness and diagnostic training programs for general health professionals in 2009 and 2011, a series of mental health clinics were established in provincial hospitals and health centres and were intended to operate one half day per week.[174] However, the prioritisation of general health services by general health professionals and the lack of ongoing training and specialist support have thwarted the success of the project.[175]

Benson in 2011 maintains the seriously mentally ill in Vanuatu—people with severe untreated schizophrenia, bipolar disorders and brief psychotic disorders—are given traditional medication and religious exorcism and cared for by their family and community.[176] The author further asserts that as an estimated 92 percent of the population practice Christianity, 'the church and pastors have always had a very important role in counselling and problem-solving for those in their congregation and have mostly been the only source of mental health care available for many people.'[177]

Young people in Vanuatu with mental health problems with nowhere to go and no capacity to seek professional help, are frequently left to resort to traditional healers and medicines. In some cases, after their behaviour has brought them to the attention of the police,

[167] Hughes and Foundation of the Peoples of the South Pacific International, above n 87, 18.
[168] Ibid 18.
[169] Ibid 20.
[170] Benson et al. above n 92.
[171] World Health Organisation, above n 2, 116.
[172] Republic of Vanuatu Ministry of Health, above n 90, 22.
[173] Email questionnaire from XY, Fiji, to Helen Ménard, 19 July 2012.
[174] Interview with Peter Kaloris, Mental Health Cordinator, Vanuatu (Port Vila, 24 June 2013).
[175] Kaloris, above n 95, 8.
[176] Benson et al. above n 92, 5.
[177] Ibid 5.

they are diagnosed and treated in the medical ward by untrained mental health care professionals, medicated for a short time and discharged with little or no follow up care.[178]

Men tend to use kava or alcohol and, if traditional medicine does not work, no further assistance is sought.[179] In provincial and rural communities 'the court of last resort of families with a disturbed mentally ill person is to seek police help to detain him or her in a police cell.'[180]

The Vanuatu Society of Disabled People only provides services for the physically and intellectually disabled.[181] The National Disability Policy and Plan of Action 2008-2018—aside from including those with 'long term mental impairments' in its definitions—makes no reference at all to mental health or mental health services.[182]

Due to a general lack of understanding of mental illness, there is no NGO network in Vanuatu to deliver culturally appropriate and acceptable mental health services nor any proper support services within the community for people with mental illness.[183] Furthermore, seven planned community workshops throughout the provinces were cancelled in 2012 due to the unavailability of funds.[184]

3.2.5. Regional Mental Health Organisations

The *Pacific Islands Mental Health Network* (PIMHnet)—an initiative of the World Health Organisation (WHO)—was established in March 2007 to assess and address some of the critical mental health issues facing countries in the Pacific Region.[185] PIMHnet identified a number of priority areas of work, including advocacy; human resources and training; mental health policy, planning, legislation and service development. Network countries meet on an annual basis to develop work plans outlining major areas for action to address these priorities, to be officially endorsed by their ministers of health.

An important stated strategy of PIMHnet is the forging of strategic partnerships with NGOs and other agencies working in the Pacific Region. This is aimed at reducing the fragmentation of mental health activities and building more coordinated and effective strategies to address the treatment gap; to improve mental health care; and put an end to stigma, discrimination and human rights violations against people with mental disorders.[186]

Nonetheless, it would seem that after the initial flurry of activity, its activities have assumed a less visible profile in the last few years and, at times, the organisation has struggled for on-going funding.[187]

A body with significant standing in the region is the *Pacific Islands Forum Secretariat* (PIFS) (formerly the South Pacific Forum)[188] which, from its membership of Pacific island

---

[178] Hughes and Foundation of the Peoples of the South Pacific International, above n 87, 27.

[179] Ibid 58, 20.

[180] Republic of Vanuatu Ministry of Health, above n 90, 26.

[181] Hughes and Foundation of the Peoples of the South Pacific International, above n 87, 16.

[182] *Government of the Republic of Vanuatu Ministry of Justice & Social Welfare and The National Disability Committee, 'National Disability Policy and Plan of Action 2008-2018' (2009) 15–17.*

[183] Kaloris, above n 95, 8.

[184] Ibid 14.

[185] WHO Regional Office for the Western Pacific Press Releases, *New Network Seeks to Improve Mental Health Care in Pacific Islands Countries* <www.wpro.who.int/NR/exeres/6C2C3583-BBA7-4E61-B64B-7BBF8372AB67.htm>.

[186] Hughes, above n 108.

[187] Radio Australia, 'Drive to Improve Mental Health Care in the Pacific,' *Pacific Beat*, 5 November 2010 (Dr Frances Hughes) <www.radioaustralia.net.au/pacbeat/stories/201011/s3057961.htm (accessed 10 April 2013)>.

countries, established the Pacific Disability Forum in 2004. This Forum—together with disabled persons' organisations (DPOs) from the member countries—organised a series of annual regional conferences culminating in the Pacific Regional Strategy on Disability 2010-2015. The Strategy is designed to comply with the terms of the CRPD and implement the human rights initiatives in the Pacific Plan,[189] while recognising that 'a rights based approach represents a paradigm shift from earlier charity or medical models.'[190] The Strategy also aims to advocate for the signing, ratification and implementation of the CRPD[191] and members of the Disability Forum are required to provide annual progress reports.[192] The Strategy makes no reference to mental health consumers as a discrete class of disabled persons and—despite the fact that Psychiatric Survivors Association is one of the affiliated DPOs in Fiji—the Disability Forum's focus appears to be on developing recommendations regarding physically, intellectually, vision and hearing impaired individuals.[193]

The *Secretariat of the Pacific Community* (SPC) (formerly the South Pacific Commission) and the WHO support the biennial Meetings of Ministers for Health for the Pacific Island Countries. The first Ministerial Conference was held in Fiji in 1995. [194] Mental health first appeared on the agenda at the Vanuatu meeting in 2007 and then not again until 2011 when it was identified as a top health priority for discussion at future meetings. The meeting noted that

> there were few data [sic] on the burden of mental health in the Pacific. No substantial progress in mental health care had occurred in the Pacific, while there were increasing trends of substance abuse, addictive behaviours, depression and suicide in many countries. For too long, mental health services have been isolated from and overlooked by health systems.[195]

---

188 Pacific Islands Forum Secretariat <www.forumsec.org/pages.cfm/about-us/partners/ (accessed 10 May 2013)>.

189 Pacific Islands Forum Secretariat, 'Forum Disability Ministers Meeting Cook Islands, Session Nine: Pacific Regional Strategy on Disability 2010-2015,' (2009) <www.forumsec.org/pages.cfm/strategic-partnerships-coordination/disability/forum-disability-ministers-meeting/fdmm-2009.html (accessed 2 December 2012)> 2.

190 Ibid 7.

191 Ibid 20.

192 Ibid 7.

193 Pacific Disability Forum (PDF) and Australia Pacific Islands Disability Support (APIDS), 'Capacity Development for Effective and Efficient Disabled Persons Organisations in Pacific Island Countries: Report on Fiji Component of Research (pilot)' (July 2011) <www.pacificdisability.org/publications.aspx (accessed 2 December 2012)> 4, 22; Pacific Disability Forum (PDF) and Australia Pacific Islands Disability Support (APIDS), 'Capacity Development for Effective and Efficient Disabled Persons Organisations in Pacific Island Countries: Report on Samoa Component of Research' (August 2011) <www.pacificdisability.org/publications.aspx (accessed 2 December 2012)> 4; Pacific Disability Forum (PDF) and Australia Pacific Islands Disability Support (APIDS), 'Capacity Development for Effective and Efficient Disabled Persons Organisations in Pacific Island Countries: Report on Vanuatu Component of Research' (March 2012) <www.pacificdisability.org/publications.aspx (accessed 2 December 2012)> 2;Pacific Disability Forum (PDF) and Australia Pacific Islands Disability Support (APIDS), 'Capacity Development for Effective and Efficient Disabled Persons Organisations in Pacific Island Countries: Report on Tonga Component of Research' (March 2012) <www.pacificdisability.org/publications.aspx (accessed 2 December 2012)>.

194 World Health Organisation and Secretariat of the Pacific Community, 'Apia Outcome Tenth Pacific Health Ministers Meeting,' (July 2013) <http://www.wpro.who.int/southpacific/pic_meeting/reports/apia_outcomefull3.pdf?ua=1 (accessed 7 September 2015)> vi.

195 World Health Organisation and Secretariat of the Pacific Community, 'Ninth Meeting of Ministers of Health for the Pacific Island Countries,' (July 2011) <http://www.wpro.who.int/southpacific/pic_meeting/reports/honiarareport.pdf?ua=1 (accessed 7 September 2015)>

Recommendations included capacity building for mental health, separate costings for mental health within health budgets, the integration of mental health services into the general health system, improved data collection and mental health human resources and updated mental health policies and legislation; and at a regional level, the need to strengthen the scope and operation of PIMHnet.[196]

At the 2013 meeting in Samoa major challenges were identified in relation to mental health including low priority in health systems, insufficient funding, poor links with overlapping health issues, lack of mental health awareness, advocacy, promotion and early intervention and a large treatment gap in undiagnosed and untreated mental health conditions.[197]

In addition to agreeing on the need to include mental health as a specific goal in the post-2015 development agenda, the meeting made the following recommendations:

a) Strengthen national and regional leadership to drive the mental health agenda, support legislation and policy, and combat stigma.

b) Strengthen the evidence base on the burden of mental disorders utilising tools and methodologies that are appropriate for the Pacific context and tailored to country needs.

c) Develop and strengthen comprehensive education and training for human resources in the region for a full range of mental health care services that respond to the various levels of need.

d) Integrate mental health into general health and community-based services.

e) Strengthen the existing network and multisectoral partnership mechanisms to promote capacity-building and coordination.

f) Expand mental health service delivery utilising existing infrastructure and tailor services to meet diverse population needs.

g) Address prevention, social determinants and risk factors and promote mental health as part of holistic well-being.[198]

3.3. Regional Policy Implementation

Political commitment is typically a product of social motivation, policy and available resources. The greater the motivation, the greater the ability to develop policy and prioritise resources. The 'lack of driving force within government's mental health team' has already been identified above as one respondent's view of the prevailing situation in Fiji.[199]

Nonetheless, implementation problems and gaps between law in theory and law in practice are not limited to countries with complex political situations or lack of resources. Very often, insufficient time for planning and implementation is allowed between commencement of the legislation and the development of necessary support mechanisms.

Other times, appropriate resources are not allocated to create the supporting infrastructure, especially in relation to community based health care models.

196 Ibid.

197 World Health Organisation and Secretariat of the Pacific Community, above n 194, 5.

198 Ibid 6.

199 Email questionnaire from AB, Fiji, to Helen Ménard, 22 March 2012.

As Rees points out, Australia's commitment to promoting human rights for the mentally ill underwent a significant shift in a relatively short period of time. In the early 1990s, following Brian Burdekin's landmark inquiry into mental health and human rights,[200] human rights were at 'the forefront of the National Mental Health Strategy.'[201] But 'within a space of 4 years a human rights based approach to advancing the interests of people with mental illness ceased to be part of the combined strategy of Australia's governments for improved mental health care.'[202] This weakening of commitment may have been partly attributable to a change of federal government in Australia in 1996 which considered that most international human rights obligations had been met—a highly debatable presumption—or alternately were not worth pursuing—equally debatable.[203]

3.3.1. Tonga

In Tonga, where the focus seems to be more on inpatient treatment, the allocation of mental health funding appears to be precarious. Staff report that, apart from serious human resource and infrastructure shortages, patients from the mental health unit are obliged to grow their own food to supplement their diet and supplied medication is frequently out of date.[204]

Despite a number of reports in Tonga that have identified needs in relation to mental health services,[205] the Ministry of Health's six priority areas in its National Health Objectives (2008-2009) did *not* include any provision for improvement of mental health services. And, aside from one reference to the construction of new facilities for mental health, there was no reference to the provision of mental health services or allocated funding in the Ministry's Corporate Plan 2008/9-2011/12. [206]

The Ministry's 2009 report had as one of its stated objectives 'to promote knowledge in mental health and dissolve misconceptions, stigmatisation, ignorance and discrimination.'[207] These were expanded in 2010 to include the establishment of a 'half way house'; to develop and improve services in outer islands; to implement provisions of the *Mental Health Act 2001* and formulate a mental health policy; and to establish a 'non-governmental community based mental health foundation to provide Mental Health Promotion and Primary Prevention for the Public.'[208]

It is unclear what provisions of the legislation were being referred to—although, in context, it is likely to relate to the community based care provisions that are largely non-operational. The reference to the establishment of a 'half-way house' is similarly ambiguous as to whether it is part of an existing or proposed community care program. While it seems that the Tongan Mental Health and Disabilities Association was established in 2010 as the

---

200 Human Rights and Equal Opportunity Commission, 'Report of the National Inquiry into the Human Rights of People with Mental Illness (Burdekin Inquiry)' (1993).

201 N Rees, 'International Human Rights Obligations and Mental Health Review Tribunals' (2003) 10(1) *Psychiatry, Psychology and Law* 33.

202 Ibid 34.

203 Ibid.

204 Loupua Sefokuli, Interview with Dr Yang Yangpin, Psychiatrist (Tonga,13 June 2012).

205 D Taylor, 'Tonga National Disability Identification Survey' (Tonga Disability Action Committee, 2006) 64; Guttenbeil-Likiliki and Foundation of the Peoples of the South Pacific International, above n 21, 43–5.

206 Kingdom of Tonga Ministry of Health, 'Corporate Plan 2008/9-20011/12 ' (2008) 3.

207 Government of Tonga, 'Report of the Minister of Health for the Year 2009' (2009) <www.health.gov.to/sites/default/files/AR2009.pdf> 70.

208 Government of Tonga, above n 31, 60.

first NGO for mental health in Tonga, it has a very low profile and there is still no national mental health policy in Tonga.

The most recent annual report of the Ministry for 2011-2012 includes the continued process of deinstitutionalisation as part of its mission statement for providing the best possible care in mental health.[209]

Corporate plans for the Ministry for 2015 -2020 are currently in draft form and detailed objectives for the mental health section have appeared for the first time. While they are positive and ambitious, they are also largely dependent on funding from external donors. Some of the more significant objectives include additional and improved infrastructure in central and regional areas; the formulation of national policies in relation to mental health, drug abuse and suicide; specialist training for mental health staff; additional specialist mental health professionals; ongoing community education pertaining to mental health; and upgrading the status of mental health within the Ministry of Health.[210]

The earlier reports cited above appear to have been developed in conjunction with a 'capacity building' aid program[211] and, to date, have failed to deliver in substance. It is hoped that with mental health now appearing as an integral part of the Ministry's strategic planning in Tonga that progress is on the horizon.

3.3.2. Samoa

The first Samoan Mental Health Policy was introduced in 2006 and, in a stated commitment to promote mental health and treat mental illness, outlined eleven key areas for action including appropriate financing; legislation and human rights; family support and focus areas for prevention and treatment—including suicide and substance abuse, sexual abuse and domestic violence.[212]

The current Samoan Health Sector Strategic Plan for 2008–2018 seeks to give effect to the aims of the Ministry, namely 'excellence in regulating the health sector and provision of articulate and appropriate health promotion and prevention services for a healthy Samoa.'[213] Yet, there is *no* reference to mental health service provision as distinct from general health services anywhere in this document.

Similarly, the National Health Promotion Policy 2010-2015[214]—developed as one of the strategies under the Health Sector Plan—makes no direct reference to mental health care except that the *Mental Health Act* and the Mental Health Policy have the potential to impact on the health of individuals and communities.[215] The Policy merely acknowledges that health is a 'state of complete physical, spiritual and mental well-being'[216]and that 'community involvement must facilitate meaningful participation of people with disabilities.'[217]

---

209 Government of Tonga, 'Report of the Minister for Health for the Financial Year 2011/2012' (2011) 32.
210 Government of Tonga, above n 31.
211 Ibid 10.
212 Hope Eseta and Foundation of the Peoples of the South Pacific International, above n 39, 16.
213 Government of Samoa Ministry of Health, above n 135.
214 Government of Samoa Ministry of Health, 'National Health Promotion Policy 2010-2015' (2008) 6.
215 Ibid 15.
216 Ibid 7.
217 Ibid 33.

Apart from a generic reference to supporting competency based training for mental health nurses, the Ministry's Corporate Plan for 2013-2016 makes no reference at all to mental health in any of its priorities, key objectives, strategic goals or work plans.[218]

The only reference to mental health in the MOH's 2010 Annual Report, is a table of statistics on suicide attempts from 1992-2010.[219] While the Report states that the decrease in the number of attempts and deaths from suicide in 2010 compared to 2009 'reflects collaborate [sic] efforts by both the government ministries and private organisations,'[220] there is no independent evidence to support this or, indeed, any published policies indicating government initiatives in this regard. The Ministry's 2011 report simply lists the number of suicides for the period and states

> [d]espite the efforts of government ministries, including the Ministry of Health, and local NGOs to conduct health promotion and awareness programs on suicide prevention, suicide remains high in mortality reporting. These high rates prompt the Ministry of Health and organisations to focus their health promotion efforts on adolescents and high risk populations, especially young men.[221]

Yet there is no evidence of any such Ministry initiatives in Samoa.

A study of Samoan youth and mental health in 2009 found that, despite the existence of the 2006 Mental Health Policy, there was still no national mental health program in existence.[222] The study recommended that further research was needed in relation to youth suicide and prevention strategies; qualitative research on mental health issues and best practice models for mental health related service providers.[223]

The national demographic health survey commissioned by the MOH in 2009, which one might have expected to report on *all* aspects of community health, makes not a *single* reference to mental health.[224]

The Samoa National Policy on Disability—first submitted to Cabinet in 2009 but not launched until 2011—did acknowledge that 'the Government of Samoa does not have any policies or national plan to address the needs of people with disabilities, except for the Mental Health Act 2007'[225] but has as part of its mission the goal to 'develop a strategy to address and provide more support for mental health and related disabilities.'[226] Part of the proposed strategy was that the MOH work with other ministries and stakeholders in the development of the Mental Health Action Plan.'[227]

---

218 Government of Samoa Ministry of Health, 'Corporate Plan 2013-2016,' (2013) <http://www.health.gov.ws/Portals/189/Approved%20MOH%20Corporate%20Plan%202013-2016.pdf (accessed 6 September 2015)> 25.

219 Government of Samoa Ministry of Health, 'Annual Report Financial Year 2009-2010' (2010) 9.

220 Ibid 9.

221 Government of Samoa Ministry of Health, above n 106, 9.

222 Hope Eseta and Foundation of the Peoples of the South Pacific International, above n 39, 35.

223 Ibid 31.

224 Government of Samoa Ministry of Health, 'Samoa Demographic and Health Survey 2009' (June 2010).

225 Government of Samoa Ministry of Women Community and Social Development, 'Samoa National Policy on Disability' (2009) (Version submitted to Cabinet in April 2009) 4; see also Pacific Disability Forum (PDF) and Australia Pacific Islands Disability Support (APIDS), above n 193.

226 Government of Samoa Ministry of Women Community and Social Development, above n 225, 18.

227 Ibid 27.

Yet, nearly ten years after the introduction of the Mental Health Policy, no Mental Health Action Plan has emerged. On this basis, it is difficult to see how the government in Samoa has progressed the implementation of its mental health policy in any significant manner.

3.3.3. Fiji

Despite the Ministry of Health's stated commitment in 2011 to develop and strengthen community mental health services, to improve mental health service delivery and to take the lead role in improving mental health service delivery and care in the region,[228] relatively speaking little has come to pass. The political situation in Fiji from 2006 to 2014 delayed the funding required from international bodies and diplomatic missions for the re-structuring and building of any new psychiatric facilities.[229] While there has been a plethora of mental health documentation produced over the last five or six years, some has never progressed beyond the draft stage, is not readily accessible and most has yet to be actioned.

The Fijian Ministry of Health's Strategic Plan 2011-2015 lists seven 'Health Outcomes,' one of which includes 'improved mental health care'.[230] Its strategic goals, outcomes and objectives in relation to mental health—without reference to any specific performance indicators—include the review of the Mental Health and Suicide Prevention Strategic Plan 2007-2011; an increase in the number of personnel trained in mental health and the provision of accessible mental health services in all regional hospitals.[231] The Ministry's 2016-2020 Strategic Plan, while maintaining mental health as a priority area for the provision of preventative, curative and rehabilitative services, essentially only refers to the integration of mental health services within primary health care in all facilities and the recording of data in relation to admission and suicide rates.[232]

The first mental health policy for Fiji was released in 2011 but does not appear to have been widely disseminated. Its vision is to provide a 'comprehensive, decentralised and community based mental health service which is coordinated at the National, Divisional and Community level and integrated into primary health care services.'[233] The policy's objectives are to

- provide mental health care in the least restrictive environment
- provide for the care, treatment, protection and rehabilitation for the people with mental disorders
- integrate mental health services into the general health services
- facilitate the development of community based mental health services
- develop, provide, and sustain psychosocial rehabilitation program and facilities as an integral part of management
- ensure that suitably qualified mental health personnel are made available through quality appropriate training

228 TemoL, above n 149.

229 Ibid.

230 Ministry of Health Fiji Islands, 'Shaping Fiji's Health: Strategic Plan 2011-2015' (2011) 14.

231 Ibid 19–22.

232 Ministry of Health and Medical Services Fiji, 'National Strategic Plan 2016-2020 Executive Version ' (2016) <http://www.health.gov.fj/PDFs/Corporate%20Plan/Strategic%20Plan%202016-2020%20Executive%20Version.pdf (accessed 4 January 2016)> 18, 20.

233 Ministry of Health Fiji - Mental Health Services, 'Mental Health Policy' (2011).

- ensure that adequate resources
- provide ongoing education, training and research in the field of mental health to support improvement of care and services.[234]

Principal objectives for action under the policy are designated as human resources and training; treatment and rehabilitation; organisation of services; availability of essential drugs; information systems; financing; advocacy; legislation and human rights; intersectoral collaboration; and research.[235] Some of the identified action areas under legislation and human rights are listed as treatment in a least restrictive environment; confidentiality; informed consent; voluntary and involuntary admissions; and review mechanisms. However, there are no strategies or performance indicators associated with these areas nor any information detailing how or when they will be implemented or evaluated. The same applies to all other stated objectives. To some extent a selection of these issues has been addressed in the Mental Health Unit Business Plan for 2015.[236]

The draft version of the National Mental Health Strategic Plan 2012-2014 contained three strategic goals being to position national mental health for long term success (including organisational structure, corporate governance and web design and development); to strengthen national mental health services (including infrastructure, practices and standards, and training of mental health professionals); and to promote mental health nationally.[237] It is unclear whether or not this plan ever progressed beyond draft form, how widely it was circulated and to what extent it has been actioned.

In September 2014 a mid-term review of the draft National Mental Health Strategic Plan 2012-2016 was submitted for endorsement. At the same time the National Mental Health Advisory Council decided to merge the National Mental Health Policy and the National Suicide Prevention Policy & Implementation Action Plan 2008-2013 into a new National Mental Health & Suicide Prevention Policy 2015-2019 (NMH&SPP).[238] The NMH&SPP links to existing policy documents and strategic plans and purports to promote the development of policies consistent with the CRPD, the provision of high quality coordinated care, the integration of mental health services into the general health system, the shift to community based mental health services, a dedicated mental health budget and specialised training for health care workers.[239]

The draft National Mental Health and Suicide Prevention Strategic Plan 2016-2020 builds on these integrated polices and outlines a series of strategies in line with the Ministry's corporate plan relating to key areas of leadership and governance; information systems; health service delivery including deinstitutionalisation and development of regional and community based services; specialist training of the health workforce and community education; provision of essential medicines; and finance.[240] It remains to be seen how these strategies will be progressed.

---

234 Ibid.

235 Ibid.

236 Ministry of Health and Medical Services Fiji, 'Mental Health Services 2015 Business Plan' (2015).

237 Ministry of Health Fiji, 'National Mental Health Strategic Plan for 2012-2014 (Draft)' (2012).

238 Ministry of Health and Medical Services Fiji, 'National Mental Health and Suicide Prevention Policy' (2015) <https://www.mindbank.info/item/5909 (accessed 5 January 2016)> 10.

239 Ibid 5.

240 Ministry of Health and Medical Services Fiji, 'National Mental Health and Suicide Prevention Strategic Plan 2016-2020' (2016)

As part of the integration policy, mental health services have been placed under the National Wellness Centre within the Ministry of Health and under the leadership of the National Mental Health Advisor.[241] Other initiatives under the NMH&SPP have had mixed results. While more than 200 primary health care professionals were trained under the WHO mhGAP program in 2014 with a further 500 projected for 2015,[242] one respondent maintains that staff selected for training did not include those from the health centres where regular weekly mental health clinics are held and that there has been no evaluation or supervision of those trained under the mhGAP program.[243]

The Ministry's Corporate Plan for 2011 outlines some performance indicators for various outcomes listed in the Strategic Plan under the 'provision of primary health care'. Despite a strategy to increase the number of mental health trained staff by November 2011,[244] the 2011 target number of mental health trainees for the year was unspecified.[245] The only other item relevant to mental health care included the development of national mental health advocacy programs by November 2011.[246]

Subsequent Corporate Plans in 2014 and 2015 contain similar unspecified aims to increase numbers of mental health trained staff.[247] Both Plans have identical strategic outcomes as 'development of a coordinated and standardised national mental health service' and 'development of mental health psychiatry and mental health clinical practice guidelines'.[248]

Again, there is no available evidence that any of these initiatives have been realised. If the implementation and operation of the Mental Health Review Board under the *Mental Health Decree 2010*—as discussed in Chapter 10—is any benchmark, the evolution of these programs will be a lengthy process.

The Ministry's infrastructure and services plan 2010-2014—referred to within the situational analysis of specialist clinical services in Fiji and under which mental health is placed—includes the creation of two regional mental health wards within existing general hospitals. This appears to be reinforcement and continuation of the established inpatient focused mental health care model; there is no mention of the development of any community based mental health services.[249]

While acknowledging that specialist psychiatric services are in high demand,[250] and that professional resources are in limited supply, the report pays little attention to any assessment

---

241 Ministry of Health and Medical Services Fiji, above n 238.

242 Ibid 15.

243 Email questionnaire from IJ, Fiji, to Helen Ménard, 18 December 2015. The WHO Mental Health Gap Action Programme (mhGAP) aims at scaling up services for mental, neurological and substance use disorders for countries especially with low- and middle-income. *www.who.int/mental_health/mhgap/en/.*

244 Ministry of Health Fiji Islands, 'Annual Corporate Plan 2011' (2011) 15

245 Ibid 14.

246 Ibid 14.

247 Ministry of Health Fiji Islands, 'Annual Corporate Plan 2014' (2014) 9; Ministry of Health Fiji Islands, 'Annual Corporate Plan 2015' (2015) 11.

248 Ministry of Health Fiji Islands, above n 247, 16; Ministry of Health Fiji Islands, above n 247, 18. An admission protocol document for St Giles was developed in 2010 but this preceded the Mental Health Decree and any formal mental health policy. See Ministry of Health Fiji, 'Admission Guideline St Giles Hospital,' (2010) <http://www.health.gov.fj/wp-content/uploads/2014/05/St-Giles-Admission-protocol_2010.pdf (accessed 5 January 2016)>

249 College of Medicine and Nursing and Health Sciences, above n 8 [4.1.7].

250 Ibid [4.2.2].

of the needs of mental health care as a discrete area of clinical services nor makes any recommendations specific to mental health.

The sole reference in the appended Clinical Services Plan 2010-2014—under its workforce planning strategies—is to 'consider the development or sourcing of appropriate training options for registrars in specialties where locally based post graduate training is not available and overseas training is not necessarily appropriate [for example mental health].'[251] However, within the substantive report, there is neither discussion of the rationale underpinning this strategy nor a plan for its implementation.

3.3.4. Vanuatu

The situation in Vanuatu is even less heartening. After the inaugural meeting of PIMHnet in Vanuatu in 2007, Vanuatu established its own National Mental Health Committee (NMHC) that required the endorsement of the Council of Ministers.[252]

The first Mental Health Policy and Plan was eventually introduced in Vanuatu in 2009 and acknowledges the challenges for mental health policy including infrastructure, lack of trained mental health professionals, limited financial resources and lack of services for mental health in primary health care.[253] The Plan outlines an ambitious range of strategies including establishment of a National Mental Health Committee (NMHC); review of mental health legislation; the provision of basic mental health care within primary health care services; the development of human resources for mental health; the availability of essential psychotropic medication; the development of information systems and data collection; promotion of mental health through advocacy and community education programs; and community involvement in mental health care delivery.[254]

When the Mental Health Policy and Plan was established in 2009, there had still been no government endorsement to enable effective functioning of the committee—a situation which remains today.[255] The NMHC continues to function in an ad hoc manner but, due to ongoing lack of government commitment and funding for mental health, AusAID has now withdrawn its support for the program.[256] AusAID had funded a full time advisory position—by way of a clinical psychologist—to assist with implementation of the Plan including 'education, clinical work, procedure and policy design and public health initiatves'. However in 2012, due to lack of government co-operation, the position was assessed as 'no longer sustainable' and was withdrawn.[257]

Currently, performance indicators and stipulated timeframes under the Plan remain largely unmet. The unendorsed NMHC can neither implement nor monitor the Plan. Drafting of new legislation—which was to have been circulated to stakeholders for discussion in 2010—has not yet commenced. As there appear to be no 'suitable candidates to draft the legislation within the State Law Office', it is proposed to seek donor funding to engage a

---

251 Ibid (Clinical Services Plan 2010-2014) 4.

252 Sections 39–40 of the *Constitution of the Republic of Vanuatu* provide that the executive power of the people of the Republic of Vanuatu is vested in the Prime Minister and Council of Ministers and the Council of Ministers shall consist of the Prime Minister and other Ministers who will not exceed one quarter of the members of Parliament.

253 Republic of Vanuatu Ministry of Health, above n 90, 4.

254 Ibid 12.

255 Ibid 8; Interview with Peter Kaloris, Mental Health Cordinator, Vanuatu (Port Vila, 24 June 2013).

256 Interview with Carlie Dodds, Clinical Psychologist, Vanuatu (Port Vila, 28 June 2012).

257 Ibid.

consultant for this task.[258] No additional services for mental health have been provided and no formal training programs are in place for mental health care professionals. Minutes from a meeting of the unendorsed NMHC in May 2012 indicate that, while a lack of funds appears to be holding up some projects, an inadequate number of people with relevant expertise have been recruited to the NMHC and the process appears to have stalled.[259] Mental health—which comes under public health in the Ministry of Health—does not feature at all, let alone as a priority, in the Ministry of Health's strategy for delivery of services from 2010- 2016.[260] Disability services which come within the Ministry of Justice and Community Services, similarly, make no specific provisions for mental health.[261]

After ratifying the CRPD in 2008, Vanuatu has yet to meet its reporting obligations as a State Party, despite a draft report being completed in 2013.[262] In 2012, the government minister responsible conceded that little progress had been made by the government in relation to the field of disability and 'NGOs prove to have been the main drivers of disability development in Vanuatu.'[263] This is particularly disappointing given that, in the lead up to the adoption of the CRPD, Vanuatu was described as 'the only Pacific island country that consistently participated in these negotiations and discussions.'[264] The ratification of the CRPD was largely due to the campaigning of one exceptionally dedicated and influential individual who led the Vanuatu Disabled Person's Association for many years and spearheaded disability rights reform in the country. Sadly, Andy Piau Lynch died in January 2011[265] and the profile of the disability rights movement in Vanuatu has now assumed far less prominence.

4. Specific Jurisdictional Issues

Disputes over ethnicity and land ownership in Fiji have resulted in four military coups in 25 years and, following the most recent coup in 2006, Fiji held its first democratic elections in 2014. While Vanuatu has not been subjected to military coups in the same way as its Melanesian neighbour, instability has been the hallmark of the political landscape since a

---

258 Kaloris, above n 95, 5.

259 Mental Health Committee Vanuatu, 'Minutes of Meeting 8 May 2012: Update on Mental Health Policy 2009-2015' (2012).

260 Government of the Republic of Vanuatu, 'Health Sector Strategy (2010-2016)' (2010) <http://www.wpro.who.int/health_services/vanuatu_nationalhealthplan.pdf (Accessed 3 September 2015)>

261 Government of the Republic of Vanuatu, 'Strategy for the Justice and Community Services Sector 2014 - 2017, Ministry for Justice and Community Services' (2014); Government of the Republic of Vanuatu, 'The National Community Based Rehabilitation (CBR) Action Plan 2014 - 2024, Ministry of Justice & Community Services' (2014)

262 Government of the Republic of Vanuatu, 'Annual Report 2013 Ministry of Justice & Community Services' (2013) <http://www.mjcs.gov.vu/images/research_database/Annual_Report_2013__05JUN14.pdf (Accessed 3 September 2015)> 18.

263 G Ligo, 'Initial Report on Disability in Vanuatu Released,' *Vanuatu Daily Post* (Port Vila, Vanuatu), 15 November 2012, 3.

264 Pacific Islands Forum Secretariat, 'Conventions and International Agreements on Disability' (2009) <www.forumsec.org/pages.cfm/strategic-partnerships-coordination/disability/conventions-international-agreements-on-disability.html (accessed 2 December 2012)>.

265 Aoteoroa New Zealand Cluster Munition Coalition, *Pacific Campaigner Andy Piau-Lynch* <www.stopclusterbombs.org.nz/2011/01/30/vanuatu-campaigner-andy-piau-lynch/ (accessed 24 March 2013)>; J Joshua, 'Influential Disability Rights Advocator Dies,' *Vanautu Daily Post* (Port Vila, Vanuatu), 2 February 2011 <www.dailypost.vu/content/influential-disability-rights-advocator-dies (accessed 24 March 2013)>.

failed political coup and the fragmentation of the Vanua'aku Pati—which had governed in its own right since independence—and its electoral loss in 1991.[266] Multi party coalitions over the past 25 years have ensured regular changes of government within every electoral term,[267] accompanied by constant rotation of ministerial portfolios—intended only to shore up coalition support rather than to guarantee any departmental leadership or expertise. Following violent pro-democracy riots in 2006, Tonga began the transition from a constitutional monarchy to democracy in 2010. All three countries also face significant challenges in relation to the logistics of service delivery across vast geographical areas.

One might be tempted to argue that these factors could be significant influences in the lack of policy development in areas not viewed as critically 'life and death'—notably, mental health care. However, the fact that Samoa does not face the same geospatial challenges and is seen as one of the more politically stable countries in the region, yet has an equally poor track record in relation to mental health policy development, tends to militate against this argument.

All countries are regularly subjected to natural disasters, the effects of which only serve to direct attention and resources away from policy development in areas perceived as less life threatening, such as mental health.[268]

The answer, therefore, must lie at a more intrinsic level. One way or another, all Pacific countries have been affected by globalisation with resultant effects on custom, culture and traditional ways of life. The capability to transcend this evolution and ensure the protection of mental health consumers' rights and their ability to access justice will depend largely on effective community education and the capacity to marry cultural beliefs and practices with modern medicine and human rights ethos.

In countries such as Vanuatu, where the literacy rates are so low, the education systems so weak, and custom and religion more deeply entrenched, the future is not promising. Another factor that distinguishes Vanuatu from the other countries under discussion is that it is a Melanesian state. Polynesian states such as Tonga and Samoa—and to a lesser extent Fiji—are more homogenous in terms of their language and culture. By contrast, Melanesian states comprise many distinct cultural groups, each with its own language and customs.[269] This makes the community awareness and engagement and social and political consensus necessary for real law reform arduous and frequently a lengthy process. This is partly why Vanuatu is still a long way from embracing mental health law reform.

---

266 H Van Trease, 'Years of Turmoil: 1987-1991' in H Van Trease (ed), *Melanesian Politics: Stael Blong Vanuatu* (Macmillan Brown Centre for Pacific Studies, University of Canterbury and Institute of Pacific Studies, University of the South Pacific, 1995) 73.

267 H Van Trease, 'Melanesia in Review: Issues and Events, 2010, Vanuatu' (2011) 23(2) *Contemporary Pacific* 511.

268 Andie Noonan, *Pacific nations must prepare for more natural disasters as El Nino takes hold, experts warn* <http://www.abc.net.au/news/2015-07-20/pacific-nations-headed-for-more-natual-disasters/6634008 (accessed 17 December 2015)>

269 G Powles, 'Law Reform in Pacific Island States' in B Opeskin and D Weisbrot (eds), *The Promise of Law Reform* (Federation Press, 2005) 404, 406.

5. CONCLUSION

Where there are insufficient mental health services and resources combined with social and political disinclination to prioritise mental health at a domestic level, the ability of mental health consumers to exercise their legislative rights—where they exist—and thereby access justice, is compromised.

As discussed in earlier chapters, the recorded prevalence of mental illness throughout the region is increasing for a variety of socio-cultural, fiscal and political reasons. All countries seem to recognise that mental health services and professional resources, at all levels, are far from adequate—in some places non existent. Their willingness to rectify the situation is less forthcoming.

While overall *health* expenditure within the region is largely within WHO guidelines, no discrete information on mental health expenditure is available in any of the target countries. Samoa, Fiji and Vanuatu have introduced formal mental health policies—Tonga has not. While Samoa has yet to develop a plan to implement its mental health policy, Vanuatu's mental health plan, developed in 2009, has not received ministerial endorsement, let alone been actioned. Strategies under the Fijian mental health plan to improve infrastructure, develop community mental health services and create mental health training programs have shown minimal progress.

Some countries face individual domestic challenges that may hinder policy development but, overall, mental health care and its contingent human rights barely feature on the Pacific landscape—and there is little cause to anticipate that change is imminent.

Part IV: Conclusion

CONCLUSION

1. OVERVIEW

This work set out to answer two questions: firstly, whether new mental health legislation in the Pacific has created or improved pathways for access to justice for mental health consumers subject to involuntary detention; and secondly, whether these new or improved pathways have conferred any real benefits on those subject to involuntary detention.

In doing so, access to justice has been measured by the delivery of the essential attributes of *information*, *representation* and *participation* within the legal mechanisms created for the admission, detention and review of detention under various mental health laws in the Pacific. Provisions of past and present statutes in four selected countries have been analsyed demonstrating that new mental health legislation—forged largely in a human rights setting—has created a variety of rights based frameworks, based on primarily Western style statutory models. However, these have failed to effect any real change for those detained under the legislation.

A number of features have been identified as contributing to this failure, including cultural ideologies in the Pacific surrounding mental health and illness, and the lower levels of acceptance of Western style human rights principles and enterprises. When mental illness is not seen as a physical condition responsive to modern—as opposed to traditional—medicine, governments have been shown to have had little incentive to prioritise it within their limited budgets when compared to the highly visible demands of physical health. In the same way, the conceptual conflict between the perceived individualism underpinning the human rights movement and the communalism of life in the Pacific frequently is viewed as justification for resisting the implementation of human rights based initiatives, especially when they are seen as tied to foreign aid and an affront to political sovereignty.

This reluctance to embrace rights based ideals is shown to be compounded by the fact that there is a dearth of professional resources and specialist mental health training opportunities in the region. Psychiatric medicine fails to attract professionals in the same way as physical medicine—especially when there are limited post graduate opportunities for psychiatry in the region—and those who do engage in study outside the region often do not return to their home countries, further depleting the specialist workforce.

All of these factors, combined with scarce economic resources and some jurisdiction specific issues, serve to create a lack of political will to prioritise and fund mental health care as part of domestic health policy.

2. The Final Score

Tonga has employed a broad tranche of rights in its revised mental health laws, notwithstanding a lack of specific reference to international mental health principles. On the other hand, its legislation—unlike its counterparts in Samoa and Fiji—is not stated to be subject to any operational qualifications. Yet, resources at every level in the country are acutely inadequate and render many of the statutory provisions unworkable. A significant resource limitation for Tonga is the geographical spread of its outer islands across a large area. A community based mental health care framework exists within the legislation—the actual product does not. Mental health care in Tonga revolves principally around inpatient care. The multi-member review tribunal conducts periodic reviews and a small number of appeals against detention, but its impartiality is compromised by the critical shortage of legal and mental health professionals available to constitute the tribunal. Despite signing the *Convention on the Rights of Persons with Disability* (CRPD) in 2007, health policy in Tonga continues to ignore mental health care. Apart from the 'usual suspects'—political will and appropriate allocation of financial resources—achieving the ideal in Tonga will depend on its ability to attract, cultivate and retain qualified mental health care professionals. With as many Tongans living overseas as at home, this challenge is considerable.

Samoa, by comparison, lacks the geographical challenges of Tonga and Fiji in relation to service delivery to outlying islands. Samoa currently has no inpatient mental health facilities and its focus is on community based mental health care with established outreach clinics on the two main islands that accommodate the entire population. The statutory framework adopts a more pragmatic approach to rights based law and appears to be aimed at the status quo despite an ambitious set of objectives to provide optimum health care services. The Act presents a model that foresees minimal interaction with formal legal systems and refrains from dealing with issues that are not part of the current treatment profile. While the 'subject to available resources' rider may reflect the reality of a poorly resourced country, it is argued that it also runs the risk of removing pressure from political institutions that play a crucial role in the allocation of resources. There is no charter for external or independent periodic review of detention orders, and appeals are heard by a single member review body located within the judiciary. It is difficult to tell how well the system is working because, comparatively speaking—for reasons as much related to culture as resources—the number of mental health consumers in Samoa presenting to formal health services is far less than its Pacific neighbours. At a policy level, ten years after the introduction of the Mental Health Policy, no Mental Health Action Plan has emerged. While a new secure inpatient centre has been under construction for several years, a number of substantive health surveys and strategies developed in Samoa over the last few years have failed to acknowledge mental health issues.

Fiji has a long-standing history of institutional mental health care. The community based mental health care policy launched under the 2010 *Mental Health Decree* has yet to be implemented in a substantive way—either by way of treatment options or rights based initiatives. Despite directly committing itself to a range of international rights based principles and signing the CRPD in 2010, Fiji appears to have been pressured into mental health law reform, for reasons that remain unclear. As with many Western countries, so far Fiji has failed to establish any supporting infrastructure to allow for effective transition to a community care model. Most of the provisions under the Decree remain untested. The limited operation of the statutory review board, due to administrative dysfunction and insufficient allocation of resources to guarantee impartiality and procedural fairness, has so far failed to deliver access to justice for mental health consumers. There are some unexplained but significant deficiencies in the rights based platform of the Decree which may have been intentional policy omissions. The future of mental health service delivery in Fiji, together with its ability to transition from an entrenched culture of inpatient care to community based care and recognition of and respect for human rights, is as uncertain as its political future.

Vanuatu has not considered mental health law reform for almost 50 years. While one or two beds at the general hospital in Port Vila are used occasionally for mental health care, until 2013 there were no formally trained mental health professionals in the country and there are still no supported community based mental health services. Individuals whose behaviour brings them to the attention of the police or who are rejected by the community are contained, untreated (and frequently subjected to violent abuse) within the prison system. With one of the highest population growth rates in the region and the lowest levels of emigration; some of the lowest levels of adult literacy and a poor education system; together with one of the lowest levels of total health expenditure per capita, Vanuatu struggles to achieve even basic levels of general health care and education. Hosting the launch of PIMHnet in 2007, drafting a mental health policy in 2009 and ratifying the CRPD in 2008 have so far amounted to little more than a smoke screen. Progressing these initiatives has been less than encouraging. The prospect of mental health care and mental health law reform assuming a position of primacy on the domestic political agenda in Vanuatu in the foreseeable future is remote.

3. Creating Future Pathways to Justice

The question that remains is how to best model legal mechanisms within mental health service delivery in the Pacific that are culturally sensitive yet legally effective and promote access to justice for mental health consumers. It is beyond the scope of this study to provide a detailed design for such models, but the need for their existence is apparent and some guiding principles can be proposed. Despite the changing nature of some Pacific communities and the infiltration of Western values, the richness of culture and tradition remains part of the vitality and uniqueness of the region and deserves to be preserved.

Tamasese argues that while mental health research has been limited, for Pacific island populations in New Zealand 'hospital statistics support the view that Pacific people delay or avoid seeking treatment from mainstream psychiatric services.'[1] He suggests that 'one reason for this delay is that the values inherent to the "western" mental health system may be viewed negatively by Pacific People.'[2]

The same author's study on culturally appropriate research methodology in mental health care in Samoa highlights the fact that 'the nuances of the Samoan language hold the key to understanding the meaning of important cultural concepts.'[3] While there was recognition by participants in his work that some mental disorders could only be treated by Western

1 K Tamasese et al. 'Ole Taiao Afua, the New Morning: A Qualitative Investigation into Samoan Perspectives on Mental Health and Culturally Appropriate Services' (2005) 39 *Australian and New Zealand Journal of Psychiatry* 300, 301.

2 Ibid.

3 Ibid.

medicine, based on physical modes of treatment, it was considered there were substantial cultural gaps in the diagnosis and treatment of mental illness.[4] In the same way that this study suggests Samoan language speakers and traditional healers need to play integral roles in effective mental health care, language and culture should also be integral components of any Pacific legal system, if justice is to be readily accessible by mental health consumers.

Lessons learned from the application of transcultural psychiatry in Tonga and working with traditional healers can also be used to facilitate greater communication between consumers and health professionals—both in the review of treatment and as a way of potentially shortening periods of detention and promoting community care. This is particularly so in Tonga where the membership of the Mental Health Review Tribunal (MHRT) should, for example, include a person with traditional knowledge and skills. This would not only enhance the capacity of the legal mechanisms to be culturally sensitive and legally effective but would go some way towards alleviating the shortage of professional membership of the tribunal and fostering procedural fairness.

MHRT hearings should also be conducted in culturally sympathetic settings rather than the formality and intimidating character of a court or hospital boardroom. This might mean communal meeting houses or other suitable places that neutralise the power balance between the decision makers and the person subject to review and facilitate openness and mutual respect. This, of course, will depend on the nature of the person's condition and its etiology —in some cases it might mean avoiding places that have some particular connection with the person's symptoms. It could even mean the placement of culturally appropriate or significant items in a meeting place, openly acknowledging certain beliefs or rituals before a hearing, conducting the hearing in a local language or allowing a person to wear traditional clothing especially where this represents respect and integrity. In other cases it might also involve the interaction of traditional healers, spiritual mentors or appropriately trained community advocates or, for example, the absence of certain family members.

In the context of Fiji and the very visible tension between human rights and traditional practices, Madraiwiwi argues that human rights provides a broader platform on which to place tradition and custom and that, in the same way that some traditional beliefs and practices have been discarded over time, the inclusiveness of human rights allows those who were previously unheard to participate and contribute to society. Madraiwiwi suggests that reconciliation must be achieved in a non-confrontational manner and—as rights exist in context and are never absolute—their synthesis depends on the recognition of aspects of 'culture, custom and tradition that can justifiably remain untouched by matters of human rights.'[5]

Any attempt to remedy the more significant impediments to the realisation of rights based legislation and to facilitate access to justice for mental health consumers, at the very least, must include the recognition and incorporation of culturally appropriate ideals as an essential part of mental health care policy and mental health legal services. This will necessitate considerable efforts to increase social awareness and acceptance of the nature and treatment of mental illness and human rights doctrines. Such systemic community education will need

---

4 Ibid 305.

5 J Madraiwiwi Ratu, 'Navigating Passage Between Human Rights and Culture in Fijian Waters' in M Powles (ed), *Pacific Futures* (Pandanus Books,The Australian National University, 2006) 50.

to originate at a government policy level and be sufficiently funded. Then, and only then, will mental health rights and services become a priority on domestic political agendas.

In 2000 New Zealand's mental health legislation was amended to include a requirement that powers be exercised and proceedings conducted under the Act with 'proper respect for the person's cultural and ethnic identity'.[6] Fiji is the only regional jurisdiction to mirror this provision. Section 6(1)(c) of the 2010 Decree states that persons and bodies exercising functions under the Decree should recognise a person's ties with family, extended family and family group and respect the person's cultural and ethnic identity. As with most provisions of this Decree, this is subject to practicality and available resources and, as with all other provisions, remains untested.[7]

At any level, information is worthless unless disseminated in a form and manner that promotes education and engages the community—particularly in areas where the community health model is in place. Legislation is merely 'an enabling tool' and 'even in countries with good legislation informal systems may subvert legislative intent.'[8] Low literacy levels in some parts of the Pacific may work against absorption of information but the challenge is to present material in a way that is easily understandable, non-threatening and culturally empathetic. For example, in Vanuatu, the highly sensitive issues surrounding HIV and AIDS have been embodied in an extremely popular television soap opera, *Love Patrol.* The series was first shown on local television in March 2007, is now into its seventh series and has Pacific wide coverage.[9]

Bartlett's writings on mental health law in Africa share a similar view. He argues that 'education and political action are equally vital parts of the road to change... [but] the argument can be overstated. Law has a symbolic as well as a functional role, and can normalise values over times, giving new ideas the gravitas of respectability.'[10]

The WHO Resource Book made an apt assessment of the challenge in much of the Pacific in the following terms:

> Mental health professionals who are not familiar with the provisions of a new law may continue with 'customary' practices in treatment provision, thus defeating the purpose of new progressive mental health legislation. Without adequate training and education—and the full involvement of a number of role players—legislation may have little impact.[11]

Regrettably, this scenario has already played out in Fiji. It is epitomised by the previously quoted observation of one respondent clearly indicating that awareness and education programs were *not* part of the preliminary stages of legislative implementation: 'The new

[6] *Mental Health (Compulsory Assessment and Treatment) Act 1992* (NZ) s 5(2)(c).

[7] *Mental Health Decree 2010* (Fiji Islands).

[8] M Freeman, *WHO Resource Book on Mental Health, Human Rights and Legislation* (World Health Organisation, 2005)17.

[9] Wan Smolbag Theatre, *Love Patrol Series* <www.wansmolbag.org/DynamicPages.asp?cid=26&navID=34 (accessed 3 September 2015)>.

[10] P Bartlett, R Jenkins and D Kilma, 'Mental Health Law in the Community: Thinking about Africa' (2011) 5(21) *International Journal of Mental Health Systems* <http://www.ijmhs.com/content/5/1/21 (accessed 5 June 2013)>.

[11] Freeman, above n 8.

decree [it] has become rather chaotic as the judiciary are still using the old [law] and the hospital kind of shifts between the two documents depending on what is convenient.'[12]

Harper writes that '[as] customary justice systems can support the legal empowerment of the poor and disadvantaged, but also block it, it is critical that justice reform and empowerment initiatives engage with community actors to maximise the system's benefits and address its weaknesses.'[13] The author also recognises that 'there is less knowledge on how customary systems might be able to contribute to legal empowerment outcomes.'[14]

The potential for some customary practices to discriminate against rather than empower marginal groups[15] must also be weighed up in considering how to improve access to justice for mental health consumers in the Pacific. When significantly vulnerable individuals—often unable to communicate their wishes effectively during periods of serious illness—are represented by the family or the community 'family', the family's cultural imperatives might not reflect the aspirations of the individual. This could impact, for example, on the willingness of the community to care for such an individual in the less restrictive environment of the community, rather than an inpatient facility, particularly where the illness is seen as a spiritual curse or a contagious form of 'black magic'.

It has not been the aim of this research to explore the advantages and disadvantages of the various health care models available for treatment of mental health consumers in the Pacific. On the other hand, the most appropriate model of care for any cohort should be closely linked to the legal model that exists to provide pathways to justice and protection of human rights arising from involuntary detention, care and treatment—whether it be in a community, supervised accommodation or a hospital setting. Poor standards of care and treatment are highly likely to be attended by infringement of human rights and limited access to justice.

Puloka, for example, maintains that in relation to youth

> mental health should be understood using a more inclusive approach that identifies the key roles that families, villages, society, schools, churches and both public and private institutions can play in the holistic healthy development of a child into youth and then adulthood.[16]

This leads us to the type of legal mechanism that best surrounds this model of service provision. Should it be equally holistic and representative of the key elements in society? This is certainly how many writers interpret the proper application of the stated mission of the CRPD.

It is not hard to find graphic examples of legal and therapeutic abuses at the extreme ends of the spectrum using any model. Nor is it realistic to expect that any chosen model will achieve optimum care and treatment for all—especially in environments that are constantly competing with the demands of primary health care and attempting to cope with the burden of increasing populations. The difficulty is finding the appropriate middle ground and a balance that ensures the greatest numbers of people are advantaged by whatever model is adopted.

---

12 Email questionnaire from AB, Fiji, to Helen Ménard, 22 March 2012.

13 E Harper (ed), *Working with Customary Justice Systems: Post-Conflict and Fragile States* (International Development Law Organisation, 2011)171, 173.

14 Ibid.

15 Ibid 172.

16 Partners in Community Development-Fiji, 'Youth Mental Stress & Violence in Fiji: Situation Analysis' (2005) 7.

The Western world abounds with horror stories from the dark days of institutionalisation involving the maladministration of electro convulsive therapy, experimental surgery, seclusion, cruelty and deprivation. Yet, many argue that modern psychiatry has merely exchanged physical restraint for chemical restraint—and, as progress, this is questionable.

As Allen contends 'mental illness sits at the intersection of several important factors in the lives of Pacific people: development, "Westernisation," migration and urbanisation.'[17] For the foreseeable future, the Pacific—which largely consists of developing countries—will be constrained by economic imperatives and fluctuating political agendas. Health expenditure struggles to provide the most basic of health care and discrete mental health expenditure rarely exists. In terms of access to justice and protection of human rights for mental health consumers, there *has* been progress. At the very least, rights based legislation driven largely by the WHO projects in the region has provided a legislative platform for change—without which there would have been little incentive at all to improve the plight of mental health consumers. The ability to build on this platform will always be subject to socio-political will and available resources regardless of the level of domestic development.

That is not to say that more developed countries are necessarily doing a better job when it comes to access to justice. The Mental Health Legal Centre (MHLC) in Victoria—one of only two specialist mental health legal centres in Australia and which had been in operation for twenty six years—lost its funding from Victoria Legal Aid in June 2013 and was threatened with closure.[18] This would have been a major setback for mental health consumers and their ability to access justice, as the MHLC has not only been a staunch advocate for consumers in Victoria but has influenced mental health policy at a national level. Fortunately, the service was able to be restructured and is still operating, supported largely by private funding. [19]

In the Pacific it will take time—possibly a long time—but this is no reason to disregard the evolutionary process. Information is now being provided to mental health consumers and some mental health community awareness programs do exist. Although legal representation for mental health consumers is currently very limited, with increasing populations there are more legal graduates being produced in the region who may eventually find their way into this area of legal practice or policy making within government. This will also provide a larger pool of professionals for the review tribunals, which will help to reduce the perception and actuality of bias. Hopefully, some graduates will become staunch advocates for the human rights of mental health consumers and will contribute to positive awareness education in their communities. There are sufficient evaluative studies of review bodies in other jurisdictions to allow the Pacific, in time, to develop best practice models that are legally effective and culturally appropriate.

Nonetheless, the role of culture in mental health cannot be ignored in the Pacific. It is a critical part of the Pacific psyche and equally critical to good mental health. While it is apparent that many Pacific Island countries are undergoing transition from traditional to Western style cultures, it is also apparent that this acculturation is a significant component in understanding mental illness among Pacific Islanders. As Aghanwa found 'the emerging

---

17 J Allen and J Laycock, 'Major Mental Illness in the Pacific: A Review' (1997) 4(2) *Pacific Health Dialog* 105 118, 116.

18 C Leslie, 'Jeopardising Access to Justice for People Experiencing Mental Ilness' (2013) <http://castancentre.com/2013/04/03jeopardising-access-to-justice-for (accessed 20 May 2013)>.

19 Mental Health Legal Centre Inc., 'Annual Report 2013 - 2014' (2014) <http://www.communitylaw.org.au/mhlc/cb_pages/annual_report_2013_2014.php (accessed 15 December 2015)>

picture of C-L [consultation liaison] psychiatry in this country [Fiji] is that expected of a society in transition, from a traditional system to Western culture.'[20] Cultural traditions cannot be erased overnight or even in a generation and neither they should be. Culture is an intrinsic part of who people are and their community connection—it is also an integral part of the rich tapestry of any society. Effective treatment of mental illness must involve a balance that is culturally sensitive and medically appropriate. In the same way that 'mental health services in [New Zealand] have traditionally focused on the medical model that prioritises disease and disorder'[21] there is now 'recognition of the need for culturally appropriate frameworks and/or services.'[22] In the same way Bartlett maintains that 'It is not merely that financial resources are not available. It is also that culturally and politically Africa is not western Europe or America'[23]— the Pacific is also not the West.

Equally, creating pathways to justice for mental health consumers in the Pacific must always be highly sensitive to and inclusive of this issue. It is not the objective to prescribe what might or might not be culturally appropriate ways of achieving access to justice in any given Pacific community. Each community must develop and own this process for itself. As a Pacific Islander living in New Zealand, Masoe explains:

> New Zealand might have been a land of milk and honey but it was also a land of isolation and strange expectations... I felt cut off from my *aiga* [extended family] and other families by the distance and walls and fences of suburbia. I think it might be hard for Palagi [foreigners] to appreciate what this environment is like for those who have not grown up with it, in the same way that a Samoan person can find it hard to understand the NZ environment...We do not see ourselves as individuals and so being cut off from our *aiga* is an unnatural and chronically stressful state.[24]

Similarly, Harper concedes that when it comes to advancing legal empowerment objectives in the context of customary justice there are no easy answers. In a series of case studies involving post conflict and fragile states, a wide range of interventions to improve access to justice were implemented, with varying degrees of success; and all were contingent upon a range of situation-specific factors—most being 'messy, unpredictable and political'.[25]

The same author also contends:

> The role customary systems should play in legal empowerment initiatives remains poorly understood. While it is clear that those advocating legal empowerment are open to the synergies that might emerge from partnering with customary justice systems, the literature proffers little practical guidance on how to engage at the customary level.[26]

---

[20] H Aghanwa, 'Consultation-Liaison Psychiatry in Fiji' (2002) 9(1) *Pacific Health Dialog* 22, 26.
[21] K Seataoai Samu and T Suaalii-Sauni, 'Exploring the 'Cultural' in Cultural Competencies in Pacific Mental Health' (2009) 15(1) *Pacific Health Dialog* 120, 124.
[22] Ibid.
[23] Bartlett, Jenkins and Kilma, above n 10.
[24] P Masoe and A Bush, 'A Samoan Perspective on Infant Mental Health' (2009) 15(1) *Pacific Health Dialog* 148.
[25] Harper, above n 13, 173.
[26] Ibid 171.

He further argues that

> whereas formal justice systems can operate to exclude certain groups, the positive attributes of customary justice systems often draw such populations towards them ... which is evident in their high levels of voluntary usage... but customary systems can also block access to justice and legal empowerment ... by compris[ing] rights to due process and an independent and fair hearing.[27]

There will never be a 'one size fits all' solution. In the same way that political systems, religious beliefs and cultural practices will never be universal, neither will legal systems. Where community based care is seen as the optimum treatment model in selected societies, the protective legal mechanism that accompanies such a model must be compatible and embrace similar underlying principles. All countries have struggled to find answers for what is proving to be a global health issue in crisis. There is no magic bullet. The best that can be achieved is a model that promotes humanity, care and treatment, and protects human rights in an empathetic, inclusive and caring society—for *all* its members.

---

[27] Ibid 172.

BIBLIOGRAPHY

ARTICLES, BOOKS, REPORTS

Aghanwa, H, 'Consultation-Liaison Psychiatry in Fiji' (2002) 9(1) *Pacific Health Dialog* 22.

Alefaoi, S, 'Reflections of a Practitioner: Purely a Journey of the Heart' (2009) 15(1) *Pacific Health Dialog* 169.

Allen, J and J Laycock, 'Major Mental Illness in the Pacific: A Review' (1997) 4(2) *Pacific Health Dialog* 105.

Asia and South Pacific Association for Basic and Adult Education Australia, Vanuatu Education Policy Advocacy Coalition, 'Education Experience Survey and Literacy Assessment: Shefa Province Vanuatu' (April 2011).

Atkinson, J M et al. 'Issues in the Development of Advance Directives in Mental Health Care' (2003) 12(5) *Journal of Mental Health* 463.

Australian Government Attorney General's Department, 'A Strategic Framework for Access to Justice in the Federal Civil Justice System, Report by the Access to Justice Taskforce' (Commonwealth of Australia, 2009).

Australian Human Rights Commission, 'Human Rights Mechanisms and the Asia-Pacific Region: Submission to the Human Rights Sub-Committee of the Joint Standing Committee on Foreign Affairs, Defence and Trade.' (December 2008).

Bartlett, P, 'The Mental Health Act: Taking Stock of the Current Position and Thinking about the Future' in *Current Legal Issues* (Oxford University Press, 2000) 537.

Bartlett, P, 'Thinking About the Rest of the World: Mental Health and Right Outside the First World' in B McSherry and P Weller (eds), *Rethinking Rights Based Mental Health Laws* (2010).

Bartlett, P, 'The United Nations Convention on the Rights of Persons with Disabilities and Mental Health Law' (2012) 75(5) *The Modern Law Review* 752.

Bartlett, P and V Hamzic, 'Reforming Mental Disability Law in Africa: Practical Tips and Suggestions' (Human Rights Law Centre, The University of Nottingham, 2010).

Bartlett, P, R Jenkins and D Kilma, 'Mental Health Law in the Community: Thinking about Africa' (2011) 5(21) *International Journal of Mental Health Systems* http://www.ijmhs.com/content/5/1/21 (accessed 5 June 2013).

Bell, S and W Brookbanks, *Mental Health Law in New Zealand* (Thomson Brookers, 2nd ed, 2005).

Benson, J, 'Mental Health in Vanuatu' (2009) *GPReview* 27.

Benson, J et al. 'A New Era in Mental Health Care in Vanuatu' (2011) 2011 *International Journal of Family Medicine*.

Bourke, T, 'Suicide in Samoa' (2001) 8(1) *Pacific Health Dialog* 213.

Bridgman, G, 'Mental Illness and Pacific People in New Zealand' (1997) 4(2) *Pacific Health Dialog* 95.

Brookbanks, W and S Simpson, *Psychiatry and the Law* (LexisNexisNZ Ltd, 2007).

Burton-Bradley, BG, 'Papua and New Guinea Transcultural Psychiatry: The First One Thousand Referrals' (1969) 3 *Australian and New Zealand Journal of Psychiatry* 383.

Cain, M et al. 'The NSW Mental Health Review Tribunal: An Analysis of Clients, Matter and Determinations' (2011).

Carney, T, 'Australian Mental Health Tribunals: 'Space' for Rights, Protection, Treatment and Governance?' (2012) 35(1) *International Journal of Law and Psychiatry* 1.

Carney, T, 'Involuntary Mental Health Treatment Laws: The 'Rights' and Wrongs of Competing Models?' in B McSherry and P Weller (eds), *Rethinking Rights Based Mental Health Laws* (Hart Publishing, 2010).

Carney, T et al. 'Advocacy and Participation in Mental Health Cases: Realisable Rights or Pipe- dreams?' (2008) 26(2) *Law in Context Special Issue: International Trends in Mental Health Laws*.

Carney, T, D Tait and F Beaupert, 'Pushing the Boundaries: Realising Rights Through Mental Health Tribunal Processes?' (2008) 30 *Sydney Law Review* 329.

Carney, T et al. *Mental Health Tribunals: Balancing fairness, freedom, protection and right to treatment?* (Themis Press, 2011).

Chang, O, 'Mental Health Care in Fiji' (2011) 3(2) *Asia Pacific Psychiatry* 73.

Chang, O, 'Mental Health Services in Fiji and the Way Forward: Pyschiatric Health in Primary Care-2' (2007) 15(2) *General Practitioner*.

Clair, F and S Fisher, 'Powering - and Empowering - Through Change: The Queensland Tribunal's Experience of Transition from Old Systems to New' (2003) 10(1) *Psychiatry, Psychology and Law* 184.

College of Medicine and Nursing and Health Sciences, 'Situational Analysis of Specialised Clinical Services in the Republic of Fiji 2010-12, Strengthening Specialised Clinical Services Program' (2012).

Commonwealth of Australia, 'Pacific 2020, Challenges and Opportunities for Growth' (2006).

Corrin Care, J, T Newton and D Paterson, *Introduction to South Pacific Law* (Cavendish Publishing Ltd, 1999).

Council on Tribunals, 'Special Report: Mental Health Review Tribunals' (2000) http://www.council-on –tribunals.gov.uk/publications/184.htm (accessed 30 November 2010).

Court, D, 'Mental Disorder and Human Rights: The Importance of a Presumption of Competence' (1996) 8(1) *Auckland U L Review*.

Cruz, Dr M, 'A Review of the Existing Functions and Responsibilities of the Fiji Ministry of Health in relation to the Care, Treatment and Rehabilitation of Mentally Ill People in Fiji (Internal Report for the World Health Organisation to Revise and Make Recommendations on the Mental Health Services in Fiji.)' (2004).

Culbertson, P, M N Agee and C Makasiale (eds), *Penina Uliuli: Contemporary Challenges in Mental Health for Pacific Peoples* (University of Hawaii Press, 2007).

Dawson, J, 'Community Treatment Orders and Human Rights' (2008) 26(2) *Law in Contex, Special Issue: International Trends in Mental Health Laws.*

Dawson, J, 'Compulsory Outpatient Treatment and the Calculus of Human Rights' in B McSherry and P Weller (eds), *Rethinking Rights-Based Mental Health Laws* (Hart Publishing, 2010).

Dawson, J, 'Psychopathology and Civil Commitment Criteria' (1996) 4 *Medical Law Review* 62.

Dawson, J and G Szmukler, 'Why Distinguish "Mental" and "Physical" Illness in Involuntary Treatment?' in M Freeman and O Goodenough (eds), *Law, Mind and Brain* (Farnham, 2009).

Department of Mental Health and Substance Abuse in Collaboration with the Victorian Health Promotion Foundation and the University of Melbourne, 'Promoting Mental Health: Concepts, Emerging Evidence, Practice. Summary Report – A Report of the World Health Organisation' (WHO, 2004).

Desjarlais, R et al. *World Mental Health: Problems and Priorties in Low Income Countries* (Oxford University Press Inc, 1995).

Deva, MP, 'Mission Report Executive Summary' (WHO Regional Office for the Western Pacific, 2003).

Donnelly, M, 'From Autonomy to Dignity: Treatment for Mental Disorders and the Focus for Patient Rights' (2008) 26(2) *Law in Contex, Special Issue: International Trends in Mental Health Laws.*

Donnelly, M 'Review of Treatment Decisions: Legalism, Process and the Protection of Rights' in B McSherry and P Weller (eds), *Rethinking Rights Based Mental Health Laws* (Hart Publishing, 2010).

Dupre-Wheeler, D, 'Bali Hai Cries for Help: World Health Organisation Regional Office of the Western Pacific Health Survey Report–Vanuatu Suicide and Related Issues Baseline Survey' (2002) http://www.inspq.qc.ca/pdf/publications/129_Trauma2002/%28J%29 Prevention Suicide.pdf (accessed 13 September 2012).

Dupre-Wheeler, D, 'Vanuatu Suicide Baseline Survey' (WHO Regional Office for the Western Pacific, 2001).

Ellard, J, 'The Madness of Mental Health Acts' (1990) 24 *Australian and New Zealand Journal of Psychiatry* 167.

Fennell, P, 'Institutionalising the Community: The Codification of Clinical Authority and the Limits of Rights Based Approaches' in B McSherry and P Weller (eds), *Rethinking Rights Based Mental Health Laws* (Hart Publishing, 2010).

Fiji Human Rights Commission, (December 2009) 8(4) *Rights Quarterly.*

Fiji Human Rights Commission, 'Correctional Centre Inspection Report 2011' (2011) http://www.fhrc.org.fj/index.php?option=com_docman&task=cat_view&gid=40&Itemid=11 (accessed 20 december 2015).

Fiji Human Rights Commission, 'Police Holding Cells Inspection Report 2012' (2012) http://www.fhrc.org.fj/index.php?option=com_docman&task=cat_view&gid=40&Itemid=11 (accessed 20 December 2015.

Fiji Law Reform Commission, 'Issue Paper No. 1 – Purpose, Principles and Definitions – Review of the Fiji Mental Treatment Act' (2006).

Fiji Law Reform Commission, 'Issue Paper No. 3 – Definition – Review Mechanisms' (2006).

Fiji Law Reform Commission, 'Issue Paper No. 5 – Advanced Treatment Statement - Review of the Fiji Mental Treatment Act' (2006).

Fiji Law Reform Commission, 'Review of the Fiji Mental Treatment Act, Issue Paper No. 5 – Advanced Treatment Statement' (2006).

Foliaki, S, 'Migration and Mental Health: The Tongan Experience' (1997) 26 *Int J Ment Health Nurs* 36.

Forbes, J R S, *Justice in Tribunals* (The Federation Press, 3rd ed, 2010).

Fraenkel, J, 'Melanesia in Review: Issues and Events, 2010, Fiji' (2011) 23(2) *The Contemporary Pacific* 456.

Freckelton, I, 'Mental Health Review Tribunal Decision –making: A Therapeutic Jurisprudence Lens' (2003) 10 *Psychiatry, Psychology and Law.*

Freeman, M, *WHO Resource Book on Mental Health, Human Rights and Legislation* (World Health Organisation, 2005).

Funk, M and N Drew, *WHO QualityRights Tool Kit: Assessing and Improving Quality and Human Rights in Mental Health and Social Care Facilities* (World Health Organisation, 2012).

George, K, 'Vanuatu: Happiest Nation on Earth, Mental Health and the Church' (2010) 18(1) *Australian Psychiatry.*

Gibbs, A et al. 'How Patients in New Zealand View Community Treatment Orders' (2005) 14(4) *Journal of Mental Health* 357.

Government of Samoa Ministry of Health, 'Annual Report Financial Year 2009-2010' (2010).

Government of Samoa Ministry of Health, 'Annual Report Financial Year 2010-2011,' (2011) http://www.health.gov.ws/Portals/189/Master%20Copy%20-%20Annual%20Report%20FY10-11.pdf (accessed 30 August 2015).

Government of Samoa Ministry of Health, 'Corporate Plan 2013-2016,' (2013) http://www.health.gov.ws/Portals/189/Approved%20MOH%20Corporate%20Plan%202013-2016.pdf (accessed 6 September 2015).

Government of Samoa Ministry of Health, 'Health Sector Strategic Plan 2008-2018' (2008).

Government of Samoa Ministry of Health, 'National Health Promotion Policy 2010-2015' (2008).

Government of Samoa Ministry of Health, 'Samoa Demographic and Health Survey 2009' (June 2010).Government of Samoa Ministry of Health, 'Samoa Mental Health Policy' (2006).

Government of Samoa Ministry of Health, 'Samoa National Health Accounts FY 2008/2009' (2012) http://www.health.gov.ws/Portals/189/News/NHA2008-09/Final%20Draft%20NHA2008-09%20-_Copy.pdf (accessed 6 September 2015).

Government of Samoa Ministry of Women Community and Social Development, 'Samoa National Policy on Disability' (January 2009).

Government of Samoa Office of the Attorney General, 'Samoa Law & Justice Sector Plan 2008-2012: Justice for a Safe and Stable Samoa' (2008).

Government of Samoa Office of the Attorney General, 'Samoa Law & Justice Sector Plan 2012-2016: Justice for a Safe and Stable Samoa' (2012) http://www.samoaljs.ws/english/images/stories/uploads/SLJS_Plan_2012-2016_English.pdf (accessed 5 September 2015).

Government of Samoa Office of the Ombudsman, 'State of Human Rights Report 2015 ' (2015) http://www.paclii.org/ws/cases/WSNHRIRp/2015/1.html#fn185 (Accessed 5 September 2015).

Government of the Republic of Vanuatu, 'Annual Report 2013 Ministry of Justice & Community Services' (2013) http://www.mjcs.gov.vu/images/research_database/Annual_Report_2013__05JUN14.pdf (Accessed 3 September 2015).

Government of the Republic of Vanuatu, 'Health Sector Strategy (2010-2016)' (2010) http://www.wpro.who.int/health_services/vanuatu_nationalhealthplan.pdf (Accessed 3 September 2015).

Government of the Republic of Vanuatu, *Ministry of Health Annual Report 2009* (2011) https://gov.vu/health.html (Accessed 3 September 2015).

Government of the Republic of Vanuatu, 'The National Community Based Rehabilitation (CBR) Action Plan 2014 - 2024, Ministry of Justice & Community Services' (2014).

Government of the Republic of Vanuatu, 'Strategy for the Justice and Community Services Sector 2014 - 2017, Ministry for Justice and Community Services' (2014).

Government of the Republic of Vanuatu, 'Universal Periodic Review (UPR) Recommendations Vanuatu, *A National Implementation Plan (2014-2018),* Ministry of Justice & Community Services' (2014) http://www.mjcs.gov.vu/images/news/disability_desk/UPR/UPR_National_Action_Plan_20142018_pdf (Accessed 3 September 2015).

Government of the Republic of Vanuatu Ministry of Health, 'Vanuatu Mental Health Policy and Plan (2009-2014)' (2009).

Government of the Republic of Vanuatu Ministry of Justice & Social Welfare and The National Disability Committee, 'National Disability Policy and Plan of Action 2008-2018' (2009).

Government of Tonga, *Laws of Tonga Revised 1967* (1967).

Government of Tonga, 'Ministry of Health Corporate Plan 2015/16-2019/20: Mental Health (Draft), ' (2015).

Government of Tonga, 'Report of the Minister for Health for the Financial Year 2011/2012' (2011).

Government of Tonga, 'Report of the Minister of Health for the Year 2009' (2009) www.health.gov.to/sites/default/files/AR2009.pdf.

Government of Tonga, 'Report of the Minister of Health for the Year 2010' (2010) www.health.gov.to/sites/default/files/AR2010.pdf.

Greig, DN, *Neither Bad nor Mad: The Competing Discourses of Psychiatry, Law and Politics* (Jessica Kingsley Publishers Ltd, 2002).

Grigor, R, 'The Physician-Specialist in Western Samoa' (1975) *New Zealand Medical Journal* 161.

Guttenbeil-Likiliki, O and Foundation of the Peoples of the South Pacific International, 'Youth and Mental Health in Tonga: A Situational Analysis' (2009).

Harper, E (ed), *Working with Customary Justice Systems: Post-Conflict and Fragile States* (International Development Law Organisation, 2011).

Harpur, P and R Bales, 'The Positive Impact of the Convention on the Rights of Persons with Disabilities: A Case Study on the South Pacific and Lessons from the U.S. Experience' (2010) 37(4) *Northern Kentucky Law Review* 362.

Haynes, RH, 'Suicide and Social Response in Fiji: A Historical Survey' (1987) 151 *British Journal of Psychiatry* 21.

Haynes, RH, 'Suicide in Fiji: A Preliminary Study' (1984) 145 *British Journal of Psychiatry* 433.

Hezel, FX, 'Cultural Patterns in Trukese Suicide' (1984) 23 *Ethnology* 193.

Hezel, F, 'What Can We Do to Prevent Suicide in the Pacific?' (1994) 1(1) *Pacific Health Dialog* 59.

Hope Eseta, F and Foundation of the Peoples of the South Pacific International, 'Youth and Mental Health in Samoa: A Situational Analysis' (2009).

Horne, WK, *Laws of Tonga,* Preface to the 1929 Edition (1929).

Hughes, D and Foundation of the Peoples of the South Pacific International, 'Masculinity, Mental Health and Violence in Vanuatu: Situation Analysis' (2004).

Hughes, F, 'Mental Health in the Pacific: The Role of the Pacific Island Mental Health Network' (2009) 15(1) *Pacific Health Dialog* 177.

Human Rights and Equal Opportunity Commission, 'Report of the National Inquiry into the Human Rights of People with Mental Illness (Burdekin Inquiry)' (1993).

Human Rights Commission Te Kahui Tika Tangata, 'Human Rights in New Zealand 2010, Nga Tika Tangata o Aotearoa 2010' (2010) www.hrc.co.nz.

Human Rights Commission Te Kahui Tika Tangata, 'Human Rights in New Zealand Today, Nga Tika Tangata o Aotearoa i Tenei Ra' (2004) www.hrc.co.nz/report/chapters/chapter 10./justice01/.html.

Hunt, P, 'Reflections on International Human Rights Law and Cultural Rights' in M Wilson and P Hunt (eds), *Culture, Rights, and Cultural Rights: Perspectives from the South Pacific* (Huia Publishers, 2000).

Ibrahim, M et al. 'Incidence v Prevalence' (June 1999) (2) *ERIC Notebook* 1.

Imrana Jalal, P, 'Pacific Culture and Human Rights: Why Pacific Island Countries Should Ratify International Human Rights Treaties' (April 2006) www.rrrt.org/images/pacific cultureandhumanrights.pdf (accessed 5 April 2013).

Imrana Jalal, P, 'Using Rights-Based Programming Principles to Claim Rights: The Regional Rights Resource Team (RRRT) Project in the Pacific Islands' (May 2005) www.rrrt.org/images/usingrightsbasedprogrammingprinciples.pdf (accesssed 5 April 2013).

Imrana Jalal, P and J Madraiwiwi (eds), *Pacific Human Rights Law Digest* (RRRT, 2005).

Imrana Jalal, P and J Madraiwiwi (eds), *Pacific Human Rights Law Digest* (RRRT, 2008).

Jowitt, A, 'Barriers to Accessing Justice: The Vanuatu Experience' in Asia Pacific Judicial Reform Forum (ed), *Searching for Success in Judicial Reform: Voices from the Asia Pacific Experience* (Oxford University Press, 2009) 137.

Kaloris, P '2012 Vanuatu Mental Health Annual Report' (Ministry of Health (Vanuatu), 2012).

Karras, M, 'Access to Justice and Legal Needs Vol. 4: On the Edge of Justice: The Legal Needs of People with a Mental Illness' (Law and Justice Foundation of New South Wales, 2006).

Kerridge, I, M Lowe and C Stewart, *Ethics and Law for the Health Professionals* (3rd ed, 2009).

Kingdom of Tonga Ministry of Health, 'Corporate Plan 2008/9-2011/12 ' (2008).

Kohn, R et al. 'The Treatment Gap in Mental Health Care' (2004) 82 *Bulletin of the World Health Organisation* 858.

Kokaua, J et al. 'Twelve-Month Prevalence, Severity and Treatment Contact of Mental Disorders in New Zealand Born and Migrant Pacific Participants in Te Rau Hinengaro: The New Zealand Mental Health Survey' (2009) 12(1) *Pacific Health Dialog* 9.

Law Commission New Zealand, 'Converging Currents: Custom and Human Rights in the Pacific, Study Paper 17' (2006).

Law Reform Commission of Victoria, 'Report No. 31: The Concept of Mental Illness in the Mental Health Act 1986' (1990).

Leslie, C, 'Jeopardising Access to Justice for People Experiencing Mental Ilness' (2013) *Castan Centre for Human Rights Law* http://castancentre.com/2013/04/03jeopardising-access-to-justice-for (accessed 20 May 2013).

Lui, D, 'Spiritual Injury: A Samoan Perspective on Spirituality's Impact in Mental Health' in P Culbertson, M N Agee and C Makasiale (eds), *Penina Uliuli: Contemporary Challenges in Mental Health for Pacific Peoples* (University of Hawaii Press, 2007) 66.

MacFarlane, P and H Ménard, *Medical Law in the South Pacific* (Kluwer Law International, 2014).

Macpherson, C and L Macpherson, *Samoan Medical Belief and Practice* (University of Hawai'i Press, 1990).

Madraiwiwi Ratu, J, 'Navigating Passage Between Human Rights and Culture in Fijian Waters' in M Powles (ed), *Pacific Futures* (Pandanus Books,The Australian National University, 2006).

Maloney, J and J R Struble, 'A New Day in Tonga: The Judiciary, The Reformers & the Future' (2007) 11(2) *Journal of South Pacifc Law* 151.

Masoe, P and A Bush, 'A Samoan Perspective on Infant Mental Health' (2009) 15(1) *Pacific Health Dialog*.

Mason, J and G Laurie, *Mason and McCall Smith's Law and Medical Ethics* (Oxford University Press, 7th ed, 2006).

Mental Health Committee Vanuatu, 'Minutes of Meeting 8 May 2012: Update on Mental Health Policy 2009-2015' (2012).

Mental Health Legal Centre Inc., 'Annual Report 2013 - 2014' (2014) http://www.communitylaw.org.au/mhlc/cb_pages/annual_report_2013_2014.php (accessed 15 December 2015).

Merkel R QC, 'Dangerous Persons': To Be Gaoled For What They Are, Or What They May Do, Not For What They Have Done' (1990) *Serious Violent Offenders: Sentencing, Psychiatry and Law Reform*.

MHDAO NSW Ministry of Health, 'Communio Final Report: Evaluation of Efficacy and Cost of the Mental Health Inquiry System' (2012).

Mila-Schaaf, K and M Hudson, 'The Interface Between Cultural Understandings: Negotiating New Spaces for Pacific Mental Health' (2009) 15(1) *Pacific Health Dialog* 113.

Ministry of Health and Medical Services Fiji, 'Mental Health Services 2015 Business Plan' (2015).

Ministry of Health and Medical Services Fiji, 'National Mental Health and Suicide Prevention Policy' (2015) https://www.mindbank.info/item/5909 (accessed 5 January 2016).

Ministry of Health and Medical Services Fiji, 'National Mental Health and Suicide Prevention Strategic Plan 2016-2020' (2016).

Ministry of Health and Medical Services Fiji, 'National Strategic Plan 2016-2020 Executive Version ' (2016) http://www.health.gov.fj/PDFs/Corporate%20Plan/Strategic%20Plan%202016-2020%20Executive%20Version.pdf (accessed 4 January 2016).

Ministry of Health Fiji, 'Admission Guideline St Giles Hospital,' (2010) http://www.health.gov.fj/wp-content/uploads/2014/05/St-Giles-Admission-protocol_2010.pdf (accessed 5 January 2016).

Ministry of Health Fiji, 'Ministry of Health Annual Report 2013' (2014) http://www.health.gov.fj/PDFs/Annual%20Report/Annual%20Report%202013.pdf (accessed 7 September 2015).

Ministry of Health Fiji, 'Ministry of Health, Annual Report 2009' (2010) <ww.health.gov.fj/PDFs/Annual%20Report/Annual%20Report%202009.pdf (accessed 10 September 2015)>.

Ministry of Health Fiji, 'Ministry of Health, Annual Report 2011' (2012) http://www.health.gov.fj/PDFs/Annual%20Report/Annual%20Report%202011.pdf (accessed 10 September 2015).

Ministry of Health Fiji, 'Ministry of Health, Annual Report 2012' (2013) http://www.health.gov.fj/PDFs/Annual%20Report/Annual%20Report%202012.pdf (accessed 9 September 2015).

Ministry of Health Fiji, 'National Mental Health Strategic Plan for 2012-2014 (Draft)' (2012).

Ministry of Health Fiji - Mental Health Services, 'Mental Health Policy' (2011).

Ministry of Health Fiji Islands, 'Annual Corporate Plan 2011' (2011).

Ministry of Health Fiji Islands, 'Annual Corporate Plan 2014' (2014).

Ministry of Health Fiji Islands, 'Annual Corporate Plan 2015' (2015).

Ministry of Health Fiji Islands, 'Fiji Health Accounts 2011-2012' (2013) http://www.health.gov.fj/PDFs/Health%20Finance/Fiji%20NHA%20Report%202011-2012.pdf (accessed 8 September 2015).

Ministry of Health Fiji Islands, 'Ministry of Health, Annual Report 2010' (2011).

Ministry of Health Fiji Islands, 'Shaping Fiji's Health: Strategic Plan 2011-2015' (2011).

Minkowitz, T, 'Abolishing Mental Health Laws to Comply with the Convention on the Rights of Persons with Disabilites' in B McSherry and P Weller (eds), *Rethinking Rights Based Mental Health Laws* (Hart Publishing, 2010).

Mohan, D, 'Mental Health Review Tribunal Decisions in Restricted Hospital Order Cases at One Medium Secure Unit, 1992-1996' (1998) 8 *Crim Behav Ment Health* 57.

Murphy, HBM, *Mental Health Trends in the Pacific Islands: A Report on a Tour of Pacific Territories* (South Pacific Commission, 1978).

Murphy, HBM, 'Rapid Social Change and the Vulnerable of Elites' (1978) 21(3) *Papua New Guinea Medical Journal* 276.

Murphy, H and B Taumoepeau, 'Traditionalism and Mental Health in the South Pacific: A Re-examination of an Old Hypothesis' (1980) 10 *Psychol Med* 471.

Narokobi, B, *Lo Bilong Yumi Yet – Law and Custom in Melanesia* (Institute of Pacific Studies of the University of the South Pacific and The Melanesian Institute for Pastoral and Socio Economic Service, 1989).

Oakley-Browne, M A, J E Wells and K E Scott (eds), *Te Rau Hinengaro: The New Zealand Mental Health Survey* (Ministry of Health, 2006).

Pacific Disability Forum (PDF) and Australia Pacific Islands Disability Support (APIDS), 'Capacity Development for Effective and Efficient Disabled Persons Organisations in

Pacific Island Countries: Report on Fiji Component of Research (pilot)' (July 2011) http://www.pacificdisability.org/publications.aspx (accessed 2 December 2012).

Pacific Disability Forum (PDF) and Australia Pacific Islands Disability Support (APIDS), 'Capacity Development for Effective and Efficient Disabled Persons Organisations in Pacific Island Countries: Report on Samoa Component of Research' (August 2011) http://www.pacificdisability.org/publications.aspx (accessed 2 December 2012).

Pacific Disability Forum (PDF) and Australia Pacific Islands Disability Support (APIDS), 'Capacity Development for Effective and Efficient Disabled Persons Organisations in Pacific Island Countries: Report on Tonga Component of Research' (March 2012) http://www.pacificdisability.org/publications.aspx (accessed 2 December 2012).

Pacific Disability Forum (PDF) and Australia Pacific Islands Disability Support (APIDS), 'Capacity Development for Effective and Efficient Disabled Persons Organisations in Pacific Island Countries: Report on Vanuatu Component of Research' (March 2012) http://www.pacificdisability.org/publications.aspx (accessed 2 December 2012).

Pacific Islands Forum Secretariat, 'Conventions and International Agreements on Disability' (2009) http://www.forumsec.org/pages.cfm/strategic-partnerships-coordination/disability/conventions-international-agreements-on-disability.html (accessed 2 December 2012).

Pacific Islands Forum Secretariat, 'Forum Disability Ministers Meeting Cook Islands, Session Nine: Pacific Regional Strategy on Disability 2010-2015,' (October 2009) < http://www.forumsec.org/pages.cfm/strategic-partnerships-coordination/disability/forum-disability-ministers-meeting/fdmm-2009.html (accessed 2 December 2012)>.

Parliament of Victoria, Social Development Committee, 'Fourth and Final Report: Inquiry into Mental Disturbance and Community Safety' (1992).

Parliament of Victoria, Social Development Committee, 'Interim Report: Inquiry into Mental Disturbance and Community Safety – Strategies to Deal with Persons with Severe Personality Disorder who Pose a Threat to Public Safety' (1990).

Partners in Community Development-Fiji, 'Youth Mental Stress & Violence in Fiji: Situation Analysis' (2005).

Pathare S and J Sagade, 'Mental Health: A Legislative Framework to Empower, Protect and Care. A Review of Mental Health Legislation in Commonwealth Member States.' (2013).

Peay, J, *Tribunals on Trial: A Study of Decision-Making under the Mental Health Act 1983* (Clarendon Press, 1989).

Poltorak, M, 'Nemesis, Speaking and Tauhi Vaha'a: Interdisciplinarity and the Truth of "Mental Illness" in Vava'u, Tonga' (2007) 19(1) *The Contemporary Pacific* 1.

Poltorak, M, 'Traditional Healers, Speaking and Motivation in Vava'u, Tonga. Explaining Syncretism and Addressing Health Policy' (2010) *Oceania*.

Polu, L, 'Cultural Rights and the Individual in the Samoan Context' in M Wilson and P Hunt (eds), *Culture, Rights, and Cultural Rights: Perspectives from the South Pacific* (Huia Publishers, 2000).

Powles, G, 'Law Reform in Pacific Island States' in B Opeskin and D Weisbrot (eds), *The Promise of Law Reform* (The Federation Press, 2005) 404.

Powles, G, 'The Legal Systems of the Region' in G Powles and M Pulea (eds), *Pacific Courts and Legal Systems* (University of the South Pacific and Faculty of Law Monash University, 1988).

Powles, G, 'Political and Constitutional Reform Opens the Door: The Kingdom of Tonga's Path to Democracy' (2012) 18 *Comparative Law Journal of the Pacific* 193.

Price, J and I Karim, 'An Evaluation of Psychiatric After-care in a Developing Country (Fiji)' (1976) 129 *British Journal of Psychiatry* 155.

Price, J and I Karim, 'Matiruku, a Fijian Madness: An Initial Assessment' (1978) 133 *British Journal of Psychiatry* 228.

Psychiatric Survivors Association, 'Strategic Plan June 2011–June 2014' (2011).

Puloka, M, 'Avanga: Tongan Concepts of Mental Illness' (1999) 6(2) *Pacific Health Dialog* 268.

Puloka, M, 'A Commonsense Perspective on Tongan Folk Healing' (1997) 2 *Int J Ment Health Nurs* 69.

Rantala, R E et al. 'Right to Health through Education: Mental Health and Human Rights' (2010) *Human Rights Education in Asia–Pacific* 188.

Rees, N, 'The Fusion Proposal: A Next Step?' in B McSherry and P Weller (eds), *Rethinking Rights Based Mental Health Laws* (Hart Publishing, 2010).

Rees, N, 'International Human Rights Obligations and Mental Health Review Tribunals' (2003) 10(1) *Psychiatry, Psychology and Law.*

Rees, N, 'Learning from the Past, Looking to the Future: Is Victorian Mental Health Law Ripe for Reform?' (2009) 16(1) *Psychiatry, Psychology and Law* 69.

Roberts, G, 'Masculinity, Mental Health and Violence in Papua New Guinea, Vanuatu, Fiji and Kiribati' (2007) 14(2) *Health Promotion in the Pacific* 35.

Roberts, G et al. 'Attempted Suicide in Western Viti Levu, Fiji' (2007) 14(2) *Health Promotion in the Pacific* 29.

Roberts, G, M Cruz and E S Puamau, 'A Proposed Future for the Care, Treatment and Rehabilitation of Mentally Ill People in Fiji' (2007) 14(2) *Health Promotion in the Pacific* 107.

Roberts G et al. 'The Fiji Islands Health System Review' (2011) 1(1) *Health Systems in Transition.*

Ross, B, 'Mental Health in Papua New Guinea' (1965) 1 *Medical Journal of Australia* 478.

Rubenstein, DH, 'An Investigative Study of Adolescent Suicides in Micronesia' (1982) 15 *Pacific Health* 2.

Schultz, R, 'Community Mental Health: Avoided by Some, Neglected by Others' (2001) 8(1) *Pacific Health Dialog* 200.

Seataoai Samu, K and T Suaalii-Sauni, 'Exploring the 'Cultural' in Cultural Competencies in Pacific Mental Health' (2009) 15(1) *Pacific Health Dialog* 120.

Seru-Puamau, E, 'Utilisation Review of First Admissions in 2002: St Giles Psychiatric Hospital, Suva, Fiji' (2006) 13(2) *Pacific Public Health* 79.

Shah, A, 'Is the Mental Health Review Tribunal Inherently Unfair to Patients?' (2010) 17(1) *Psychiatry, Psychology and Law.*

Shea, P *Defining Madness* (Hawkins Press, 1999).

Singh, S et al. 'WHO Profile on Mental Health in Development (WHO proMIND): Fiji.' (World Health Organisation, 2013) http://www.who.int/mental_health/policy/country/countrysummary/en/index.html (accessed 2 January 2016).

Sione, V et al. 'Walking Apart Towards the Same Goal? The View and Practices of Tongan Traditional Healers and Western Trained Tongan Mental Health Staff' (2009) 15(1) *Pacific Health Dialog* 89.

Smith, RKM, *Textbook on International Human Rights* (Oxford University Press, 2nd ed, 2005).

South Pacific Lawyers Association, 'Needs Evaluation Survey for South Pacific Lawyer Associations - Final Report' (2011).

Suaalii-Sauni, T et al. ' Exploration of Pacific Perspectives of Pacific Models of Mental Health Service Delivery in New Zealand' (2009) 15(1) *Pacific Health Dialog* 18.

Tamasese, K et al. 'Ole Taiao Afua, the New Morning: A Qualitative Investigation into Samoan Perspectives on Mental Health and Culturally Appropriate Services' (2005) 39 *Australian and New Zealand Journal of Psychiatry* 300.

Tarivonda, L et al. 'WHO Profile on Mental Health in Development (WHO ProMIND); Vanuatu' (World Health Organisation, 2012).

Taufe'ulugaki, A, 'Cultural Rights in the Tongan Context: Some Issues' in M Wilson and P Hunt (eds), *Culture, Rights, and Cultural Rights: Perspectives from the South Pacific* (Huia Publishers, 2000).

Taylor, D, 'Tonga National Disability Identification Survey' (Tonga Disability Action Committee, 2006).

Then, Shih-Ning, 'Evolution and Innovation in Guardianship Laws: Assisted Decision Making' (2013) 35 *Sydney Law Review* 133.

Tiatia, J, 'Young Pacifican Suicide Attempts: A Review of Emergency Department Medical Records, Auckland, New Zealand' (2001) 8(1) *Pacific Health Dialog* 124.

Tiatia, T, 'New Zealand-born Samoan Young People, Suicidal Behaviours and the Positive Impact of Spirituality' in P Culbertson, M N Agee and C Makasiale (eds), *Penina Uliuli: Contemporary Challenges in Mental Health for Pacific Peoples* (University of Hawai'i Press, 2007) 94.

Toafa, V, R Moata'ane and B Guthrie, 'Traditional Tongan Medicine and the Role of Traditional Tongan Healers in New Zealand' (2001) 8 *Pacific Health Dialog* 78.

Tobin, J, 'Melbourne Legal Studies Research Paper No.562, Introduction: The Right to Health in International Law' (2011) *Melbourne Law School* http://ssrn.com/abstract=1948850.

Topp, V, M Thomas and M Ingvarson, 'Lacking Insight: Involuntary Patient Experience of the Victorian Mental Health Review Board' (2008).

Turner-Tupou, F, 'Using Mea-alofa in a Holistic Model for Pasifica Clients: A Case Study' in P Culbertson, M N Agee and C Makasiale (eds), *Penina Uliuli: Contemporary Challenges in Mental Health for Pacific Peoples* (University of Hawai'i Press, 2007) 149.

UNICEF, 'State of Healthy Behaviour and Lifestyle of Pacific Youth – Kingdom of Tonga Report' (2001).

United States Department of State Bureau of Democracy Human Rights and Labor, 'Country Reports on Human Rights Practices for 2013 - Fiji' (2013).

Vaka, S et al. 'Walking Apart Towards the Same Goal? The View and Practices of Tongan Traditional Healers and Western Trained Tongan Mental Health Staff' (2009) 15(1) *Pacific Health Dialog*.

Van Trease, H, 'Melanesia in Review: Issues and Events, 2010, Vanuatu' (2011) 23(2) *The Contemporary Pacific* 511.

Van Trease, H, 'Years of Turmoil: 1987-1991' in H Van Trease (ed), *Melanesian Politics: Stael Blong Vanuatu* (Macmillan Brown Centre for Pacific Studies, University of Canterbury and Institute of Pacific Studies, University of the South Pacific, 1995) 73.

Vanuatu Law Commission, 'Ombudsman Act - Issues Paper No 1 2015 ' (2015).

Vanuatu Law Commission, 'Public Health Act Legislative Review 2013' (February 2013) http://www.lawcommission.gov.vu/images/stories/public%20health%20act-%20report.pdf (accessed 5 April 2013).

Vanuatu National Statistics Office Ministry of Finance and Economic Management, *National Census of Population and Housing Summary Release* http://www.vnso.gov.vu/images/stories/2009_Census_Summary_release_final.pdf (accessed 1 April 2013).

Victorian Law Reform Commission, 'Guardianship: Final Report 24' (2012).

Vivili, P, S Finau and E Finau, 'Suicide in Tonga, 1982-1997' (1999) 6(2) *Pacific Health Dialog* 211.

Watchirs, H and G Heesom, 'Report on Right Analysis Instrument for use in Evaluating Mental Health Legislation' (1996).

Weller, P, 'Lost in Translation: Human Rights and Mental Health Law' in B McSherry and P Weller (eds), *Rethinking Rights Based Mental Health Laws* (Hart Publishing, 2010).

Weller, P, 'Supported Decision Making and the Achievement of Non Discrimination: The Promise and Paradox of the Disabilities Convention' (2008) 26(2) *Law in Context Special Issue: International Trends in Mental Health Laws.*

WHO, Geneva, 'A Mentally Healthy Nation with Accessible Care for All, The Country Summary Series. Vanuatu, Mental Health Improvements for National Development' (2009).

WHO, 'Report on the Workshop on Human Resource Development for Mental Health in Pacific Island Countries' (WHO, Regional Office for the Western Pacific, 2003).

Williams, V, 'The Challenge for Australian Jurisdictions to Guarantee Free Qualified Representation Before Mental Health Tribunals and Boards of Review: Learning from the Tasmanian Experience' (2009) 16(1) *Psychiatry, Psychology and Law* 108.

Wilson, G, ''Europeanisation' and Admission to a Mental Hospital in the Fiji Islands' (1965) 64 *NZMed J* 364.

Wilson, M and P Hunt (eds), *Culture, Rights, and Cultural Rights: Perspectives from the South Pacific* (Huia Publishers, 2000).

Wilton, NM, 'Mental Health in the Republic of Vanuatu' (WHO Regional Office for the Western Pacific, 1997).

Woolf, L, 'Access to Justice: Final Report (UK)' (1996) www.justice.gov.uk (accessed 5 March 2012).

World Health Organisation, 'Expert Opinion on Barriers and Facilitating Factors for the Implementation of Existing Mental Health Knowledge in Mental Health Services' (2007).

World Health Organisation, 'Human Resources for Health, Country Profiles: Tonga,' (2014) http://www.wpro.who.int/hrh/documents/publications/wpr_hrh_country_profiles_tonga_upload.pdf (accessed 2 January 2016).

World Health Organisation, 'Mental Health Action Plan 2013 - 2020' (2013).

World Health Organisation, 'Mental Health Care Law: Ten Basic Principles' (1996).

World Health Organisation, 'Regional Strategy for Mental Health' (WHO, Western Pacific Region, 2002).

World Health Organisation, 'Report on the Mental Health Policy Project: First International Training Forum on Mental Health Policy and Services' (WHO, 2002).

World Health Organisation, 'Situational Analysis of Mental Health Needs and Resources in Pacific Island Countries' (WHO, Centre for Mental Health Research, Policy & Service Development, 2005).
World Health Organisation, 'WHO Country Cooperation Strategy for Samoa' (2003).
World Health Organisation, 'WHO Mental Health Atlas 2011' (2011).
World Health Organisation, 'World Health Report' (WHO, 2001).
World Health Organisation Western Pacific Region, 'Fiji Country Profile' (2011) http://www.wpro.who.int/countries/fji/7FIJpro2011_finaldraft.pdf (accessed 2 June 2013).
World Health Organisation Western Pacific Region, 'Samoa Country Profile' (2011) http://www.wpro.who.int/countries/wsm/29SMApro2011_finaldraft.pdf (accessed 2 June 2013).
World Health Organisation Western Pacific Region, 'Tonga Country Profile' (2011) http://www.wpro.who.int/countries/ton/33TONpro2011_finaldraft.pdf (accessed 2 June 2013).
World Health Organisation Western Pacific Region, 'Vanuatu Country Profile' (2011) http://www.wpro.who.int/countries/vut/35VANpro2011_finaldraft.pdf (accessed 2 June 2013).
World Health Organisation and Secretariat of the Pacific Community, 'Apia Outcome Tenth Pacific Health Ministers Meeting,' (July 2013) http://www.wpro.who.int/southpacific/pic_meeting/reports/apia_outcomefull3.pdf?ua=1 (acessed 7 September 2015).
World Health Organisation and Secretariat of the Pacific Community, 'Eighth Meeting of Ministers of Health for Pacific Island Countries' (2010).
World Health Organisation and Secretariat of the Pacific Community, 'Ninth Meeting of Ministers of Health for the Pacific Island Countries,' (July 2011) http://www.wpro.who.int/southpacific/pic_meeting/reports/honiarareport.pdf?ua=1 (accessed 7 September 2015).
Zuckerberg, J 'Mental Health Law and its Discontents: A Reappraisal of the Canadian Experience' in B McSherry and P Weller (eds), *Rethinking Rights Based Mental Health Laws* (Hart Publishing, 2010).

Cases

Acting Public Prosecutor v Uname Aumane & Others [1980] PNGLR 510; [1980] PGSC 5.
AG v B [2001] QCA 169.
Attorney General v Crichton [2014] WSCA 8.
Attorney General v Garry David (aka Garry Webb) [1992] 2 VR 46.
Buxton v Jayne (1960) 2 All ER 697.
Crown v Manu [2011] TOSC 34.
Fa'aoso v Paongo [2006] TOSC 37.
Gorce v Miller [2003] TOSC 46.
In re Application under Part VI of the Mental Treatment Act, Gokal v Gokal [2004] FJHC 28.
In the Matter of the Constitution and the Laws of Tuvalu Act 1987, No.4 /1989 (unreported, High Court of Tuvalu, Donne CJ).

Iosefa v Tuvalu Red Cross [2012] TVHC 9.
Joli v Joli [2003] VUCA 27.
Kable v Director of Public Prosecutions (NSW) (1996) 189 CLR 51; [1996] HCA 24.
Kirby v Leather (1965) 2 All ER 441.
Malette v Shulman (1990) 67 DLR (4th) 321.
Nadan & McCoskar v State [2005] FJHC 252.
Police v Auvailiili [2010] WSSC 88.
Police v Fanueli [1993] WSSC 3.
Police v Fono [1999] WSSC 51.
Polites v Commonwealth (1945) 70 CLR 60.
Public Prosecutor v Kalon [2008] VUSC 9.
Public Prosecutor v Nicholls [2003] VUSC 8.
Public Service Board of NSW v Osmond (1986) 159 CLR 656.
R (on the application of JB) v RMO, Dr Haddock [2005] EWHC 921 (Admin).
R (on the application of JB) v RMO, Dr Haddock [2006] EWCA Civ 961.
R v Colgan (1959) SR (NSW) 96.
R v M'Naghten (1843) 10 Cl & Fin 200 HL.
R v Vola [2005] TOSC 31.
Re Application by Kama [2007] Tonga LR 76.
Rex v Taufa [2004] TOSC 66.
Schloendorf v Society of New York Hospital 105 NE 82,93 (NY1914).
Statement of Reasons in the Appeal of Gary Ian Patrick Webb (also known as Garry Ian Patrick David) a Security Patient at Aradale Hospital, Mental Health Review Board No. 230190:X01:300512, 9 May 1990.
Tangata v Speaker of the Legislative Assembly [1997] CKHC 1.
Tone v Police [2004] TOSC 36.
Wagner v Radke [1997] WSSC 6.
Waitemata Health v Her Majesty's Attorney General & Ors [2001] NZCA 312.

LEGISLATION

1914 Protocol relating to the New Hebrides between Britain and France.
Act of Constitution (Amendment) (No. 2) Act 2010 (Tonga).
Act of Constitution (Amendment) (No. 3) Act 2010 (Tonga).
Act of Constitution (Amendment) Act 2010 (Tonga).
Administration of Justice Decree 2009 (Fiji Islands).
Administration of Justice (Amendment) Decree 2009 (Fiji Islands)
Administration of Justice (Amendment) (No.3) Decree 2010 (Fiji Islands).
Civil Law Act [Cap 25] (Tonga).
Community Protection Act 1994 (NSW).
Community Protection (Amendment) Act 1991 (Vic).
Constitution (Amendment) Act 1997 (Fiji Islands).
Constitution Amendment Act (No. 2) 1997 (Samoa).
Constitution of the Independent State of Western Samoa 1960.

Constitution of the Republic of Fiji.
Constitution of the Republic of Vanuatu.
Constitution of the Sovereign Democratic Republic of Fiji 1990.
Constitution of Tonga.
Consultation Draft, *Mental Health Bill 2007* (Fiji Islands).
Convention Against Torture And Other Cruel, Inhuman Or Degrading Treatment Or Punishment (Ratification) Act 2010 (Vanuatu).
Convention On The Rights Of Persons With Disabilities (Ratification) Act 2008 (Vanuatu).
Convention On The Rights Of the Child (Ratification) Act [Cap 219] (Vanuatu).
Cook Islands Act 1915 (New Zealand).
Crimes Decree 2009 (Fiji Islands).
Crimes Ordinance 1961 (Samoa).
Criminal Offences Act [Cap 18] (Tonga).
Criminal Procedure Decree 2009 (Fiji Islands).
Executive Authority of Fiji Decree 2009 (Fiji Islands).
Fiji Constitution Amendment Act 1997 Revocation Decree 2009 (Fiji Islands).
Fiji Independence Order 1970.
Fijian Affairs (Amendment) Decree 2010 (Fiji Islands).
Human Rights Commission Act 1999 (Fiji Islands).
Human Rights Commission Decree 2009 (Fiji Islands).
Law Commission Act [Cap115] (Vanuatu).
Law Reform Commission Act 2008 (Samoa).
Lunacy Act 1890.
Lunatics Detention Act [Cap 80] (Tonga).
Media Industry Development Decree 2010 (Fiji Islands).
Medical Services Act [Cap 76] (Tonga).
Mental Defectives Act 1911 (NZ).
Mental Health Act 1911 (NZ).
Mental Health Act 1930 (UK).
Mental Health Act 1959 (UK).
Mental Health Act 1983 (UK).
Mental Health Act 1986 (Vic).
Mental Health Act 1990 (NSW).
Mental Health Act 1992 (Tonga).
Mental Health Act 1993 (SA).
Mental Health Act 1996 (Tas).
Mental Health Act 1996 (WA).
Mental Health Act 1998 (NT).
Mental Health Act 2000 (Qld).
Mental Health Act 2001 (Tonga).
Mental Health Act 2007 (Samoa).
Mental Health Act 2007 (UK).
Mental Health Act 2009 (SA).
Mental Health Act 2014 (Vic).
Mental Health Amendment Act 1954 (NZ).
Mental Health (Compulsory Assessment and Treatment) Act 1992 (NZ).

Mental Health Decree 2010 (Fiji Islands).
Mental Health Ordinance 1961 (Samoa).
Mental Health and Related Services Amendment Act 2007 (NT).
Mental Health (Treatment Order Forms) Notice 2007 (Samoa), S.R.2007/26 & 27 (7 June 2007).
Mental Hospital Act [Cap 38] (Vanuatu).
*Mental Treatment Ac*t [Cap 103] (Solomon Islands).
Mental Treatment Act [Cap 113] (Fiji Islands).
Mental Treatment Ordinance [Cap 37] (Tuvalu).
Mental Treatment Ordinance [Cap 56] (Kiribati).
Mentally Disordered Persons Ordinance 1963 (Nauru).
New Hebrides Orders in Council (1922-1970).
Nuie Act 1966 (NZ).
Ombudsman (Komesina o Sulufaiga) Act 2013 (Samoa).
Penal Code [Cap 26] (Solomon Islands).
Penal Code [Cap 135] (Vanuatu).
Prisons Act [Cap 86] (Fiji Islands).
Prisons and Corrections Act 2006 (Fiji Islands).
Ratification and Validation of the Declaration and Decrees of the Fiji Military Government Decree 2007 (Fiji Islands).
Reprint of Statutes Act 1972 (Samoa).
Samoa Act 1921 (NZ).
Tonga Orders in Council 1952-1955.
Western Pacific (Courts) Order 1961 (UK).

TREATIES AND OTHER INTERNATIONAL INSTRUMENTS

CESCR Committee, *General Comment No.14: The Right to the Highest Attainable Standard of Health (Art. 12 of the ICESCR),* 22nd sess, UN Doc E/C.12/2000/4 (8 November 2000).
CESCR, *Limburg Principles on the Implementation of the International Covenant on Economic, Social and Cultural Rights*, E/C.12/2000/13, 24th sess, Provisional Agenda Item 3, (10 February 2000).
Convention against Torture and Other Cruel, Inhuman or Degrading Treatment or Punishment, opened for signature 10 December 1984, 1465 UNTS 85 (entered into force 26 June 1987).
Convention on the Elimination of all Forms of Discrimination Against Women, opened for signature 1 March 1980, 1249 UNTS 13 (entered into force 3 September 1981).
Convention on the Rights of Persons with Disabilites, opened for signature 13 December 2006, 2515 UNTS 3 (entered into force 3 May 2008).
Convention on the Rights of the Child, opened for signature 20 November 1989, 1577 UNTS 3 (entered into force 2 September 1990).
ESCR Committee, *General Comment No. 3: The Nature of States Parties Obligations (Art. 2, para. 1 of the Covenant),* 5th Sess, UN Doc E/1991/23 (4 December 1990).

Hague Convention on the Civil Aspects of International Child Abduction, opened for signature 25 October 1980, 1343 UNTS (entered into force 1 December 1983).

International Covenant on Civil and Political Rights, opened for signature 16 December 1966, 999 UNTS 171 (entered into force 23 March 1976).

International Covenant on Economic, Social and Cultural Rights, opened for signature 16 December 1966, 993 UNTS 3 (entered into force 3 January 1976).

Office of the High Commissioner for Human Rights, *Principles for the Protection of Persons with Mental Illness and the Improvement of Mental Health Care*, GA Res 46/119, (17 December 1991).

Office of the High Commssioner for Human Rights, *CESCR General Comment 5: Persons with Disabilities,* 11th sess, UN Doc E/1995/22 (12 September 1994).

Optional Protocol to the Convention on the Rights of Persons with Disabilities, opened for signature 13 December 2006, Doc.A/61/611 (entered into force 3 May 2008).

UN Commission on Human Rights, *The Siracusa Principles on the Limitation and Derogation Provisions in the International Covenant on Civil and Political Rights*, E/CN.4/1985/4, (28 September 1984).

Universal Declaration of Human Rights, GA Res 217A (III), UN GAOR, 3rd sess, 183rd plen mtg, UN Doc A/810 (10 December 1948).

World Health Organisation Sixty-Fifth World Health Assembly, Comm A, 1st report, 9th plen mtg, Res WHA65.4, WHA65/2012/REC/1 (adopted 25 May 2012).

OTHER

Advocacy Tasmania Inc., http://www.advocacytasmania.org.au/mentalhealth.htm (accessed 11 April 2013).

Aoteoroa New Zealand Cluster Munition Coalition, *Pacific Campaigner Andy Piau-Lynch* http://www.stopclusterbombs.org.nz/2011/01/30/vanuatu-campaigner-andy-piau-lynch/ (accessed 24 March 2013).

Auckland District Law Society, *Tongan Lawyers Looking for Reform after King's Death* http://www.adls.org.nz/resources/news-details?NewsId=444076d5-7653-4d57-8f07-3e91d3598690 (accessed 14 June 2012).

Carney, T, 'Mental Health Tribunals – Rights, Protection or Treatment? Lessons from the ARC Linkage Grant Study?' (Paper presented at the Rights Responsibilities Rhetoric - Unpacking the Policy and Practice Issues in Mental Health Law, Guardianship and Trusteeship, Adelaide, October 2009).

'Commission Reports 'Below Standard Performance,' *Samoa Observer* (Apia, Samoa), 12 October 2014 http://www.samoaobserver.ws/home/headlines/11856-commission-reports-below-standard-performance (accessed 6 September 2015).

Deidre Taotua Fanene, 'There Is No Health, Without Mental Health,' *Samoa Observer* (Apia, Samoa), 1 June 2014, http://www.samoaobserver.ws/other/community/10367-there-is-no-health-without-mental-health (accessed 6 September 2015).

Deva, MP 'Matters of the Mind,' *The Fiji Times ONLINE* (Online), Tuesday August 28, 2012 2012 http://www.fijitimes.com/story.aspx?id=210296 (accessed 4 October 2012).

Fiji Bureaus of Statistics, < http://www.statsfiji.gov.fj/ (accessed 31 August 2012)>.

Fiji Disabled Peoples Association http://www.fdpa.org.fj/ProjectsAndServices.aspx (accessed 3 April 2012).

Fiji Human Rights and Anti - Discrimination Commission, http://www.fhrc.org.fj/ (accessed 18 December 2015).

Fiji Islands Bureau of Statistics http://www.statsfiji.gov.fj/Census2007/Release%201%20-%20Population%20Size.pdf (accessed 3 September 2012).

Fiji Law Reform Commission, *Mental Health Act Reviews Resumes* <www.lawreform.gov.fj/common/default.aspx?Page=mentalRev> (accessed 19 February 2008)>.

Fiji Times, 'Mind Matters,' *Vanuatu Daily Post* (Port Vila, Vanuatu), Thursday July 19 2012, 6.

Fiji Times, 'Woman Locked for 30 Years,' *Vanuatu Daily Post* (Port Vila), Saturday, June 15, 2013.

Fiji Village, *Proposed Fiji Labour Party Legal Challenge of Political Party Decree Dismissed* (15 March 2013) Island Business Magazine http://www.islandsbusiness.com/news/fiji/634/proposed-fiji-labour-party-legal-challenge-of-poli/ (accessed 4 June 201D Treaties3).

Garae, L, 'Family Offers Boy as Reconciliation,' *Vanuatu Daily Post* (Port Vila, Vanuatu), Saturday August 20, 2011.

Goshen Trust Mental Health Services Samoa, < http://www.sungo.ws/index.php?option=com_content&view=article&id=83&Itemid=156 (accessed 28 May 2012)>.

Government of Samoa Ministry of Health, 'Summary of Recommendations' (Paper presented at the National Symposium on Mental Health Issues in Samoa, Kitano-Tusitala Hotel, Apia, 2003).

Grigor, J, 'A Psychiatrist's View of Recent Mental Health Legislation' (Paper presented at the Professional Responsibility in Psychiatry, Psychology and Law: Proceedings of the 7th Annual Congress of the Australian and New Zealand Association of Psychiatry, Psychology and Law, Melbourne, Australia, 1986).

'Health Looks into New Mental Clinic,' *Samoa Observer* (Apia, Samoa), 24 January 2013, http://www.samoaobserver.ws/local-news/28-health-/3063-health-looks-into-new-mental-clinic (accessed 6 September 2015).

Hill, B, *Fiji Police Accused of Destroying Draft Constitution* (28 December 2012) ABC News Pacific Beat http://www.abc.net.au/news/2012-12-28/fiji-police-accused-of-destroying-draft-constitution/4446542 (accessed 2 June 2013).

Joshua, J, 'Influential Disability Rights Advocator Dies,' *Vanautu Daily Post* (Port Vila, Vanuatu), February 2, 2011 http://www.dailypost.vu/content/influential-disability-rights-advocator-dies (accessed 24 March 2013).

Karan, M, 'Hospital Lack Psychiatry Services,' *Fiji Times ONLINE* (Online), Tuesday, March 08, 2011 < http://www.fijitimes.com/story.aspx?id=167763 (accessed 29 March 2011)>.

Kolotita Talatalaga, 'Boxing Day Tragedy at Tafa'igata,' *Samoa Observer* (Apia, Samoa), 3 January 2013 http://www.samoaobserver.ws/home/headlines/2710-boxing-day-tragedy-at-tafaigata (accessed 9 March 2013).

Lanuola Tupufia, 'Man Charged for Death of Hans Dalton,' *Samoa Observer* (Apia, Samoa), 18 January 2013 http://www.samoaobserver.ws/local-news/police-and-prison/2956--man-charged-for-death-of-hans-dalton (accessed 9 March 2013).

Ligo, G, 'Initial Report on Disability in Vanuatu Released,' *Vanuatu Daily Post* (Port Vila,

Vanuatu), Thursday November 15, 2012, 3.
Ligo, G, 'Problems in Health is Huge: Ken,' *Vanuatu Daily Post* (Port Vila, Vanuatu), Wednesday 27 February 2013.
Member States of the United Nations https://www.un.org/en/members/index.shtml (accessed 31 December 2012).
Ménard H, *LW112 Legislation Course Book* (Course Materials School of Law, University of the South Pacific, Suva, Fiji, Rev. July 2011) 4.5.
Michael Field, 'Family Sues Samoa over Hans Dalton's Prison Death' (17 September 2014) http://www.stuff.co.nz/world/south-pacific/61303199/family-sues-samoa-over-hans-daltons-prison-death (accessed 6 September 2015).
Ministry of Health and Medical Services Fiji, *Mental Health* http://www.health.gov.fj/?page_id=1424 (accessed 5 January 2016).
Ministry of Health and Medical Services Fiji, *Suicide* http://www.health.gov.fj/?page_id=2420 (accessed 5 January 2016).
Ministry of Health and Medical Services Fiji, 'World Suicide Prevention Day' (2015) http://www.health.gov.fj/?p=4705 (accessed 5 January 2016).
Moore, Marj, 'So Who Killed Hans Dalton?,' *Samao Observer* (Apia, Samoa), 10 February 2014 http://www.samoaobserver.ws/editorial/9232-so-who-killed-hans-dalton (accessed 6 September 2015).
Noonan, Andie, *Pacific nations must prepare for more natural disasters as El Nino takes hold, experts warn* http://www.abc.net.au/news/2015-07-20/pacific-nations-headed-for-more-natual-disasters/6634008 (accessed 17 December 2015).
Oceania Map www.geographicguide.com (accessed 30 December 2012).
Pacific Islands Forum Secretariat http://www.forumsec.org/pages.cfm/about-us/partners/ (accessed 10 May 2013).
Psychiatric Survivors Association, http://www.fdpa.org.fj/Psychiatric_Survivors_Association.aspx (accessed 3 April 2012).
Radio Australia, 'Drive to Improve Mental Health Care in the Pacific,' *Pacific Beat*, 5 November 2010 (Dr Frances Hughes).http://www.radioaustralia.net.au/pacbeat/stories/201011/s3057961.htm (accessed 10 April 2013).
Samoan Police Officers Fired after New Zealander's Death http://www.3news.co.nz/Samoan-police-officers-fired-after-New-Zealanders-death/tabid/417/articleID/285936/Default.aspx (accessed 9 March 2013).
Secretariat of the Pacific Community http://www.spc.int/en/about-spc/history.html (accessed 10 May 2013).
Secretariat of the Pacific Community, *Statistics for Development Division, Pacific Islands Populations Estimates, Mid-year 2015* http://www.spc.int/nmdi/population (accessed 2 January 2016).
Secretariat of the Pacific Community, *Statistics for Development Program, Pacific Islands Populations Estimates, Mid-year 2013* http://www.spc.int/ (accessed 13 May 2013).
Shing, G, 'Access to Justice Has Failed Considerably: Salwai,' *Vanuatu Daily Post* (Port Vila, Vanuatu), 28 August 2012 www.dailypost.vu/print/8377.
Sofaia Koroitanoa, 'President Made Appointments to PSC and Human Rights and Anti Discriminatory Commission,' *FijiOne* (Suva, Fiji), 8 May 2015 http://fijione.tv/president-made-appointments-to-psc-and-human-rights-and-anti-discriminatory-commission/ (accessed 18 December 2015).

StatPac Survey Sampling < http://www.statpac.com/surveys/sampling.htm (accessed 19 December 2013)>.

'Taskforce Looks at Mental Health,' *Samoa Observer* (Apia, Samoa), 19 January 2014 http://www.samoaobserver.ws/local-news/28-health-/8915-taskforce-looks-at-mental-health (accessed 6 Septemeber 2015).

TemoL, *St Giles Hospital to Be Turned into a Regional Mental Health Institute* (Fri, 23/10/2009,0936) < http://www.connectme.com.fj/news/national/St-Giles-Hospital-to-be-turned-into-a-regional-mental-health-institute (accessed 29 March 2011)>.

The Fijian Government, 'Heath Committed Towards Mental Health,' 7 November 2014 http://www.fiji.gov.fj/Media-Center/Press-Releases/HEATH-COMMITTED-TOWARDS-MENTAL-HEALTH.aspx (accessed 21 December 2015).

United Nations Treaty Collection http://treaties.un.org/Pages/ViewDetails. aspx?src= TREATY&mtdsg_no=IV-4&chapter=4&lang=en (accessed 9 November 2012).

United Nations Treaty Collection, Participant Search http://treaties.un.org/pages/Treaty ParticipantSearch.aspx?tab=UN (accessed 9 Nov 2012).

United Nations Treaty Collection, State Reports http://www.ohchr.org/EN/HRBodies/ CRC/Pages/CRCIndex.aspx (accessed 17 December 2015).

Vanuatu http://www.mapsofworld.com/country-profile/vanuatu-information-geography-history.html (accessed 30 June 2012).

Vanuatu Law Commission, < http://www.lawcommission.gov.vu/index.php?option=com_ content&view=article&id=19&Itemid=3 (accessed 14 June 2012)>.

Wan Smolbag Theatre, *Love Patrol Series* http://www.wansmolbag.org/DynamicPages. asp?cid=26&navID=34 (accessed 2 June 2013).

Wexler, D B, *International Network on Therapeutic Jurisprudence, Therapeutic Jurisprudence: An Overview* http://www.law.arizona.edu/depts/upr-intj/ (accessed 25 May 2013).

WHO Regional Office for the Western Pacific Press Releases, *New Network Seeks to Improve Mental Health Care in Pacific Islands Countries* http://www.wpro.who.int/NR/exeres/ 6C2C3583-BBA7-4E61-B64B-7BBF8372AB67.htm.

WHO Western Pacific Region, *Fiji* www.wpro.who.int/countries/fij/2010/FIJ.htm (accessed 14 March 2011).

WHO, Western Pacific Region, 2010, Fiji www.wpro.who.int/countries/fij/2010/FIJ.htm (accessed 14 March 2011).

WHO, Western Pacific Region, 2010, Samoa www.wpro.who.int/countries/sma/(accessed 14 March 2011).

WHO, Western Pacific Region, 2010, Tonga www.wpro.who.int/countries/ton/2010/TON.htm (accessed 14 March 2011).

WHO, Western Pacific Region, 2010, Vanuatu www.wpro.who.int/countries/van/ 2010/VAN.htm (accessed 14 March 2011).

World Health Office, Regional Office for the Western Pacific, *Press Release: New Network Seeks to Improve Mental Health Care in Pacific Islands Countries* (17 July 2007) www.wpro.who.int/NR/exeres/6C2C3583-BBA7-4E61-B64B-7BBF8372AB67.htm.

World Health Organisation, *Mental Health Advocacy* http://www.who.int/mental_health/ advocacy/en/ (accessed 11 June 2012).

Respondents and Interviewees

Email questionnaire from AB, Fiji, to Helen Ménard, 22 March 2012.
Email questionnaire from AB, Fiji, to Helen Ménard, 10 April 2012.
Email questionnaire from Dr Ian Parkin, Psychiatrist Samoa, to Helen Ménard, 15 April 2011.
Email questionnaire from Dr Ian Parkin to Helen Ménard, 8 March 2012.
Email questionnaire from Dr Ian Parkin to Helen Ménard, 22 January 2013.
Email questionnaire from Dr Ian Parkin, Psychiatrist Samoa, to Helen Ménard, 10 January 2016.
Email from Dr Mike Poltorak, Kent University, to Helen Ménard 12 June 2013.
Email from Dr Odille Chang, Fiji National University, to Helen Ménard, 12 June 2013.
Email from Dr Odille Chang, Fiji National University, to Helen Ménard, 10 January 2016.
Email questionnaire from EF, Fiji, to Helen Ménard, 16 January 2013.
Email questionnaire from IJ, Fiji, to Helen Ménard, 18 December 2015.
Email questionnaire from John Obed Alilee, Supreme Court Registrar, Vanuatu, to Helen Ménard, 15 July 2013.
Email questionnaire from Loupua Sefokuli, Lawyer Tonga, to Helen Ménard, 10 March 2012.
Email questionnaire from Ma'afu Sefokuli, Court Clerk Tonga, to Helen Ménard, 20 June 2011.
Email questionnaire from Salesi Mafi, Senior Magistrate Tonga, to Helen Ménard, 16 September 2011.
Email questionnaire from Salesi Mafi, Senior Magistrate Tonga, to Helen Ménard, June 2012.
Email questionnaire from Tony Lawson to Helen Ménard, 20 May 2011.
Email questionnaire from XY, Fiji, to Helen Ménard, 19 July 2012.
Interview with Carlie Dodds, Clinical Psychologist, Vanuatu (Port Vila, 28 June 2012).
Interview with Jane Laycock, Clinical Nurse Educator, Vanuatu (Port Vila, xx June 2013).
Interview with Loupua Sefokuli, Law Graduate, (Port Vila, November 2010).
Interview with Peter Kaloris, Mental Health Cordinator, Vanuatu (Port Vila, 24 June 2013).
Loupua Sefokuli, Interview with Dr Yang Yangpin, Psychiatrist (Tonga, 13 June 2012).
Loupua Sefokuli, Interview with Ilaivatu Mafi, Sister in Charge MHU (Tonga, 13 June 2012).

ANNEXES

No. 1. Konga X Kupu 89-99 (Tongan Translation of Parts of Sections 89–99 of the *Mental Health Act 2001*)

LAO KI HE FAKALELEI 'ATAMAI FIKA 8, 2001

KONGA X KUPU 89 – 99

NGAAHI TOTONU 'A E KAU MAHAKI MO E NGAAHI FOUNGA LAUNGA.

Ko e fakapa'anga 'e he Kautaha Mo'ui 'a Mamani (WHO) ma'a e Va'a Fakalelei 'Atamai 'a e Falemahaki Vaiola.

taha ko ha taha mahaki 'i ha, pe na'e fai hono faito'o 'i ha, fale fakalelei 'atamai pe fale tokangaekina 'o e mo'ui pea fekau'aki mo e natula pe ngaahi fakaikiiki kehe 'o e fakahū pe faito'o ko ia kuo pau 'e 'ikai ke fakaha ia, fakahangatonu pe ta'efakahangatonu, ki ha taha kehe tukukehe kapau ko e fakakakato 'o ha fiema'u 'i he Lao nip e ha lao kehe.

(5) Ka 'i ai ha taha 'oku ne maumau'i 'a e kupu ni kuo pau 'e ala mo'ua 'oku halaia ki ha tautea pa'anga 'e 'ikai laka hake 'i he $500.

KUPU 93 : NGAAHI TUKUKEHE

Kuo pau 'e 'ikai ke ngaue'aki ha fakataputapui ki he fakaha ha fakamatala 'i he kupu 92 ki hano 'oatu 'o e fakamatala –

(a) kapau 'oku tomu'a loto ki ai 'a e toko taha 'oku kau ki ai 'a e fakamatala pe, kapau kuo pekia 'a e toko taha ko ia, 'i he loto ki ai 'a hono kainga ofi taha;
(b) 'i hano fiema'u 'e he Fakamaau'anga lolotonga ha hopo hia;
(c) fekau'aki mo e hokohoko atu 'a e tokanga'i mo/pe faito'o ki ha kainga pe ha taha 'oku pehe 'oku fengaue'aki ofi 'i he hokohoko atu 'a hono tokanga'i pe faito'o 'o e toko taha ko ia, kapau 'oku fiema'u 'a e fakaha ko ia ki hono malu'i 'a e toko taha ko ia;
(d) ki he ngaahi taumu'a fakatotolo fakafaito'o pe fakasosiale, ka kuo pau ke fiemalie 'a e Minisita 'oku fiema'u ke fakaha pea 'oku 'ikai ke kaunga kovi ki he lelei 'a e toko taha ko ia 'a ia 'oku kau ki ai 'a e fakamatala; pe
(e) kapau 'oku fakakaukau 'a e Minisita 'oku kau lelei ki he kakai.

KUPU 94 : NGAAHI FOUNGA FAI 'O E NGAAHI LAUNGA

Kuo pau ke fakapapau'i 'e he toketa 'atamai fakamafai'i 'o ha fale fakalelei 'atamai pe 'e he taha pule 'o ha fale tokangaekina 'o e mo'ui 'oku fokotu'u ha ngaahi founga ngaue 'oku ala faka'aonga'i ki hono fai 'o e ngaahi launga.

KUPU 95 : FAKA'ILONGA'I 'O E LAUNGA

Kuo pau ke fakapapau'i 'e he toketa 'atamai fakamafai 'o ha fale fakalelei 'atamai pe 'e he taha pule 'o ha fale tokangaekina 'o e mo'ui 'e ma'u 'e ha taha na'a ne fai ha launga 'i he kupu 94, 'i he vave taha 'e ala lava, ha tohi faka'ilonga'i pea ke fakaha ma'u pe ki ai 'a e tu'unga 'o e fakatotolo pe ha ngaue kehe ki he launga.

KUPU 96 : ME'A FAKATOHI 'O E NGAAHI LAUNGA

Kuo pau ke fakapapau'i 'e he toketa 'atamai fakamafai 'o ha fale fakalelei 'atamai pe 'e he taha pule 'o ha fale tokangaekina 'o e mo'ui 'oku kakato mo tonu 'a e ngaahi me'a fakatohi 'o e ngaahi launga kotoa pe, kau ai 'a e natula 'o e launga mo ha fakatotolo pe ngaue kehe kuo fai 'o fekau'aki mo ia.

No. 2. Ki He Kau Psychiatric Assistants (PA) (Tongan Brochure on the Different Types of Mental Illness) (English Translation)

From the Psychiatric Unit

To psychiatric assistants (PA) or such related person(s)

Preface

Side effects of Psychosis (there are two psychotic illnesses namely Schizophrenia & Bipolar disorder)

It is important that you know these by heart when carrying out your duties to our psychiatric patients.

As you are all aware of, one can die from committing suicide due to side effects from anti-psychotic medication (Haloperidol, Stelazine etc)

These are the types of side effects of the medication.

(1) Akathesia: (body and mind wants to move all the time)

A person who is unfamiliar with psychotic patients usually thinks that this side effect is one of the signs of psychotic illness. The fact is that it is one of the side effects of the anti-psychotic medicine.

The patient feels the urge to move all the time and sometimes he or she would feel in his or her head, chest, feet, brain or soul the urge to move and go. At the same time he or she experiences anxiety therefore results in some of them ending up committing suicide.

The patient does not know what is going on with his or her body. He or she often tries so hard to do something to stop such feelings. As a result one would climb a coconut tree, jump down and, would be lucky to survive the fall.

Therefore, it is important for the P.A to explain this to the patient, his or her family or relatives.

Please note that it is our task (doctor, nurse, MHWO, PSW and PA) to inform the patient, his or her family or relative about akathesia and its side effects pursuant to the Mental Health Act, 2001.

The purpose for taking of tablets namely Artane and Cogentin is to calm the patient and to decrease the side effects of anti- psychotic medication.

It is most important for the P.A, nurse, PSW and the MHWO to inform the doctor if a patient has akathesia or if the patient is still not calm after taking either Artane and Cogentin.

(2) Dystonia

This usually happens in a sudden manner and it is noticeable when they stretch their neck to a stiff position at times bending to the side and upwards causing their upper body to bend backward with eyes rolling in the same position.

The cure is to give them a shot of I/M Cogentin 2mg once STAT and to be done in accordance with our guiding chart.

It is important for the staff to relay this to the patient, his or her family or relative so that they can predict such incident at home so that they could bring the patient to the hospital to be given a shot.

This cannot cause death but it will cause panic amongst the patient and his or her family when it happens at home.

(3) Parkinsonism

A lot of our patients suffer from Parkinsonism and it is up to a stage that they cannot do any work. It can cause an accident such as falling from a high place that would cause death.

Parkinsonism can decrease or be prevented when the patient takes Artane and Cogentin. Parkinsonism can cause a patient to feel stiffness in his or her joints especially their hands and feet and it is likely that their feet and hands have been locked therefore difficult to walk and move. They tend to walk stiffly and slow.

Taking of tablets namely Artane and Cogentin can decrease stiffness of movement and also calm the patient.

There are other side effects such as Tardive Dyskinesia but we will end here.

Thank you very much
Dr.Mapa H. Puloka
Senior Medical Officer in Charge of Psychiatric Unit,
VAIOLA HOSPITAL.

No. 3. KO E Fale Fakalelei 'Atamai (Tongan Brochure on the Facilities in the Mental Health Care Unit at Vaiola Hospital in Nuku'alofa) (English Translation)

PSYCHIATRIC UNIT

It is important to call the ward 'Psychiatric Unit' rather than calling it a ward for the mentally disturbed or retarder's house.

This Unit is still commonly called and known by civil servants and the public as the mentally disturbed or retarder's house. I hereby urge you all not to use those terms again and to call it the Psychiatric Unit.

The fact is, in using the words mentally disturbed or retarder's house it does not give a positive implication or reflect positive opinion towards this group of people, who are experiencing these problems. In using the Psychiatric Unit, it reflects positive views and hopes for something good in the future. The using of the Psychiatric Unit accords with the name of our hospital, VAIOLA. According to Tongan myths ,Vaiola was a curing flowing water in Pulotu. It was a source of life and cure therefore, it is important that we reflect positive opinions and sense of hope rather than ridiculing and putting forward negative hopes for the future.

The purpose of this ward is to rehabilitate patients and not to despise them as mentally disturbed or retarded. If we bear this concept in mind then it will give us a more positive view on what the purpose of this house is.

The idea of self-fulfilling prophecy also applies to this situation. It means that we sort of predict something beforehand and even though that has not happened we tend to adjust our behaviour in accordance with what we expect to happen. A clear example of this is amongst teachers. A teacher would say beforehand that a student will fail the exams on the basis that the teacher knows that such student is not very smart. The outcome will be that the teacher's attitude towards such student will be negative and it seems like he or she is trying to make such student fail the exam just to make his or her earlier prediction come true.

It applies to the using of the words 'house for mentally disturbed patients or retarder's house'. The continuance use of such words will take control of what we think about these people and the result would be our view will be people are mentally disturbed and retarded.

If we use the words mental health then we will think, see and behave in a rehabilitated way towards these people who have suffered some mental illness and are admitted to the psychiatric ward. In using the words mental health it is like planting something good and in the end we will reap good results.

Another principle from the science of psychology which is obviously natural in our Tongan way of living, it is called HALO EFFECT. It happens when we notice one particular behaviour and we take that to judge a person's overall character but it is incorrect. Unfortunately, it is commonly perceived to be such person's character but the fact about that person's true character is not what we think it is. It is quite unfortunate that such view has been part of our society and, it has become a state of mind that we have contributed to its expansion. When a person is mentally ill, usually such person will always be known for being mentally ill rather than being known for all the good deeds shown and done by this person. Not only that, but such person's immediate family and relatives are called and stigmatized about their relative's mental illness. Therefore, it becomes ridicule in the society. It not only affects relatives of such person but sometimes it affects people that has no relation whatsoever to the mentally ill patient. In addition, people tend to expand the ridicules towards the patient's house, properties, land and even animals.

Continuing to use negative impressions towards psychiatric patients will bury whatever good that was left in them therefore, deteriorates the patient's condition. After all, such good that was in that patient would have been maintained and developed and some patients may have been fully cured.

It is my hope that the people in the society will change their state of mind, view, attitude and behavior towards mentally ill patients. They can do so, by acknowledging and appreciating whatever it is good in the patient and label him or her with it in the society. In doing so, such good(s) will undermine whatever negative recognition or label the society has given this patient just because he or she is mentally ill. It will give the patient a positive image in society.

Support from the society is vital because the negative and positive effects of the patient's illness usually happen within the society. When they tend to label patients with whatever good(s) they have, it will give the patient positive hope which might form a positive character within the patient and there is hope that the result would be that some will be cured.

On the other hand, there are some words that encourage, build self esteem, calming and that includes rehabilitate. In comparing rehabilitation and the negative words mentioned earlier, heal a patient, it has great power to calm or even heal a mentally disturbed patient.

The power of the word rehabilitate is so great that it can convey to cure mental illness which is a BLESSING unlike the use of the words 'mentally disturbed or retarded' which would seem more like a curse.

Using of words ' mentally disturbed or retarded' are seemingly satanic and reveals a curse but using the words 'rehabilitate or mental health' sounds hopeful, calming for it contains overflowing power of healing that can cure a mentally ill patient which is a blessing.

Written by Dr. Mapa Ha'ano Puloka
Psychiatric Unit, Vaiola Hospital

No. 4. Statement of Patients' Rights to Apply to Review (Inpatient) Order (English) under *Mental Health Act 2007* (Samoa)

Statement of Patients Rights to Apply to Review Order

Application to Review Inpatient Treatment Order

On the making of an Inpatient Treatment Order each of the following persons may apply to the District Court, for leave to review the Inpatient Treatment Order.

(a) the patient;

(b) any other person who satisfies the District Court they have a proper interest in the matter.

If any such person wishes to apply to the Review Tribunal, that person may seek help from:

(a) a health care professional;

(b) a mental health care professional;

(c) his or her lawyer.

Steps to be taken for Review

An application for a review shall be:

(a) in a form as may be prescribed from time to time;

(b) processed by a health care professional or mental health care professional who becomes aware of a request for a review by the person subject to the order or by any other person with a bona fide interest in the persons welfare;

(c) filed with the Registrar of the District Court, within 14 days of the making of the Order.

Finding of District Court

The District Court provided that leave is granted, shall review the Order. Upon hearing a review, the Court shall revoke the Order unless the Court is satisfied that:

(a) the person subject to the Order continues to meet the criteria under section 13 of the Mental Health Act 2007; and

(b) the Order continues to be required in all of the circumstances.

Further Information

For further information about the Review, see sections 21 and 22 of the Mental Health Act 2007.

Issued under the authority of the Regulations Ordinance 1953.
Notice – Samoa Observer: 8th June 2007
These Regulations are administered by the Ministry of Health.

Copies of these Regulations can be purchased from the Office of the Clerk of the Legislative Assembly.

Printed by the Clerk of the Legislative Assembly, by authority of the Legislative Assembly.

No. 5. Statement of Patients' Rights to Apply to Review (Inpatient) Order (Samoan) under *Mental Health Act 2007* (Samoa)

2007/26 *Faasilasilaga o (Pepa Faatumu o Poloaiga mo Togafitiga) mo Tulaga Maloloina o le Mafaufau 2007* 10

Faamatalaga o Aia Tatau a Gasegase ina ia Talosaga se Toe Iloiloga o le Poloaiga

Talosaga ina ia Toe Ilotlo le Poloaiga mo Togafitiga o Gasegase Taofia i Falemai

I le faia o se Poloaiga mo Togafitiga o Gasegase Taofia i Falemai e mafai e so o se tagata ua taua mulimuli ane ona talosaga i le Faamasinoga Faa-Itumalo, mo se faatagaga e toe iloilo ai le Poloaiga mo Togafitiga o Gasegase Taofia i Falemai:

(a) le tagata mai;

(b) so o se isi lava tagata o ia lea ua faamalieina le Faamasinoga Faa-Itumalo e faapea e talafeagai le latou aia i le mataupu.

Afai e i ai se isi tagata e manao e talosaga i le Komisi Faamasino mo Toe Iloiloga, e mafai e lena tagata ona saili le fesoasoani mai:

(a) se tagata tomai faapitoa tau soifua maloloina;

(b) se tagata tomai faapitoa tau tulaga maloloina o le mafaufau;

(c) lana loia.

Laasaga e ao ona faia mo le Toe Iloiloga

O se talosaga mo se toe iloiloga e tatau ona:

(a) faia i se pepa faatumu e pei ona faatonuina mai lea taimi i lea taimi;

(b) ia faia e se tagata tomai faapitoa tau soifua maloloina po o se tagata tomai faapitoa o tulaga maloloina o le mafaufau o lo o ia silafia se talosaga mo se toe iloiloga e le tagata o lo o i ai lana aia i le agaga lelei i le olaga manuia o le tagata;

(c) ia faatoai i le Resitara o le Faamasinoga Faa-Itumalo i totonu o le 14 aso talu ona faia le Poloaiga.

Sailiiliga a le Faamasinoga Faa-Itumalo

O le Faamasinoga Faa-Itumalo pe afai ua tuuina atu se faatagaga, e tatau ona toe iloiloina le Poloaiga.

I le fofogaina ai o se toe iloiloga, e tatau i le Faamasinoga ona faaleaoga le Poloaiga seia vagana ai ua faamalieina le Faamasinoga e faapea:

(a) o le tagata o lo o noatia i le Poloaiga e faaauau pea ona faamalieina le taiala faavae i lalo o le fuaiupu 13 o le Tulafono o Tulaga Maloloina o le Mafaufau 2007; ma

(b) o lo o faaauau pea ona manaomia le Poloaiga i tulaga aliae uma.

Isi Faamatalaga

Mo nisi faamatalaga e uiga i le Toe Iloiloga, silasila i fuaiupu 21 ma le 22 o le Tulafono o Tulaga Maloloina o le Mafaufau 2007.

Tuuina atu i lalo o le pule faataga a le Tulafono o Tulafono Faatonutonu 1953.

Faasilasilaga - Samoa Observer: 8 Iuni 2007

O nei Tulafono Faatonutonu o lo o faafoe i le Matagaluega o le Soifua Maloloina.

O ata o nei Tulafono Faatonutonu o lo o mafai ona faatauina atu, mai le Ofisa o le Failautusi o le Fono Aoao Faitulafono.

Lolomiina e le Failautusi o le Fono Aoao Faitulafono, i le pule a le Fono Aoao Faitulafono.

No. 6. Statement of Patients' Rights to Apply to Review (Community) Order (English) under *Mental Health Act 2007* (Samoa)

2007/26 *Mental Health (Treatment Order Forms) Notice 2007* 15

Statement of Patients Rights to Apply to Review Order

Application to Review Community Treatment Order

Following the making of a community Treatment Order each of the following persons may apply to the District Court for leave to review the Community Treatment Order:

(a) the patient;

(b) any other person who satisfies the District Court they have a proper interest in the matter.

If any such person wishes to apply to the District Court, that person may seek help from:

(a) a health care professional;

(b) a mental health care professional;

(c) his or her lawyer.

Steps to be taken for Review

An application for a review shall be:

(a) in a form as may be prescribed from time to time;

(b) processed by a health care professional or mental health care professional who becomes aware of a request for a review by the person subject to the order or by any other person with a bona fide interest in the persons person welfare;

(c) filed with the Registrar of the District Court.

Finding of District Court

The District Court provided that leave is granted, shall review the Order. Upon hearing a review, the Court shall revoke the Order unless the Court is satisfied that:

(a) the person subject to the Order continues to meet the criteria under section 10 of the Mental Health Act 2007; and

(b) the Order continues to be required in all of the circumstances.

Further Information

For further information about the Review, see section 19 and 20 of the Mental Health Act 2007.

No. 7. Statement of Patients' Rights to Apply to Review (Community) Order (Samoan) under *Mental Health Act 2007* (Samoa)

Faamatalaga o Aia Tatau a Tagata e Talosaga ai ma ia Toe Iloilo le Poloaiga

Tusi talosaga ina ia Toe Iloilo le Poloaiga mo Togafitiga o Tagata Lautele

Ina ua maea le faia o se Poloaiga mo Togafitiga o Tagata Lautele, e mafai e tagata taitoatasi ua taua mulimuli ane ona talosaga i le Faamasinoga Faa-Itumalo mo se faatagaga e toe iloilo ai le Poloaiga mo Togafitiga o Tagata Lautele;

(a) le tagata mai;
(b) so o se isi lava o ia lea ua faamalieina le Faamasinoga Faa-Itumalo e faapea e talafeagai lo latou aia i le mataupu.

Afai e i ai so o se isi tagata e fia talosaga i le Faamasinoga Faa-Itumalo, e mafai e lena tagata ona saili le fesoasoani mai:

(a) se tagata tomai faapitoa tau soifua maloloina;
(b) se tagata tomai faapitoa tau tulaga maloloina o le mafaufau;
(c) sana loia.

Laasaga e faia mo le Toe Iloiloga

E tatau ona faia se talosaga mo le toe iloiloga:

(a) i se pepa faatumu e mafai ona faatonuina mai lea taimi i lea taimi;
(b) ia faia e se tagata tomai faapitoa tau soifua maloloina po o se tagata tomai faapitoa o tulaga maloloina o le mafaufau o ia lea o lo o silafia se talosaga mo se toe iloilolga a le tagata o lo o noatia i le poloaiga po o e so o se isi tagata e i ai sana aia i le agaga lelei i le soifua manuia o le tagata;
(c) ia faatoai atu i le Resitara o le Faamasinoga Faa-Itumalo.

Sailiiliga a le Faamasinoga Faa-Itumalo

O le Faamasinoga ae vagana ai e faapea ua tuuina atu le faatagaga, e tatau ona toe iloiloina le Poloaiga.
I le fofogaina o se toe iloiloga, e tatau i le Faamasinoga ona faalēaogā le Poloaiga seia vagana ai ua faamalieina le Faamasinoga e faapea:

(a) o le tagata o lo o noatia i le Poloaiga o lo o faaauau pea ona faamalieina le taiala faavae i lalo o le fuaiupu 10 o le Tulafono o Tulaga Maloloina o le Mafaufau 2007; ma
(b) o lo o faaauau pea le manaomia o le Poloaiga i tulaga uma e aliae mai.

Isi Faamatalaga

Mo nisi faamatalaga e uiga i le Toe Iloiloga, silasila i le fuauiupu 19 ma le fuaiupu 20 o le Tulafono o Tulaga Maloloina o le Mafaufau 2007.

No. 8. Brochure on Sadness/St Giles Hospital, Fiji

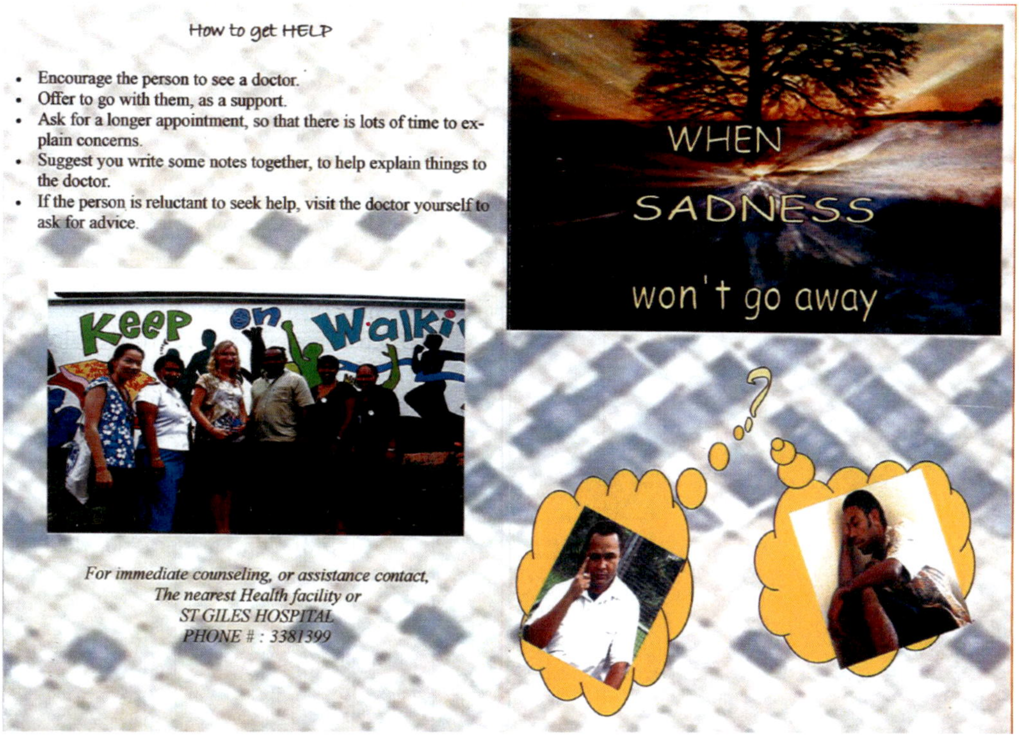

How to get HELP

- Encourage the person to see a doctor.
- Offer to go with them, as a support.
- Ask for a longer appointment, so that there is lots of time to explain concerns.
- Suggest you write some notes together, to help explain things to the doctor.
- If the person is reluctant to seek help, visit the doctor yourself to ask for advice.

For immediate counseling, or assistance contact,
The nearest Health facility or
ST GILES HOSPITAL
PHONE # : 3381399

WHEN SADNESS won't go away

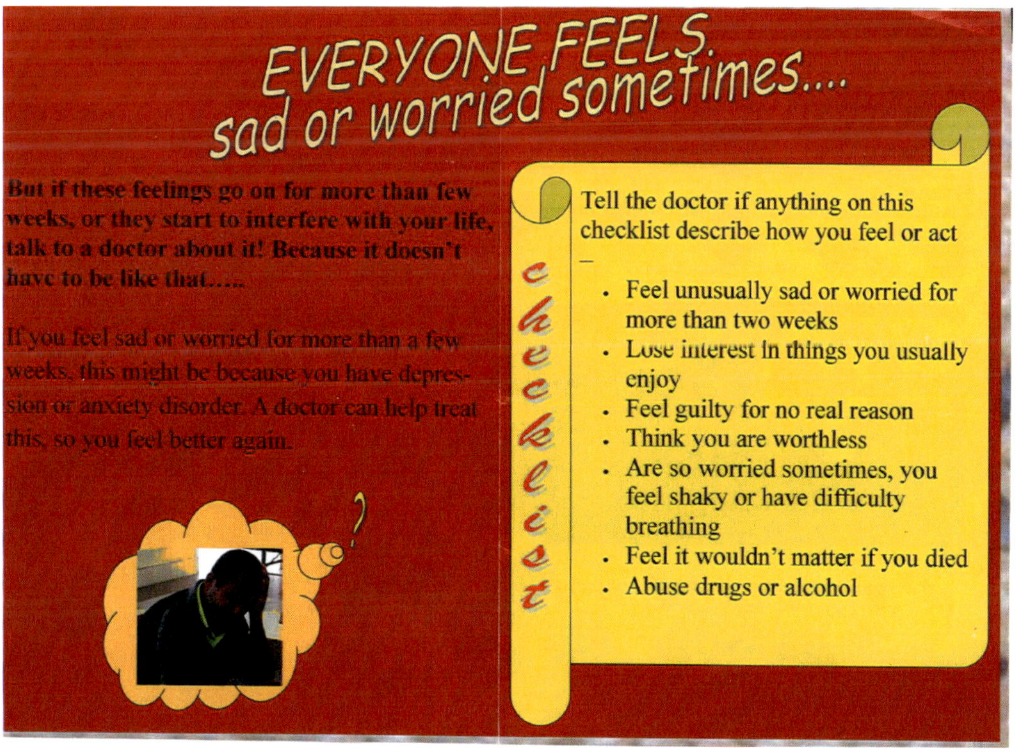

EVERYONE FEELS sad or worried sometimes....

But if these feelings go on for more than few weeks, or they start to interfere with your life, talk to a doctor about it! Because it doesn't have to be like that.....

If you feel sad or worried for more than a few weeks, this might be because you have depression or anxiety disorder. A doctor can help treat this, so you feel better again.

checklist

Tell the doctor if anything on this checklist describe how you feel or act –

- Feel unusually sad or worried for more than two weeks
- Lose interest in things you usually enjoy
- Feel guilty for no real reason
- Think you are worthless
- Are so worried sometimes, you feel shaky or have difficulty breathing
- Feel it wouldn't matter if you died
- Abuse drugs or alcohol

No. 9. Brochure on Stigma and Mental Illness/ St Giles Hospital, Fiji

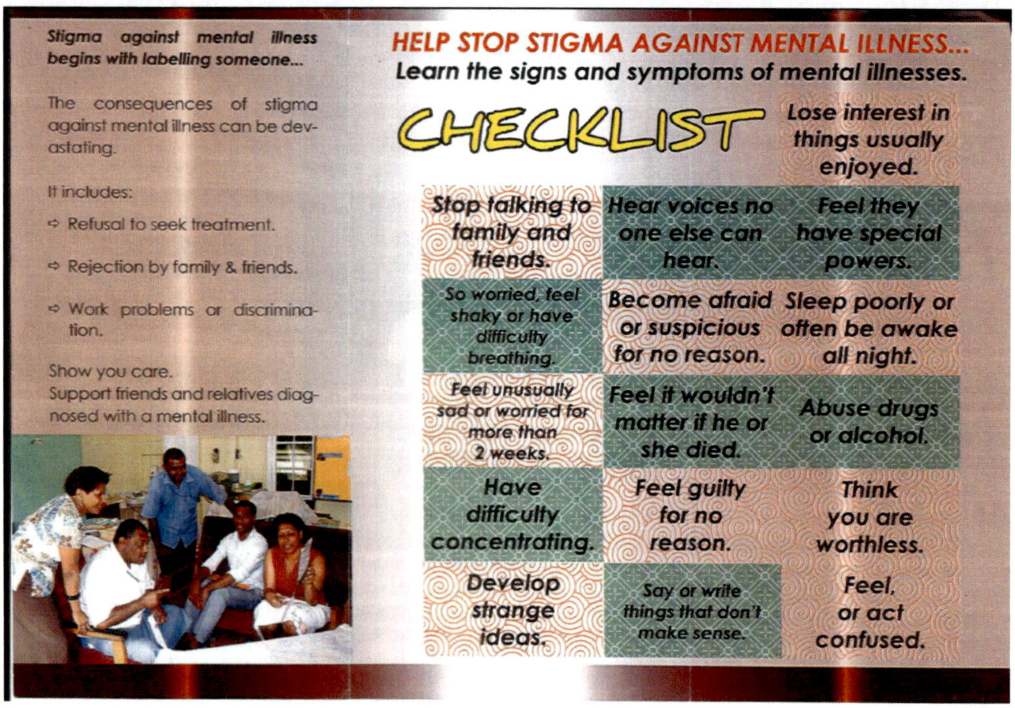

No. 10. Brochure on Mental Illness/St Giles Hospital, Fiji

MENTAL HEALTH

What is mental health?

Mental health is more than just the absence of illness or disorder, it is:

- *Having the emotional and spiritual resources that allows us to enjoy life and cope/survive pain, disappointment, and sadness*
- *A positive sense of wellbeing and underlying belief in our own worth and other's self-worth*
- *Ability to initiate, nurture & sustain mentally satisfying personal & spiritual relationships*
- *When an individual can think clearly and work towards solving problems they face in life*

Education is key to reducing the negative attitude towards mental health and mental illness

GETTING TO KNOW YOUR MENTAL HEALTH...

Our brain is a very important part of our body, just like our heart or lungs. It controls our body and affects how we think, feel and behave.

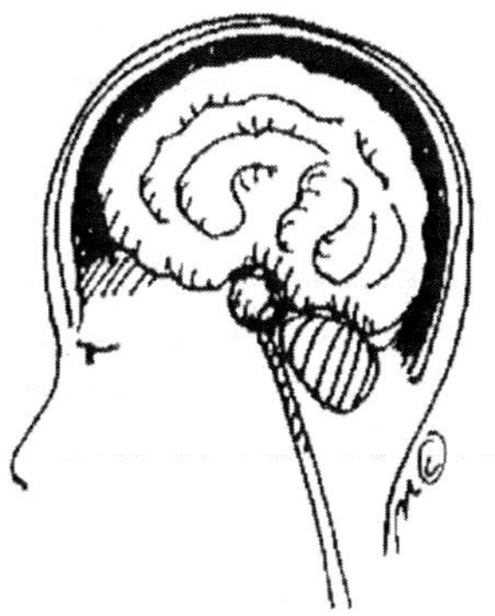

However, the health of the brain is often forgotten. Different life situations can put pressure on our brain and it is important to know how to look after it in order to cope with these situations.

What is stress?

Stress is a reaction to difficult situations. Sometimes it is a good thing as it pressures us to change a situation. However, if the stress is felt for a long period of time it can start to effect our physical and mental health.

It disrupts nearly every system in your body – raising blood pressure, suppressing the immune system, increasing the risk of heart attack and stroke, reducing fertility, increasing aging, it can even affect the brain leaving you more vulnerable to developing mental illness.

Know the signs of Stress Overload!

Increased heart rate	Irritability
Stomach pains	Aggression
Faster breathing	Crying often/ unexpectedly
Choking feeling	Difficulty being around people
Headaches	Lack of energy
Chest pains	Moodiness

SUICIDE

We know that globally 90% of people who commit suicide have a mental illness. Many people who experience suicidal ideas don't know why they feel that way and they are frightened.

So getting help quickly is very important.

TIPS FOR HELPING

1. Tell the person that you are noticing changes in their character/behaviour and tell them you are worried
2. Encourage the person to talk about how they are feeling
3. Do not underestimate if someone says they feel like dying/hurting themselves, always listen to the person and take them seriously
4. Reassure the person that there is help available and that they can gain support to get through this
5. Accompany them to a health service

For further information:

St Giles Hospital or visit the hospital on Reservoir Rd. Suva Ph 3381399

Pacific Counseling and Social Services. Ph. 3100191

Youth Champs 4 Mental Health: Facebook/email: youthchamps4mentalhealth@gmail.com. Ph 8620146

Psychiatric Survivors Association Fiji National Council for Disabled People, Brown St. Suva Ph. 3319043

Fiji Alliance for Mental Health (FAMH) Ph. 92033[illegible]

STIGMA

Stigma is a negative attitude towards something/someone. It usually occurs because of lack of education or awareness of the issue.

People with mental illness often experience stigma and describe it as difficulty being accepted by other people. They find it difficult to find friends, housing and work because others discriminate against them. Sometimes they find that their old friends are uncomfortable being around them and they feel cut off from society.

FIGHTING STIGMA

People with mental illness should not be blamed for their condition any more than people with diabetes be blamed for having diabetes. As long as that person is able to receive the right care and treatment, that person can lead a normal life. The same goes for mental illness.

Some illnesses are more severe than others and require the person to have treatment all their life, but most recover to lead happy and productive lives. **However, stigma can prevent that person from achieving this.**

MENTAL HEALTH

10 TIPS TO REDUCING STRESS

1. Take deep breaths. Focusing on your breathing takes your mind off the stress cause and calms you, sending more oxygen into your body.

2. Make time to practise RELAXATION techniques. Don't wait for stress to hit you, instead start the day calm and in control. Do breathing exercises for ten minutes before you start your day.

3. Talk to a friend or counsellor about specific problems that feel too big for you to manage. A problem shared is truly a problem halved.

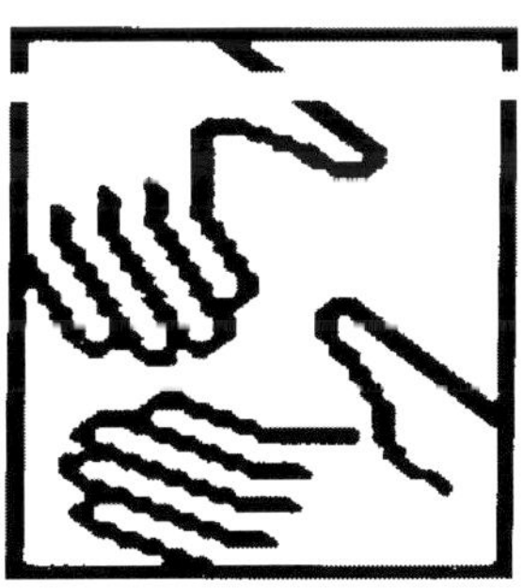

4. Pray or read something inspirational - whatever makes you feel more in tune with your spiritual side and reminds you of your worth.

5. Watch your thoughts and make a habit of catching those "dark clouds" and replacing them with something positive.

6. Stress is often caused by feelings of inadequacy. Remind yourself of your strengths and accomplishments

7. Each day visualize what you want to happen, not on your weaknesses. We all have things that are difficult to do or to cope with, but we don't need to make them the focus of our attention.

8. BALANCE is the key. Eat a healthy balance of foods—cut down on sugary foods and salt. Have a balance of activity – make sure you leave time for activity that gives you pleasure.

9. Have a good laugh. Humour and stress relief go hand in hand.Try art, music, or dancing to explore your creative side for relaxation and enjoyment.

10. Keep moving. The benefits of EXCERCISE for stress relief are many. Make a point of some daily exercise.

WHAT IS MENTAL **ILLNESS** ?

Know how to spot the signs and symptoms...

Everyone goes through happy sad angry times in their life However if a person is, for example, sad for more than 2 weeks and it starts to impact on their daily activities, including sleep patterns, or affects their relationships - it is important to check with a doctor.

Mental illness is anything that affects a person's thoughts, emotions or behaviour that results in:

1 A significantly negative effect on the person or those around them

2. An obvious change in their personality.

3 Friends or relatives feel that what is happening to the person is strange and hard to understand.

4 Not coping with situations you would normally cope with

There are different types of mental illness Some illnesses affect your mood and some affect your thinking, your senses or a combination of these. Some illnesses are more severe than others.

A person may be able to overcome a mild illness through simple lifestyle changes, others may require medication, counselling and even hospitalisation.

WHAT CAUSES MENTAL ILLNESS?

What causes mental illness?

This is a very good question! We know that most mental illnesses are caused by a chemical imbalance in the brain, but we don't always know what causes the chemical imbalance. However, we do know of lots of things that make mental illness **more likely** to happen, including:

mental illness.

- Having problems early on in life; a mother being very ill during her pregnancy, problems during the birth of a baby and a child being seriously ill when they are growing up.
- Having had a serious head injury
- The use of illicit drugs
- The use of too much
- Any kind of big stress. For example unemployment, homelessness, divorce, exams, childlessness or death of a loved one
- Any kind of serious physical illness.

We think that these things combine to create a chemical imbalance in the brain. It is this chemical imbalance that leads to mental

Some common Types of Mental Illness:

Depression
Schizophrenia
Anxiety
Bipolar Disorder
Personality Disorders
Psychosis

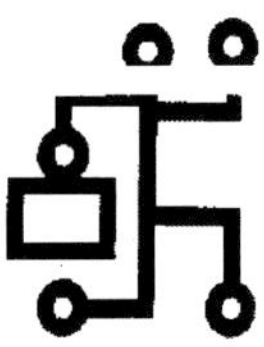

WHAT TO DO IF SOMEONE IS ACTING STRANGELY...

GETTING HELP

If someone has a sudden change of character, is acting strangely or has sadness or over-excitement that is not going away, **you can help!**

Supporting the person to go to a doctor is important. St Giles Hospital is a specialist service that can give advice and treatment. You can guide them to assistance.

Some people may need to be admitted but most people can be seen as an outpatient.

The important thing is not to ridicule the person, but to support them to get help.

Recovery and Mental Illness

The Recovery Journey

Life is full of ups and downs and illnesses especially remind us of this. Working towards recovery from an illness is an important process for people .

The recovery journey becomes particularly important and is about regaining the aspects of life that we value the most and about gaining back our identity.

The recovery from an episode of mental illness can be a journey, but it is all the more effective if there are others to 'keep on walking' alongside us.

The recovery journey is different for each individual, but common to all is a process of development and change and regaining of a sense of self and health.

Rehabilitation is one aspect of working towards recovery after mental illness. It usually starts in the hospital and needs to be continued into the home and community.

Unfortunately, with mental illness there is a stigma attached. This stigma means that people identify the person by their illness and forget that they are a person first.

This is when the person, health professionals, and carers work together to learn how to manage the illness so that the person can get on with their life.

Getting back into daily activities—new and old

Special points of interest:

- ☺ Understanding is the key
- ☺ Support for people who are ill and their carers is essential
- ☺ Community acceptance of all types of people with all types of abilities is vital to a happy healthy community

Common impairments and Mental Illness

Mental illness can affect people in different ways depending on the type of illness and its severity.

Most people will recover after an illness, but it can take some months. Needing to adjust to medication side-effects like drowsiness, nausea, etc.

Some people will experience ongoing impairments such as reduced concentration, slowed thinking, difficulty expressing self verbally, difficulty organizing self and daily tasks, etc.

Some people might continue to hear voices or have strange ideas.

However, if we can help people to manage these symptoms they can get on in their life despite them.

St Giles Hospital 2011 Fact Sheet

Unlocking Disability

Disability refers to when a person is unable to do certain things that most others can do. It can be described in three different parts:

Impairment

When there is an abnormality in a body.

Limitation in Activity

When the impairment affects our ability to do a certain activity.

Limitation in Participation

When the community structure prevents a person participating in an activity because of their impairment.

Sometimes mental illness can lead to an impairment. For example, slower information processing (thinking time). It may affect their activities because it takes the person longer to answer a question during a conversation.

If the community is aware and they give extra time during the conversation for the person to answer then there is no limitation on participation in social activities.

However, if the community does not understand and they stop the conversation and stop talking to the person then their participation in important conversations is stopped and they become excluded from the community social activities.

Education = Understanding = Inclusion

How has the illness affected you...and how do we get around it?

It is important to get to know yourself again after experiencing an illness, whether it be physical or mental. Through trying out different activities you can explore how the illness may have affected your usual day.

Sometimes its just a matter of practice to get back the skills, other times you may have to change the way you do the activity but you can still reach the end goal.

Sometimes, its not possible or you don't want to do the same activities anymore and you might like to try different activities in your day to find a sense of purpose and enjoyment.

We all want to be productive citizens and its important to work together to discover new potentials following an illness.

Understanding, patience, and support during this discovery time is very important. Self esteem is needed for discovering new potentials.

Its important not to blame someone for changes in abilities...

instead turn it around by working together to find new potentials...

Tips for support

1. Give the person and their family/ friends time to talk about their illness and how it has affected their lives.

2. Let the person know you love and care for them.

3. Gentle encouragement to keep trying is important as its hard work learning new ways of doing things.

4. Never ridicule the person because of what they cant do—focus on what they can do, no matter how small that might seem...sometimes the small things are the most special.

5. Even if you do not understand what a person is saying to you, give that person attention and if you notice emotions let the person know that you have noticed ("you seem sad/happy about that").

6. If you see someone who is doing something that puts them at risk, don't stand back—help them or contact someone who can help

7. Offer carers support, help them to find ways to take a break in their day. Just talking about their day can lift the load on a persons shoulders. We have to look after carer's mental health too.

8. Don't forget that we are people first and the illness comes second.

Page 2 Recovery

No. 11. Brochure on Services Provided by St Giles Hospital, Fiji

ervices Provided in the Hospital

Inpatient Services
Out patient services
Occupational Therapy
Counseling Services/family Therapy
Pharmaceuticals Services
Day care and Rehabilitation
Community Psychiatric Nursing
Forensic Services
Psycho social Rehabilitation
Suicidal care
Mental Health Training and Awareness

you are admitted to the Hospital you are equested to bring the following;

Toiletries
Change of clothes

void the following;

harp instrument e.g. scissors, knives and razor blades
having gear to be left with the Sister In Charge

aluables such as cash, jewelery, mobile phones are not to e kept in the wards. Will be taken to the Hospital dministrator or given back to the relatives.

isiting Hours

om –3pm Weekdays and Public Holidays

MINISTRY of Health
Shaping Fiji's Health

NCHP

04/02/09

St Giles Hospital

There is no Health without Mental Health

St Giles Hospital is the national specialist hospital for psychiatric clients. It was established in 1884 and situated on Reservoir Road in Suva. The Hospital has grown in 120years since and now caters for the whole of Fiji and patients even come from the region.

There are 136 beds/78 males /58 females who are cared for in our male and female wards. A multidisciplinary team of doctors, nurses, medical orderlies, counselor and social worker provides the patient care being led by the Medical Superintendent.

Telephone No-3381399/3381464/3381476

1.Why are patients admitted to St Giles?

- Assessment round the clock-set information
- Place of safety-Family unable to manage patient at home.
- Introduction of Medication and monitor progress
- Build up a picture of patient
- Respite care
- To offer Occupational Therapy

2.How long will I stay in the Hospital?

The average length of stay is 72days.However some patients may be discharged after a week or two. Some patients need to be at St Giles much longer. This will depend on the following factors:

- Doctors/nurses need more time to treat the patient
- Risk of violence or self harm
- Nowhere to go/Lack of support in the community
- Stigma of Mental Health
- Nature and duration of the illness

3. What is CPN and what does she/he do?

Community Psychiatric Nurse is a nurse who sees patients in their own home.

- Monitor care [see how he/she is coping at home]
- Get a picture of a patient's home and family
- Get a chance to talk about problems and talk about possible answers
- Give feedback or reports to doctors and nurses in St Giles
- Give medication/Modecate injection and replace tablets.
- Monitor to see if patients are taking the right number of tablets at the right time.
- Build up trust
- Look for side effects and sign of relapse.
- Support the family members

Sign of Relapse

- Poor Sleeping
Talkative and talking to self
- Neglecting personal Hygiene
- Isolative
- Irritable and angry [for no appropriate reason]

4. Why am I being given an injection?

- It is longer lasting /you may only need injection every 2 or 4weeks.
- Saves you having to remember to take tablets 2 or 3 times a day
- Its more practical and may save you time and money

5. How long am I expected to take medications?

- You may need to carry on taking medications even after you feel
well or until your doctor/Nurse and you agree that you no longer need to take it
- But you should talk to your CPN about this

6. What are the side effects and what I should I do if I get them?

Side effects could be;
- Rolling eyes
- Drooling [excessive salivation]
- Drowsiness
- Tremor
- Stiffness [especially upper body]
- Restlessness
- Lock jaw
- Dry Mouth
- Blurred vision
- Slurred speech
- Involuntary tongue movements
Shuffling gait

Talk to your Doctor [CPN]

7. What should I do if I am unhappy with the way I am treated?

- At St Giles we take patients seriously and wait to hear any complaints if possible talk to the person you are unhappy with
- If you are unhappy with what they say talk to their senior nurse/Doctor

If you still unhappy talk to the Matron/Medical Superintendent.

About the Author

Helen J. Ménard
International Legal Consultant
Picnic Bay, Queensland, Australia
Email: menardcamp@hotmail.com
helenjmenard@gmail.com

Helen J. Ménard holds a PhD in Law, a Graduate Diploma in Insurance Law, and a B.Juris and LL.B.

She has been admitted to practice as a barrister and solicitor of the Supreme Court of Victoria; the High Court of Australia; the National Court of Justice of Papua New Guinea; and the Supreme Court of Vanuatu.

As a lawyer the author has worked across a broad spectrum of the legal profession in Australia including private practice, the corporate sector, public mental health, legal aid and community legal services. She has practised predominantly in the areas of civil litigation, medical law and mental health law.

Prior to admission to legal practice, the author held certificates in General Nursing, Midwifery and Operating Theatre Management and worked extensively within the health profession.

The author commenced as a fulltime academic at the School of Law, University of the South Pacific, Vanuatu in 2004 and since 2014 has continued to teach there on a consultancy basis, along with various other tertiary institutions in Australia.

Her primary area of legal research is health law and ethics, specifically the South Pacific region and has co-authored several editions of a text on medical law in the South Pacific.

She is currently a legal consultant on mental health law reform with the World Health Organization (WHO) and has been engaged as an international legal consultant with International Development Law Organization (IDLO).

LEGISLATION AND TREATIES INDEX

E

F

H

I

L

M

N

O

P

R

S

U

W

Cases Index

A

B

C

F

G

I

J

K

M

N

P

R

S

T

W

General Index

A

B

C

D